Aktuelle Materialien zur Internationalen Politik

herausgegeben von der
Stiftung Wissenschaft und Politik, Berlin

Band 73

Benedikt Zanker

On the Viability of an
International Lender of Last Resort

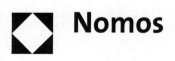 

Die Deutsche Bibliothek verzeichnet diese Publikation in
der Deutschen Nationalbibliografie; detaillierte bibliografische
Daten sind im Internet über http://dnb.ddb.de abrufbar.

Die Deutsche Bibliothek lists this publication in the Deutsche
Nationalbibliografie; detailed bibliographic data is available
in the Internet at http://dnb.ddb.de.

ISBN 978-3-8329-2568-0

1. Auflage 2007
© Nomos Verlagsgesellschaft, Baden-Baden 2007. Printed in Germany. Alle
Rechte, auch die des Nachdrucks von Auszügen, der fotomechanischen Wieder-
gabe und der Übersetzung, vorbehalten. Gedruckt auf alterungsbeständigem
Papier.

Table of Contents

	Acknowledgements	13
1.	**Introduction and Theory**	15
1.1	**Introduction**	15
1.2	**Theory**	20
1.2.1	Regime Theory	21
1.2.2	Public Choice Theory	25
1.2.2.1	Global Public Goods	27
1.2.2.2	Moral Hazard Problems	29
1.2.2.3	Principal-Agent Problems	31
1.2.3	Financial Market Theory	33
1.2.3.1	The Efficient Markets Hypothesis	34
1.2.3.2	The Financial-Instability Hypothesis	37
1.2.3.3	Rational Herding	39
1.3	**Structure of the Analysis**	42
2.	**Financial Crisis Theory**	47
2.1	**Financial Crises in an International Context**	49
2.1.1	Four Types of Currency Crises	50
2.1.2	The Problem of Contagion	52
2.2	**Three Generations of Financial Crisis Models**	53
2.2.1	First Generation Models	54
2.2.2	Second Generation Models	56
2.2.3	Third Generation Models	58
2.2.3.1	Macroeconomic Feedback Models	58
2.2.3.2	Bank-run and Liquidity Models	59
2.2.3.3	Models of Expectations Formation and Herding Behaviour	60
2.3	**Evidence and Evaluation**	62
2.3.1	Empirical Evidence	62
2.3.2	Evaluation	63
2.3.3	Lessons and Implications	66
3.	**Selected Proposals to Increase Global Financial Stability**	68
3.1	**General Proposals to Increase Global Financial Stability**	68
3.1.1	Improved Transparency and Higher Regulatory Standards	68
3.1.2	An International Credit Insurance	71

3.1.3	The Tobin Tax	72
3.1.4	A Global Central Bank	74
3.1.5	A World Currency	75
3.2	**Proposals Addressing the Role of the IMF**	76
3.2.1	A Sovereign Debt Restructuring Mechanism	77
3.2.2	The Calomiris Proposal	78
3.2.3	The Report by the Independent Task Force	80
3.2.4	The Meltzer Report	84
3.2.5	The Köhler Approach: Procedural Changes	86
3.3	**Conclusion**	88
4.	**The Lender of Last Resort: The Concept in Theory**	90
4.1	**The Importance of Foreign Currency**	90
4.1.1	Enhancing Access to Foreign Currency	91
4.2	**The Concept of a Lender of Last Resort**	92
4.2.1	Henry Thornton (1760–1815)	93
4.2.1.1	Issues in Last Resort Lending	94
4.2.1.2	Individual Institutions versus the Monetary System	96
4.2.1.3	Contemporary Response	97
4.2.2	Walter Bagehot (1826–1877)	98
4.2.2.1	Lending Freely	100
4.2.2.2	Penalty Rates	101
4.2.2.3	The Collateral	102
4.2.2.4	Financial Stability after 1866	103
4.3	**An International Lender of Last Resort**	104
4.3.1	Theoretical Considerations	105
4.3.2	The Case for an International Lender of Last Resort	107
4.3.3	Fundamental Differences between International and Domestic Settings	109
4.3.4	The IMF as International Lender of Last Resort	111
4.3.5	The Fund's Record as Crisis Manger	113
5.	**The Lender of Last Resort: The Concept in Practice**	117
5.1	**The Panic of 1907**	117
5.1.1	The Setting	118
5.1.2	The Run on Banks and Trust Companies	120
5.1.3	Pressure on Money, Stock and Call Loan Markets	121
5.1.4	Lessons of 1907	123
5.2	**The 1960s Sterling Crisis**	124

5.2.1	The Setting	124
5.2.2	The Crisis	125
5.2.3	Lessons of the Sterling Crisis	128
5.3	**Emerging Market Crises in the 1990s**	129
5.3.1	The Mexican Peso Crisis	130
5.3.2	The Asian Financial Crisis	131
5.3.2.1	Crisis in Thailand	133
5.3.2.2	Crisis in South Korea	134
5.3.2.3	Crisis in Indonesia	136
5.3.3	The Asian Crisis' Aftermath	138
5.3.3.1	The Rouble Crisis	138
5.3.3.2	Crisis in Brazil	140
5.3.3.3	Crisis in Argentina	142
5.3.4	Lessons from Emerging Market Crises	143
6.	**The Principle of Lending Freely**	146
6.1	**The Fund's Resources**	147
6.1.1	Current Funding Needs of the IMF	150
6.2	**Funding Needs of an International Lender of Last Resort**	153
6.2.1	Lending-in-last-resort as Input in Monetary Policy	155
6.2.2	Lending-in-last-resort as Input in Banking Policy	157
6.2.3	Necessary Funding for an International Lender of Last Resort	160
6.2.4	Estimating Short-term External Obligations in the Developing World	161
6.2.5	Liquidity Gaps in the Past	166
6.3	**Conclusion and Implications**	170
7.	**The Collateral Question**	173
7.1	**The Concept of Collateral**	174
7.2	**Assets Acceptable as Collateral**	176
7.2.1	Financial Assets	177
7.2.1.1	Argentina's Contingent Repurchase Facility	179
7.2.2	Collateralising Equity	181
7.2.2.1	Privatisation in Latin America	182
7.2.2.2	Privatisation in East Asia	184
7.2.2.3	Privatisation in China	186
7.2.2.4	Privatisation in Russia	187
7.2.3	Securitisation of Future Flow Receivables	188
7.2.3.1	Securitising Natural Resources	189

7.2.3.1.1	The US-Mexican Framework Agreement	190
7.2.3.2	Securitising Alternative Foreign Currency Receivables	192
7.2.3.2.1	Telephone Receivables	193
7.2.3.2.2	Workers' Remittances	194
7.2.3.2.3	Credit Card Receivables	196
7.2.3.2.4	Taxing Export Earnings	196
7.3	**Problems Arising from the Imposition of Strict Collateral Requirements**	199
7.4	**Implications for the Viability of an International Lender of Last Resort**	201
8.	**Pre-qualification**	203
8.1	**Advantages of Pre-qualification**	203
8.2	**Pre-qualification Criteria**	206
8.2.1	Transparency Criteria	207
8.2.2	Criteria Ensuring Financial Sector Stability	211
8.2.2.1	Capital Adequacy Requirements	212
8.2.2.2	Minimum Reserve Requirements	216
8.2.2.3	Internationalisation of the Financial Sector	217
8.2.2.4	Deposit Insurance	220
8.2.3	Criteria Indicating Sustainable Sovereign Indebtedness	222
8.2.3.1	Solvency Ratios	224
8.2.3.2	Liquidity Ratios	226
8.3	**Conclusion: Pre-qualification Is the Way Forward**	228
9.	**Moral Hazard**	230
9.1	**IMF Induced Moral Hazard**	231
9.2	Empirical Evidence on Moral Hazard Issues	233
9.2.1	Evidence on Creditor-side Moral Hazard	234
9.2.2	Evidence on Debtor-side Moral Hazard	241
9.3	**Catalytic Finance**	244
9.3.1	Empirical Evidence on Catalytic Finance	246
9.4	**Instruments Mitigating Moral Hazard Problems**	249
10.	**Principal-Agent Problems**	253
10.1	**The Actors' Interests**	253
10.1.1	Interests of Borrowing Countries	254
10.1.2	Interests of International Investors	255

10.1.3	Creditor Country Interests	255
10.1.3.1	Foreign Policy Objectives	256
10.1.3.2	Financial Sector Interests	257
10.1.3.3	Creditor Country Costs	258
10.1.4	Evidence on IMF Lending Arrangements	259
10.2	**The Distribution of Voting Power at the IMF**	260
10.2.1	IMF Voting Weights	261
10.2.2	Voting Power at the IMF	264
10.2.2.1	Voting Power at the Board of Governors	266
10.2.2.2	Voting Power at the Executive Board	269
10.2.2.3	Constituencies at the Executive Board	272
10.2.2.4	The Power of Industrialised and Developing Countries at the IMF	273
10.3	**The Case for Reforming IMF Governance Structures**	275
10.3.1	Governance Reform Proposals	277
10.3.2	Political Difficulties	279
10.3.3	Governance Reform and Pre-qualification	281
11.	**Sovereign Debt Restructuring**	283
11.1	**Debt Restructuring in the Past**	283
11.1.1	New Money Approach	284
11.1.2	The Brady Plan	286
11.2	**The Changed Environment**	287
11.2.1	Successful Restructurings	288
11.2.2	Problems due to Renegade Creditors	290
11.2.3	Need for Reform	293
11.3	**Proposals to Facilitate Sovereign Debt Restructuring**	294
11.3.1	A Code of Good Conduct	294
11.3.2	Collective Action Clauses	297
11.3.3	A Sovereign Debt Restructuring Mechanism	300
11.4	**SDRM versus CAC and Code of Conduct**	303
11.4.1	Concerns on the Effectiveness of Collective Action Clauses	304
11.4.2	Market-based Approach as the Way Forward	309
12.	**A Proposal**	311
12.1	**Underlying Principles**	311
12.1.1	Principles for Effective Liquidity Assistance	312
12.1.2	Principles for Effective Monitoring and Supervisory Work	313
12.2	**Membership Rules for a Restructured IMF**	315
12.2.1	General Membership	315

12.2.2   Access to Large-scale Liquidity Assistance 317
12.2.2.1   Sovereign Stability Criteria 319
12.2.2.2   Criteria Indicating Financial Sector Stability 320
12.3   **Lending Rules Governing IMF Facilities** 322
12.3.1   Lending Rules Governing PRGF and SBA Facilities 322
12.3.2   Lending Rules Governing ELA Facilities 323
12.3.2.1   Ensuring Liquidity Assistance in Sufficient Amounts 323
12.3.2.2   Ensuring Liquidity Assistance Is Employed Effectively 325
12.3.2.3   Reigning In on Debtor-side Moral Hazard 326
12.4   **Funding Issues and Transition Period** 327
12.4.1   Funding Issues 328
12.4.2   Transition Period 328

13.   **Epilogue: Chances of Implementation** 331

13.1   **Opposition to Reform** 332
13.1.1   Opposition by Developed Countries and the G-7 332
13.1.2   The Lacking Clout of Developing Economies 336
13.2   **The Potential for Gradual Reform** 337
13.2.1   Regional Monetary Cooperation 338
13.2.2   Changes Inside the IMF 341

Appendix 345
Abbreviations 345
Bibliography 347

Illustrations

Table 2.1	Net Capital Flows to Developing Countries and Emerging Economies 1994–2004	48
Table 6.1	IMF Financial Resources 2002–2004	147
Table 6.2	General Quota Reviews	148
Table 6.3	GAB Participants and Credit Amounts	149
Table 6.4	NAB Participants and Credit Amounts	149
Figure 6.1	Currency Depreciation Cycle	158
Table 6.5	Consolidated Claims of Reporting Banks on Individual Countries	162
Table 6.6	International Debt Securities by Nationality of Issuers	163
Table 6.7	International Liquidity of Crisis Economies	168
Box 7.1	Assets Eligible as Collateral under Basel II	178
Table 7.1	Chinese SOEs in 2004 Global Fortune 500	186
Table 7.2	Government Shares in Selected Oil & Gas Producers	191
Table 7.3	Collateral Preferences	193
Table 7.4	Top 10 Developing Country Recipients of Workers' Remittances	195
Table 7.5	Potential Export Tax Revenues of Selected Exporting Nations	198
Table 8.1	Thresholds for Sustainable Levels of External Indebtedness	225
Box 8.1	Pre-qualification Requirements for Liquidity Assistance	229
Table 10.1	Selected Quotas and Voting Shares in the Board of Governors	262
Table 10.2	Quotas and Voting Shares in the Executive Board	263
Table 10.3	Board of Governors and Voting Power	265
Table 10.4	Differences between Simple and Supermajority Requirements Selected Members in the Board of Governors	267
Table 10.5	Executive Board and Voting Power	268
Table 10.6	Differences between Simple and Supermajority Requirements: Executive Board	269
Table 10.7	Constituencies and Voting Power in the Executive Board	270
Box 12.1	Principles for Effective Liquidity Assistance	313
Box 12.2	Principles for Effective Monitoring and Supervision	314
Box 12.3	Conditions for General Membership	316
Table 12.1	Thresholds for Sustainable Levels of External Indebtedness	320
Box 12.4	Conditions for Advanced IMF Membership	322
Box 12.5	Lending Rules Governing Extended Liquidity Assistance	327
Table 13.1	Foreign Currency Reserves in East Asia	339

11

Acknowledgements

I am indebted to Professor Dr. Michael Kreile at Humboldt-Universität zu Berlin and Dr. habil. Heribert Dieter at Stiftung Wissenschaft und Politik for their helpful supervision. Financial support has been generously provided by the Fritz Thyssen Stiftung für Wissenschaftsförderung. For the unique opportunity to spend two years with the Research Unit Global Issues at Stiftung Wissenschaft und Politik I am particularly grateful to Dr. Albrecht Zunker and Dr. Friedemann Müller. Publication in the SWP Series *Aktuelle Materialien zur Internationalen Politik* has been made possible by Dr. Günther Maihold.

Berlin, November 2006

Benedikt Zanker

1. Introduction and Theory

1.1 Introduction

Since 1944, when 730 delegates from the 44 allied nations convened at the Mount Washington Hotel in Bretton Woods, the global financial system has changed dramatically. Established to regulate the international political economy, in the first three decades after its inception the Bretton Woods system provided a level of exchange rate stability unmatched anytime thereafter and thereby contributed significantly to the vast expansion in international trade and investment during the postwar years. The founding members were able to maintain their currencies at fixed rates to the dollar because capital controls protected them from violent capital flow reversals. When currencies came under pressure nevertheless, the newly created IMF provided foreign currency loans until the storm was weathered. In case of *fundamental disequilibria* the Bretton Woods Agreement allowed for an exchange rate adjustment given consent by the IMF.

Today, the international monetary system is fundamentally different. President Nixon's decision to close the gold window[1] and abolish the Bretton Woods System led to a significant increase in the volatility of asset prices and set off a process of decreasing capital controls and increasing capital mobility that has defined the post-Bretton Woods era of financial integration ever since[2]. Moreover, while only few selected countries and industry sectors participated in the international monetary system in the past, today a vast number of developing countries and emerging economies are involved in the global financial system. Likewise, not only firms from almost any industrial sector but even households have started borrowing and investing abroad. As a result, international capital flows have multiplied several times over and exposure to the global financial system has become all but universal.

While financial integration has brought many benefits to both industrial and developing countries, it has led a substantial loss in stability. The liberalisation of capital flows increased the flow of foreign savings into emerging economies several-fold but at the same time created the problem of violent capital flow reversals. As a result the frequency of financial crises has risen. A study by Barry Eichengreen and Michael Bordo identifies 38 financial crises for the period between 1945 and 1971, but 139 for the years between 1973 and 1997. The increase in crisis frequency has

---

1 Under the gold standard the United States stood ready to redeem dollar notes for gold thereby opening a so-called *gold window* for the holders of those notes.
2 See Susan Strange. 1986. *Casino Capitalism.* Oxford: Blackwell: 38–43

been particularly alarming in developing countries which had to cope with some form of financial crisis only 17 times before 1973, but 95 times thereafter. But even in industrial countries the frequency of financial crises has more than doubled during the post-Bretton Woods era, from 21 between 1945 and 1973 to 44 thereafter[3]. However, since the EMS crises of the early 1990s, financial crises have occurred only in developing countries and emerging economies. Indeed, currency crises, banking crises and twin crises are by now almost universally associated with the emerging economies of Latin America, Asia, Russia and Turkey.

The costs of financial crises are high: For the people of Thailand, Korea, and Indonesia the Asian Crisis meant deep recessions, rising unemployment and increased poverty. In 1998 real GDP declined 6.7 percent in Korea, 10.8 percent in Thailand and 13.2 percent in Indonesia. As a result, from 1997 to 1999 unemployment climbed from 4.7 to 5.5 percent in Indonesia, from 2.6 to 6.8 percent in Korea and from 0.9 to 3.4 percent in Thailand[4]. In the same period real wages fell by 7 percent in Thailand, 10 percent in Korea and an astonishingly 30 percent in Indonesia while the share of population classified as living in poverty more than doubled in Korea, shot up from 11.4 to 15.9 percent in Thailand and rose to 18.2 from 11.3 percent in Indonesia[5]. But while financial crises afflict hardest losses on the countries they strike, financial globalization means that industrial countries suffer negative consequence alike. In contrast to financial crises in earlier periods, contemporary emerging market crises have the ability to destabilise the global financial system. Contagion not only means that a crisis originating in Southeast Asia can spread to Latin America and Central Asia, but also that the financial systems of advanced industrial economies can become exposed to severe disruptions. The demise of Long-Term Capital Management is a paramount example of how financial institutions' exposure to emerging markets can threaten mature financial systems even in advanced industrial economies.

Volatile capital flows and financial crises are an inevitable consequence of open capital accounts. Without a re-regulation of short-term capital flows, they cannot be prevented. And indeed, a selective implementation of capital controls may go a long way in reducing the frequency of financial crises in vulnerable developing and emerging economies. If implemented, experience in trade policy suggests such regulations should be based on tariffs rather than trying to implement volume

---

3 See Michael Bordo and Barry Eichengreen. 2002. *Crises Now and Then: What Lessons from the Last Era of Financial Globalization?* NBER Working Paper No. 8761. Washington, DC: National Bureau of Economic Research: 41

4 See ADB. 2001. *Key Indicators 2001: Growth and Change in Asia and the Pacific.* Manila, Philippines: Asian Development Bank

5 See ESCAP. 2002. *Bulletin on Asia-Pacific Perspectives 2002/03.* Bangkok, Thailand: United Nations Social and Economic Commission for Asia and the Pacific: 40

restrictions[6]. However, vested interests in both industrial and developing countries render a widespread re-implementation of even limited capital account controls and similar measures to stabilize capital flows to emerging markets unlikely[7]. Conceding the fact that financial crises will remain a more or less regular feature of a global financial system therefore demands to explore instruments that would be effective in at least reducing their frequency and severity.

The International Monetary Fund was established as just such an instrument and until recently remained the pre-eminent international institution to combat financial crises and maintain global financial stability. During the post-war era its existence contributed to an unprecedented period of economic growth. By lending to countries in balance of payments problems the IMF effectively contributed to maintain the system of fixed exchange rates that lasted until 1971. It could do so because balance of payments difficulties usually originated in the current account as a consequence of temporary shocks to trade while capital controls to a large extent prevented destabilising speculative capital flows. The Articles of Agreement not only prohibited lending to meet large or sustained capital outflows but also explicitly allowed for the Fund to impose capital controls as a condition for liquidity assistance.

The re-emergence of Western Europe and Japan as major economic powers, rapid growth in emerging markets and the increase in private capital flows have fundamentally changed the global economy. Since 1973 the Bretton Woods system of fixed exchange rates has given place to an environment cohabitated by fixed, flexible and adjustable peg regimes. While its objectives remain the same, in the post-Bretton Woods system the Fund's role in providing temporary liquidity assistance during current account crises has lost in importance. Growing private capital markets and steep increases in cross-border capital flows mean that the majority of financial crises today originate in the capital account. To address capital account crises requires liquidity assistance on a far larger scale than to redress temporary imbalances in the current account. Meanwhile, IMF membership has risen to 184 and split into two groups whose interests at times diverge: Advanced industrial countries that make up the group of IMF net creditors—the United Kingdom being one of the last advanced industrial countries to borrow from the Fund in 1976—and developing countries and emerging market economies as the Fund's debtors.

---

6 See Ludger Schuknecht. 1999. "A Trade Policy Perspective on Capital Controls." *Finance and Development.* Vol. 36, No. 1. Washington, DC: International Monetary Fund

7 For a thorough overview of alternative measures to stabilize capital flows to emerging market economies see John Williamson. 2005. *Curbing the Boom-Bust Cycle: Stabilizing Capital Flows to Emerging Markets.* Policy Analyses in International Economics 75. Washington, DC: Institute for International Economics

The IMF attempted to stay abreast of these changes: Compared to the post-war era and in response to the Latin American Debt Crisis, the transition from planned to market economies of central European countries and the 1990s emerging market crises it has expanded its mandate considerably. During the early years of its existence the Fund's jurisdiction was restricted to oversee the abandonment of exchange controls regarding the current account; during the Asian Crisis the conditions it attached to its financial assistance included a wide range of prescriptions not only in terms of fiscal and monetary policy but also regarding structural reforms; conditions imposed by the IMF were based almost exclusively on the so-called Washington Consensus—highly controversial in both academic and policy-making circles.

However, the record of IMF involvement in recent emerging market crises has been ambiguous at best. While the Mexican rescue in 1995 can be perceived as successful intervention, the Fund's involvement during the Asian Crisis has been far less effective. Liquidity assistance was advanced not only too late but at insufficient amounts and thus failed to restore investor confidence. Furthermore, there is a wide consensus that the Fund's austerity programs caused unnecessary hardship on the countries' populations and were bad economics due to their pro-cyclical nature. While restrictive fiscal and monetary policies contributed to output contraction, the Fund's insistence on continuing privatisation, liberalisation and deregulation has fuelled suspicions in the developing world that the Fund's policies represent foreign policy and private sector interests of its major industrialised shareholders.

As a result, the institution's legitimacy and credibility has been eroded among many borrowing members while its influence on economic policies of countries that do not require its emergency assistance has declined. Asian economies have piled up vast amounts of foreign currency reserves, at least partly to reduce their dependence on IMF support should financial difficulties arise in the future. Argentina's recovery from the crisis following default in December 2001 further eroded the Fund role as the world's pre-eminent institution to combat financial crises as growth resumed despite a rejection of the Fund's policy demands[8]. Moreover, Argentina even temporarily defaulted on its debt service obligations to the IMF without becoming a pariah to the financial community as countries like Congo or Iraq; as a consequence, the Fund's status as sacrosanct lender has been damaged to an considerable degree. Nevertheless, as the problem of financial crises is bound to re-emerge at some stage in the future and global imbalances continue to threaten the world economy, the international community cannot dispense with an effective institution to respond to crises and foster global financial stability.

---

8 See Mark Weisbrot. 2005. "The IMF Has Lost Its Influence." *International Herald Tribune.* September 23, 2005

The debate on a reform of the global financial architecture and the Bretton Woods institutions that has developed since the Asian Crisis produced a vast array of proposals to increase global financial stability. Recommendations range from gradually reforming IMF lending policies to abolishing the Fund entirely. An alternative proposition has been to restructure the IMF into an international lender of last resort. The concept of a lender of last resort draws on a central banking principle popularized by Walter Bagehot in the late nineteenth century. It suggests that during financial crises central banks should provide generous short-term liquidity assistance to distressed but fundamentally solvent banks in order to arrest the crisis and mitigate its impact on the real economy. Applied to the international monetary system it would require the IMF to serve as lender of last resort to its sovereign members during debt, currency or banking crises. Although several factors make the provision of effective lender of last resort services more difficult on an international than on a domestic level, the fundamental reasoning behind the concept seems suggestive. If financial integration and the deregulation of capital flows lead to a globally integrated financial system, a failure to create the instruments necessary to maintain financial stability domestically make a reduction in the frequency of financial crises difficult to achieve.

Restructuring the IMF into an international lender of last resort would be attractive at least on two accounts. First, it would significantly enhance the institution's capacity as crisis manager. To effectively arrest financial crises liquidity assistance needs to be provided timely and in sufficient amounts. Both proved difficult under the Fund's current lending procedures. One the one hand, IMF conditionality policy requires lengthy negotiations between IMF and borrowing country on the terms and conditions of stability programs. On the other, when liquidity assistance is disbursed in tranches upon meeting specific reform milestones, immediate external assistance often proves insufficient to arrest a crisis and restore market confidence since investors remain unsure whether amounts pledged by the official sector will actually be disbursed. If the IMF would provide ample and unconditional liquidity assistance to distressed members in a similar way as a central bank does as lender of last resort to the domestic economy, financial crises could be addressed far more effectively. Violent capital flow reversals might even be prevented in the first place if international investors render the Fund's commitment to provide short-term liquidity assistance credible and thereby feel fewer incentives to rush for the exit.

Second, by operating similar to an international lender of last resort the IMF would be able to address its legitimacy problem in developing countries and emerging market economies alike. Disbursing loans according to clear and predictable principles would reduce suspicions that the IMF uses foreign currency loans as policy instrument to further its major shareholders' interests; members' access to large-scale liquidity assistance would end to be influenced by geo-political considerations in G-7 treasury departments but become increasingly based on economic reasoning. Operating as international lender of last resort the Fund would abandon conditionality and lend to all illiquid, but fundamentally solvent economies thereby abandoning its controversial strategy of ex-post conditionality. By ceasing to interfere in members' sovereign right of economic policy making the Fund's acceptance in its client countries would be greatly enhanced; as a result, cooperation with the Fund's surveillance and technical assistance activities would be likely to increase the effectiveness of crisis prevention. In return, members in the process of turning away from the Fund and attempting to organise regional self-help mechanisms may be induced to maintain their involvement and contribute to halt the Fund's declining influence on economic policy-making at its emerging market members.

The differences between the domestic and the international economic environment make the operation of an effective international lender of last resort inherently difficult. Consequently the majority of policy-makers dismiss the concept of an international lender of last resort as practically unfeasible. This dissertation attempts to provide an analysis of the concept of an international lender of last resort and to assess its practical viability.

1.2 Theory

As an attempt is made to examine the concept's viability from several different angels, it is a practically oriented analysis, not a theory test. Consequently, formal theory, specifically international relations theory is neither the focus nor central to the argument of this study. Nevertheless, every analysis and argument rests on theoretical foundations. On the one hand, underlying assumptions of any argument are inevitably based on some form of theory. On the other, the approaches and instruments employed to examine the subject of interest also originate from a body of theoretical work. Often, underlying assumptions and individual approaches can be attributed to an implicit body of theory. But just as often, assumptions stem from empirical evidence difficult to allocate to a specific body of economic, political or international relations theory.

Both is the case in this analysis for which three broad strands of theory can be identified. Underlying the whole analysis is the belief that international cooperation can be an effective way for countries to address issues impossible to tackle autonomously. As such the argument is founded on neo-liberal institutionalism and regime theoretic assumptions. Furthermore, moral hazard and principal-agent considerations are identified as fundamental to the concept of an international lender of last resort.

These issues highlight the importance of rational or public choice concepts to this endeavour. Finally, many of the conclusions and suggestions that will follow are based on the findings of numerous empirical studies undertaken by researchers at universities, the IMF, and other economic or financial institutions. These sources cannot be attributed to a specific theory or school of thought individually. Implicit assumptions are certainly present, but they draw on the vast pool of economic and financial market theory and differ from case to case. However, the line of reasoning these sources are utilized to bolster rests on specific assumptions regarding financial markets and the occurrence of financial crises.

1.2.1 Regime Theory

Analysing whether restructuring the IMF into an international lender of last resort could enhance global financial stability implicitly assumes that international cooperation is possible. Furthermore, it implies a fundamental belief in the effectiveness of international institutions in realising objectives that cannot be achieved by unilateral action alone. Typically, such objectives arise in the context of global issues. The problem of global financial instability is a prime example. It affects countries universally but no country can effectively address it alone. Unilateral efforts can neither ensure nor even significantly improve global financial stability since international financial crises can result from the breakdown of a single economy. Only when all states participating in the international monetary system cooperate by ensuring that a crisis will not erupt from within their economy, can global stability be enhanced. Similarly, arresting a financial crisis requires a combined effort of several actors: the crisis country must improve its economic policies, the official sector needs to provide short-term liquidity assistance and international investors need to roll-over loans or participate in debt restructurings. Again, without cooperation, stability cannot be restored. In the field of international monetary relations cooperation between sovereign states has taken place in the past and continues to do so. While neo-realist theories of international relations struggle to convincingly explain these patterns of cooperation, neo-liberal institutionalism and regime theoretic explanations are more successful.

Like realist and neo-realist theories, neo-liberal institutionalism perceives sovereign states as independent units interacting with each other in an anarchic environment. Consequently, states are perceived as the central actors in international relations. In both realist and neo-liberal institutional theory states are modelled as rational actors selecting strategies to maximize individual utility[9]. While neo-realists

---

9 See Robert Keohane. 1989. *International Institutions and State Power.* Boulder, CO: Westview Press: 7–8

predominantly focus on the high politics of security affairs, neo-liberal institution-alism acknowledges the importance of social and economic issues in the interaction among states.

Although both schools share fundamental assumptions about states and their role in the international realm, their conclusions regarding the possibilities for cooper-ation diverge: In contrast to neo-realists like Kenneth Waltz, neo-liberal institu-tionalism assesses the opportunities for international cooperation as relatively favourable. In the neo-realist view of the world cooperation among states almost exclusively occurs under hegemonic stability: Without a hegemon willing to coerce other states into contributing to common efforts, the opportunities for international cooperation become limited. Consequently, international institutions are understood primarily as instruments by which hegemonic powers exercise their dominance. In neo-liberal institutionalist accounts the scope for international cooperation is much wider. When interdependent actors feel that objectives can be realised more effec-tively by cooperative than by unilateral efforts, international cooperation becomes a realistic option. International institutions can facilitate the process of cooperation and thus have a much wider role than serving as policy instrument for hegemonic powers.

These distinct stances on international cooperation result from diverging assumptions regarding states' utility functions. The neo-liberal school of thought assumes that states consider only their own gains and losses; absolute gains are suf-ficient to make cooperation worthwhile. Neo-realists in contrast point out that states not merely consider their own gains from cooperation, but also those of other states. Own gains are significantly diminished when other states also benefit from co-operation. To be attractive, cooperation must yield relative gains on other states. As a result, realists view opportunities for cooperation as far more limited.

The implicit assumptions regarding cooperation among sovereign states under-lying the argument presented in this analysis draw on neo-liberal institutionalist approaches, specifically on the theoretical framework laid out by Robert O. Keohane. Keohane takes the existence of mutual interests between sovereign states as both a given and an opportunity for cooperation, despite retaining the funda-mental neo-realist assumptions about the international realm. International regimes, defined by Stephen Krasner as *implicit or explicit principles, norms, rules, and decision-making procedures around which actors' expectations converge in a gciven area of international relations*[10], can facilitate cooperation. As other inter-national institutions like conventions or international organizations they establish a

---

10 Stephen Krasner. 1983. "Structural Causes and Regime Consequences: Regimes as Intervening Variables." In Stephen Krasner (Ed.). 1983. *International Regimes.* Ithaca, NY: Cornell Uni-versity Press: 2

form of legal liability between individual states[11]. Because there is no supranational authority to enforce agreed rules and practices, they are similar to agreements among oligopolistic firms or public conventions: rules are not broken as long as all other actors adhere to them. Consequently, the primary objective of international institutions is not to establish enforceable contractual obligations among states but to create stable expectations on and confidence about other actors' behaviour and to establish a working relationship among sovereign states[12]. International regimes contribute to achieving this objective by increasing information and by reducing the costs involved in reaching cooperative agreements.

The most important function of conventions or regimes is to reduce uncertainty among actors[13]. Given the lack of contract enforcing authorities in the international realm, the greatest barrier to cooperation arises from uncertainty on whether other actors will keep their commitments. Due to problems of asymmetric information, actors are often unsure whether the commitments they are expected to make are ultimately favourable to their own interests. If other negotiating parties are in possession of superior information, bargaining outcomes may be less advantageous than they initially appear. Furthermore, moral hazard effects may provide additional incentives for the negotiating parties to alter their behaviour once an agreement has been reached. As a result, expected benefits of participating in cooperative agreements may not be forthcoming as expected. Cooperation is further hampered when states fear that others take on irresponsible commitments. No matter whether states make commitments they know ex-ante are impossible to keep or assume responsibilities they cannot discharge due to over-optimistic assumptions, for states doubting the ability of bargaining parties to fulfil their obligations it can be rational to decide against cooperation. International regimes reduce such uncertainties by coordinating a better dispersal of information, by reducing moral hazard incentives and by shaping the expectations on other states' behaviour.

International regimes also reduce the transaction costs involved in international cooperation[14]. For one thing, international regimes reduce the costs arising from the bargaining process itself by providing for infrastructure and clear bargaining rules. Negotiations and agreements can be concluded much faster when agreements on participants and the fundamental objectives of cooperation have been made in

---

11 International organisations often exist within a regime and are an instrument to implement a regimes rules and procedures. As the distinction between different types of international institutions does not add to the argument in this context, the terms will be used interchangeably. For a thorough discussion on the definition of international regimes see Andreas Hasenclever, Peter Mayer and Volker Rittberger. 1997. *Theories of International Regimes.* Cambridge: Cambridge University Press: 8–22
12 See Robert Keohane. 1984. *After Hegemony.* Princeton, NJ: Princeton University Press: 89
13 See Keohane (1984): 92–96
14 See Keohane (1984): 89–92

advance and need not to be negotiated for every issue anew. Once a regime has been created, marginal costs of addressing additional problems are significantly less than those arising when negotiating outside of a regime. Similarly, the costs of monitoring members' behaviour and adherence to the rules and norms established under a regime are internalized and so shared by all members: Monitoring costs for individual states are thus significantly reduced. In addition, arrangements on various distinct issue areas tend to be what Keohane calls *nested* within a regime. This allows for linking different issues together and enhances states' ability to bargain with each other; in monetary terms, by linking issues regimes improve the liquidity of side-payments in the bargaining process. At the same time, shirking commitments becomes more expensive and increases incentives for participants to keep their part of the bargain. All these channels of transmission allow international regimes to reduce the costs of cooperation among sovereign states, increasing net benefits and making cooperation a more attractive strategy.

Although mutual interests among states make international cooperation possible, cooperation often fails despite their existence. Therefore shared interests are a necessary but not a sufficient condition for cooperative behaviour among states. For international cooperation to be realised, the benefits arising from coordinating actions among actors must clearly outweigh the coordination costs involved. The higher the net gains derived from cooperation, the higher the probability that coordination will be realised and international regimes created. Several factors influence the size of net gains that can be derived from cooperation: First and foremost, gains from cooperation depend on the level of interdependence between states and on the density of issues within individual policy areas. In economic relations, the density of issues is generally high. Consequently, gains from cooperation exceed those in policy areas with lower issue density. The large number of economic and financial regimes is a direct result. In policy areas characterised by limited interdependence and low issue density, the probability for institutionalised cooperation to develop will be small; here ad-hoc agreements can become preferable because transaction costs arising from organizing international regimes can be avoided.

Costs of creating international regimes are also related to the number of participants. The more players participate, the harder and more expensive it will be to control members' adherence to agreed rules and principles. In regimes with very large numbers of participants additional instruments for control become necessary; as a result costs of cooperation rise and reduce the attractiveness of creating international regimes. Aside from costs and benefits, the probability of international cooperation is also influenced by the balance of power between actors. Although the existence of a hegemonic power is no necessary requirement for cooperative behaviour, it increases the likelihood that international regimes will be formed. For a hegemonic power within a specific problem area, the benefits of international cooperation can be substantial and may exceed the costs of creating a regime unilaterally. Countries with less exposure to specific policy areas gain proportionally less from cooperation; but even relatively limited benefits from cooperation may induce a country to join a regime if the expenses of creating a regime are covered by the hegemon.

Neo-liberal institutionalist theories of international regimes do not explain cooperation among states equally well for all areas. Regarding issues of international security, neo-realist approaches often appear more suggestive, as may cognitive approaches in other policy areas. However, in accounting for international cooperation on economic and financial issues, neo-liberal institutionalist frameworks as laid out by Keohane have the greatest explanatory power. Regarding the issue of global financial stability, the two main strands of critique on neo-liberal institutionalism fail to significantly undermine the theory's applicability. The realist critique that Keohane's approach fails in taking into account states' concentration on relative gains rather than absolute gains[15] is not convincing since the costs of financial instability make cooperation worthwhile not only for industrialised countries, but for emerging markets and developing countries alike[16]. The point of contention that interests or utility functions of states are not exogenous but influenced by participation in international regimes[17] does not contravene Keohane's conclusions regarding the opportunities for international cooperation. Although both arguments can be applied to cooperation on selected economic and financial issues, in the policy area of this analysis both issues of contention are of limited relevance.

1.2.2 Public Choice Theory

Public choice provides the methodological background to this analysis. *Public choice theory* analyses issues in the field of politics based on economic concepts; it applies economic principles to problems of individual and collective decision-

---

15 See Joseph Grieco. 1988. "Anarchy and the Limits of Cooperation: A Realist Critique of the Newest Liberal Institutionalism." *International Organization.* Vol. 42, No. 3: 485–507

16 While an increase in global financial stability would benefit countries universally, for a selected group of actors within countries more stability would involve detrimental effects: Actors concerned are those who gain from financial instability either directly through speculation, primarily hedge funds, or by selling insurance against volatility, e.g. institutions selling and marketing options or interest and currency swaps. See Heribert Dieter. 2003. "Das globale öffentliche Gut Finanzielle Stabilität: Wege zur Reduzierung der Turbulenzen auf den internationalen Finanzmärkten." In: Achim Brunnengräber (Ed.). 2003. *Globale öffentliche Güter unter Privatisierungsdruck: Festschrift für Elmar Altvater.* Münster, Germany: Westfälisches Dampfboot: 93

17 See Alexander Wendt. 1992. "Anarchy Is What States Make of It: The Social Construction of Power Politics." *International Organization.* Vol. 46, No. 2: 391–425

making and may thus be understood as a research agenda rather than discipline in itself[18]. Public choice approaches draw on essentially three building blocks: Methodological individualism, rational choice and the belief that politics can be modelled as exchanges among actors. As such public choice has numerous roots and antecedents including Max Weber's sociology, John Stuart Mill's utilitarism and Adam Smith's classical economics. Beginning in the 1950s it developed into a coherent approach and has become widely respected at least since it won James Buchanan the Nobel price in economics in 1986. Public choice theory has developed numerous models and concepts to analyse a wide range of issues in the public domain such as voting behaviour, collective action problems, bureaucracies or public goods.

Like neo-liberal institutional theories of international relations, public choice theory rests on rational choice assumptions. In this sense neo-liberal institutionalism as theoretic framework to explain international relations and public choice theory as methodological tool set are ideal complements. Rational choice theory assumes individuals are goal-oriented, purposive and have hierarchically ordered preferences. Individuals' actions are based on rational calculations aiming at the maximization of utility. This includes determining the utility foregone by rejecting alternative actions and identifying associated costs. Consequently, social patterns, collective behaviour and collective decisions are perceived as the outcome of rational choices made by utility-maximizing individuals. At the same time, theses social patterns provide the setting for subsequent rational decisions by individuals, determining the distribution of resources and the alternative actions individuals can choose from[19].

Rational choice theory is often associated with methodological individualism and its explicit focus on the individual as the unit of analysis[20]. However, even when methodological individualism is rejected, rational choice assumptions can be retained. As in both realist and neo-liberal institutionalist approaches to the analysis of international relations, states can be selected as the unit of analysis and assumed to determine their course of action in accordance with rational choice assumptions. Similarly, public choice concepts can be successfully employed to analyse the behaviour of and relations among individual states or groups like emerging economies, developing and industrial countries or international investors. Three public choice concepts are of particular relevance when analysing whether the IMF could be restructured into an international lender of last resort: The concept of global public goods, the concept of moral hazard, and principal agent models.

---

18 See James Buchanan. 2001. *The Origins and Development of a Research Program*. Webpage. Fairfax, VA: Public Choice Society. http://www.pubchoicesoc.org/about_pc.html
19 See Jonathan Turner. 1991. *The Structure of Sociological Theory*. Belmont, CA: Wadsworth: 354
20 See Mark Bonchek and Kenneth Shepsle. 1997. *Analysing Politics: Rationality, Behavior and Institutions*. New York, NY: W. W. Norton: 19

1.2.2.1 Global Public Goods

The concept of public goods can be traced back to the eighteenth century: David Hume and Adam Smith both discuss public or common goods within their work. In contrast to the majority of goods, public goods are not provided by the private sector. This is due to two particular qualities: Public goods are non-excludable and non-rivalrous. Impure public goods fulfil these qualities only partially: Club goods, one type of impure public goods, are non-rivalrous, but excludable in consumption. Common pool resources, another type, are non-excludable, but rivalrous in consumption. Due to the existence of free-rider problems, the market often fails to provide public goods at sufficient quantities. Because rational actors have the incentive to consume public goods complementarity and due to their quality of non-excludability, providers of public goods cannot effectively ensure payment by the consumers of public goods; as a consequence, the private sector is unwilling to provide them. Because public goods can be essential for social welfare, the government often takes on the responsibility for their provision.

While the need for public goods like security or broadcasting can be catered for nationally, the provision of other non-rivalrous and non-excludable goods cannot be ensured by national governments alone. Global warming is a prime example. To qualify as global public good, the good's benefits must occur to more than one group of countries and to a broad spectrum of the world's population—without jeopardizing the needs of future generations[21]. As in the case of non-global public goods, depending on the degree to which these qualities are fulfilled, pure and impure global public goods can be distinguished. A further distinction can be made between *final global public goods* such as a healthy environment, peace or international stability and *intermediate global public goods* like international regimes or other institutions created to facilitate the provision of final global public goods[22]. The need for international regimes is a consequence of the difficulties involved in the provision of global public goods. Domestically, the state can coerce individuals to pay for the consumption of publicly provided goods. Global public goods can be consumed universally, but there is no supranational institution to ensure that its beneficiaries contribute to the costs of provision. To facilitate the cooperation required for the provision of global public goods, the existence of international regimes can be essential.

---

21 See Inge Kaul, Isabelle Grunberg and Marc Stern. 1999. "Defining Global Public Goods." In Inge Kaul, Isabelle Grunberg and Marc Stern (Eds.). *Global Public Goods.* Oxford: Oxford University Press: 10
22 See Inge Kaul, Isabelle Grunberg and Marc Stern (1999): 13

Global financial stability should be regarded as global public good since instability has all characteristics of global public bads[23]. Global financial instability imposes heavy costs on all countries involved: The financial crisis in Thailand had repercussions not only on the geographical region of Southeast Asia, but also on emerging economies in Central Europe and Latin America. Industrial countries not only suffered large losses in the value of their foreign assets, but had to face the threat of an international credit freeze and slowing economic growth. Excessive volatility and over-reaction by markets can be perceived as a negative externality of financial markets' function to price risks. It occurs when financial panics and herd behaviour lead to sharp movements in asset prices which cannot be justified by currently available information[24]. Financial market failures originate from information asymmetries inherent in the relationship between lenders and borrowers and can result in problems of moral hazard and adverse selection. Moreover, a vulnerable financial system can result in multiple equilibria[25] and self-fulfilling financial crises. At the international level these problems are exacerbated: Due to liberalised capital markets, instability within one economy can quickly spill over to others. Information asymmetries are aggravated due to different degrees of transparency, accounting practices and monitoring difficulties. As increased safety and regulatory requirements imposed by national authorities reduce financial sector profitability, a competitive reduction of regulations may occur between regulatory authorities of individual countries which try to ensure their domestic financial sector's international competitiveness.

A lack of financial stability imposes significant costs onto society: As the failure of a single bank can endanger the whole financial sector, failing banks are normally bailed-out by the government; costs of bank bail-outs typically involve amounts between 15 and 20 percent of GDP, but can rise up to 50 percent as in Argentina during the early 1980s[26]. In addition, international credit crunches resulting from global financial instability can slow economic growth significantly, not only in developing countries and emerging economies, but in industrialised countries as well. In developing countries negative growth and the economic reforms necessary

---

23 In contrast to global public goods, global public bads produce socially undesirable outcomes that are non-rival and non-excludable across countries. Typical examples include acid rain, global warming or war.

24 See Charles Wyplosz. 1999. "International Financial Instability." In Inge Kaul, Isabelle Grunberg and Marc Stern (Eds.). *Global Public Goods.* Oxford: Oxford University Press: 153

25 Multiple equilibria arise in situations where variables can converge on more than one stable combination. This is the case when functions are non-linear and intersect at two or more points. In most instances the real world is described more accurately by multiple than by simplifying single-equilibrium models.

26 See Andrew Crockett. 1997. "Why Is Financial Stability a Goal of Public Policy?" In Federal Reserve Bank of Kansas City. 1997. *Maintaining Financial Stability in a Global Economy.* Kansas City, MO: Federal Reserve Bank of Kansas City: 13

to restore stability can provoke backlashes by the public and endanger political stability. As such, the adverse effects of financial instability are felt universally, not only within the crisis country or its geographic region.

Modelling financial stability as a global public good highlights the importance of two sets of issues in the analysis of whether the IMF could operate as international lender of last resort: Examining the factors contributing to financial instability points to the area on which reform efforts should concentrate. Analysing the difficulties associated with the provision of global public goods facilitates the identification of the key problems which make coordinated international efforts to increase global financial stability so demanding. The central problems for international cooperation are problems of moral hazard and principal-agent relationships.

1.2.2.2 Moral Hazard Problems

Moral hazard problems can be identified in almost all parts of this analysis: On the one hand the existence of moral hazard is an important factor contributing to the difficulties in providing public goods. On the other, moral hazard considerations are the foundation of claims that liquidity assistance by the official sector contributes to rather than mitigates the problem of financial instability. Last, not least, the concept of moral hazard is a fundamental building block of both neo-realist and neo-liberal theories of international relations. As moral hazard in the international credit markets will be discussed in depth in chapter 9, a short description of the concept here suffices.

A typical definition provided by microeconomic textbooks describes moral hazard as *the tendency whereby people expend less effort protecting those goods which are insured against theft or damage*[27]. Another asserts that *Moral Hazard arises when individuals, in possession of private information, take actions which adversely affect the probability of bad outcomes*[28]. Consequently, for moral hazard to be present, the actor in question must undertake a hidden action which increases the probability of an unwanted outcome. The concept of moral hazard, long identified in the insurance industry, was introduced to economics by Kenneth Arrow in 1963. Analysing the particularities of the medical care sector, Arrow identified several problems impeding the effectiveness of insurance for health care. The most important finding was that insurance influences incentives of the insured party and can thus alter the probability of the insured event unless it is outside the control of the insured party:

---

27 Robert Frank. 1991. *Microeconomics and Behavior.* New York, NY: McGraw-Hill: 193
28 Douglas McTaggart, Christopher Findlay and Michael Parker. 1992. *Economics.* Sydney, Australia: Addison-Wesley: 440

What is desired in the case of insurance is that the event against which insurance is taken be out of control of the individual. Unfortunately, in real life this separation can never be made perfectly. The outbreak of fire in one's house or business may be largely uncontrollable by the individual, but the probability of fire is somewhat influenced by carelessness, and of course arson is a possibility, if an extreme one[29].

Two types of moral hazard can be distinguished: Arrow's example refers to so-called ex-ante moral hazard. It implies that once insurance has been taken out, the insured event becomes more likely as the insured party has fewer incentives to prevent the event from occurring. Ex-post moral hazard refers to situations where the insured event is not more likely to occur, but once it occurs the insured party is more likely to claim damages. In this case the insured party would claim payments e.g. for the repair of minor damages to an insured car he would have left unrepaired without insurance. Another type of ex-post moral hazard can take place via misrepresentation, i.e. when insurance benefits are claimed despite a lack of damage or the insured party misrepresents damage to make it eligible for insurance payments. Again, both cases result from information asymmetries; without privileged information, the insured party would be unable to profit from moral hazard behaviour for given perfect information the insurer could price contracts adequately. A related problem resulting from asymmetric information is that of adverse selection, identified by George Akerlof in the so-called *lemon problem*[30]. Adverse selection is a result of ex-ante misrepresentation and describes a situation where the inability of one actor to assess the quality of other actors in the same market leads to a predominance of poor-quality actors.

The insurance industry has developed a number of ways to reduce moral hazard incentives by adding specific provision to insurance contracts: The two most important are provisions for deductibles and provisions for co-payments[31]. Both instruments reduce the attractiveness of moral hazard behaviour since the insured party incurs a loss when the insured item is damaged. Deductibles require the insured party to pay for the initial damage up to a specific amount. They increase incentives for the prevention of damage and reduce transaction costs as claims are made only for damages in excess of the deductible amount. Because deductibles reduce the likelihood that an insured event will occur, they primarily address ex-ante moral hazard. Provisions for co-payments safeguard that the insured party con-

29 Kenneth Arrow. 1963. "Uncertainty and the Welfare Economics of Medical Care." *The American Economic Review*. Vol. 53, No. 5: 941–969
30 See George Akerlof. 1970. "The Market for Lemons: Quality Uncertainty and the Market Mechanism." *Quarterly Journal of Economics*. Vol. 84, No. 3: 488–500
31 See David Hyman. 1993. *Microeconomics: Analysis and Applications*. Boston, MA: Irvin: 603

tributes a certain percentage to all damage claimed. Co-payment provisions create incentives to keep the size of damage claimed low; as such they are most effective at mitigating ex-post moral hazard problems. A third common procedure is to limit payouts by placing a quantity limit on the damage covered by the insurance[32]. While quantity limits reduce the amounts of damage payments claimed by the insured party, they are less effective in reducing the number of claims on the insurer.

The importance of moral hazard considerations in the context of global financial instability is based on the widespread claim that in its efforts to mitigate financial crises the IMF has exacerbated moral hazard problems and so made future crises more likely. Two potential moral hazard effects of international liquidity assistance can be identified. Debtor moral hazard suggests that the fact that liquidity from the official sector is available in times of crisis reduces borrowing countries' incentives to pursue responsible economic policies. Creditor-side moral hazard implies that IMF bail-outs have increased the incentives of private lending institutions to make irresponsible loans. As imprudent lending and irresponsible economic policies are the root cause of many financial crises, moral hazard considerations are central to a discussion of the Fund's role in increasing the stability of the global financial system.

1.2.2.3 Principal-Agent Problems

Like moral hazard, principal-agent problems are a result of asymmetries in information between contracting parties. The concept has its origins in attempts to address moral hazard in the insurance industry by designing optimal contracts; the seminal paper by Spence and Zeckhauser from the early 1970s is the work most widely known in this area[33]. The term principal-agent theory was coined by Stephen Ross in 1973[34]. By applying the concept in their *Theory of the Firm*[35], Jensen and Meckling developed principal-agent considerations into a *more general positive theory of firm-like relationships*[36]. Since then, principal-agent models have been employed successfully to analyse a wide array of other institutions including public sector entities and international organisations.

---

32 See Edgar Browning and Jacquelene Browning. 1992. *Microeconomic Theory and Applications*. New York, NY: Harper Collins: 454

33 See Michael Spence and Robert Zeckhauser. 1971. "Insurance, Information and Individual Action." *American Economic Review*. Vol. 61, No. 2: 380–387

34 See Stephen Ross. 1973. "The Economic Theory of Agency: The Principal's Problem." *American Economic Review*. Vol. 63, No. 2: 134–139

35 See Michael Jensen and William Meckling. 1976. "Theory of the Firm: Managerial Behaviour, Agency Costs and Ownership Structure." *Journal of Financial Economics*. No. 3: 303–360

36 Barry Mitnick. 1992. "The Theory of Agency and Organizational Analysis." In Norman Bowie and Edward Freeman. 1992. *Ethics and Agency Theory*. Oxford: Oxford University Press: 78

Principal-agent problems can arise in almost every institutional setting and occur when one party, the principal, hires another, the agent, to act on his behalf but cannot ensure that the agent acts fully in alignment with his interests. Miller and Moe define principal-agent models as *an analytical expression of the agency relationship, in which one party, the principal, enters into a contractual agreement with another, the agent, in the expectation that the agent will subsequently choose actions that produce outcomes desired by the principal*[37]. Two basic assumptions underlie agency theory: Firstly, both principals and agents are self-interested maximizers of their individual utility functions. And secondly, the agent is assumed to be more risk averse than the principal. Without a divergence of interests between principal and agent, problems of moral hazard and adverse selection could not arise.

Principal-agent problems arise as due to information asymmetries the principal cannot sufficiently monitor his agent's actions. This deficit on behalf of the principal enables the agent to shirk from its responsibilities when shirking maximizes his utility. Four types of information asymmetry can be distinguished: When choosing its agent, the principal is subject to ex-ante information asymmetries: Due to the existence of *hidden characteristics* of agents, the principal lacks the ability to ensure that the agent chosen possesses the qualification to effectively represent the principal's interests. Even if aware of the agent's qualifications, the principal may still be uncertain regarding the agent's *hidden intentions*. Ex-post information asymmetries describe the principal's difficulty in monitoring the agent's actions: *Hidden action* refers to the problem that an agent has privileged information regarding his own actions. As such, the agent's behaviour is difficult to monitor because the principal lacks accurate information regarding the agent's actions. In case of *hidden information* the principal is aware of the actor's actions, but lacks the expertise to assess these actions' quality; prime examples are expert services provided by lawyers or physicians. In both cases monitoring difficulties arise because the principal cannot establish to what degree specific outcomes are the result of the agent's actions.

Several ways exist how a principal can mitigate his agents' ability to shirk their responsibilities and limit divergences from his interests; agency theory focuses on this area. One possibility is to align agents' interests with the principal's objectives by inserting specific incentives into contracts. Another is to design an effective mechanism to monitor the agent's actions. In addition, the principal can pay the agent directly for refraining from specific actions which are harmful to the principal's interests. To address the problem of hidden characteristics, a screening process can be established and signalling devices can be employed. However, all

---

37 Gary Miller and Terry Moe. 1986. "The Positive Theory of Hierarchies." In Herbert Weisberg (Ed.). 1986. *Political Science: The Science of Politics.* New York, NY: Agathon Press

instruments are nevertheless subject to asymmetries in information; as such, their effectiveness is often limited. Furthermore, each instrument involves transaction costs which have to be born by the principal: Information costs to instruct the agent of the principal's interests, monitoring costs to control the agent's actions and motivating or policing costs to influence the agent's incentives by reward and punishment[38]. Jensen and Meckling point out that apart from the transaction costs incurred by the principal, principal-agent relationships can also involve costs on behalf of agents. So-called bonding costs refer to expenditures incurred by the agent in an attempt to ensure the principal that he will refrain from certain actions harmful to the principal's interests[39]. The existence of transactions costs implies that principal-agent relationships inevitably involve some form of welfare loss.

Principal-agent models can be effectively applied to model relationships within international relations and in the area of international monetary relations specifically. Regarding principal-agent problems at the IMF, Vaubel has analysed both the relationship between national governments and their executive directors at the Fund and that between executive board and IMF staff[40]. Tirole models the problems of global financial instability as a *common agency problem* between international investors and emerging market borrowers. According to his analysis, international investors face a dual agency problem as the return on their investments is influenced not only by the actions of private borrowers but also by the behaviour of emerging market governments. As such he identifies the Fund's role as that of a *delegated monitor* reducing the transactions costs involved in the relationship between international creditors and emerging market debtors[41]. In this analysis an even wider perspective chosen: In the discussion of legitimacy problems at the IMF, member countries represented by their executive directors are modelled as agents, while the international community at large is perceived as the principal with the overriding objective to improve global financial stability.

1.2.3 Financial Market Theory

Financial crises are a main source of global financial instability. In contrast to proponents of the efficient markets hypothesis in its purest form who exclude the possibility of financial crises occurring in sophisticated and well-regulated financial

---

38 See Ronald Duska. 1992. "Why Be a Loyal Agent? A Systemic Ethical Analysis." In Norman Bowie and Edward Freeman. 1992. *Ethics and Agency Theory*. Oxford: Oxford University Press: 152

39 See Jensen and Meckling (1976): 306

40 See Roland Vaubel. 2003. *Principal-Agent-Probleme in internationalen Institutionen*. HWWA Discussion Paper 219. Hamburg: Hamburgisches Welt-Wirtschafts-Archiv: 11–13

41 See Jean Tirole. 2002. *Financial Crises, Liquidity, and the International Monetary System*. Princeton, NJ: Princeton University Press: 47–51, 97–128

markets, underlying this analysis is the belief that although markets are generally efficient in the long run, they can overtrade and lead to inefficiencies in the short-term. Following Charles Kindleberger it is assumed that *markets work well on the whole, and can normally be relied upon to decide the allocation of resources and, within limits, the distribution of income, but that occasionally markets will be overwhelmed and need help*[42].

Financial crises are not attributed to the claim that financial markets are fundamentally inefficient or inherently unstable as argued by George Soros[43], but to evidence that financial market participants sometimes deviate from typically rational decision-making. In addition it is acknowledged that financial crises can result even from rational behaviour on behalf of investors. Although these assumptions are incompatible with the strong efficient markets hypothesis, in its semi-strong form efficient markets theory constitutes a suggestive framework to think about financial markets. Drawing on three concepts of financial market theory, the efficient markets hypothesis, the financial instability theorem and rational herding models, the understanding of financial markets underlying this analysis resembles that laid out by Charles Kindleberger in his work on manias, panics and crashes.

1.2.3.1 The Efficient Markets Hypothesis

Efficient markets theory originates in Maurice Kendall's 1953 finding that stock prices follow a *random walk*[44]. Instead of identifying a related pattern of stock price movements, changes in security prices were shown to be independent of previous movements[45] and reacting only on entirely new information impossible to forecast by analysing past prices. Efficient markets theory explains this finding through the existence of arbitrage. Although the fundamental concept has been propagated since the nineteenth century, today it is most commonly associated with the work of Eugene Fama[46]. Fama and other proponents of the efficient markets hypothesis argued that if information on past prices would allow for more accurate expectations on future movements of asset prices, investors would instantly trade away the difference between current and expected future asset prices.

---

42 Charles P. Kindleberger. 2000. *Manias, Panics and Crashes: A History of Financial Crises*. 4th Edition. New York, NY: John Wiley & Sons: 4
43 George Soros. 2003. *The Alchemy of Finance*. Hoboken, NJ: John Wiley & Sons: 333
44 If a variable's path over time follows no predictable pattern, its behaviour is referred to as a random walk.
45 See Maurice Kendall. 1953. "The Analysis of Economic Time Series, Part I. Prices." *Journal of the Royal Statistical Society* 96: 11–25
46 See Eugene Fama. 1970. "Efficient Capital Markets: A Review of Empirical Work." *Journal of Finance* 25: 383–417

The central postulate of the efficient market hypothesis is that asset prices determined in financial markets reflect all available information. This implies not only that markets process information fully, rationally and timely, but also that there are no systemic errors. Three degrees of market efficiency can be distinguished according to the degree of information incorporated in asset prices: In *weak* efficient markets asset prices reflect all information included in past price movements; as prices follow a random walk, superior returns cannot be achieved by analysing past asset prices. The *semistrong* form of market efficiency assumes asset prices not only reflect all information in past prices, but almost instantly adjust to all public information such as earnings statements, merger proposals, official releases or any other information published in newspapers or by financial information systems. Consequently, only insider knowledge and secretive information would enable investors to outperform the market. In its *strong* form the efficient market hypothesis proposes that market prices incorporate all types of information, including information unavailable to the public like company secrets and insider knowledge. Proponents of strong market efficiency consequently attribute investment performance to luck and deny that professional fund managers are more likely to outperform the market than the proverbial monkey selecting stocks by throwing darts on a newspaper's financial pages.

There is a wide consensus that the market efficiency hypothesis in its strong form cannot be upheld. On the one hand, it rests on assumptions incompatible with reality: Information is assumed to be costless[47], market participants are assumed to be always rational and financial markets are assumed to be perfect due to atomistic competition and the absence of transaction costs. Income claims are assumed to be perfectly divisible and tradable. Moreover, in perfect asset markets lending and borrowing takes place at a single and uniform rate of interest and governments refrain from interfering. There is ample evidence that these conditions fail to resemble reality. On the other, empirical studies have identified several cases contradicting the claim that movements in asset prices are entirely random. There is evidence for a positive correlation between stock price movements over periods of up to eight months[48]; at the same time, for a period of over 50 years, five-year returns for stocks were found to be negatively correlated[49]. Other anomalies incompatible with strong market efficiency include excess volatility, exchange-rate

---

47 More realistically, Jensen suggested that information is included in asset prices up to the point where the marginal costs of gathering additional information equals its marginal informational benefit. See Michael Jensen. 1978. "Some Anomalous Evidence Regarding Market Efficiency." *Journal of Financial Economics*. Vol. 6, No. 2 and 3: 95–101

48 See Narasimhan Jeegadesh and Sheridan Titman. 1993. "Returns to Buying Winners and Selling Loosers: Implications for Stock Market Efficiency." *Journal of Finance*. Vol. 48: 65–92

49 See Eugene Fama and Kenneth French. 1988. "Dividend Yields and Expected Stock Returns." *Journal of Financial Economics*. Vol. 22, No. 1: 3–25

overshooting or the finding that small firms tend to outperform larger firms. Evidence has further been presented that stocks with low price-earnings ratios outperform stocks expensive in terms of earnings[50] and that shares with low price-to-book ratios performed significantly better than those comparatively expensive in terms of assets[51]. An additional anomaly is the so-called January effect which describes the phenomenon that particularly small capitalisation stocks tend to have significantly higher returns in January than in all other months[52].

Taking into account 20 years of empirical evidence on the efficient market hypothesis, Fama proposed to replace his initial classification of market efficiency into weak, semistrong and strong forms by a taxonomy based on distinct empirical evidence[53]. Studies on the weak form of market efficiency, testing time-series or cross-sectional predictability of stock price movements, were either compatible with market efficiency or could be discarded due to the joint-hypothesis problem[54]. Event studies, testing how quickly prices incorporate new information also generally support the efficient market hypothesis in its semistrong form, regardless of whether analysing stock splits, initial public offerings, mergers or buy-backs. In terms of strong market efficiency testing for private information suggests that insiders can indeed beat the market and that at times professional research can improve investment returns. In a similar vain, analysing the performance of actively managed funds suggests that overall active portfolio management fails to outperform the market.

These findings suggest that while financial markets are generally efficient, inefficiencies and anomalies nevertheless occur occasionally. Claims that markets are perfectly efficient are thus not persuasive. Consequently, support for the strong efficient market hypothesis has fallen continuously since the concept's height of acceptance during the 1970s[55]. Semistrong market efficiency, in contrast, describes modern financial markets quite successfully and several of its predictions can be identified in practice: Compared to past price movements, asset prices appear to follow a random walk. Moreover, they react to and price in new information very

---

50 See Sanjoy Basu. 1977. "The Investment Performance of Common Stocks Relative to Their Price-Earnings Ratios: A Test of the Efficient Markets." *Journal of Finance.* Vol. 32, No. 3: 663–682

51 See Eugene Fama and Kenneth French. 1992. "The Cross Section of Expected Stock Returns." *Journal of Finance.* Vol. 47: 427–466

52 See Michael Rozeff and William Kinney. 1976. "Capital Market Seasonality: The Case of Stock Returns." *Journal of Financial Economics.* Vol. 3: 379–402

53 See Eugene Fama. 1991. "Efficient Capital Markets: II." *Journal of Finance.* Vol. 49, No. 3: 283–306

54 As any deviation of asset prices from the fundamental asset value requires an asset pricing model, irregularities in asset prices can be attributed to either market inefficiency or to a faulty pricing model. As such, it can be claimed that asset prices reflect the fundamental value while the faulty pricing model sets an inaccurate price.

55 See Robert Shiller. 2002. *From Efficient Market Theory to Behavioural Finance.* Cowles Foundation Discussion Paper No. 1385. New Haven, CT: Yale University: 3–4

quickly; at the same time, arbitrage opportunities have been strongly diminished in modern financial markets. In addition, both fundamental as well as technical trading strategies in most instances fail to consistently outperform asset indices. As such, the vast majority of empirical evidence contradicts the claim that *all financial prices accurately reflect all public information at all times*[56]—although prices adjust very rapidly to new information[57]. Despite numerous well-known anomalies the efficient market hypothesis, in its semistrong form, is the most suggestive analytical framework to study financial markets.

Financial crises are due to the fact that markets are not efficient all the time; particularly in the short-term inefficiencies can arise. These inefficiencies occur because occasionally both firms and individuals tend to engage in overtrading. Over-trading involves purely speculative behaviour, an overestimation of returns or excessive gearing[58]. As overtrading is a self-reinforcing process it can lead to speculative manias or bubbles when the majority of financial market participants engage in such practices. Most of the time manias and bubbles result in panics, crashes and financial crises. In his financial-instability hypothesis, Hyman P. Minsky conceptualises how speculative manias and bubbles can develop in originally stable economies.

1.2.3.2 The Financial-Instability Hypothesis

The financial-instability hypothesis offers a basic framework for understanding and interpreting financial crises. It regards financial crises as an inherent component of any capitalist system and emphasises the importance of financial relations in advancing economic theory. According to Minsky, the critical element in explaining why financial instability occurs is the development over historical time of liability structures that cannot be validated by market-determined cash flows or asset values[59]. In Minsky's model, this insight is derived from a micro-economic analysis of businesses' balance-sheet structures.

Hyman Minsky describes a sequence of events that lead a robust economy into a state of fragility where financial crises are most likely to occur. Induced by displacement, Minsky's term for an exogenous shock, new profit opportunities of sufficient scope foster an increase in investment and production. Increased investment and

---

56 See Robert Shiller. 2001. *Irrational Exuberance*. New York, NY: Broadway Books: 171
57 See Eugene Fama, Lawrence Fisher, Michael Jensen and Richard Roll. 1969. "The Adjustment of Stock Prices to New Information." *International Economic Review*. Vol. 10, No. 1: 1–21
58 See Kindleberger (2000): 15
59 See Hyman P. Minsky. 1982. "The Financial Instability Hypothesis: Capitalistic Processes and the Behaviour of the Economy." In Charles P. Kindleberger and Jean-Pierre Laffargue (Eds.). 1982. *Financial Crises: Theory, History and Policy*. Cambridge: Cambridge University Press: 13

production leads to steady growth in output, income and consumption—a self-reinforcing mechanism pushing the economy towards full employment. The resulting boom is fuelled by monetary easing and credit expansion, enticing ever more investment and production. As this process strengthens, continuous appreciation in prices leads to investments not only to increase production capacity but also for speculative reasons: In such a situation of *euphoria* market participants start deviating from typical rational behaviour and engage in overtrading. Firms increasingly shift from operating in sound and healthy financial—so-called *hedge* positions—to *speculative* or *ponzi positions*. Operating in *speculative positions* occasionally requires firms to raise short-term bridge financing, although over the full investment period a positive net present value is given. In a *ponzi position* a firm faces higher debt demands than investment receipts for all periods except the final one. In this case, a rise in interest rates is likely to lead to a negative present value of the whole investment project. The higher the ratio of companies operating in *speculative* or *ponzi positions*, the higher the degree of fragility of the financial system.

As the economy approaches full employment, attractive investment opportunities become scarce. Businesses experience difficulties in repaying short-term debt obligations by investment income alone and are forced to increase their debt positions further. In a state of fragility, the economy is in greatest danger of crisis and a self-enforcing downward trend of credit rationing and rising interest rates that causes insolvencies and bankruptcies. Actual crises either result from changes in economic variables, external shocks, fire-sales of assets in order to repay loans or just from selling pressure by early investors doubting the current state's viability. If an increasing number of investors' attempt to switch out of real or long-term financial assets into money, the crisis gets under way and can lead to a debt-deflation cycle of falling lending, borrowing, investment, output and income. In recession, the weakest and most debt-laden companies fail; others restructure their balance sheets and thereby contribute to a self-healing process that eventually leads the financial system from a state of fragility back to a state of robustness.

According to Minsky, this process is natural to any capitalist economy; consequently financial crises are understood as normal patterns of the economic cycle. Although derived for a closed economy, the model can be extended to an open economy perspective by introducing international capital flows as the central factor pushing economies in a state of fragility in which they are particularly prone to currency crises. Applied to an open economy, the model offers useful insights on the development of capital flow volatility, currency crises and observed boom-and-bust patterns in emerging economies[60].

Overtrading and speculative excesses[61] suggest that financial market participants, both firms and individual investors, occasionally deviate from the rational behaviour attributed to them in most economic models. This does not imply that the assumption of rational actors must be abolished. As efficient markets theory provides the best framework to analyse the movement of asset prices, rational choice theory remains the most suggestive approach to analyse the majority of decisions taken by political and economic actors. But as in its strong form the efficient markets hypothesis cannot be upheld and semistrong market efficiency resembles reality closer, the neo-classical assumption of perfectly rational actors is an ideal and actors are better described by the notion of bounded rationality. The concept of bounded rationality allows for a relaxation of the most problematic rational choice assumption, namely that of perfectly informed and accurate decision-making, by acknowledging that actors' cognitive abilities can be subject to limitations[62]. Nevertheless, although Kahneman and Tversky and Richard Thaler convincingly identify many instances where investors fail to act rationally[63], overall rational choice theory more successfully accounts for market reactions than behavioural finance approaches. While the latter accounts for a minority of observances, rational choice theory convincingly describes the majority of market reactions. In the same way financial crises should be perceived as exceptions, not as the typical state of financial markets.

1.2.3.3 Rational Herding

While proponents of the financial-instability hypothesis associate overtrading and speculative manias with *general irrationality or mob psychology*[64], herd-like behaviour can also be interpreted as a rational reaction of individuals taking into

60 See Jose Ricardo da Costa e Silva. 2002. *Currency Crises in Emergent Markets and Minsky Financial Fragility Theory: Is There a Link?* WU Working Paper. St. Louis, MO: Washington University

61 Overtrading refers to the phenomenon that at times investors engage in overly frequent buying or selling operations despite a lack of additional information. Speculative excesses denote investments decisions based on speculative rather than valuation-based considerations that drive asset prices to historically unusual high levels.

62 Herbert Simon defines theories of bounded rationality as *theories that incorporate constraints on the information-processing capacity of the actor.* Herbert Simon. 1982. *Models of Bounded Rationality.* Cambridge, MA: MIT Press: 162

63 See Daniel Kahneman and Amos Tversky. 1979. "Prospect Theory: An Analysis of Decision under Risk." *Econometrica.* Vol. 47, No. 2: 263–291 or Richard Thaler. 1992. *The Winner's Curse: Paradoxes and Anomalies of Economic Life.* Princeton, NJ: Princeton University Press

64 Kindleberger (2000): 26

account the judgments of others. But such behaviour, while perfectly rational on behalf of the individual, can lead to fundamentally irrational group behaviour. Since 1992 a large economic literature on herding phenomena has emerged. The majority of models attribute rational herding to one or more of three effects: Pay-off externalities, principal-agent issues and informational cascades[65].

Models of *informational cascades* set off research in the field of rational herding. The canonical models were developed in 1992 by Banerjee and Bikhchandani and Hirschleifer and Welch. In both models individuals receive private signals but can also observe other actors' decisions. When assuming that others are in possession of superior information, it becomes a rational strategy to ignore own information and act in accordance to the behaviour observed by the majority of actors. As a result, actors' decisions end up being based not on private information but on the self-reinforcing behaviour of the majority. Banerjee's model conceptualises how acting on the majority of actors' information rather than on one's own can become an optimizing decision rule[66]; Bikhchandani, Hirschleifer and Welch suggest that localized conformity and the fragility of mass behaviour can be attributed to informational cascades[67]. Informational externalities and cascades explain a wide range of financial market phenomena such as both demand and supply for initial public offerings, merger waves or the observation that firms tend to raise capital in identical ways over specific periods of time.

Models based on *pay-off externalities* show how individual actors' payoffs can be positively correlated with the number of other actors taking the same decisions. A typical example for herd behaviour due to the existence of pay-off externalities are bank runs discussed in detail in a later chapter: Because banks only keep a certain percentage of deposits and lend on the majority of depositors' funds, they are unable to repay depositors all at once. Without external assistance during a banking panic, a bank can repay only a fraction of its depositors before becoming illiquid. In their seminal model on bank runs Diamond and Dybvig show that under a system of fractional reserve banking it can be a rational strategy for individual depositors to start running at banks because the earlier a depositor demands repayment, the higher the probability that the bank will be able to accommodate his request[68]. For a group this strategy is irrational: Without a bank run, the eventual repayment of all deposits

65 See Andrea Devenow and Ivo Welch. 1996. "Rational Herding in Financial Economics." *European Economic Review*. Vol. 40: 603–615

66 See Abhijit Banerjee. 1992. "A Simple Model of Herd Behaviour." *Quarterly Journal of Economics*. Vol. 107: 797–817

67 See Sushil Bikhchandani, David Hirshleifer and Ivo Welch. 1992. "A Theory of Fads, Fashion, Custom, and Cultural Change in Informational Cascades." *Journal of Political Economy*. Vol. 100: 992–1026

68 See Douglas Diamond and Philipp Dybvig. 1983. "Bank Runs, Deposit Insurance, and Liquidity." *Journal of Political Economy* 91: 401–419

would be ensured. Another example of pay-off externalities can be observed in the functioning of stock exchanges and trading systems. The more liquid an exchange, the easier and less costly it is for traders to execute their transactions. As a result, market participants tend to converge to trade on a limited number of exchanges or trading platforms where sufficient liquidity ensures that transactions can be smoothly executed. Admati and Pfleiderer even show how strategic considerations cause traders to concentrate their trading activity on particular time periods during individual trading days[69].

Finally, *principal-agent approaches* argue that it may be an optimal strategy for agents taking decisions in an environment of uncertainty to follow other actors' strategies in order to reduce the principal's ability to accurately evaluate their actions. Principal-agent explanations of herding behaviour are based on the experience that individual performance is often evaluated in relation to the performance of comparable actors. Scharfstein and Stein show that portfolio managers concerned about their reputation in the labour market can be well advised to disregard their private information and copy the investment strategies of their competitors[70]. If performance disappoints the fund manager will be less likely to suffer sanctions when all other managers also underperformed than in case he would disappoint while his peers performed satisfactorily. The same reasoning explains why even the majority of actively managed funds allocate assets in close resemblance to individual benchmark indices. If market performance disappoints, a portfolio manager is unlikely to be fired as a result of equally disappointing performance. But if a manager underperforms the market he can be expected to face negative consequences.

Models of rational herding suggest that allegedly irrational decisions by financial market participants can be the result of perfectly rational decisions on behalf of individuals. The existence of rational herding does not imply that market inefficiencies are never due to irrational behaviour by financial market participants. In contrast, many market excesses are more convincingly explained by bounded rationality and a relaxation of rational choice assumptions. The arguments laid out in the following chapters are based on the belief that financial markets exhibit a semi-strong form of market efficiency and that the majority of financial crises arises from short-term market inefficiencies. These inefficiencies can be due either to temporary irrationality on behalf of financial market participants or to rational herding phenomena.

69 See Anat Admati and Paul Pfleiderer. 1988. "A Theory of Intraday Patters: Volume and Price Variability." *The Review of Financial Studies.* Vol. 1, No. 1: 3–40
70 See David Scharfstein and Jeremy Stein. 1990. "Herd Behaviour and Investment." *The American Economic Review.* Vol. 80, No. 3: 465–479

1.3 Structure of the Analysis

The analysis is structured into 12 chapters and an epilogue. Chapter 2 attempts to clarify the concept of financial crisis. It indicates that recent emerging market crises are a negative consequence of an otherwise welcomed increase in cross-border capital flows and provides a general definition. After distinguishing four types of currency crises, three generations of financial crisis models are introduced and discussed. The discussion is followed by a review of empirical evidence on how financial crises develop and a short introduction to the problem of contagion. The chapter ends with an evaluation of the applicability of various crisis models and briefly indicates selected implications that can be drawn from studying the different approaches to explain the phenomenon of currency crises. Its primary purpose is to lay the groundwork for the analysis developed over the following chapters.

Chapter 3 provides a short overview of current proposals to reform the global financial architecture. Its aim is not to provide a comprehensive literature review, but to introduce selected alternative proposals addressing the problem of financial instability. About half of the proposals introduced list various measures to increase global financial stability in general; they include measures to increase data dissemination and transparency, the introduction of a Tobin tax, Soros' suggestion to create an international credit insurance corporation, and the idea to create a world currency and a world central bank The remainder comprises the group of recommendations and proposals more specifically related to the role of the IMF as crisis manager. In this context Anne Krueger's proposal to create a sovereign debt restructuring mechanism, the Calomiris proposal and the recommendations made by the Independent Task Force are summarized. In addition, the chapter describes the reform agenda suggested by the Meltzer Commission and highlights recent procedural changes at the IMF under the directorship of Horst Köhler.

Chapter 4 introduces the theoretical concept of a lender of last resort and its historic antecedents. After laying out the importance of liquidity in preventing and mitigating financial crises, the concept's origins in nineteenth century Britain are explored concentrating on the contributions by Henry Thornton and Walter Bagehot. Taking note of both authors' central arguments allows for a deeper understanding of the theoretical concept and highlights that a lender of last resort is by no means a fad in crisis literature but has been fundamental for the functioning of financial systems for over 150 years. While Thornton put the concept of a lender of last resort into a coherent theoretical framework, Bagehot is credited with popularizing it and drawing attention to the concept's most important features. Following the introduction to Thornton's and Bagehot's work, the chapter's remainder highlights the difficulties of transferring the concept of an lender of last resort to an international setting and identifies the central differences between a domestic and an international lender of last resort. It concludes with the finding that the international monetary system lacks an international lender of last resort since current IMF policies contradict the essential principles Bagehot defined for an effective lender of last resort.

Chapter 5 adds real world examples to the theoretical discussion in the previous chapter. The objective is to provide for a better understanding of the concept of a lender of last resort. Three crisis episodes and their resolution are described in depth: The financial crisis that occurred in 1907 in the United States, the 1960s Sterling Crisis and the emerging market crises that erupted since 1995. Each crisis took place under different monetary arrangements: In 1907 the United States were on the gold standard. In the 1960s the Bretton Woods system of fixed exchange rates and capital controls had just started operating. Recent crises in Asia and Latin America, finally, occurred in the post Bretton Woods environment of floating exchange rates and adjustable pegs. While the crisis of 1907 provides a showcase for the development of bank runs and banking panics and the Sterling Crisis serves as example for a pure currency crisis, recent emerging market crises should be perceived as a hybrid form. The episodes chosen show that for the resolution of financial crises the existence of a lender of last resort is essential but that the responsibilities of a lender of last resort can be discharged by various actors. The chapter concludes by asserting that without the existence of a institutionalised lender of last resort, the resolution of financial crises is dependent on ad-hoc arrangements and the existence of individuals able to co-ordinate rescue efforts.

Chapter 6 analyses the viability of Bagehot's first principle that an effective lender of last resort should lend freely in times of crisis. It establishes that unless an international lender of last resort has sufficient resources to lend freely, its capacity to mitigate financial crises and restore confidence will be limited. After taking count of the resources currently available to the IMF, the chapter attempts to provide rough estimates how much funding would be required for the IMF to function as international lender of last resort. In this context the difference between *lending-in-last-resort as an input in monetary policy* and *lending-in-last-resort as an input in banking policy* is introduced. While the former would require unlimited amounts of hard currency, lending-in-last-resort as an input in banking policy can be realised with a far less resources indicating that the viability of an international lender of last resort does not depend on the ability to issue hard currency. When restricting its mandate to enable developing country central banks to act as lenders of last resort for their financial systems, a funding range between USD 250 and USD 350 billion appears sufficient.

Chapter 7 assesses the viability of introducing Bagehot's collateral requirement in an international context. Drawing on his original argument the two central functions a collateral requirement serves are identified: It provides security to the lender and allows for a rough solvency test on the borrower. The chapter argues that only the latter function is relevant in an international setting since extracting collateral from sovereign debtors is unfeasible in practice. A subsequent analysis of the assets available to sovereign borrowers for collateral use suggests that due to a lack of suitable assets a strict collateral requirement would permanently exclude many developing countries from liquidity assistance by the official sector: Only a fraction of the Fund's 182 members owns significant natural resources or retains sufficiently large stakes in domestic industries to put up collateral in the amounts required to mitigate capital account crises. The chapter ends by arguing that two alternative approaches, pre-qualification and ex-post conditionality, can substitute a collateral requirement in providing a rough test on borrowers' solvency.

In Chapter 8 pre-qualification is examined in depth as ex-post conditionality is discarded on grounds of efficiency and legitimacy. The analysis yields that opting for a pre-qualification approach would not only enhance the Fund's effectiveness as crisis manager, but also create strong incentives for countries to follow sound economic policies. A pre-qualification approach as suggested in the chapter would make eligibility for large-scale liquidity assistance conditional on members meeting several requirements that are discussed subsequently. IMF members would have to commit to strict transparency requirements, to ensure minimum standards of financial sector stability and to keep sovereign indebtedness at sustainable levels. Financial transparency would be ensured by requiring members to join the Fund's Special Data Dissemination Standard. To ensure financial sector stability members would require financial institutions to adhere to prudent capital adequacy and cash reserve requirements and to open the banking sector for international competition. Regarding sovereign indebtedness members would need to observe the maximum ceiling established under the Fund's debt sustainability framework, maintain an adequate level foreign currency reserves and avoid excessive levels of short-term obligations in their debt structures.

Chapter 9 addresses moral hazard problems raised by liquidity assistance through the official sector. After distinguishing between debtor-side and creditor side moral hazard, empirical evidence on the matter is analysed in depth. The analysis yields that while IMF lending practice during the 1990s has inevitably resulted in some degree of moral hazard, empirical evidence is ambivalent and suggests that the scope of moral hazard problems resulting from official sector lending is more limited than asserted by its opponents. In particular, creditor-side moral hazard seems to have declined to acceptable levels as a result of the Fund's decision to resist further loans to Russia in 1998 and Argentina in 2001. After arguing that a certain degree of moral hazard can be desirable due to the concept of catalytic finance, the chapter concludes by making the case for penalty interest rates on all emergency loans by the official sector as an adequate instrument to keep remaining debtor-side moral hazard in check.

Following the discussion of moral hazard problems, Chapter 10 deals with principal-agent problems at the IMF. The analysis concentrates on the diverging interests between two groups of IMF members: the group of developing countries and emerging economies and the group of creditor countries entailing primarily advanced industrial economies. An analysis of members' quota allocation and voting shares establishes that advanced industrial countries exert a dominant influence over IMF policies: Developing countries not only command significantly less voting share, but are also underrepresented at the Fund's executive board. The chapter argues that the under-representation of developing countries has considerable costs in terms of the institution's legitimacy and effectiveness and highlights the most promising reforms that could be undertaken to redress this imbalance. It is acknowledged however, that although desirable, political considerations make a re-allocation of quotas, voting weights and seats at the executive board a very difficult undertaking.

Chapter 11 addresses the problem of how to deal with economies that seem to be insolvent and should thus disqualify for large-scale liquidity assistance by the official sector. It is argued that those countries should be supported in efforts to restructure their debt burdens to sustainable levels. Subsequently statutory and market-based approaches to restructure sovereign debt burdens are discussed. It is suggested that an increasing introduction of collective action clauses in combination with a widely accepted code of good conduct is likely to address the problem as effectively as would a formal sovereign debt restructuring mechanism. The examination of a number of empirical studies suggests that collective action clauses have little impact on the terms under which developing economies can borrow from international capital markets. The chapter concludes by asserting that while both statutory and market-based approaches would clearly improve on the current practice of dealing with unsustainable sovereign debt burdens; the latter emerges as preferable due to reasons of practicability.

Chapter 12 converges the arguments developed over the preceding chapters and concludes that an international lender of last resort operating strictly according Bagehot's principles is practically infeasible. It then presents a pragmatic proposal how the Fund's lending policies could be reformed to nevertheless allow the IMF to operate far more similar to an international lender of last resort than it currently does. The proposal centres on a pre-qualification approach for large-scale liquidity assistance to improve the Fund's capacity as crisis manager. Countries not meeting pre-qualification conditions would still have access to the Fund's regular facilities but be excluded from liquidity assistance in excess of the current overall ceiling of 300 percent of a member's quota. The epilogue assesses the political viability of this proposal. It argues that although reform will be slow and difficult, there are several indicators pointing to an increased likelihood that the proposal's central parts may be implemented in the future.

2. Financial Crisis Theory

Financial integration has been accompanied by an unprecedented period of economic growth in the developing world. While empirical studies struggle to establish a robust causal relationship between financial integration and economic growth, there is evidence that financial globalisation enhances economic growth in developing countries with a certain degree of stability. The data suggests that countries with a minimum level of good governance and macroeconomic stability clearly benefit from increased cross-border capital flows[1]. Empirical evidence also shows that the volatility of output growth has fallen during the 1990s while financial integration increased relative to the three preceding decades[2]. At the same time, financial openness was found to be associated with an increase in consumption volatility relative to the volatility of income growth up to a certain threshold when the correlation turns negative[3]. Analysing the impact of financial liberalisation on stock market volatility yields similar results: While in the long-run stock market cycles are not extended by financial liberalisation, in the short-run particularly emerging economies can find themselves exposed to stronger and more frequent stock market volatility[4].

These findings imply that for many countries—at least in the short-term—the benefits of financial integration are alleviated by increased volatility. Particularly destabilising is the volatility of capital flows into developing countries and emerging market economies. Violent capital flow reversals make it increasingly difficult for developing countries to pursue sustainable economic policies; financial crises are a direct result. Table 2.1 indicates the high volatility of net private capital flows to developing countries which declined from USD 196 billion in 1996 to USD 76 billion in 1998 and USD 66 billion in 2001 before recovering to over USD 230

---

1   See Eswar Prasad, Kenneth Rogoff, Shang-Jin Wei and M. Ayhan Kose. 2004. *Financial Globalization, Growth and Volatility in Developing Countries.* NBER Working Paper No. 10942. Cambridge, MA: National Bureau of Economic Research

2   M. Ayhan Kose, Eswar Prasad and Marco Terrones. 2003. *Financial Integration and Macroeconomic Volatility.* IMF Working Paper No. 03/50. Washington, DC: International Monetary Fund

3   The relative volatility of consumption to income is preferable as a measure of welfare than income volatility alone given that economic actors derive their utility primarily from consumption. The finding that relative volatility of consumption to income is at first positive and thereafter negatively correlated to financial integration implies that an increase in income smoothing capabilities arises only after a certain level of capital inflows. Up to this threshold, an increase in financial integration increases relative consumption growth volatility thus making populations in developing countries worse off.

4   See Graciela L. Kaminsky and Sergio L. Schmunkler. 2002. *Short-Run Pain, Long-Run Gain: The Effects of Financial Liberalization.* Working Paper No. 2912. Washington, DC: The World Bank: 29–30

billion in 2004. The data shows that while net direct investment increased continuously over that period, portfolio investment and bank credits have been extremely volatile.

Table 2.1
Net Capital Flows to Developing Countries and Emerging Economies 1994–2004

USD billion	1994	1995	1996	1997	1998	1999	2000	2001	2002	2003	2004
Total Private Capital	151,7	192,8	196,7	191,7	76,2	86,0	74,3	66,2	68,1	158,2	232,0
Direct Investment	80,6	101,5	116,0	146,2	158,6	173,2	167,0	178,6	142,7	153,4	189,1
Portfolio Investment	113,0	23,9	86,3	60,8	42,6	69,5	21,0	−83,6	−87,6	−7,3	64,0
Other Investment	−41,9	67,4	−5,6	−15,3	−125,0	−156,7	−113,7	−28,8	13,0	12,1	−21,1
Offical Flows	3,5	49,5	−6,8	28,4	56,0	18,3	−52,1	−0,6	10,6	−61,7	−81,0

Source: IMF World Economic Outlook 2002, 2003, 2005.

Particularly countries with relatively underdeveloped financial sectors, limited macroeconomic stability or irresponsible fiscal policies have experienced financial crises so severe as to almost eliminate the initial gains in economic growth. In contrast to crises experienced in the 1970s or the EMS crises in the early 1990s, emerging market crises since 1995 impacted the real economy to a considerable extent. Sharp exchange rate devaluations and declines in asset prices during the Asian Crisis pushed regional economies into severe recessions with output in 1998 contracting by double digit rates and unemployment rates multiplying in Thailand, South Korea and Indonesia[5]. To a large extent the effects of currency crises on the real economy were transmitted via the banking sector[6]. A massive increase in non-performing loans led banks to reduce lending activities and starve the private sector of capital. Cash-starved companies were unable to profit from increased competitiveness in the world markets while foreign denominated loans increased liquidity pressures and led to wide-spread bankruptcies. The harsh declines in living standards resulting from the economic slump were felt particularly strong in countries that had only recently grown out of underdevelopment and turned into fast growing emerging market economies. The devastation felt in Argentina after its

---

5 Joseph Stiglitz. 2001. *Globalization and Its Discontents*. London: Allen Lane: 97
6 See Piti Disyatat. 2001. *Currency Crises and the Real Economy: The Role of Banks*. IMF Working Paper No. 01/49. Washington, DC: International Monetary Fund

default in December 2001 is only the latest case in a long list of casualties of financial crisis.

Financial crises not only strike at excessively indebted countries that pursue irresponsible fiscal policies; even relatively healthy emerging economies can be plunged into crisis as a consequence of financial panics. The benefits of increased financial integration thus come at a price, at least up to a certain level of economic and financial development: it is a higher likelihood of experiencing financial crisis and its painful effects on the real economy[7]. While the occurrence of financial crises can be reduced by a number of initiatives and instruments, the possibility that financial crises occur cannot be eliminated without sacrificing the beneficial effects on economic growth that arise from increasing cross-border capital flows. In order to assess which instruments and policies seem promising to at least reduce frequency and severity of financial crises, a rudimentary review of the major economic crisis models is in order. It highlights that over the last decades different types of financial crises have occurred as a consequence of distinct economic and financial weaknesses. The implication is that instruments and policies adequate to mitigate financial crises in the past will not necessarily be suited for the breed of crises experienced today.

2.1 Financial Crises in an International Context

In the New Palgrave Dictionary of Economics a financial crisis is defined

> as a sharp, brief, ultra-cyclical deterioration of all or most of a group of financial indicators—short-term interest rates, asset (stock, real estate, land) prices, commercial insolvencies and failures of financial institutions[8].

Michael Bordo attempts to clarify the concept by listing the central elements of a typical financial crisis: He suggests that financial crises are generally associated with a change in expectations regarding the economic environment, doubts on the solvency of selected financial institutions and widespread attempts to convert illiquid assets into money. Moreover, during a financial crisis the solvency of even fundamentally sound financial institutions may be under threat as the value of their portfolios declines in accordance with falling assets prices that precipitate depositor panics and bank runs. As a consequence of banking panics, financial crises often

---

7 See Sergio L. Schmukler, Pablo Zoido and Marina Halac. 2003. *Financial Globalization, Crises, and Contagion.* Working Paper. Washington, DC: The World Bank: 24
8 John Eatwell, Murray Milgate and Peter Newman (Eds.). 1991. *The New Palgrave: A Dictionary of Economics.* London: Macmillan: 339

result in a decline of the money supply causing a reduction in economic activity, falling profits and an increasing number of bankruptcies. This process can be exacerbated by deflation and resulting debt crises. In the majority of cases ending financial crises requires liquidity support by an official sector institution that increases the money supply by granting emergency loans or undertaking open market operations[9].

While several different types of financial crisis are identified in the academic literature, common to all of them is the rush of investors to switch out of real or longer-term financial assets into money, based on a change in perceptions about future economic development. In an international context, financial crises are most often experienced in form of currency crises. The discussion about the possibility and merits of an international lender of the last resort revolves almost exclusively around currency crises of the type experienced in Mexico 1994–95, in Asia in 1997–98 or Russia in 1998. Such currency crises can arise under a number of different scenarios and due to a wide variety of economic or financial reasons. What the recent types of currency crises have in common is a violent reversal of capital flows, for which developing and emerging economies are rarely prepared and struggle to cope with. Nevertheless, financial crises can develop even without the problems violent capital outflows pose to developing economies.

2.1.1 Four Types of Currency Crises

The focus of this paper is on international financial crises and currency crises for it is only in an international context that the need for an international lender of last resort arises; at the national level domestic central banks can take on lender of last resort responsibilities. Causes responsible for setting off currency crises are numerous. While in the post-war period most currency crises developed out of current account problems, recent crises in Latin America, South East Asia and Russia originated from violent capital flow reversals. Martin Feldstein identifies four kinds of currency crises[10]:

A current account crisis is associated with an overvalued fixed exchange rate causing a rising trade deficit as exports become too expensive and imports too cheap. Reasons for an overvaluation include high domestic inflation and the devaluation of trading partners' currencies. In a system of fixed exchange rates, the

---

9 See Michael Bordo. 1986. "Financial Crises, Banking Crises, Stock Market Crashes and the Money Supply: Some International Evidence, 1870–1933." In Forrest Capie and Geoffrey Wood. 1986. *Financial Crises and the World Banking System*. New York, NY: St. Martin's Press: 191

10 See Martin Feldstein. 1999. *Self-Protection for Emerging Market Economies*. NBER Working Paper No. 6907. Cambridge, MA: National Bureau of Economic Research

peg may even initially be set to high. In order to maintain the domestic currency at its overvalued level, the central bank is using up its international currency reserves. Since foreign currency reserves are inevitably limited, speculative attacks may eventually lead to devaluation after reserves have been exhausted. The devaluation of Thailand's Bhat in July 1997 is an exemplary case for this pattern.

A balance sheet crisis can occur under all exchange rate regimes and without the presence of current account deficits. It is likely to be induced by short-term liquidity problems in case an economy's foreign-currency denominated short-term liabilities exceed its foreign currency reserves. A debtor country may thus be solvent in the long-term due to expected export earnings, but still face devaluation pressure as either private or government debtors face temporary financing gaps and investors fear default. If lenders are willing to roll over debt agreements and extend lending, a currency crisis does not need to occur. But if investors doubt the debtors' ability to secure bridge-financing in order to service current liquidity demands, they may face violent capital flow reversals as experienced by Mexico in 1994–95 or Korea in 1997–98.

The state of a country's banking system is another potential trigger for currency crisis. Initial exchange rate depreciation may leave domestic banks with excessive foreign currency liabilities in regard to domestic currency assets. In addition, a bank's share of bad loans may sharply increase as local businesses face insolvency due to the rising value of foreign-currency denominated loans matched by local currency income alone. In this respect bank failures represent balance sheet problems at the micro-level. When depositors doubt banks' ability to pay out deposits, bank-runs are likely to develop. If all depositors demand repayment of their deposits at once, the bank's withdrawal reserve—sufficient in non-crisis times—is run down, realising the depositors' fear of loosing their deposits. As depositors lack the information whether banks are illiquid or insolvent, even the existence of a lender of last resort may fail to prevent a bank run in case it only supports solvent institutions. Financial sector weakness played a particularly important role during the turmoil in South East Asia.

Even without balance sheet problems, current account deficits or bank failures, a currency may face severe selling pressure generated purely by changed market expectations, whether founded or not. Contagion spreading a crisis from one country to another is only one of several reasons for markets' sudden reversal of investment strategies, which can lead to some or all of the problems mentioned above. As in 1998 when the Russian crisis spread to Latin America, contagion may occur by geographic or structural connotations by investors, by adjusted portfolio strategies, margin calls or simply changes in investment preferences. An initial sell-off, even if irrational, can thus induce a self-enforcing mechanism of downward pressure on a country's currency, leading to widespread bank failures and debt-deflation cycles. It is especially during a currency crisis induced by supposedly irrational behaviour that sufficient amounts of liquidity can stabilise exchange rates until irrational fears have subsided.

2.1.2 The Problem of Contagion

An important feature of recent currency crises has been the experience of contagion. Not only seemed the crisis in Mexico to have a *tequila effect* on other Latin American economies, the Thai turbulence spread quickly to both other East Asian economies and later to Russia and even Latin America. A variety of factors are used to explain the contemporaneous development of financial distress in several emerging market economies. The so-called *monsoon thesis* ascribes the coincidence to external factors impacting all economies in a similar pattern, such as a change in macroeconomic variables of industrialised economies, e.g. a hike in U.S. interest rates. Another explanation comes in the form of spill-over effects in terms of trade, such as changes in demand due to currency impacts on exports and imports[11]. While these forms of transmission successfully explain contagious effects during the 1970s and 1980s, neither *tequila effect* nor the *Asian flu* can exclusively be reduced to spill-over or monsoon effects.

Goldstein[12] suggests that individual financial crises function as *wake-up call* to problems formerly overlooked by the markets. Accordingly, the Thai financial crisis in 1997 alerted the market to problems of weak financial institutions and crony capitalism. This led to a re-assessment of other Asian economies' attractiveness and a change in sentiment towards the whole region. While this certainly has been a factor contributing to the *Asian flu*, it seems unlikely to be the sole determinant when looking at Latin America: The economies of Argentina and Brazil were very different from the Mexican economy, so increased consideration of factors responsible for the malaise in Mexico struggles to plausibly explain the negative sentiment towards the rest of Latin America.

Kodres and Pritsker[13] argue that perceived contagion can also be attributed to portfolio re-balancing effects caused by an initial crisis. Market losses generated in

---

11 For a discussion see Barry Eichengreen, Andrew Rose and Charles Wyplosz. 1996. *Contagious Currency Crises*. NBER Working Paper No. 5681. Cambridge, MA: National Bureau of Economic Research

12 Morris Goldstein. 1998. *The Asian Financial Crisis: Causes, Cures, and Systematic Implications*. Policy Analysis in International Economics 55. Washington, DC: Institute for International Economics

13 Laura E. Kodres and Matthew G. Pritsker. 1998. *A Rational Expectations Model of Financial Contagion*. Board of Governors of the Federal Reserve Finance and Economics Discussion Series 98–48. Washington, DC: Federal Reserve

one economy may force fund managers to sell off investments in other markets in order to satisfy capital demands and margin calls by investors redeeming their funds. Portfolio losses may similarly force hedge funds to adjust their portfolios as the reduced asset value of their funds reduces their capacity to leverage. Assuming asymmetric information, cross-market portfolio re-balancing may mistakenly be attributed by other market participants as caused by fundamental reasons potentially triggering an excessive self-enforcing process of capital flow reversals.

The variety of plausible explanations suggests that contagion can arise due to many different reasons. While not all are applicable to each observed case of contagion, hardly any contagious effects are caused by one reason alone. As most authors willingly concede, there exist a variety of transmission channels which make economies receptive to spill-overs from countries in crisis. Development of policies to address this problem must take into account all possible transmission channels in order to reduce vulnerability to contagion.

2.2 Three Generations of Financial Crisis Models

All four types of currency crises discussed above are compatible with three approaches that attempt to model the development of currency crises. Current account and balance sheet problems are the key determinants in fundamental explanations advanced initially in 1979 by Krugman[14] and more recently by Corsetti, Pesenti and Roubini[15] as well as Burnside, Eichenbaum and Rebello[16]. Bank runs, as described by Diamond and Dybvig[17] and contagion are aligned with *panic* or *multiple equilibria* approaches put forward by authors like Obstfeld[18], Cole and Kehoe[19] or Chang and Velasco[20].

---

14 Paul Krugman. 1979. "A Model of Balance-of-Payment Crises." *Journal of Money, Credit and Banking* 11: 311–325
15 Giancarlo Corsetti, Paolo Pesenti and Nouriel Roubini. 1998. *What Caused the Asian Currency and Financial Crisis*. Part I and Part II. NBER Working Papers No. 6833 and 6844. Cambridge, MA: National Bureau of Economic Research
16 Craig Burnside, Martin Eichenbaum and Sergio Rebelo. 1998. *Prospective Deficits and the Asian Currency Crisis*. NBER Working Paper No. 6758. Cambridge, MA: National Bureau of Economic Research
17 Douglas Diamond and Philipp Dybvig. 1983. "Bank Runs, Deposit Insurance, and Liquidity." *Journal of Political Economy* 91: 401–419
18 Maurice Obstfeld. 1994. *The Logic of Currency Crises*. NBER Working Paper No. 4640. Cambridge, MA: National Bureau of Economic Research
19 Harold L. Cole and Timothy J. Kehoe. 1998. *Self-Fulfilling Debt Crises*. Research Department Staff Report 211. Minneapolis, MN: Federal Reserve Bank of Minneapolis
20 See Roberto Chang and Andrés Velasco. 1998. *Financial Crises in Emerging Markets: A Canonical Model*. NBER Working Paper No. 6606. Cambridge, MA: National Bureau of Economic Research and *Financial Fragility and the Exchange Rate Regime*. NBER Working Paper No. 6469. Cambridge, MA: National Bureau of Economic Research

2.2.1 First Generation Models

First generation models explain currency crises as inevitable consequence of economies' fundamental weaknesses such as current account problems or budget deficits, but also structural, institutional or political deficiencies. In this view a run on a country's currency is an inevitable and rational behaviour by forward-looking investors trying to minimise speculative losses and maximise financial gains.

Key representative of this type of explanation is Paul Krugman's 1979 *Model of Balance of Payment Crisis* and its 1984 extension by Flood and Garber[21]. It builds on Salant and Henderson's analysis of the viability of government intervention to stabilise the price of gold[22]. Their key assumptions are that speculators are willing to hold any kind of commodity only if an expected increase in its price at least equals the return on other assets of comparable risk and that commodity prices increase over time by the rate of inflation as in Hotelling's 1931 model on the *Economics of Exhaustable Resources*[23]. If a government tries to fix the commodity's price by announcing its willingness to buy or sell it at a specific rate, rational speculators will buy the commodity at prices below and sell at prices above the peg. Assuming government tries to fix the price above the current market level, it will initially have to buy up all stocks offered by speculators and thus be building a large reserve. As the shadow price (the price in absence of intervention) is assumed to rise in line with inflation, it will eventually surpass the peg inducing unlimited demand by speculators and forcing the government to sell its reserves. Speculators, aware that government's reserves are limited, will rationally rush to buy the commodity until reserves are liquidated and the government is no longer able to fix the commodity's price at a specific level.

Krugman's model follows the same rationale with foreign exchange modelled as the exhaustible resource under the assumption of limited government reserves. Assuming that the government will seignorage its constant fiscal deficits and thus continuously increase the money supply, the value of domestic currency will steadily decline. Because rational investors expect in advance the run on foreign currency when the peg is reached, they will immediately sell off domestic currency and force the government to liquidate its limited resources. This behaviour brings forward the moment where the shadow price reaches the peg and thus triggers the crisis.

---

21 Robert Flood and Peter Garber. 1984. "Collapsing Exchange-Rate Regimes: Some Linear Examples." *Journal of International Economics* 17: 1–13
22 Stephen W. Salant and Dale W. Henderson. 1978. "Market Anticipations of Government Policies and the Price of Gold." *Journal of Policitical Economy* 86: 627–648
23 Harold Hotelling. 1931. "The Economics of Exhaustable Resources." *Journal of Political Economy* 39: 137–175

The reason is backward induction: any delay would offer an opportunity for capital gains, so individual investors have an incentive to purchase the stock ahead of the expected crisis date; and in doing so, they advance that crisis date, until it occurs at the earliest possible moment[24].

The characterising feature of first generation models is the inconsistency between government's goal to fix the exchange rate and its economic policies, i.e. the attempt to finance budget deficits by increasing the money supply leading to a rise in the shadow price of foreign exchange. Following this argument a currency crisis is the inevitable outcome of fundamental flaws in government policy. Given a fundamental weakness of the economy, a currency crisis only quickens the process, but does not cause it. This implies further that a currency crisis does not lead to a downturn in the real economy but only exposes a fundamental flaw already present in the system. Accordingly, fundamental models fail to explain cases where currency crises have a severe impact on the real economy.

Although the explanatory power of first generation models may appear limited in regard to the Asian Crisis, a number of studies nevertheless suggest fundamental economic weaknesses as its main reason. Corsetti, Pesenti and Roubini describe the Asian financial crisis as a consequence of fundamental problems in both the financial and the corporate sector. Following this reasoning a belief in stable currencies and government bail-outs led to imprudent and unprofitable overinvestment and excessive borrowing in foreign currencies until the debt burden became unsustainable[25]. Burnside, Eichenbaum and Rebello interpret the event as a classic type of Krugman's balance-of-payments crisis: They suggest the Asian meltdown was caused by excessive prospective benefits due to implicit bail-out guarantees to the indebted banking sector. Rational investors thus fled the currency in the belief that governments were unwilling to increase taxes or reduce budget deficits and were likely to rely on printing money[26].

In a similar approach Dooley highlights the importance of reserves for the government not only for reasons of self-insurance, but also as resources for offering implicit government guarantees for depositors and financial institutions[27].The large capital inflows into emerging economies since the early 1990s are attributed to governments offering investors implicit guarantees on their loans. Due to implicit

---

24 Paul Krugman. 2001. *Crises: The Next Generation*. Draft prepared for Razin Conference at Tel Aviv University. March 25–26, 2001: 3

25 Giancarlo Corsetti, Paolo Pesenti and Nouriel Roubini. 1998.*Paper Tigers? A Model of the Asian Crisis*. NYU Working Paper. New York, NY: 28

26 Burnside, Eichenbaum and Rebelo (1998): 27

27 Michael P. Dooley. 1998. *A Model of Crises in Emerging Markets*. International Finance Discussion Papers 630. Washington, DC: Federal Reserve:4

guarantees rational actors flooded Latin American and South East Asian economies with liquidity when these investments became more attractive than assets in industrial economies. As first doubts over the governments' levels of reserves arose, implicit guarantees appeared unlikely to be realisable. In response, investors withdrew funds because lacking government guarantees the higher yields would have come at the cost of higher risk. Each bailout in any emerging economy would then be perceived as reducing the amount of funds available for governments to bail out other institutions and thus made government guarantees less and less credible.

Fundamental models are successful in explaining financial crises during the early 1970s, as in their aftermath no strong deterioration of the real economy was observed. Currency crises of the 1980s and 1990s, however, did have deep impacts on the real economy. Furthermore, currency crises also occurred in countries, whose economy appeared sound, neither exhibiting particularly large fiscal nor current account deficits; fundamental approaches struggle to present suggestive explanations for these observations. In addition, the crisis of the European Monetary System in 1992–93 underlined that countries' currencies can be brought down without the assumption of limited foreign exchange reserves. The abandonment of fixed exchange rates for the Swedish Krona in 1992 was not forced by a depletion of foreign currency reserves. The Riksbank could choose from a variety of options to increase their stock of reserves and was able to fend of speculative attacks on the Krona during August and September, before announcing the float of their currency in November 1992. To explain currency crises with this kind of features, a new approach became necessary.

2.2.2 Second Generation Models

Second generation models describe currency crises as a consequence of markets moving from one equilibrium to another. Multiple equilibria exist, as speculators have imperfect information on governments' willingness to defend a peg and allocate resources in different ways depending on their current expectations of government behaviour. In this view, currency crises are essentially self-fulfilling, as markets' behaviour according to expected government policies may force the government to react in exactly this way. In contrast to the fundamental approach, currency crises can occur in countries with healthy economies and need not necessarily take place in economies with significant macroeconomic weaknesses.

The model devised by Maurice Obstfeld in 1994 rests on the belief that first generation models simplify the role of government. Instead of merely financing deficits by printing money, governments are modelled as rational actors with the choice to either abandon or to defend an exchange rate peg. Government's dependency on foreign currency reserves is assumed to be limited due to their ability to borrow in international capital markets and due to the existence of alternative strategies to defend a fixed exchange rate. A more potent government closely resembles the role of European states during the EMS crises of the early 1990s. For emerging economies, however, the level of international reserves continues to play an important role because their access to capital markets is generally limited due to their weaker borrower status.

For a currency crisis to occur in Obstfeld's model several conditions must be fulfilled: There must be sound reasons for the government to abandon its currency peg, there must be reasons to defend the peg and the costs of defending the peg must rise if markets doubt the viability of the fixed exchange rate system. A typical motivation for abandoning a currency peg is the desire by governments to service debt obligations by seignorage. Even without the existence of public debt, expansionary monetary policy can be desirable in order to provide stimulus for an ailing economy. However, to build credibility in its economy, to facilitate trade or solely due to reasons of national pride associated with a strong currency, governments are often willing to suffer considerable pain in order to defend fixed exchange rates. When investors expect a currency depreciation to be likely, they will demand more interest for lending money to compensate for increased risk: This in turn increases the government's difficulty to service debt obligations without resorting to currency devaluation. Under these circumstances speculators can induce governments to abandon exchange rate pegs by increasing interest demands to account for expected devaluation and crises become self-fulfilling.

As first generation models proved successful in describing currency crises during the 1970s, second generation multiple equilibria models fare better at explaining EMS crises of the early 1990s. But in regard to recent emerging market crises both models seem lacking some aspects. Regarding fundamental explanations, the state of East Asian economies was not particularly troubling in terms of macroeconomic variables. Current account deficits were either absent or small; neither were economies troubled by excessive fiscal deficits given generally austere fiscal policies. Multiple equilibria approaches equally struggle to fit observations on recent emerging market crises sufficiently. While during the boom phase large amounts of foreign investments flooded the region, governments were not as independent on international reserves as argued by Obstfeld[28]. Especially when there are doubts about an economy's sustainability, governments can find it much harder to draw on other resources than international reserves when trying to maintain a fixed exchange rate. Mexico's devaluation was forced by its inability to roll over short-term debt and place a sufficient amount of tesobonos; there was no opportunity to borrow else-

---

28 See Obstfeld (1994)

where. In response, a variety of new approaches, a third generation of multiple equilibria models, has developed to fit more closely the experiences made in Latin America and South East Asia since the mid 1990s.

2.2.3 Third Generation Models

Approaches developed to improve on first and second generation models can be classified into three broad types: Macroeconomic feedback models, liquidity and bank-run models and models of information acquisition and expectations formation[29]. Both fundamental and self-fulfilling multiple equilibria approaches fit handsomely into this taxonomy, since both include macro-economic feedback elements. However, this classification seems most helpful when applied to the so-called third generation of models developed in reflection of the emerging market crises in the 1990s second half[30]. These models reject purely fundamental explanations, but differ widely in identifying key determinants of recent capital account crises. Employing Krugman's taxonomy helps to structure the large number of attempts to explain financial turmoil in Mexico, Southeast Asia, Russia, Brazil and Argentina. Each class of model has several representatives, one of which will be introduced respectively below.

2.2.3.1 Macroeconomic Feedback Models

In macroeconomic feedback models crises can become self-fulfilling as investor's expectations and behaviour have effects on the real economy. Their behaviour in turn confronts governments with a new situation where they may be forced to react in a way validating investors' initial expectations. Expectations by investors that the government may depreciate its currency can lead them to demand higher interest on loans. Higher interest rates in turn may make government's debt burden unsustainable, essentially triggering the expected devaluation. A representative model of this class is the approach developed by Cole and Kehoe[31] to explain the Mexican debt crisis during 1994–95, where investors' fear of default lead them to refrain from rolling over short-term debt and substantially increased the probability of default.

Central to their model is the government's inability to roll-over short-term debt, because lenders expect it to default. A crisis is most likely when a government finds

---

29 See Paul R. Masson. 1999. *Multiple Equilibria, Contagion and the Emerging Market Crises.* IMF Working Paper No. 99/164. Washington, DC: International Monetary Fund: 5

30 See Krugman (2001)

31 Harold L. Cole and Timothy J. Kehoe. 1996. A *Self-Fulfilling Model of Mexico's 1994–95 Debt Crisis.* Research Department Staff Report 210. Minneapolis, MN: Federal Reserve Bank of Minneapolis

itself in a *crisis zone*, where amount and maturity of government and private sector debt are above a certain threshold. In their dynamic, stochastic general equilibrium model Cole and Kehoe[32] show that it may be optimal for the government to default if it finds itself unable to roll over its debt obligations, notwithstanding that without liquidity problems the optimal strategy would have been to continue servicing its debt. In their approach self-fulfilling crises and multiple equilibria occur given a certain degree of fundamental weakness.

Introducing a random sunspot variable they further establish that while a particular combination of high debt and short maturity is a necessary condition, even then a crisis does not necessarily occur. But in a crisis zone any economy is at risk and non-fundamental variables such as market expectations may be enough for a self-fulfilling crisis to develop. Regarding the case of Mexico, Cole and Kehoe advance exactly this argument: The central bank failed to roll-over its debt by placing bonds in the market when the country found itself in a crisis zone: Although Mexico's debt levels were sustainable in the medium to long-term and fiscal policies responsible, the debt's short maturity made the country excessively vulnerable.

2.2.3.2 Bank-run and Liquidity Models

In Bank-run and liquidity models self-fulfilling crises occur as lenders or depositors try to react optimally given imperfect information on other lenders' or depositors' behaviour. If banks face deposit demands in excess of their liquidity reserves, they become illiquid as soon as all depositors want to withdraw their funds at once. Depositors' optimal action is thus dependent on the behaviour of all other depositors. If other depositors withdraw their funds and force banks into default, loss minimizing depositors will rationally do the same: trying to withdraw their funds as long as the bank is still liquid. If other depositors refrain from running, the optimal strategy is to refrain from running as well, since default would be averted reducing the probability of deposit loss to zero. In essence, lenders are facing a classic prisoner's dilemma and crises result from a failure to co-ordinate. Representatives of this class of models include the attempt by Sachs, Tornell and Velasco[33] to explain the Mexican Crisis, Radelet and Sachs[34] who argue that the Asian crisis was mainly

---

32 See Cole and Kehoe (1998)
33 Jeffrey Sachs, Aaron Tornell and Andrés Velasco. 1995. *The Collapse of the Mexican Peso: What Have We Learned?* NBER Working Paper No. 5142. Cambridge, MA: National Bureau of Economic Research
34 See Steven Radelet and Jeffrey Sachs. 1998. *The East Asian Financial Crisis: Diagnosis, Remedies, Prospects.* Brookings Papers on Economic Activity No. 1. Washington, DC: The Brookings Institution and *The Onset of the East Asian Financial Crisis.* NBER Working Paper No. 6680. Cambridge, MA: National Bureau of Economic Research

caused by financial panic and the canonical model developed by Chang and Velasco.[35]

Chang and Velasco attribute financial crises primarily to financial system fragility: Indeed, in Thailand, Malaysia, Korea, Indonesia and the Philippines' excessive short-term debt and M2 to international reserves ratios were observed for the pre-crisis period. Building on Diamiond-Dybvig type bank run models Chang and Velasco show the possibility of bank-runs in cases of *international illiquidity*, a situation where short-term foreign-denominated debt exceeds the amount of international reserves available to a country's financial system. The concept of international illiquidity seems similar to Cole and Kehoe[36] *crisis zone* in describing the conditions under which financial crises are most likely to occur.

In the model banks are assumed to transform debt maturity by receiving liquid deposits and partly investing them in illiquid longer-term assets. While pooling risk, they also open the possibility of self-fulfilling bank-runs as in an open economy a bank rescue by the government depends on the stock of reserves. In a system of fixed exchange rates, a depletion of reserves or seignorage is likely to lead to speculative attacks and eventual devaluation. Chang and Velasco also show that, depending on the structure of international debt, a simultaneous bank-run by both domestic depositors and international investors may lead the economy to a new equilibrium at a depreciated domestic currency. Devaluation in turn may on the one hand cause other bank-runs to happen and on the other increase their effects on the real economy via balance-sheet problems in the non-tradable goods sector.

2.2.3.3   Models of Expectations Formation and Herding Behaviour

Given the fact that financial crises occurred even in economies with sound fundamentals, another route of explanation concentrates on herding behaviour and expectations formation. In an environment with imperfect and asymmetric information it may be rational for actors not only to rely on limited private information but to also include clues derived from the behaviour of other investors. Bikhchandani, Hirschleifer and Welch[37] showed that in the case of investors acting sequentially and incorporating the actions of their predecessors in their decision making, situations can occur where private signals are overwhelmed by the information of other actors' decisions. As this process is self-enforcing it allows for herding behaviour that causes and re-enforces violent capital flow reversals.

---

35   See Chang and Velasco (1998)
36   Cole and Kehoe (1998)
37   Bikchandani, Hirschleifer and Welch (1992) and Banerjee (1992)

In the model put forward by Chari and Kehoe[38] in 2001 currency crises occur because lenders react to small signals in an environment of imperfect information. Two types of government are introduced: A *competent* government acts efficiently in times of distress and never defaults. In contrast, an *incompetent* government will default in times of crisis. Both types of government will act equally efficient in non-crisis times, making it difficult for international investors to decide whether they are investing in a country with competent or incompetent government. Only in times of crisis a government shows its true colours.

Lenders decide whether to invest in a syndicated project in a particular borrowing country or in the rest of the world and receive private signals about the likelihood of a potential crisis. Frictions of information are introduced by assuming that lenders sequentially decide whether to invest in the borrowing country's project or abstain by placing their funds somewhere else. Given these assumptions Chari and Kehoe show that if lenders are uncertain about the borrowing country's competence it only takes small signals to set off herd behaviour in the form of violent capital flows. If on the other hand lenders are convinced that a specific government would never default, large capital inflows would continue.

The model also underlines the importance of fundamentals. If macroeconomic variables are weak, a crisis is more likely than if the economy is in good shape. However, a weak economy does not necessarily lead to violent capital flow reversals. Crisis occurs if the economy is in a fragile condition, investors are uncertain whether government will default in times of crisis and a particular combination of small signals triggers herd behaviour. Chari and Kehoe highlight two aspects in their approach. Firstly, times of financial distress are to be understood as stress test, or *tests of fire*, for governments to prove their competence. If they default, it will hurt their reputation and render them as *incompetent* in times of crisis; capital outflows will result as a consequence. In contrast, by surviving crisis without default, a government can prove its resilience and gain credibility in the market place. Assuming crises function as signalling device implies that bailouts by a third party can deprive competent governments of the possibility of proving its resilience to the market place. So even if unanticipated bailouts may not have costs in terms of moral hazard, they may still be costly due to so-called *signal-jamming* costs.

---

38 V. V. Chari and Patrick J. Kehoe. 2001. *Hot Money*. Research Department Staff Report 228. Minneapolis, MN: Federal Reserve Bank of Minneapolis

2.3 Evidence and Evaluation

As the previous discussion has shown, the increasing number of international financial crises experienced since the collapse of the Bretton Woods regime has led to large amounts of models and theories trying to shed light on the subject of currency crises. The growth of contributions to the field has further accelerated in the aftermath of the Asian crisis. As a consequence, our knowledge on fundamental reasons and potential triggers for currency crises has increased substantially. However, each generation of models evolved from an effort to improve on existing models regarding most recent crisis experiences. As such every currency crisis has triggered the development of models and theories particularly successful in explaining specific crises[39]. At the same time, these models' applicability regarding less recent experiences declined. Notwithstanding, empirical studies have identified a number of macroeconomic variables correlated to various kinds of crises over several decades.

2.3.1 Empirical Evidence

Empirical evidence testing the correlation of specific macroeconomic variables with the emergence of currency crises is growing. Eichengreen, Rose and Wyplosz construct a measure of weighted changes in exchange rate, international reserves and interest differentials and analyse the evidence of over 20 OECD economies since 1959[40]. Crises are found to occur often in economies easing their monetary policy, experiencing increasing inflation and growing losses in international reserves. Furthermore, before a crisis develops, current accounts often turn negative while capital flows decline. Kaminsky, Lizondo and Reinhart have analysed the correlation between speculative attacks and banking crises for a period between 1975 and 1995[41]. In their sample of 20 economies in Europe, Asia, Latin America and the Middle East, financial crises tend to be preceded by falling exports, output and equity prices, rising money supply and high interest rates. Banking crises are an additional indicator for currency crises. Frankel and Rose[42] test a larger sample of over 100 emerging economies for the period from 1971 to 1992. Here low growth in output, high growth in domestic credit and high foreign interest rates emerge as

---

39 See Eichengreen, Rose and Wyplosz (1995) and Krugman (2001): 1–2

40 Barry Eichengreen, Andrew Rose and Charles Wyplosz. 1996. "Exchange Rate Mayhem: The Antecedents and Aftermath of Speculative Attacks." *Economic Policy* 21: 249–312

41 Graciela Kaminsky, Saul Lizondo and Carmen M. Reinhard. 1997. *Leading Indicators of Currency Crises*. IMF Working Paper No. 97/79. Washington, DC: International Monetary Fund

42 Jeffrey A. Frankel and Andrew K. Rose. 1996. *Currency Crashes in Markets: Empirical Indicators*. NBER Working Paper No. 5437. Cambridge, MA: National Bureau of Economic Research

leading indicators preceding currency crises. In addition, Frankel and Rose identify a correlation between low ratios of foreign direct investment to total debt and a high likelihood of currency crisis.

Berg and Patillo have tested how warning indicators identified in empirical surveys fare when trying to predict turmoil in South East Asia[43]. Two out of three models tested failed to provide any significant results in forecasting the crisis; only the indicators identified by Kaminsky, Lizondo and Reinhart had limited success. While types of samples and periods chosen vary considerably, a number of leading indicators emerge and are identified in several empirical studies including those cited above. Currency crises typically occur in periods of overvalued exchange rates, strong growth in domestic credit and growing current account deficits. In the aftermath of crisis, economies are often left with an undervalued exchange rate, high interest rates, inflation and declining current account deficits. Furthermore, currency crises in emerging economies do often coincide with high interest rates in less risky developed countries. However, high domestic asset prices and fiscal policies do not emerge as leading indicators for currency crises[44].

2.3.2 Evaluation

When unique equilibrium models by Krugman and Flood and Garber emerged in the late 1970s there were widespread doubts on the sustainability of the international financial system. While the currencies of Germany and Japan faced persistent buying pressure, the currencies of the old industrial powers appeared overvalued. In 1968 the United Kingdom and France surrendered to speculative attacks and devalued their currencies, while Germany reacted to the increased demand by modestly adjusting the Deutschmark upwards in the following year[45]. By 1970 similar pressures on the U.S. Dollar were strengthening. The unpopularity of the war in Vietnam made it difficult for the administration to increase taxes and it responded by increasing the money supply thereby fuelling inflationary pressures. By 1971 foreign-held reserves by far exceeded U.S. gold reserves and Nixon was forced to abandon convertibility of the dollar into gold and with it the Bretton Wood system. Being developed in the aftermath of these developments, Krugman's model fares very well in describing how currency crises develop as result of the incompatibility

---

43 Andrew Berg and Catherine Pattillo. 1999. *Are Currency Crises Predictable? A Test.* IMF Staff Paper 46/2. Washington, DC: International Monetary Fund

44 Charles Wyplosz. 1998. *Globalized Financial Markets and Financial Crises.* Paper presented at the conference "Coping with Financial Crises in Developing and Transition Countries: Regulatory and Supervisory Challenges in a New Era of Global Finance" organised by the Forum on Debt and Development. Amsterdam, March 16–17, 1998

45 See Barry Eichengreen. 1996. *Globalizing Capital.* Princeton, NJ: Princeton University Press: 132

of attempts by the government to tackle deficits by printing money and at the same time maintaining a fixed currency regime. However, taking into account the very different kind of crises experienced during the 1980s, the model's simplistic view of government makes it less suitable to interpret subsequent financial crises in Europe, Latin America and South East Asia[46].

Similarly, second generation multiple equilibria approaches evolved as a reaction to speculative attacks on currencies in the European Monetary System. Attacks on European currencies became an attractive investment strategy as the economic slump and high rates of unemployment in Europe during the early 1990s undermined the credibility of official commitments to defend the exchange rates agreed under the EMS. Obstfeld's description of governments' policy choices clearly reflects the state of the European economy at the time. The perceived overvaluation of European currencies was painful in terms of both unemployment and high interest rates which were required to maintain the currencies within EMS bands. But to abandon efforts maintaining currencies within the EMS band under the Maastricht Treaty meant disqualification from the European Monetary Union and could prove costly in terms of reputation. Given high unemployment and weak financial institutions the markets started questioning the determination of central banks and governments to maintain the fixed exchange rates as agreed under the EMS. With Denmark's rejection of the Maastricht Treaty fears about governments' willingness to defend overvalued exchange rates strengthened since for any country a rejection of the Maastricht Treaty considerably reduced the motivation to maintain the peg for the sake of EMU eligibility. European central banks were forced to drastically raise interest rates and many European central banks exhausted their international reserves only to eventually surrender and devalue. Obstfeld's central assumption of central banks' policy choice to defend or abandon a fixed exchange rate regime does handsomely describe these developments. However, in subsequent emerging market crises in Latin America, Asia and Central Europe, governments didn't have this choice. When governments eventually abandoned their pegs, it was not to reduce unemployment in their economy, but simply a result of lacking foreign exchange reserves.

Likewise, third generation approaches that attempt to explain financial crises in Latin America and Southeast Asia are a product of the experiences made since the mid 1990s. Each model stresses particular features of recent emerging market crises. The role of excessive short-term debt and fears of illiquidity is key determinant in Cole and Kehoe's model aimed explicitly at explaining the Tequila Crisis. Chang and Velasco emphasize the importance of stability within the domestic financial

---

46 See Paul Krugman. 1996. *Are Currency Crises Self-fulfilling?* NBER Macroeconomics Manual. Washington, DC: National Bureau of Economic Research

system: These factors were pre-eminent during financial turmoil in Southeast Asia. What emerging market crises had in common was their inability to withstand violent capital flow reversals. But the reasons triggering such capital flow reversals differed from case to case. Macroeconomic feedbacks, bank runs, debt structures, financial system instability and herding behaviour all account to some degree for recent emerging market crises; only the weight of these factors varies, depending on the economy concerned. This consequently reduces third generation models' explanatory power regarding balance-of-payments crises during the 1970s and speculative attacks on currencies under the EMS during 1992–93.

Despite some similarities financial crises have come in various forms, and a successful one-size-fits-all approach is unlikely to evolve. The existence of a vast array of models and theories demands concentration on aspects of particular importance regarding the most recent type of financial crisis: Therefore lessons and implications of third generation models should provide the primary theoretical framework underlying the formulation of policy prescriptions to reduce both frequency and severity of financial crises in developing countries and emerging economies.

Notwithstanding, although first generation balance-of-payments models have been of limited explanatory power regarding the Mexican and Asian crises, fundamental economic variables such as levels of sovereign debt or foreign currency reserves retain exceptional relevance; their importance is underlined by the empirical surveys mentioned above and the role fundamental variables have played in virtually every theory on financial crises. Most plausibly, fundamentals seem at work when generating an environment of financial fragility where financial crises are most likely to occur. For the understanding of financial crises the concept of *crisis zones* as suggested by Cole and Kehoe seems a helpful feature, particularly when defined not only in terms of short-term debt but including the key macroeconomic variables identified by Eichengreen, Rose and Wyplosz, Kaminsky, Lizondo and Reinhart and Frankel and Rose.

While the existence of a *crisis zone* is a necessary—although not sufficient—condition for liquidity problems to occur, what triggers a crisis eventually is impossible to generalise. Experiences made during past crisis episodes have drawn attention to a wide variety of potential sources, but none can be claimed essential in all instances. Herding behaviour may or may not occur, bank runs are never inevitable and macroeconomic feedback loops can lead to self-fulfilling financial crises but they don't always do so. Consequently, one may have to accept that the most any additional explanatory approach on financial crisis can yield is to add to a list of factors likely to trigger a crisis under particular circumstances. While the quest for all encompassing models is likely to continue, the prescription of policy guidelines to reduce frequency and strength of financial crises does not depend on the development of a fourth generation of models[47]. Existing models and theories, particularly those of the third generation, and the experiences made so far already allow drawing the most relevant lessons regarding policy prescriptions to increase global financial stability.

2.3.3 Lessons and Implications

A large number of implications and policy advice have been suggested in the debate on causes and remedies regarding the problem of financial crises. Not surprisingly, each approach to explain how financial crises develop emphasises particular policy responses, depending on the model advanced. Fundamental approaches will underline the importance of macroeconomic factors, while multiple equilibria approaches add a variety of suggestions on how to avoid the move from good to bad equilibria. Each generation of models developed with a particular type of crisis in mind suggests policies fitting to those particular experiences. Despite the subjectivity of policy proposals, four lessons appear less dependent on the particularities of specific crisis models[48].

First and foremost, the improvement of monitoring and information systems regarding the state of individual economies is of crucial importance. Fundamental variables play an important role in all models explaining financial crises, either as reason by themselves or as foundation for an environment where crises are likely to occur. Despite the existence of refined monitoring mechanisms, the number of variables included in preventive monitoring may have to be widened considerably to include information on economies' debt structure, reserve depletion and country specific structural weaknesses.

The emergence of global capital markets has further strengthened the important role the financial sector plays in any economy. Its role in transforming debt maturity and efficiently channelling funds to its best uses is essential particularly in emerging economies. But it is vital that sufficient regulation and supervisory structures are in place in order to prevent financial institutions from taking on excessive levels of risk in terms of default, exchange rate volatility and debt maturity.

Experience from a large number of currency crises further underlines the danger of committing to a system of fixed exchange rates. A currency peg seems to be viable only when governments are clearly in a position to maintain it. Sound macroeconomic policies alone have proven to be insufficient, and a strong developed financial system and a large pool of foreign currency reserves appear to be the

---

47 See Krugman (2001) who suggests how a fourth generation model might look like.
48 Bijan B. Aghevli. 1999. "The Asian Crisis: Causes and Remedies." *Finance and Development.* Vol. 36, No. 2. Washington, DC: International Monetary Fund

minimal requirement. These conditions are hard to attain, and in practice render a fixed exchange rate regime imprudent for a majority of emerging economies.

The timing and sequencing of capital market liberalisation has been very important particularly for Asian economies. While capital market liberalisation itself has beneficial effects on the development of most economies, the way it is done is very important. Experience suggests that a gradual opening is the most prudent way: foreign direct investment should be liberalised before short-term capital flows are freed from regulation. Moreover, the liberalisation of capital flows should go hand in hand with structural liberalisation of the financial system, in essence the opening of the market for foreign financial institutions with more experience in due diligence execution and risk management.

These four lessons allow for the formulation of specific policy advice. Some policies will be suitable for all economies, namely those regarding the prevention of an economy entering a *crisis zone*. Others may be less applicable and depending on the state of the particular economy and its financial system. Regarding causes that can trigger a currency crisis, comparative studies identifying features and similarities between economies that have experienced currency crises in the past may be a useful source for alerting to dangerous developments and devising potential policy responses. As such, economic history may become a more important source of policy formulation than it is at present.

The measures identified above almost exclusively serve the goal of crisis prevention. But even the strongest efforts in crisis prevention cannot eliminate the possibility of future financial crises. When surrendering to the fact that financial crises seem an inherent feature of the global financial system, it is equally important to develop effective strategies to mitigate financial crises once they are under way. An international lender of last resort is one of several instruments which could enable the international community to enhance its ability to manage inevitably occurring financial crises.

3. Selected Proposals to Increase Global Financial Stability

As both character and origin of financial crises can vary considerably, it is not surprising that numerous proposals and recommendations have been made on how to increase global financial stability and reduce crises' frequency and severity. Very often, proposals address specific aspects of countries' vulnerability to financial crises. Therefore alternative proposals to increase the stability of the international monetary system do not necessarily contradict each other. Indeed, very often recommendations could be implemented in combination. Enhancing data dissemination and financial transparency, for example, does not interfere with the creation of a sovereign debt restructuring mechanism. Similarly, a Tobin tax does not eliminate the case for reforming the IMF into an international lender of last resort. While some of the proposals described below are designed to exclusively address the problem of financial crises, others are merely useful measures to enhance global financial stability in general. A selection of recommendations and proposals is described below. The selection does not claim completeness; it merely intends to provide a background for the subsequent discussion on the feasibility of one specific proposal: The suggestion to reform the IMF into an international lender of last resort. For the sake of clarity, the proposals presented below are classified into two categories: One comprises general proposals to increase global financial stability; the other, proposals specifically addressing the role of the IMF[1].

3.1 General Proposals to Increase Global Financial Stability

3.1.1 Improved Transparency and Higher Regulatory Standards

To increase transparency regarding governments' and banking institutions' financial position is the most uncontroversial measure to increase global financial stability. If the real level of indebtedness of governments is known, lending decisions by international creditors are likely to be more aligned with economic realities. High transparency standards raise the costs and thus reduce the attractiveness for governments to build-up unsustainable debt burdens; if data transparency would include derivative transactions and off-balance sheet obligations so often overlooked until

---

1 This structure follows that chosen by Barry Eichengreen. 1999. *Towards A New International Financial Architecture: A Practical Post-Asia Agenda.* Washington, DC: Institute of International Economics. His study is the most conclusive presentation of alternative proposals to increase global financial stability. However, since publication 1999 some proposal have lost in relevance and are accordingly omitted in the presentation above. Other have entered the debate and will consequently be indicated.

the Asian Crisis, creditors' ability to assess borrowers' capacity to service their debt obligations would be further enhanced. As a consequence, international investors could assess the risks associated with individual loans more accurately and price them accordingly. While international investors would be likely to reduce the volume of loans to countries saddled with excessive debt burdens, given higher interest costs the attractiveness for borrowers to take out further loans would simultaneously decline: Both would increase market discipline. As a result of more informed and prudent lending decisions, unsustainable debt structures and violent capital flow reversals would occur less frequently than in the past.

The same reasoning applies to financial sector regulation. If financial institutions are forced by supervisory authorities to regularly publish accurate information on their assets and liabilities, vulnerabilities would be exposed earlier and could be addressed more effectively. By imposing adequate capital standards[2], financial sector vulnerability can be further reduced since banks' ability to take on large numbers of projects with unfavourable risk-reward characteristics would decline. As such, a global regulatory institution, e.g. a super-regulator as proposed by Kaufman, although practically infeasible would indeed substantially increase global financial stability[3]. As in the case of government indebtedness, greater transparency in the financial sector increases market discipline and contributes to reducing the willingness of international creditors to engage in excessively risky lending.

The need for improvements in transparency has been acknowledged by the Group of 22 report on transparency and accountability in 1998 already. At the time, the working group recommended improvements in the *coverage, frequency and timeliness* of *data on foreign exchange reserves, external debt and financial sector soundness* and suggested that the IMF should publish *transparency reports* describing how individual countries meet international standards of disclosure[4]. At the same time it highlighted the importance of accurate, relevant and timely financial information to be published by the private sector, particularly regarding the exposures of investment banks, hedge funds and institutional investors. In a corresponding report, the G-22 identified several principles and policies to increase financial sector stability[5]. Today a number of initiatives have been implemented resulting in various standards on data and policy as well as on financial sector transparency: The IMF developed the *Special Data Dissemination Standard* and the

---

2 Chapter 8 discusses the determination of adequate capital requirements at greater length.
3 See Henry Kaufman. 1998. "Preventing the Next Global Financial Crisis." *The Washington Post.* January 28, 1998
4 Group of 22. 1998. *Report of the Working Group on Transparency and Accountability.* Washington, DC: G-22
5 See Group of 22. 1998. *Report of the Working Group on Strengthening Financial Systems.* Washington: G-22

General Data Dissemination System, the *Code of Good Practices on Fiscal Transparency* and the *Code of Good Practices on Transparency in Monetary and Financial Policies.* Financial sector standards have been developed by several organizations: They include the Basel Commission on Banking Supervision's *Basel II Revised International Capital Framework,* the *Objectives and Principles for Securities Regulation* by the International Organization of Securities Commissions, the International Association of Insurance Supervisors' *Insurance Supervisory Principles,* the Committee on Payments and Settlements Systems' *Core Principles for Systematically Important Payment Systems* and the *40+8 Recommendations* for anti-money laundering and combating the financing of terrorism by the Financial Action Task Force. Furthermore, there exist a number of standards to safeguard market integrity such as the OECD's *Principles of Corporate Governance, International Accounting Standards* by the International Accounting Standards Board, the International Federation of Accountants' *International Standards on Accounting* and the World Bank's *Principles and Guidelines for Effective Insolvency and Creditor Rights Systems.* Adherence to these standards is monitored by IMF and World Bank in their *Reports on the Observance of Standards and Codes* (ROSC) and often as part of the *Financial Sector Assessment Program* (FSAP).

The standards and codes itemized above are all voluntary; nevertheless a large number of countries already subscribe to many of them. However, due to a lack of know-how not all countries are in a position to provide sufficient data on all aspects of sovereigns' and their banking sector's financial position. Increasing targeted development and technical assistance would go a long way in ensuring that at least a majority of countries provide accurate and timely data. Nevertheless, there will always remain financial market participants, governments as well as investors or financial institutions, with strong incentives to provide inaccurate information: Governments may want to disguise the dire state of their finances, banks can fear closure by domestic regulators, and investment mangers might attempt to prevent massive outflows of their funds under management. Perfect information will therefore be neither available in the recent future nor in the medium term. As a result, there will always be different degrees of information between different participants in financial markets for *information asymmetries are intrinsic to financial markets*[6]. Improving the availability of accurate financial data is an important task and will contribute to improving market discipline. But it cannot prevent financial panic and crises from occurring occasionally. Consequently, the implementation of transparency standards should be understood as a complementary measure to other instruments; as a stand-alone solution it is insufficient.

---

6 Eichengreen (1999): 80.

3.1.2 An International Credit Insurance

While the Asian Crisis was still ongoing, George Soros suggested the creation of an international credit insurance corporation (ICIC) alongside the IMF[7]. Its task was to provide at reasonable cost guarantees for international loans. Under the proposal a new institution would define a threshold for sustainable indebtedness and require each country to provide accurate and timely data on all borrowing transactions by public and private sectors alike. International loans would be insured only up to a pre-defined maximum threshold; any loans to either public or private sector institutions above this threshold would remain uninsured. As a consequence, interest costs for all loans below the threshold would be at very favourable rates. Interest charges on loans surpassing the threshold would command large premiums to take into account the credit risk in case of default and thus loose attractiveness for borrowing countries. In case of default, insured loans would be fully repaid by the credit insurance while the loss of uninsured loans would be carried in full by private sector lenders. Ideally, the proposal would result in a reduction of excessive lending while up to a sustainable level encouraging capital flows to developing countries at little interest cost. More importantly, the majority of international creditors would feel no incentives to flee a country in financial difficulties since its loans would be insured. At the same time, moral hazard problems would be reduced given the absence of official sector bail-outs for uninsured loans. In Soros' proposal, the new institution would be funded by issuing Special Drawing Rights (SDRs); alternatively, funding could be put up by borrowing countries directly via a fee payable at the time of issuance[8].

Despite its initial suggestiveness, the creation of an international credit insurance corporation has never been seriously considered. Several difficulties inherent in the proposal are responsible: First, monetary policy makers fear the effects an issuance of SDRs might have on inflation[9]. Furthermore, if uninsured loans are substantial in size, a default could still cause systemic risks to the financial system. Consequently, the credibility of the official sector to refrain from bail-outs would remain limited. Other concerns arise with regard to the practical operability of an international credit insurance corporation. The problem of determining the threshold of indebtedness up to which loans would be insured alone would not disqualify the proposal: A frame-

---

7 See George Soros. 1997. "Avoiding a Breakdown: Asia's Crisis Demands a Rethink of International Regulation." *The Financial Times.* December 31, 1997
8 See Eichengreen (1999): 86
9 Soros argues that their issuance would not be inflationary since SDRs would only be created in case a borrowing country defaults; and given a default, newly issued SDRs would only supplant the capital lost in the default but not increase the money supply. See George Soros. 1998. *The Crisis of Global Capitalism.* New York, NY: Public Affairs: 178

work along the lines of the debt sustainability framework developed by IMF and IDA could address this issue[10]. More difficult would be to determine which loans would be insured and which would not if demand for debt significantly exceeds the previously defined ceilings of sustainability. Moreover, the belief that the existence of an international credit insurance corporation would result in higher capital flows to developing countries is questionable. As suggested by Jeffrey Frankel, higher capital flows would most likely occur only when international lending is in decline[11]. If international lending is forthcoming in times of economic growth, increased interest costs for uninsured loans would curtail developing countries' ability to borrow without increasing the debt service portion of revenues to un-sustainable levels. Depending on the yield spread between insured and uninsured debt, the creation of an international credit insurance corporation could thus result in an increase in interest costs for the world's poorest economies.

3.1.3 The Tobin Tax

The Tobin Tax is arguably the most widely discussed instrument to reduce specu-lative currency transactions. Proposed in 1972 and reiterated in 1978 by James Tobin, the idea of taxing currency transaction did not receive wider attention until the 1990s when emerging market crises let NGOs re-discover the idea[12]. The proposal's central idea is to levy taxes on currency transactions in order to curb incentives for currency speculation. Proponents argue that exchange rate volatility and short-term capital flows would be reduced as an increase in transaction costs would leave market participants with fewer incentives to engage in speculative cur-rency transactions. While short-term capital flows would be reduced, long-term capital flows are assumed to remain stable since discounted over a longer period transaction costs would become insignificant. Although numerous versions of the proposals are circulating, most discuss an excise duty on currency transactions of 5 to 25 basis points; taxes would be enacted by national authorities in multinational cooperation. Given a daily volume of currency transactions of nearly USD 2000 billion, tax revenue could amount to anywhere between USD 50 and USD 300 bil-lion annually. While a by-product of the initial proposal, worldwide lobbying for a

---

10 See IDA and IMF. 2004. *Debt Sustainability in Low-Income Countries – Proposal for an Oper-ational Framework and Policy Implications.* February 3, 2004. Washington: International Monetary Fund

11 See Jeffrey Frankel. 1999. "Soros' Split Personality: Scanty Proposals from the Financial Wizard." *Foreign Affairs.* Vol. 78, No. 2

12 See James Tobin. 1999. "Prologue." In Mahbub ul Haq, Inge Kaul and Isabelle Grunberg (Eds.). 1996. *The Tobin Tax: Coping with Financial Stability.* Oxford: Oxford University Press

Tobin Tax by NGO's seems primarily motivated by the opportunities for development assistance such revenues would generate.

Several reasons explain why the idea of taxing currency transactions has not been realised despite widespread support. For one, there is a large degree of scepticism whether a Tobin tax would make a difference to capital transactions; if it would, it is doubtful that the effects would be desirable as they might include a reduction not only of speculative capital flows but also of beneficial direct investment. Assuming a Tobin tax would be desirable, its realisation may still be infeasible. Given the problems involved with multilateral cooperation on far less controversial issues, a universal agreement on taxing foreign currency transactions appears unrealistic. If only some countries would introduce a Tobin tax, capital flows would not be altered but merely move to those jurisdictions where currency transactions remain tax-free. All three issues address the question of whether a Tobin tax would be effective in reducing the volatility of international capital flows; they do not deal with the question of whether a tax on currency transactions would be a sensible way of raising revenues for increased development assistance or similar purposes.

If excise levies would be imposed in a range of between 5 and 25 basis points, it is unlikely that the current pattern of currency transactions would be considerably altered; most likely both exchange rate and capital flow volatility would remain unchanged. Martin Wolf has argued that volatility may even rise as hedging would become relatively less attractive[13]. Furthermore, during financial panics, violent capital flow reversals will not be prevented via increasing transaction costs by miniscule amounts; if taxes levied were high enough to make a difference, they would severely impede the functioning of financial markets.

Moreover, even if a Tobin tax would influence the pattern of currency transactions, the effects would not necessarily be desirable. For one, a tax on currency transactions would be unable to discriminate between beneficial and speculative international capital flows; therefore it might not only curb speculative but also unequivocally desirable flows of capital between countries. In addition, there is little empirical evidence for the claim that speculative capital flows and speculation per se is necessarily destabilizing. Friedman argued that it is not since speculators would hurt themselves by speculating and thus go bankrupt[14]. Even if assuming that speculation is destabilizing and thus undesirable, increasing transaction costs may not solve the problem. Bubbles occur in real estate markets despite substantially higher

---

13 See Martin Wolf. 2004. *Why Globalization Works*. New Haven, CT: Yale University Press: 303
14 See Milton Friedman. 1953. *A Case for Flexible Exchange Rates*. Essays in Positive Economics. Chicago, IL: University of Chicago Press

transactions costs. Similarly, there is no evidence that asset markets with higher transactions costs are less volatile than those with little or no costs[15].

The most important reason why a Tobin tax has not been implemented at least nationally to raise additional revenues is the fact that it is practically and politically unfeasible. If one government would impose it on all transaction executed within its domestic financial centres, transactions would simply be executed abroad. This is against national interest and would be strongly opposed by domestic interest groups. If a majority of nations would introduce the measure, trading would move to off-shore centres like the Caymans. To prevent transactions from fleeing to non-tax jurisdictions, a Tobin tax would have to be implemented almost universally and require cooperation by all the world's sovereign entities. Leaving aside that the world's largest financial centres have no intention to join a coordinated effort, universal cooperation on this issue appears unlikely at best. Furthermore, financial markets constantly generate innovative products. It would be surprising if financial markets would struggle to devise innovative instruments allowing to trade currencies without becoming liable to transaction taxes.

3.1.4 A Global Central Bank

One of the most radical proposals put forward has been the creation a global central bank as suggested by Jeffrey Garten[16]. His suggestion is based on the belief that the IMF cannot deal with several crises simultaneously and cooperation between the world's major central banks or finance ministries would fail as the needs of national economies would override all other considerations. A global central bank would inject liquidity to foster economic growth, address issues of debt sustainability in developing economies and even universally monitor the health of financial institutions. Its most important function would be to act as true lender of last resort and engage in open-market operations on an international level. As such it would buy debt instruments of countries in crisis and sell them back once the country has recovered. Funding would be provided either by credit lines with national central banks or by taxing international trade or currency transactions. Under Garten's proposal, the global central bank would be controlled by a board of governors consisting of representatives of the G-7 and eight emerging market economies.

Several reasons render the creation of a global central bank unrealistic. Most importantly, nation states are unlikely to cede so many essential functions to an international institution they cannot fully control. Even if a number of nations would

---

15 See Dieter (2002): 14
16 See Jeffrey Garten. 1998. "Needed: A Fed for the World." *The New York Times.* September 23, 1998

be willing to participate, the chances of universal participation are minimal. While members of the European Union have given up the prerogatives of monetary policy and created a single currency, they remain unwilling to cede national authority on financial sector regulation. Furthermore, monetary integration in Europe evolved from a process of integration which lasted several decades and has been motivated politically as much as economically. If on the other hand national central banks would keep important prerogatives, the effectiveness of a global central bank would be severely impaired by national central banks vetoing all decisions of limited relevance to national interests. If a global central bank would be made independent with the mandate to maintain global financial stability, a task of immense importance would lie with an unaccountable bureaucracy not necessarily more qualified than staff at national central banks[17]. Finally, without a global currency, the creation of a global central bank would be unlikely to sufficiently reduce both number and frequency of financial crises and face the same difficulties as the International Monetary Fund today.

3.1.5 A World Currency

In contrast to most proposals that try to find ways of dealing with the consequences of exchange rate volatility, the creation of a world currency would address the problem of currency crises at its roots. Only the creation of a single currency can eliminate the problems arising from excessive exchange rate volatility. As one of the idea's early proponents Richard Cooper in 1984 suggested *the creation of a common currency for all of the industrial economies, with a common monetary policy and a joint Bank of Issue to determine that monetary policy*[18]. His proposal was based on the belief that steady growth in international trade and capital flows would lead to a corresponding increase in the problems caused by exchange rate volatility. The system he advocates is similar to that created by the European Monetary Union, with participants including essentially all members of the OECD. Members would cede their prerogative of monetary policy to an independent supranational institution, governed by representatives of member states whose voting weights correspond to their nation's share in the combined gross national product of all member economies. As monetary financing of budget deficits would become impossible, capacity for national economic policy would be reduced to fiscal policy.

---

17 See George Selgin. 1999. "We Need a Global Fed? It Just Ain't So!" *The Freeman: Ideas on Liberty.* Vol. 49, No. 2
18 See Richard Cooper. 1984. "A Monetary System for the Future." *Foreign Affairs.* Vol. 63, No. 1

The proposal to create a world currency is an extension of the idea of creating a global central bank with functions similar to those of national central banks and the European Central Bank today. No matter whether participation would be limited to the world's major industrial economies and emerging economies or universal, a world currency is unrealistic for the same reasons as Garten's proposal of a world central bank. Nation states are far away from being willing to grant such extensive powers to a supranational organisation they cannot control, particularly if participating countries and their economies would be as diverse as universal membership implies. The lack of an adequate solution to the problem of checking the power of an independent institution without impeding its effectiveness alone disqualifies the proposal as politically viable measure to increase global financial stability: A global central bank would have to determine its monetary policy to benefit the majority of its members; members in other stages of the economic cycle than the majority would suffer under a monetary policy aggravating its economic problems.

While a global currency would eliminate the problems created by exchange rate volatility, financial crises stemming from mismatches in debt structures or unstable financial systems would still occur. A common currency would be likely to transmit these problems even faster than they are transmitted today. Furthermore, while negative effects of exchange rate volatility for corporations are undisputable, the degree by which exchange rate fluctuations hurt the real economy is controversial. According to Rogoff, its effects are far less substantial than often assumed[19]. However, benefits for the real economy have to be very large to make the cost of ceding authority over national policy worthwhile. Another argument suggests that the elimination of competition between currencies would reduce innovation and thus entail a reduction in economic growth and development. While the creation of a world currency will remain unrealistic in the near future, the development of regional currency blocs similar to the EMU is a more realistic possibility for the medium to long-term. For countries with similar economic and financial characteristics like members of ASEAN or Mercosur a common currency has already been deliberated.

3.2 Proposals Addressing the Role of the IMF

A number of proposals to enhance global financial stability attempt to improve the Fund's ability to prevent and mitigate financial crises specifically. While the creation of a sovereign debt restructuring mechanism would add to the functions

---

19 Rogoff, Kenneth. 1999. *International Institutions for Reducing Global Financial Instability.* NBER Working Paper 7265. Cambridge, MA: National Bureau of Economic Research

currently performed by the IMF, other proposals aim at fundamentally reassessing the Fund's responsibilities and significantly restructuring its operational procedures.

3.2.1 A Sovereign Debt Restructuring Mechanism

The creation of a sovereign debt restructuring mechanism would enhance the stability of the global financial system by facilitating the process of restructuring the debt burden of unsustainably indebted economies. It thus specifically addresses the problem of how to deal with countries when short-term liquidity assistance is unlikely to solve the problem of unsustainable indebtedness. A formal debt restructuring mechanism modelled along the lines of U.S. insolvency law was originally suggested by Kunibert Raffer in 1990[20]. A decade later, the idea re-entered the debate when it was taken up by IMF First Deputy Managing Director Anne Krueger to create incentives for countries burdened by unsustainable levels of sovereign debt to restructure their obligations in an orderly way, ideally before plunging into a financial crisis. The existence of a formal mechanism for sovereign debt restructuring—Anne Krueger argued—would encourage both creditors and debtors to work out sustainable agreements on their own accord thereby avoiding having to resort to the formal mechanism. Reacting to a multitude of objections, the Fund's original proposal was altered several times before it was effectively dropped when the Treasury made its opposition official[21].

Under the Fund's original proposal, a formal debt restructuring mechanism would entail four features. Most importantly, it would offer the debtor country a limited period of legal protection from creditors trying to undermine a restructuring by calling on national courts. At the same time, the mechanism would ensure creditors that during the standstill period debtor countries would pursue prudent economic policies and negotiate in good faith with its creditors. In case the debtor country would reach a restructuring agreement with the vast majority of creditors, the mechanism would ensure than a minority of hold-out creditors would be bound to its terms and not seek full repayments through the courts. To enable countries to raise new loans and meet immediate financing needs, the restructuring framework would provide for the possibility of granting new lenders a preferred creditor status, ensuring they would be repaid before all other creditors. The mechanism would be

---

20 See Kunibert Raffer. 1990. "Applying Chapter 9 Insolvency to International Debts: An Economically Efficient Solution with a Human Face." *World Development*. No. 18: 301–311

21 For the original proposal see IMF. 2001. *A New Approach to Sovereign Debt Restructuring: Preliminary Considerations*. November 30, 2001. Washington, DC: International Monetary Fund. Initial objections were taken into account in IMF. 2002. *A Sovereign Debt Restructuring Mechanism – Further Reflections and Future Work*. Washington, DC: International Monetary Fund

set in motion on the request of the debtor country and be subject to endorsement by the IMF.

Although addressing a fundamental problem of international monetary relations, several difficulties make the practicability of a formal sovereign debt restructuring mechanism questionable. For one, it would need the universal force of law as otherwise hold-out creditors could sue in jurisdictions where the mechanism's rules do not apply. As argued before, the necessary universal participation for such a mechanism to function is politically unfeasible. Similar efforts like the creation of an international criminal court underline the fact that not even all of the most advanced economies may necessarily subscribe to the framework, not to mention offshore heavens like the Cayman Islands or the Bahamas. Another important objection stems from the prominent role the IMF would take under the proposal. Not only would the Fund decide on whether a country should be allowed to activate the mechanism, but it would also be the institution monitoring whether the debtor country fulfils its duties during the standstill period. On the one hand, the Fund disqualifies as a neutral arbiter as in most instances it will be a creditor of the country asking for a standstill. Given its preferred creditor status, private sector creditors are unlikely to perceive the Fund's neutrality as credible. In addition, the existence of many different categories of claims begs the question whether an orderly and timely restructuring process could be realised. Notwithstanding, to be effective the standstill and binding-in of creditors would have to include both domestic claims on the sovereign as well as external obligations owed by the private sector. Finally, although the proposal goes to considerable length in ensuring that the final diction on a debt restructuring proposal will rest with creditors and debtors and not the IMF or any other international body, without strong incentives to reach an agreement either party may simply refuse to consent to any proposal until the standstill period has passed. By including collective action clauses in sovereign debt contracts, the process of restructuring sovereign debt burdens can be significantly facilitated without the existence of an institutionalised framework. The issue of sovereign debt restructuring will be discussed in depth in chapter 11.

3.2.2 The Calomiris Proposal

Charles Calomiris' *Blueprints for a New Financial Architecture* suggest to replace the IMF and all other forms of international crisis lending by a framework similar to an international lender of last resort. All current lending facilities provided by the IMF to countries facing liquidity problems would be abolished. A new IMF would provide liquidity assistance exclusively to countries qualifying ex-ante by following prudent economic and financial policies. Countries failing to fulfil these conditions would be excluded from membership and thus from liquidity assistance by the official sector. As emergency loans could be provided instantly to qualified countries and current conditionality policy would be abandoned, the effectiveness of international liquidity assistance in preventing and mitigating financial crises would be considerably enhanced. At the same time, the proposal goes a long way in minimising moral hazard problems that result from the availability of official sector liquidity assistance.

To qualify for membership at the new IMF, countries would have to meet several conditions. The first set of conditions aims at ensuring a credible regulation of the banking sector while the second defines specific rules for the behaviour of national authorities. Regarding the former, membership requires countries to meet four conditions. First, national authorities must force banks to meet prudent capital requirements for enhanced stability. A central addition to this condition is the demand that banks raise a fraction of their capital by issuing subordinated debt to ensure monitoring by the private sector. Second, governments would have to require banks to meet adequate reserve requirements consisting in holding a minimum share of assets in cash and marketable securities. Like capital adequacy requirements, reserve requirements aim at reducing banks' vulnerability when liquidity is scarce. In order to eliminate the risk of bank runs, IMF membership would also require governments to introduce explicit deposit insurance. In addition, governments would have to ensure that their financial sectors are open to international competition and foreign investment, not only for the sake of tapping alternative sources of capital but also because competition increases the quality of banking practices. To ensure the effectiveness of the subordinated debt requirement in fostering market discipline, to qualify for membership governments would have to refrain from recapitalizing insolvent banks. To avoid maturity mismatches in sovereign debt structures, countries would need adhering to sustainable upper ceilings on the portion of short-term debt within total sovereign indebtedness. Countries operating a system of fixed exchange rates would have to keep sufficient foreign currency reserves as a share of high powered money and should allow banks to offer accounts both in domestic and foreign currency.

Only countries meeting the requirements listed above would be admitted to membership at the IMF. Countries facing speculative attacks on their currencies could borrow foreign currency from the Fund without any further conditions. The IMF would lend in alignment with the rules Bagehot defined for an effective lender of last resort: As such it would lend freely, at penalty interest rates and against good collateral only. Collateral would consist of all types of sovereign debt priced in the market and be no less than 125 percent of the amount borrowed; a quarter of the overall amount pledged would have to be in form of foreign sovereign debt securities. Maturity of loans would be 90 days, extendable only once by a super-majority of executive directors. To finance its lending, the Fund would borrow cash from central banks issuing hard currency; loans would be collateralized by the same countries' government bonds since all contributions to the Fund would be made in government paper. During a transitional period international development banks would support developing countries in modernizing their banking systems and enable them to meet the criteria necessary for membership.

Among the objections made to this proposal de-facto suggesting the creation of an international lender of last resort, three have considerable weight. For one, opponents argue that without the ability to issue hard currency an international lender of last resort cannot exist. Funds committed by the international community are assumed to be inevitably insufficient for an international lender to lend as freely as suggested by Bagehot. In addition, granting unconditional access to countries meeting pre-specified stability requirements, is widely perceived as excessively increasing moral hazard problems. Once pre-qualified countries received liquidity assistance, it is argued, they would lack incentives to continue pursuing prudent policies while a deterioration in fiscal and monetary responsibility would mean that countries become unable to repay their debts to the international community. Finally, opponents question the instrument of pre-qualification central to Calomiris' proposal by arguing that the international community cannot credibly commit to stand idle when the default of a country not qualified for international liquidity assistance would threaten a systemic breakdown[22].

3.2.3 The Report by the Independent Task Force

In contrast to other proposals, the report by the Task Force on the Future of the International Financial Architecture sponsored by the Council of Foreign Relations does not suggest the creation of a new international institution but offers seven policy recommendations to increase the stability of the global financial system[23]. Their findings are particularly interesting as they represent the views of scholars, former politicians, international bureaucrats and market participants alike. The independent task force was headed by former U.S. Secretary of Commerce and Blackstone chairman Peter Peterson and former Trade Representative Carla Hills and included academics Barry Eichengreen, Martin Feldstein and Paul Krugman as well as Paul Volcker, George Soros, AIG's Maurice Greenberg and several other

---

22 See Eichengreen (1999): 102
23 See Council on Foreign Relations. 1999. *Safeguarding Prosperity in a Global Financial System: The Future International Financial Architecture.* Independent Task Force Report. New York, NY: Council on Foreign Relations

prominent public and private sector representatives. The report underlines the importance of increasing incentives for both emerging market creditors and debtors to pursue prudent borrowing and lending policies identified as the key to enhanced global financial stability. The recommendations are designed to attain several objectives: To encourage emerging economies to strengthen their efforts in crisis prevention, to promote fair burden sharing among borrowers, private sector and official sector creditors, to introduce market-based incentives for crisis prevention and resolution, to refocus IMF and World Bank on the mandates there are best suited to achieve, to allow for international capital to flow to countries and enterprises offering the highest returns and to ensure that industrialised countries contribute adequately in the struggle to increase international financial stability. The report underlined that the recommendations summarized below are likely be met by considerable opposition from vested interests, particularly in industrial economies, and that the success of implementation would fundamentally depend on the degree of ownership affected countries would develop.

To provide incentives for countries to pursue prudent economic policies, the task force recommends a number of initiatives increasing the rewards for what it terms *Joining the Good Housekeeping Club*. By publishing regular reports on countries' adherence to international financial standards and by commenting on the quality of members' economic policies, the IMF would contribute to the creation of an environment where countries following sound policies and taking active steps to prevent financial difficulties are rewarded by easier and less costly access to international capital. These efforts would be enhanced by making banks subject to less stringent capital requirements for loans made to countries following sound policies. Since the report's publication in 1999, the IMF has come a long way in implementing many of the suggestions, but may initiatives remain that would add to the steps already taken.

Acknowledging the vulnerability caused to developing economies by excessive short-term indebtedness, the task force suggested a number of policies to facilitate a reduction of the short-term portion of international capital flows. Countries vulnerable to violent capital flow reversals are advised to follow Chile's example of taxing capital flows which leave the country after extremely short durations. The report further argues that capital adequacy requirements in industrialised countries should be amended to avoid discriminating against longer-term investments by making short-term loans to developing countries comparatively attractive and by lifting taxes and similar restrictions on capital flows directed at medium and long-term investment. Addressing the problems caused by short-term strategies pursued by highly speculative investors and hedge funds, the task force proposed to initially increase the demands on risk management at prime brokerages; in case the desired effects would fail to materialise, higher capital requirements for loans to offshore financial centres—where the majority of hedge funds is incorporated—should be imposed by regulatory authorities.

The report also addressed the difficulties in restructuring the obligations of countries burdened by unsustainable levels of sovereign debt. To facilitate the process, all IMF members are encouraged to include collective action clauses in all debt securities issued to the public thereby ensuring that a majority of creditors can agree on a restructuring in spite of opposition by minority hold-outs. G-7 countries could facilitate this process by requiring that all sovereign debt issued within their jurisdiction must include such clauses. By encouraging debtors to maintain accurate and inclusive directories of their creditors and creditors to voluntarily form standing committees, the negotiation process could be further facilitated. In addition, the task force recommended the IMF to encourage developing economies to implement adequate deposit insurance schemes and abstain from assisting in restructuring efforts when a debtor country does not commit to engage in good faith negotiations. This includes the insistence that during the negotiation process no discrimination between different types of debt holders would be acceptable. As a general rule, the IMF would grant emergency loans only when there is a realistic chance that balance of payment problems can be successfully addressed by temporary liquidity assistance.

The choice of the adequate exchange rate system is identified as a crucial factor determining the vulnerability of emerging economies to financial crises. Regarding an optimal regime the report is strict: Developing economies should avoid employing adjustable peg regimes and opt instead for managed floating. Currency boards and monetary unions are argued acceptable under exceptional circumstances only. This stance is based on the argument that despite some attractive features adjustable peg regimes proved to be one of the main culprits for the financial crises in Asia, Latin America and Russia since 1995. Not only should the IMF strictly advise countries to avoid such regimes, but it should also refrain from providing liquidity assistance to help countries supporting a peg.

Regarding the adequate size of liquidity assistance, the report argues in favour of limiting the size of emergency loans the IMF can grant to member countries in financial distress. IMF loans should reduce the impact financial crises have on the real economy and facilitate necessary reforms, but not ensure that countries can meet all short-term external debt obligations as this would increase moral hazard problems. To achieve the former, current borrowing limits of 100 to 300 percent of a member's quota are perceived sufficient. Consequently, the taskforce recommended the Fund to generally abstain from making emergency loans above these thresholds as it did in Mexico, Thailand, Indonesia, Brazil and Korea. Only under exceptional circumstances when crises are assumed systemic, should the Fund make additional resources available. Such so-called *systemic back-up facilities* would be subject to a supermajority support in the executive board and differ depending on the causes a systemic crisis is attributed to. For crises resulting from a country pursuing irresponsible policies, funds would be made available by drawing on General and New Agreements to Borrow; they would be subject to entering an IMF stability program that addresses the most important policy flaws. Distressed countries that follow prudent policies and are perceived as being the victim of contagion and investor uncertainty would be granted an alternative facility financed by a one-off allocation of SDRs. Such facilities would be disbursed timely and not require the borrower to design an IMF approved stability program; they would nevertheless be subject to interest charges above the market rate.

The task force further called for a refocusing of both IMF and World Bank to the functions they are most likely to discharge successfully. The central mandate of the IMF should be to act as a crisis lender and to monitor members' adherence to international financial standards; the World Bank's role was seen as lying in the reduction of poverty and the facilitation of economic development. The Fund should reduce its lending activities and increase its efforts in crisis prevention. It should restrict its role to monitor and provide advice regarding fiscal and monetary policy, exchange rate regimes and financial sector reform. The World Bank should engage in longer-term structural reform projects and facilitate progress in social aspects of economic development; in this context particular emphasis was put on the task to support the creation of adequate safety nets in developing countries. According to the task force, the Bank should not be required to contribute to emergency loans put together by the IMF in an effort to halt or prevent financial crises.

The recommendations by the Independent Task Force are currently the most pragmatic proposal to increase global financial stability. As the report does not develop a coherent framework but rather lists the lessons learned from past financial crises, it circumvents typical flaws and is less prone than other proposals to the objection that its suggestions are incompatible with reality. At the same time, recommendations often lack concreteness or fail to address problems of implementation. The suggestions regarding the introduction of incentives for *good housekeeping* share many similarities with Calomiris' proposal, although in a watered down form. Nevertheless, the recommendations made by the task force would go a long way in reducing both frequency and severity of financial crises. Although their success in implementation has been as limited as that of more radical proposals, the introduction of individual recommendations into existing frameworks appears the most promising way to increase global financial stability.

3.2.4 The Meltzer Report

The International Financial Institutions Advisory Commission (IFIAC) was established by Congress as part of the legislation that authorised USD 18 billion additional funding for the IMF[24]. Its mandate consisted in advising U.S. policy makers on improving the functioning of seven international financial institutions: The IMF, World Bank, Inter-American Development Bank, Asian Development Bank, African Development Bank, the Bank for International Settlement and the WTO. Strongest emphasis was put on adapting the IMF and the World Bank to an environment fundamentally different to that existing at the time when the Bretton Woods organisations were established in 1944. To improve effectiveness and accountability, the Meltzer Commission identified as most important need a redefinition and separation of both institutions' functions. Accordingly, the Meltzer report published in March 2000 proposes wide-ranging reforms for the seven organisations analysed[25]. Most central to the stability of the global financial system are the suggestions made regarding the International Monetary Fund.

On IMF reform the core recommendations are threefold; they are designed to improve the stability of the global financial system, to enhance the functioning of markets and to assist countries in pursuing prudent economic policies. To achieve these objectives, the commission proposed the Fund's mandate to be narrowed to three essential functions. First, the IMF should function as *quasi international lender of last resort*. In this role it would provide short-term emergency loans to fundamentally healthy countries facing liquidity crunches. Second, the Fund should gather and disseminate economic and financial data on its member countries' economies to provide financial markets with the information necessary to reach informed investment decisions. Lastly, it would continue to provide under Article IV consultations non-binding advice to member countries on how to improve the stability and effectiveness of their economies.

Under the IFIAC proposal membership at the IMF would require countries to report on their economic and financial position timely and accurately. As the majority of developed countries already report to the OECD and discuss financial sector issues at the Bank for International Settlements, OECD members would be allowed to opt out of Article IV consultations with the IMF. The publication of

---

24 The Commission chaired by Alan Meltzer of Carnegie Mellon University was made up of 12 members from academia, politics and the private sector, including IIE director Fred Bergsten, Charles Calomiris and Jeffrey Sachs of Columbia University.

25 See International Financial Institution Advisory Commission. 2000. *Report of the International Financial Institution Advisory Commission.* Washington, DC: Senate Committee on Banking, Housing, and Urban Affairs

reports on Article IV consultations with all other members would become mandatory.

As quasi international lender of last resort the IMF would provide liquidity assistance to members meeting minimum prudential standards. A credit limit would be set at the level of a country's annual tax receipts. Countries meeting these minimum requirements would receive immediate assistance without any further conditions. The Fund would cease its practice of negotiating policy reforms and stability programs but liquidity assistance would be restricted to fundamentally solvent borrowers. The use of IMF funds to bail-out insolvent financial institutions and protect foreign investors from losses would be excluded. Large industrial economies issuing hard currency would refrain from approaching the IMF for liquidity assistance as resources are insufficient for this purpose and hard currency issuing central banks are in a position to act as lender of last resort to their economies without external assistance.

The Meltzer Commission defines four minimum prudential standards qualifying members for liquidity assistance by the IMF. First, members must open their financial sectors to foreign competition and refrain from inhibiting operations by foreign competitors. Open and competitive financial sectors are expected to limit corruption, increase stability and enhance banking practice. Foreign banks would profit as portfolio diversification reduces default risk and earnings volatility. Second, national authorities would need to ensure that commercial banks' capitalisation is sufficient to reduce the vulnerability of domestic banking sectors and increase market discipline. To achieve this objective, national authorities should insist that financial institutions maintain an adequate equity base and issue subordinated debt. In addition, all members receiving IMF assistance would be required to accurately and timely disclose the maturity structure of sovereign and publicly guaranteed debt obligations including off-balance-sheet liabilities. Lastly, to be eligible for liquidity assistance member countries would have to meet adequate fiscal requirements defined by the IMF. This aims to ensure that members refrain from employing IMF resources to maintain irresponsible budget policies. In this respect, the commission highlighted that the responsibility of a lender of last resort is to the market and not to individual institutions; it should therefore refrain from bailing-out insolvent entities and restrict its assistance to illiquid, but fundamentally solvent borrowers.

Terms applicable for liquidity assistance are devised to safeguard that members draw on the IMF only if private sector resources are unavailable. Accordingly, emergency loans would be subject to a penalty interest charge above the market rate; the latter is to be determined by the yield on the member's sovereign debt seven days before approaching the IMF for assistance. Furthermore, liquidity assistance should be disbursed exclusively for the short-term as liquidity crises are assumed to generally last for no more than a number of weeks; only under exceptional circumstances would liquidity assistance become necessary for a longer period. Maturity for emergency loans suggested by the Meltzer Report is set at a maximum of 120 days, with a roll-over being permitted only once. To retain the Fund's ability in acting as quasi international lender of last resort, IMF loans should be given repayment priority over all other obligations, both secured and unsecured. This requires that borrowing countries exempt the IMF from the application of potential negative pledge clauses for all sovereign debt issues and ensure that borrowers defaulting on IMF loans automatically disqualify for assistance by multilateral development institutions or alternative bilateral grants or loans.

3.2.5 The Köhler Approach: Procedural Changes

In response to the experiences made during the 1990s, then newly-appointed IMF managing director Horst Köhler at the annual meetings in Prague announced his intention to increase the Fund's effectiveness and legitimacy by refocusing it on its core mandate: to foster macroeconomic stability by promoting sound economic policies and structural reforms and to oversee the international financial system in order to safeguard its functioning[26]. The agenda of reform embarked upon led to substantial improvements regarding crisis prevention and surveillance. The IMF has become more transparent and both quality and quantity of financial information released by its members have increased. In its surveillance role the IMF has strengthened its focus on international capital markets and members' institutions and financial sectors; at the same time it has increased its efforts in addressing financial sector vulnerability and unsustainable indebtedness. A new International Capital Markets Department has been established as has the Capital Markets Consultative Group. In this context the *Financial Sector Assessment Program* (FSAP) has been expanded enhancing the Fund's ability in identifying financial sector vulnerabilities. In its *Reports on the Observance of Standards and Codes* (ROSC) the IMF comments on members' adherence to various standards of data transparency.

Regarding crisis management, improvements in IMF effectiveness have been more limited, despite the implementation of several initiatives. Nevertheless, a number of the problems experienced in East Asia and Latin America have been addressed and enhance the Fund's effectiveness and legitimacy as a crisis lender. Following a review on its conditionality policies, the IMF has streamlined and focussed the conditions attached to its lending facilities; both number and scope of

---

26 See Horst Köhler. 2000. *Address to the Board of Governors of the Fund.* Prague, September 26, 2000

conditions have been reduced substantially and will enhance the ownership in programs felt by countries implementing them. During the crisis in Indonesia, the IMF made the disbursement of liquidity support contingent on the country's success in meeting 140 individual conditions; the *Guidelines on Conditionality* approved by the Board in 2002 abolished this excessive form of micromanagement by the Fund. The new approach is based on five principles: National ownership of reform programs, parsimony in the application of program-related conditions, tailoring programs to members' specific circumstances, better cooperation with other international organizations and increased clarity of conditions[27]. While streamlining and reducing fiscal, monetary and structural conditions, the IMF continues to rely on conditionality policy as its central instrument of ensuring the effectiveness of its programs and safeguarding the Fund's resources.

Another important, although eventually unsuccessful initiative to increase the Fund's capacity in crisis management has been the creation of *Contingent Credit Lines* (CCL). Contingent Credit Lines were intended to provide a precautionary line of credit to fundamentally healthy economies experiencing financial distress despite pursuing sound economic policies. To be eligible for liquidity support under the CCL, members had to fulfil four conditions: First, the member must not be expected to require IMF support for reasons other than financial contagion. Second, the member must follow prudent policies and show progress in adhering to internationally accepted standards. To qualify, a country would also have had to be in good relations with its private creditors and show improvements in reducing external vulnerabilities. Countries were nevertheless required to put in place an adequate economic program and commit to a further adjustment of policies. Funds would have been provided on a stand-by basis for up to a year. Despite the lack of a specific access limit, facilities were expected be provided in a range of between 300 and 500 percent of the qualified members' quota. Although the CCL would have greatly enhanced the Fund's effectiveness in preventing contagion, its conditions proved unattractive to IMF members. As a result, the facility remained unused. After adjusting the terms a year later to make the facility more attractive, it was withdrawn in 2003.

The *framework for exceptional access*, approved by the executive board in September 2002, represents an effort to increase clarity and predictability of IMF funding decisions for both its members and market participants[28]. It applies specifically to the type of capital account crises experienced in the recent past where

---

27 See IMF. 2002. *Guidelines on Conditionality.* September 25, 2002. Washington, DC: International Monetary Fund: 8

28 See IMF. 2002. *Access Policy in Capital Account Crises.* Report prepared by the Policy Development and Review and Treasurer's Departments. July 29, 2002. Washington, DC: International Monetary Fund

IMF liquidity support substantially surpassed its traditional limits on lending. Exceptional access refers to all loans above the Fund's regular access limit of 100 percent of a member's quota in a single year and 300 percent in total. The framework defines several conditions which must be met for the Fund to approve liquidity assistance above this ceiling. First, the member must face exceptional balance of payments difficulties arising from the capital account which cannot be met by arrangements within regular access limits. Second, there must be a high probability that the member's indebtedness will remain at a fundamentally sustainable level. Good prospects must exist that the member will regain access to international capital markets during the emergency loan's duration. Finally, the adjustment program needs to have a high probability of success requiring not only the government's willingness to reform but also the necessary policy and institutional capacity to implement adjustments. If successfully implemented into IMF decision-making, these minimum criteria for exceptional access would go a long way towards ensuring that emergency loans above the regular level are granted only if exceptional liquidity assistance is likely to be an effective instrument. Since the framework became operational in early 2003, exceptional access to the Fund's resources has been approved in two cases: Argentina and Brazil. As an internal evaluation has found, neither Argentina nor Brazil met all four criteria[29] which reduces the framework's credibility considerably.

3.3 Conclusion

All proposals described above aim at increasing the stability of the global financial system by reducing the frequency and severity of financial crises. Proposals to introduce a Tobin tax and approaches focussing on data dissemination standards and financial transparency are attempts to reign in on violent capital flow reversals. As such, they primarily serve the purpose of crisis prevention. Other proposals attempt to increase the capacity of the international community to mitigate financial crises once they are under way; their focus is on crisis management rather than crisis prevention. The majority of proposals for a new international financial architecture include measures for crisis prevention as well as measures to enhance crisis management. This applies to Meltzer Report, Calomiris Proposal as well as to the recommendations made by the Independent Task Force. A central aspect of crisis management is the provision of emergency loans during financial crises because only by

---

29 See IMF. 2004. *Review of Exceptional Access Policy.* Report prepared by the Policy Development and Review and Finance Departments. March 23, 2004. Washington, DC: International Monetary Fund: 3

providing sufficient liquidity to the financial system can crises be mitigated and eventually brought to a hold.

In a domestic economy this function is generally provided by the central bank acting as lender of last resort. A lender of last resort provides liquidity in situations where capital markets cease functioning effectively but liquidity assistance is necessary to prevent widespread bankruptcies and a collapse of the financial sector. The global financial system cannot rely on such an institution since an international lender of last resort does not exist.

The existence of an international lender of last resort would allow for more effective crisis management than is possible today and thus considerably strengthen the stability of the global financial system. To assess the viability of an international lender of last resort in practice is the aim of this analysis. As background to the argument, the following chapter provides a definition and discusses the theoretical concept of a lender of last resort and its origins.

4. The Lender of Last Resort: The Concept in Theory

Economic growth requires a functioning financial sector that channels funds to their most effective uses and provides firms with the capital they need. Without liquidity, the financial sector cannot fulfil this role. Without access to capital, firms are unable to refinance their obligations, have to declare bankruptcy, and the economy contracts. Preventing financial panics from turning into fully fledged financial crises and ending liquidity crises once they have developed, requires access to sufficient amounts of liquidity. The role of a lender of last resort is to provide that liquidity when no other institution is willing or able to do so. To take on this responsibility, a lender of last resort needs access to substantial financial resources. In most countries the central bank acts as lender of last resort for its own economy. Given its ability to issue money, it can access almost unlimited amounts of currency. While in industrialised countries financial crises can be ended by providing sufficient amounts of domestic currency, in developing countries and emerging market economies restoring stability often requires large amounts of foreign currency, predominantly dollars, yens, or euros.

4.1 The Importance of Foreign Currency

Responsible for this dependence on foreign currency are differences in borrowing capacity and capital market access between industrial and developing countries. In industrial countries both the private and the public sector can satisfy their capital needs in domestic currency. If a domestic central bank runs out of currency reserves, it can rely on its ability to issue additional money by starting the printing press. In most emerging markets, both public and private sectors can borrow from capital markets in hard currency, i.e. in dollar, euro, yen, and sterling, only. To arrest a financial crisis, emergency loans by developing country central banks must therefore be made not merely in local, but primarily in foreign currency. While domestic currency can be issued if scarce, foreign currency can only come from reserves, credit lines with commercial banks, the IMF or other forms of external assistance.

Foreign currency reserves enable governments to counter pressures on their currency through intervention in foreign exchange markets. By selling and buying foreign against domestic currency, central banks can defend an exchange rate peg and manipulate the market price of their currency in any direction. The knowledge that the central bank has access to ample amounts of international currency alone can be enough to deter speculative attacks, as short-selling currencies involves high costs in terms of interest rate differentials and lending fees. Moreover, it increases market confidence about the government's determination and ability to maintain an announced currency peg. Sufficient foreign currency reserves can also facilitate an orderly devaluation process in case a government intends to devalue voluntarily. However, access to international currency for self-protection against speculative attacks and currency crises is often restricted for developing countries and emerging economies. Nevertheless, developing country governments have a number of policy options to increase their access to international liquidity.

4.1.1 Enhancing Access to Foreign Currency

The most direct method for governments to increase their capacity to provide liquidity during financial crises is by accumulating foreign currency reserves through trade surpluses. But storing away export earnings to bolster reserves means incurring opportunity costs in terms of investing in the domestic economy and increasing long-term output and consumption. It also comes at the cost of higher interest rates since emerging market yields usually exceed the yields available from investing in treasuries or other safe industrial countries' paper. A preferable strategy is thus to borrow foreign currency at medium or long-term maturity and investing it in liquid short-term securities, the strategy China pursued to shore up its foreign currency reserves[1]. However, while allowing for the re-investment of export earnings to foster economic growth, this strategy can be costly in terms of interest charges since long-term emerging market debt usually yields several hundred basis points more than U.S. treasuries.

Another strategy to reduce the likelihood of liquidity crises as a result of capital markets' unwillingness to roll-over short-term loans in times of crisis is to avoid excessive short-term and foreign currency borrowing in the first place. The Mexican crisis in 1994–95 was primarily the result of international investors' unwillingness to roll over tesobonos and Mexico's inability to service its short-term debt obligations without external support[2]. At the same time restructuring short into medium and long-term debt is costly given maturity-based interest rate differentials. An alternative strategy to reduce the likelihood of sharp capital flow reversals is to discourage speculative capital flows by imposing temporary duties. In 1991 Chile introduced regulations requiring borrowers to park 20 percent of foreign-denominated loans at the central bank at zero interest for a period of six months. While this

---

1 See Feldstein (1999): 15
2 See United States General Accounting Office. 1996. *Mexico's Financial Crisis: Origins, Awareness, Assistance, and Initial Efforts to Recover*. Report to the Chairman, Committee on Banking and Financial Services, House of Representatives. Washington, DC: United States General Accounting Office: 143

strategy increased the ratio of long-term to short-term loans, the overall amount of capital inflows remained stable[3].

A market-based strategy for governments to ensure access to international reserves is negotiating short-term callable credit lines with commercial banks. In order to induce international lenders to commit to such credit lines, the provision of adequate collateral is inevitable, especially when trying to obtain commitments from consortia including private lenders like commercial banks or other financial institutions. Collateral may come in form of secure export earnings or revenues from natural resources like oil as in the case of Mexico in 1994–95. This issue will be analysed in depth in chapter 7. Securing credit lines with international lenders may be the least costly strategy to ensure government's credibility in maintaining a currency peg as long as the facility is large enough and remains undrawn. While during crisis such credit lines may prove costly as well, they still allow for credit at a time when other commercial lenders are unwilling to provide loans.

Most ways to increase international reserves or secure instant access at times of crisis are available to a limited number of emerging economies only. Many developing countries have only limited access to international capital markets and lack assets suitable as collateral to negotiate credit lines with commercial banks. For these countries building-up large amounts of foreign currency reserve albeit costly, is the only viable strategy to protect against sovereign default due to liquidity problems. However, the fact that liquidity crises are an exception rather than the rule and unlikely to occur in all emerging economies simultaneously, suggests a co-operative approach to the problem: Pooling international currency reserves can provide countries in liquidity problems with instant access to foreign currency and reduces participants' vulnerability to speculative attacks and currency crises.

On a national level such co-operation has been realized since the nineteenth century when central banks increasingly took on the responsibility of acting as lender of last resort during liquidity crises. At Bretton Woods the IMF was created to fulfil a similar function for the international monetary system. But in its current structure, the Fund is ill equipped to fill this role. In order to understand why, a deeper analysis of the concept of a lender of last resort and its development is necessary.

4.2 The Concept of a Lender of Last Resort

The concept of a lender of last resort originates in nineteenth century England and emerged as a response to then frequent banking panics and bank runs. In order to

---

3 Salvador Valdes-Prieto and Marcelo Soto. 1997. *The Effectiveness of Capital Controls: Theory and Evidence from Chile*. Working Paper. Santiago de Chile: Pontificia Universidad Católica de Chile

prevent resulting bank failures and the bankruptcies of other commercial enterprises, a common response was sought to arrest the effects the failure of even a single bank can have on the real economy. Economic thinkers like Thornton or Bagehot suggested that the Bank of England should act as lender of last resort to the British economy. In this function the Bank was to provide emergency loans to financial institutions during liquidity crises thereby preventing bank failures and the effects those failures can have on the real economy.

The role of a lender of last resort is based on two specific characteristics of modern monetary systems, fractional reserve banking and the governmental monopoly to issue money. Fractional reserve banking refers to the practice of banks of lending on large parts of the cash they receive by depositors. It builds on the assumption that depositors are unlikely to withdraw their full deposit all at once. Lending on a share of its deposits in return for interest payments, banks can pay interest to depositors and create profit for stockholders. This practice increases the money supply via the deposit creation multiplier but also allows for the development of bank runs in case all depositors demand to withdraw the full amount of their cash deposits at once. A bank's failure to satisfy all withdrawal demands simultaneously can result in bankruptcy, subsequent failure of the bank's corporate clients and the development of financial crises.

The existence of a governmental monopoly to issue money is the reason why banks can nevertheless practice a system of fractional reserve banking. As the sole institution with the ability to issue money, only the central bank can guarantee the convertibility of deposits into currency. This allows banks to lend on parts of their deposits trusting in the central bank's willingness and capacity to provide money if liquidity problems arise.

4.2.1 Henry Thornton (1760–1815)

Although mentioned already 1797 in Sir Francis Baring's *Observations on the Establishment of the Bank of England*, the concept of a lender of last resort was first developed by Henry Thornton at the beginning of the nineteenth century. In his 1802 *Enquiry into the Nature and Effects of the Paper Credit of Great Britain* he rigorously analysed the Bank of England's functions and characteristics as lender of last resort.

Thornton drew attention to the Bank of England's position as ultimate provider of liquidity to the economy in times of crisis. On one hand, it served as custodian for the central gold reserve available to all other banks. On the other, it held a monopolistic role as the sole issuer of legal tender in the form of universally accepted paper notes; as a consequence, it could draw on unlimited amounts of money to inject into the financial system in times of financial distress and money contraction.

Thornton expected the Bank of England not only to prevent uncertainty about the unlimited availability of liquidity, but also to safeguard the central gold reserve in times of rapid depletion due to excessive external demand. In case of excessive internal demand, the Bank was to provide liquidity by issuing notes. In order to prevent external depletion by inflationary pressures and in line with fellow Bullionists, Thornton generally advocated a strictly controlled creation of paper money. Notwithstanding, he underlined the importance of maintaining a sufficiently large liquidity reserve in order to react to short-term balance-of-payments shocks. In describing the functions of the Bank of England, Thornton went to great lengths in pointing out the dangers of pro-cyclical behaviour in a situation when gold was leaving the country due to temporary shocks to the real economy. When suffering a temporary depletion of gold reserves, the prudent reaction was to inject liquidity into the system for the sake of preventing monetary contraction, a corresponding decline in economic activity, and a worsening of the trade balance and particularly exports as the prime source of gold inflows.

Following this line of reasoning, Thornton underlined the public duties the role as lender of last resort entailed. In contrast to commercial banks, as lender of last resort the Bank of England was to aim for stability of the whole economy instead of considering solely its own liquidity needs. Moreover, anti-cyclical behaviour should be its mode of action: When the economy was facing monetary contraction and private banks reduced their lending activities, the lender of last resort was to counteract monetary contraction by massively injecting cash into the financial system. In this way it could prevent solvent, but illiquid banks from collapsing and taking other institutions with them. A contraction of the real economy as a consequence of widespread bank failures could thus be averted. In order to be able to act this way, the Bank of England needed far larger amounts of liquidity reserves than regular commercial banks.

4.2.1.1 Issues in Last Resort Lending

Thornton's work discusses several issues regarding the Bank of England's function as lender of last resort[4]. One is the alleged contradiction of a prudent control of the money supply with tasks expected by the bank when carrying out lender of last resort responsibilities. In general, Thornton advocated a restrictive and controlled stance in regard to monetary expansion. In order to avoid domestic inflation in the

---

4 See Thomas M. Humphrey and Robert E. Keleher. 1984. "The Lender of Last Resort: A Historical Perspective." *Cato Journal*. Vol. 4, No. 1: 275–318

case of flexible exchange rates or a continuous outflow of gold reserves into foreign economies under a fixed rate regime, the rate of monetary expansion was to be prevented from rising excessively. Instead it was supposed to rise gradually and in accordance to the growth in trade and output. In order to achieve non-inflationary growth the Bank of England should follow the long-term policy

> To limit the total amount of paper issued, and to resort for this purpose,
> whenever the temptation to borrow is strong, to some effectual principle
> of restriction; in no case however, materially to diminish the sum in
> circulation, but to let it vibrate only within certain limits; to afford a slow
> and cautious extension of it, as the general trade of the kingdom enlarges
> itself[5].

Only continuous external drains on gold might require monetary contraction to reduce inflationary pressures and support the current account by limiting demand for imports and supporting growth in exports. In times of financial distress, however, the lender of last resort function demands an extension of the monetary base, in spite of long-term stability targets. Injection of liquidity is needed in cases of domestic banking crises when depositors withdraw gold reserves from commercial banks in excessive amounts. Monetary expansion was also advocated in the case of real shocks temporarily distorting the balance of payments and when due to depleted reserves the usual mechanism of self-adjustment failed. In this case, the lender of last resort's duty was to *allow of some special, though temporary, increase in the event of any extraordinary alarm or difficulty, as the best means of preventing a great demand at home for guineas*[6].

Short-term expansion of the monetary base above the rate of long-term output growth does not contradict the intention of long-term monetary restraint and stability if restricted to extraordinary periods. It should be understood as temporary measure to prevent monetary contraction from hurting the economy by hindering growth in trade and output. Long-term stability in monetary expansion will be distorted only little and potentially even not at all in case the belief that a lender of last resort is willing to inject liquidity if needed actually prevents a bank-run from developing in the first place.

---

5   Henry Thornton. 1939. *An Enquiry into the Nature and Effects of the Paper Credit of Great
    Britain.* New York, NY: Rinehart and Company: 259
6   Thornton (1939): 259

4.2.1.2 Individual Institutions versus the Monetary System

Thornton further specified the main target of last resort lending. As he ascertained, the Bank of England's responsibility lies in stabilising the whole economy, not in protecting particular institutions within it. Accordingly, he was not concerned about the failure of individual institutions, especially if they were insolvent, but only with the repercussions such failures might have on the stability of the monetary system. Regarding the extension of money supply Thornton pointed out the central inherent moral hazard problem: Injecting liquidity into distressed banks may lead to irresponsible and excessive lending practices, as banks include potential liquidity support into their decision making.

> It is by no means intended to imply, that it would become the Bank of England to relieve any distress which the rashness of country banks may bring upon them: the bank, by doing this, might encourage their improvidence[7].

Thornton advises not to bail out banks which behaved irresponsibly and took on excessive risks, except in cases where a failure would have adverse impacts on the whole economy. But in his view this scenario was unlikely to occur. If it did, lending should be restrained and on unattractive terms. Nevertheless, he warned that bailing-out failed institutions based on potential effects bank bankruptcies can have on the financial system may open the door for continuous demands by any bank. Accordingly, he prefers insolvent institutions to fail and their assets to be re-allocated.

> There seems to be a medium at which a public bank should aim in granting aid to inferior establishments, and which it must often find very difficult to be observed. The relief should neither be so prompt and liberal as to exempt those who misconduct their business from all the natural consequences of their fault, so scanty and slow as deeply to involve the general interests. These interests nevertheless, are sure to be pleaded by every distressed person whose affairs are large, however indifferent or even ruinous may be their state[8].

Bank runs and fiscal distress are usually triggered by shocks to the monetary system. Thornton cites rumours about an invasion or the failure of a large financial institution as typical examples. Preventing those shocks in the first place would thus appear the key in preventing financial crises from emerging. While it is impossible

---

7 Thornton (1939): 188
8 Thornton (1939): 188

to prevent all exogenous shocks to the system, there may be the opportunity of preventing at least some, e.g. to bail out a failing commercial bank. But in Thornton's view shock prevention is not the lender of last resort's responsibility. Instead of trying to prevent the shocks themselves, he perceives the central bank's task as to prevent financial crises from developing as a consequence of such macroeconomic shocks by flooding the financial system with liquidity to prevent monetary contraction and its effects on the real economy.

> If any one bank fails, a general run on the neighboring ones is apt to take
> place, which if not checked at the beginning by a pouring into circulation
> a large quantity of gold, leads to very extensive mischief[9].

He even argues that it are not exogenous shocks that are responsible for financial crises and monetary contraction, but rather the failure of the central bank to fulfil its function as lender of last resort. Would the central bank promptly inject sufficient amounts of liquidity into the system, a crisis would not develop. Consequently, he blames Great Britain's financial crises of 1793 and 1797 on the incompetent reaction by the Bank of England.

Henry Thornton describes the primary function of a lender of last resort as the provision high-powered money, namely gold and Bank of England notes, to the financial system. In contrast to the duties currently ascribed to the International Monetary Fund, Thornton's lender of last resort has a purely monetary role. Rather than monitoring risks and arranging bailouts to prevent the failure of important entities, the lender of last resort should concentrate on the provision of liquidity. The importance Thornton attributes to liquidity stems from his believes regarding the way financial crises affect the real economy, that is via excessive monetary demand rather than through credit-rationing by the banks. It is the excessive demand for high-powered money that subsequently leads to a contraction of the monetary base. And it is this monetary contraction and the malfunction of the money multiplier which causes a decline in output and employment.

4.2.1.3 Contemporary Response

For the larger part of the nineteenth century Thornton's belief in the Bank of England's duties as lender of last resort was strongly opposed by members of the Currency School[10]. Its followers advocated full convertibility and a strictly regulated issuance of paper money at all times. Because it perceived the Bank of England as no different from commercial banks, the Currency School was particularly critical of

---

9 Thornton (1939): 180
10 See Thomas Humphrey and Robert Keleher (1984)

its role as lender of last resort. The opposition can be explained by the fact that members of the Currency School failed to distinguish between different types of drains on the central bank's gold reserves; financial crises were exclusively attributed to an over-issuance of notes, in which case the suggested cause of action was to curtail the money supply as soon as gold reserves came under pressure. Following this argument, during times of crisis the Bank of England was to behave like any commercial bank and limit credit and the issuance of notes. Consequently, members of the Currency School saw no need for the Bank of England to hold higher reserves than commercial banks.

Members of the Banking School instead subscribed to the majority of Thornton's theses. They acknowledged the Bank of England's special responsibility in times of crisis and fully endorsed its function as lender of last resort. They also believed in the distinction of different types of drain on gold reserves and supported expansionary action in case internal or temporary external drains got out of hand. Like Thornton, members of the Banking School expected the Bank of England to maintain higher reserves than commercial banks enabling it to react on short-term balance-of-payments difficulties.

The Bank Charter Act of 1844 essentially implemented the Currency School's position and thus was opposed by members of the Banking School. It divided the Bank of England into two departments: The Issuing and the Banking Department. While granting the Bank of England the monopoly of money creation, the Bank Charter Act strictly restrained the issuing department's ability to issue currency. Above a specified level, notes could only be issued if fully backed by gold reserves. This removed the Bank's ability to react in different ways to distinct types of liquidity shortages and made the lender of last resort function de facto impossible. In practice, the Bank Charter Act of 1844 failed to prevent subsequent financial crises; in 1847, 1857 and 1866 the government was forced to suspend its rules in order to accommodate the need for liquidity and prevent a collapse of the financial system. As a consequence of these experiences, the need for a lender of last resort function became more widely supported during the second half of the nineteenth century with Walter Bagehot its most ardent supporter.

4.2.2 Walter Bagehot (1826–1877)

Although the theoretical concept had been developed by Thornton around 70 years earlier, Walter Bagehot is the economic thinker most widely associated with the central principles of last resort lending. Bagehot's core achievement was to popularise and suggestively present the concept rather than to create it from scratch[11]. While his argument did not differ substantially from that of Thornton and the majority of his points were not novel, he clarified and restated the key issues and revived the case for the Bank of England to take on the duties of a lender of last resort during liquidity crises. Bagehot also extended on Thornton's early work by defining the core principles a lender of last resort should adhere to when discharging its responsibilities; these principles have subsequently been cited in almost every discussion on the lender of last resort function: They proclaim that a lender of last resort should lend freely at a high rate against good collateral[12].

In Lombard Street Bagehot made the case for the Bank of England to officially accept its duty as lender of last resort to England's economy. Unlike other joint-stock banks[13], in its operational conduct the Bank of England was responsible not only for its own affairs but also had to safeguard the stability of the monetary system. Like Thornton and members of the Banking School, Bagehot distinguished between internal and persistent external drains on the Bank's gold reserves. External drains encompassed claims from abroad to meet foreign payment requisite to pay large and unusual foreign debts;[14] while internal drains referred to extra demand for liquidity at home to meet sudden apprehension or panic arising in any manner, rational or irrational[15]. Regarding the former case, Bagehot advocated monetary expansion; regarding the latter, he advised an increase in lending rates. To meet extraordinary demand, the Bank of England was to maintain larger gold reserves than ordinary banks in order to accommodate internal and temporary external out-flows while maintaining the stability of the domestic money supply.

In addition, Bagehot drew attention to several issues either only sparsely dis-cussed or wholly neglected by Henry Thornton. A point in case is his insistence that the duties of a lender of last resort go beyond the provision of liquidity in times of crisis. As quoted below, he drew attention to its role in creating an environment of public confidence. By transparently confirming its willingness to provide ample liquidity if necessary, the Bank of England would be able to prevent many crises from occurring in the first place. Failing to explicitly state its intention to generously

---

11 See Frank Whitson Fetter. 1965. *The Development of British Monetary Orthodoxy 1797–1875*. Cambridge, MA: Harvard University Press

12 See for example Charles Goodhart and Gerhard Illing (Eds.). 2000. *Financial Crises, Contagion, and the Lender of Last Resort. A Reader*. Oxford: Oxford University Press: 1

13 Joint-Stock Banks refers deposit banks whose business is mainly in the United Kingdom: The term includes banks which are member of the British Bankers' Association, like clearing banks or domestic banks of England, Scotland, Northern Ireland.

14 As example of such an external drain Bagehot cites the large withdrawals by Germany of gold reserves from London to realise the value of French reparations negotiated after 1870–71.

15 Walter Bagehot. 1999. *Lombard Street: A Description of the Money Market*. New York, NY: John Wiley & Sons 43.

advance credit in times of crisis, he argued the Bank of England would forfeit a key function of a lender of last resort. While it could still prevent banks from failing and endangering the monetary system, the Bank of England would fail to enhance public confidence and prevent financial panics from developing:

> In fact, to make large advances in this faltering way is to incur the evil of making them without obtaining the advantage… To lend a great deal and yet not give the public confidence that you will lend sufficiently and effectually, is the worst of all policies[16].

As Dr. Strangelove put it to the Soviet ambassador in Stanley Kubrick's Dr. Strangelove or How I Learned to Stop Worrying and Love the Bomb, the whole point of having a Doomsday Machine is lost if you keep it a secret[17].

4.2.2.1   Lending Freely

Bagehot argued that only by generously providing liquidity to the market the Bank of England as lender of last resort would be able to prevent financial panics bringing down the monetary system and eventually the whole economy. While banks were likely to be the key recipients of Bank of England loans, lending was not to be restricted to financial institutions; during a period of monetary strain, the failure of any commercial entity had the power to offset a financial panic in the money market, no matter whether bank, merchant or trading company.

> A Panic, in a word, is a species of neuralgia, and according to the rules of science you must not starve it. The holders of the cash reserve must be ready not only to keep it for their own liabilities, but to advance it most freely to the liabilities of others. They must lend to merchants, to minor bankers, to "this man and that man," whenever the security is good. In wild periods of alarm, one failure makes many, and the best way to prevent the derivative failures is to arrest the primary failure which causes them[18].

The lender of last resort is thus perceived as responsible to the whole economy, not for only a selected sector or interest group within it. Confidence could be maintained only if all creditors in the economy expected their loans to be repaid by their debtors. As soon as doubt or alarm set in about the solvency of a specific debtor, a

---

16 Bagehot (1999): 64–65
17 See Paul Strathern. 2001. *Dr Strangelove's Game: A Brief History of Economic Genius.* London: Penguin Books: 1
18 Bagehot (1999): 51

rush for cash could set in exposing the weakness of the system. In order to prevent a situation where the Bank of England's reserves were not sufficient to pay every creditor, it had to act decisively and quickly before initial alarm would develop into panic. By advancing loans freely, initial confidence in the money market could be restored since creditors felt their funds to be safe and instantly accessible.

> What is wanted and what is necessary to stop a panic is to diffuse the impression, that though money may be dear, still money is to be had. If people could be really convinced that they could have money if they wait a day or two, and that utter ruin is not coming, most likely they would cease to run in such a mad way for money[19].

4.2.2.2 Penalty Rates

Extending Thornton's work, Bagehot also insisted on the importance of charging an interest premium over the market rate for any loans provided by the Bank of England in its capacity as lender of last resort. While lending freely in times of crisis was a lender of last resort's primary function, as argued by Thornton and the Banking School, it should do so at a rate above the market—a penalty rate.

> These loans should only be made at a very high rate of interest. This will operate as a heavy fine on unreasonable timidity, and will prevent the greatest number of applications by persons who do not require it. The rate should be raised early in the panic, so that the fine may be paid early; that no one may borrow out of idle precaution without paying well for it; that the Banking reserve may be protected as far as possible[20].

Accordingly, the penalty rate was supposed not only to channel available resources to its most efficient uses but also to secure distributional equality. High interest was also to help the maintenance of the gold reserve by attracting foreign inflows of capital and supporting the current accounts via deflation of the domestic price level. In addition, high rates were expected to quicken the process of borrowers paying back their loans thus allowing for a smoother return to the long-term goal of controlled monetary expansion. Penalty rates on emergency loans could so serve as deterrent to cautious borrowers amassing inefficiently high gold reserves and entice borrowers to first assess every other possibility of satisfying liquidity needs before turning to the Bank of England. Moreover, as Humphrey and Keheler suggest,

---

19 Bagehot (1999): 65–65
20 Bagehot (1999): 197

penalty rates can implicitly serve the function of a market test regarding the borrower's solvency status[21].

4.2.2.3 The Collateral

The third component of Bagehot's Principles is the insistence on loans to be made against good collateral only. By providing adequate collateral, borrowers can signal that while in need of liquidity, they are fundamentally solvent for no advances need be made by which the Bank will ultimately loose[22]. Fully aware that during financial panics asset prices are often severely impaired and that to calm financial panics generous lending is required, Bagehot poses few restrictions on the assets acceptable as collateral; any asset valuable in normal times was to qualify. Consequently, reduced asset prices during crisis should not have constituted an obstacle to lending, as the crisis lender should consider the asset's value in normal times. In order to maintain monetary stability the lender of last resort should be able to lend with minimal restrictions in terms of borrowers' eligibility and collateral suitability "for it is ready lending which cures panics, and non-lending or niggardly lending which aggravates them"[23]. Clearly, to advance cash freely was the overriding principle in efforts to prevent financial crisis from deepening; it was not the issue whether collateral assets are attractive to the lender of last resort at that particular period of time.

Like Thornton, Bagehot strongly opposed the provision of liquidity to poorly managed and insolvent banks. The lender of last resort's responsibility was to be not on individual institutions, but on the whole monetary system. The hostility towards bailing-out insolvent banks may reflect Bagehot's awareness of the moral hazard problems the existence of a lender of last resort can pose. Consequently, the Bank of England was not to attempt preventing the collapse of an individual insolvent institution, but to try to contain any effects the failure of that institution might have on the money market and thus on fundamentally solvent institutions in the economy. In addition to advocating the lender of last resort function, Bagehot stressed the importance of good governance in financial institutions and was optimistic regarding market pressures pushing banks towards prudent lending and sufficient reserves. Increasing the stability of joint-stock banks was perceived as essential since the higher individual institutions' stability, the less pressure would be exerted on the Bank of England's limited reserves.

> As these ... suggestions are designed to make the Bank as strong as possible, we should look at the rest of our banking system, and try to

---

21 See Humphrey and Keleher (1984): 39
22 Bagehot (1999): 198
23 Bagheot (1999): 316

reduce the demands on the banks as much as we can. The central machinery being inevitably frail, we should carefully and as much as possible diminish the strain upon it[24].

4.2.2.4 Financial Stability after 1866

While financial crises occurred frequently until the Overend Gurney Crisis in 1866, the following decades saw a period of financial stability that lasted until the Great Depression. Incipient panics in 1878, 1890 and 1914 were prevented from developing into severe financial crises. During the same period the United States experienced financial crises in 1873, 1893 and 1907–08. A number of authors attribute this period of stability in Great Britain to a change in policy by the Bank of England[25]. According to this view, the Bank of England adopted monetary policies following the principles advocated by Bagehot in Lombard Street. Widespread awareness that the Bank of England would act as lender of last resort during periods of monetary pressure was credited with achieving a sense of security that prevented continuous bank runs, financial panics, and subsequent financial crises from occurring[26]. In contrast, the United States lacked a central institution with the mandate to provide ample credit to rescue banking panics. Efforts by local clearing houses to provide liquidity via the issuance of loan certificates were of limited success in addressing the problem. Successful prevention of banking panics turning into severe financial crises by lender of last resort operations in Canada, France and Germany are further evidence that increased stability at least in part has been a consequence of central banks assuming the function of a lender of last resort[27].

Weakening this case is the fact that the Bank of England had acted as lender of last resort long before 1873 and even before Thornton made its case in 1802. But never had the Bank of England explicitly stated that it would interfere and provide liquidity in times of crisis—a central point of Bagehot's critique on the institution as discussed above. Due to reasons of moral hazard, the Bank continued its practice of creative ambiguity even following the publication of Lombard Street. While it successfully provided liquidity when banking panics arose, it refrained from explicitly committing to this responsibility. Furthermore, a number of problems triggering banking panics in the preceding decades had receded when the period of financial stability in Great Britain commenced after 1866. Crop failures occurred

---

24 Bagehot (1999): 74
25 See Michael Bordo and Lars Jonung. 2000. *Lessons for EMU from the History of Monetary Unions*. London: Institute of Economic Affairs
26 Michael D. Bordo. 1983. *The Lender of Last Resort: Some Historical Insights*. NBER Working Paper 3011. Washington, DC: National Bureau of Economic Research
27 Bordo (1989): 16–17

less frequently in the second half of the nineteenth century and their impact on both the economy and the financial system declined due to lower shipping costs and increased supply from the United States. In the financial sector, bigger and better managed joint-stock and deposit banks replaced the large number of small and vulnerable country banks; as a consequence, stability of the financial sector increased and bank failures became less common. In addition, a reduced military involvement and improved government finances reduced pressures on the Bank of England to provide reserves to the government. Wood argues that the period of financial stability has to be attributed primarily to a combination of those three factors, claiming that the one thing of which we can be certain is that the stability was not a consequence of the Bank of England's conversion to Bagehot's rule[28].

While less frequent crop failures, a healthier financial sector and sounder government balances doubtlessly contributed to financial stability after 1866, it is unlikely that more frequent lender of last resort operations by the Bank of England have played no part in these developments. The debate stirred up by Bagehot led to a renaissance of the concept and Bank of England officials were forced to deliberate and comment on the subject. In spite of ardent opponents, the majority position was to maintain constructive ambiguity but to assure that the Bank of England had assumed its responsibility in the past and was unlikely to fail doing so in the future. It thus seems likely that after 1873 the public was at least more reassured of the Bank's potential role during crisis periods than before. The fact that it indeed took on that responsibility at several occasions can only have hardened this belief. Furthermore, lender of last resort operations have been undertaken during financial panics at numerous occasions ever after, contemporary examples including the bailout of Credit Lyonnais by the Bank de France and the rescue organised by the New York Federal Reserve to prevent the reverberations of a failure of Long-Term Capital Management. At a domestic level, evidence supports the soundness of the concept: The existence of a lender of last resort indeed reduces the likelihood of financial panics developing in to severe financial crises and can help to mitigate the impact on the real economy once a crisis has arisen.

4.3 An International Lender of Last Resort

While the concept of a lender of last resort has been analysed in depth in a domestic setting, contributions regarding the possibility of an international lender of last resort have been incoherent and often superficial. There is agreement that an international lender of last resort would be somehow modelled on the role central banks perform

---

28 John H. Wood. 2003. "Bagehot's Lender of Last Resort: A Hollow Hollowed Tradition." *The Independent Review.* Vol. 7, No. 3: 343–351

in domestic economies. Further consensus exists that its mandate would be to reduce frequency and severity of financial crises in emerging economies and increase the stability of the global financial system. But there is no common understanding how an international lender would operate to achieve its goals. Two central questions form the core of the debate that has arisen in the aftermath of emerging market crises since 1995: Firstly, is there a need for an international lender of last resort? And secondly, if so, can there be an international lender of last resort or is the concept either theoretically or practically infeasible?

4.3.1 Theoretical Considerations

The success of central banks acting as lender of last resort in fostering domestic financial stability raises the question to what extent similar approaches could be employed to increase global financial stability. Interpreting international currency crises in terms of domestic banking panics, emerging economies can be argued to face dangers similar to those of banks in a vulnerable financial system: Asymmetric information and herd behaviour by international investors trying to pull out all their funds at once can create situations where even fundamentally sound public and private sector institutions are threatened by default due to a lack of international liquidity. During financial panics, institutions that in non-crisis times have no difficulties in rolling-over their loans have to repay maturing obligations simultaneously; without third-party emergency assistance they can be forced into bankruptcy. By providing short-term liquidity an international lender of last resort could prevent fundamentally solvent entities from bankruptcy and arrest the negative effects bankruptcies have on individual economies. Moreover, financial panics within a single economy could be prevented from spreading to other economies via contagion and spill-over effects as in the case of Southeast Asia, Russia and Brazil.

Central banks in industrial economies are able to act as a lender of last resort given effectively unlimited access to liquidity. Since debt obligations tend to be denominated in domestic currency[29], by issuing currency central banks can provide liquidity assistance even when reserves are limited. As debt structures of developed economies have longer maturities than those in developing countries, short-term liquidity problems are likely to remain an exception rather than the rule. When a lack of liquidity in money markets arises, the central bank can increase the money

---

29 See Frederic S. Mishkin. 2000. *The International Lender of Last Resort: What Are the Issues?* Paper prepared for the Kiel Week Conference "The World's New Financial Landscape: Challenges for Economic Policy." June 19–20, 2000. Kiel, Germany: Kiel Institute of World Economics

supply which raises the price level and reduces debt burdens. Liquidity problems can thus be eased and widespread bankruptcies prevented.

Debt obligations in emerging economies instead are often denominated in foreign currency and debt maturities are often short rather than long-term. In order to mitigate financial panics, a lender of last resort must be able to provide sufficient liquidity in both domestic and foreign currency. While for domestic banking panics local currency loans may be sufficient to prevent widespread bankruptcies, obligations to international investors have to be repaid in foreign currency. However, domestic central banks can issue domestic currency only as the international community has strong reservations regarding countries that print other countries' currency. Foreign currency denominated debt service obligations must thus be met by reserves. When currency reserves are limited, central banks in emerging economies struggle to function as effective lender of last resort to their economies.

An international lender of last resort could overcome this problem by providing foreign currency loans to central banks and enabling them to stabilize their economies in two non-exclusive ways: One is to provide both domestic and foreign currency denominated loans to prevent the bankruptcy of domestic institutions and default by the official sector; the other is to attempt stabilizing the exchange rate of its currency by intervening in international currency markets. Moreover, the mere existence of an international lender of last resort may be sufficient to increase confidence in the markets and reduce the attractiveness of speculative attacks on currencies of fundamentally healthy economies.

Most importantly, emergency loans by an international lender of last resort would enable domestic central banks to provide short-term liquidity assistance to their economies not only in domestic, but also in foreign currency. Banks as well as non-financial institutions may at times require external assistance not due to mismanagement and excessive indebtedness, but due to changes in investor sentiment. This is particularly problematic in terms of foreign currency denominated debt when a change in expectations leads international investors to simultaneously recall most of their maturing loans. Even fundamentally solvent institutions may go bankrupt when failing to raise the necessary funds to repay their debt obligations on time. Violent capital outflows exacerbate liquidity shortages by exerting pressure on domestic exchange rates: As investors try to pull out their funds, the value of domestic currency depreciates thereby raising the burden of foreign-denominated debt. Accordingly, unlimited access to domestic currency is generally insufficient to arrest financial panics in emerging economies. Only additional and sufficient amounts of foreign currency can mitigate financial panics involving not only domestic creditors but also international investors and prevent fundamentally solvent banks from failing.

An alternative conception of an international lender of last resort entails its role in enabling central banks to intervene in foreign exchange markets. The provision of foreign currency would thus allow domestic central banks to uphold exchange rate pegs or at least prevent the domestic currency from excessive depreciation. Since a substantial depreciation can trigger financial crises via balance-sheet effects, by stabilizing domestic exchange rates central banks could so prevent widespread bankruptcies resulting from increased debt burdens of institutions indebted in foreign currency. Although the intervention in currency markets has often proved to merely postpone the problem, it has been the dominant use of IMF emergency loans during the crisis in 1997–98.

As the central task of an domestic lender of last resort does not lie in preventing the collapse of individual institutions but rather in preventing the effects those bankruptcies have on the financial system, the importance of an international lender of last resort would not rest on supporting individual economies, but on its role in providing stability to the global financial system.

4.3.2 The Case for an International Lender of Last Resort

The case for an international lender of last resort is powerful: More than a hundred years of experience have shown how a lender of last resort substantially increases the stability of domestic financial systems. As argued above, a lack of foreign currency reserves often prevents central banks in emerging economies from fulfilling a similar role. An international lender of last resort with access to sufficient amounts of hard currency could alleviate this problem. As financial crises in emerging economies have proven to be destabilizing for the international monetary system, not only developing but industrial countries alike would benefit from a reduction in the frequency and severity of financial crises.

Nevertheless, a number of economists contest the need for an international lender of last resort. Anna Schwartz denies that in a world with flexible exchange rates the institution of an international lender of last resort is necessary[30]. According to her reasoning if local central banks discharge their responsibilities as domestic lender of last resort, stability of the international financial system can be achieved without a supra-national institution. Domestic central banks can prevent monetary contraction in their economies by issuing their own currency; if foreign currency is needed, markets would be willing to provide the necessary loans if debtors are worthy of credit. Schwartz further argues that financial crises can only be ended by a com-

---

30 Anna J. Schwartz. 2000. "Earmarks of a Lender of Last Resort." In Charles Goodhart and Gerhard Illing (Eds.). 2000. *Financial Crises, Contagion, and the Lender of Last Resort. A Reader.* Oxford: Oxford University Press

bination of several strategies; liquidity provision alone would be insufficient. Accordingly, only emerging market countries themselves could end financial crises within their economy; in this perception, there is neither a need nor a role for an international organization in fostering the stability of the global financial system.

Another view rejects the creation of an international lender of last resort on the grounds that it curtails beneficial international competition between currencies. According to the Free Banking School[31] the existence of central banks is the key source of financial instability; without them, banks competing with each other would regulate themselves far more successfully since competition that characterizes a decentralized system wins out over the policy edicts of a central bank largely because of the absence of key perversities that are inherent in central control[32]. A universal reserve currency would relieve local central banks from competitive pressures to pursue prudent monetary policies; similarly, the existence of an international lender of last resort would prevent competition between domestic central banks in fulfilling the role of a lender of last resort. Moreover, without the existence of central banks, governments would be unable to amass excessive debt burdens in the first place since markets would stop advancing loans after indebtedness surpasses a sustainable level; government debt is priced as riskless only given central banks' ability to monetize debt if necessary. Authors like Kroszner therefore argue that free banking might be a suggestive model particularly regarding emerging economies[33].

General opposition to the creation of international institutions is further based on public choice models that question the possibility to control a supra-national bureaucracy with the power to create international reserves. Accordingly, like all types of national or international bureaucracies, an international lender of last resort would be impossible to control but fundamentally motivated to maximize its influence and resources. Indeed, bureaucracies have been frequently observed to divert from original mandates to follow policies increasing own power and influence. The IMF is an exemplary case: Its multiple mandate enlargements since the collapse of the Bretton Woods System and frequent quota increases underline the suspicion that once created international organisations attempt to increase both their mandate and budget. From a public choice perspective, without effective monitoring the creation of new international institutions should be resisted.

---

31 For a introduction to Free Banking see Lawrence H. White. 1984. *Free Banking in Britain: Theory, Experience, and Debate, 1800–1845*. New York, NY: Cambridge University Press
32 Roger W. Garrison. 1996. "Central Banking, Free Banking, and Financial Crises." *Review of Austrian Economics*. Vol. 9, No. 2: 109–127
33 Randall S. Kroszner. 1995. *Free Banking: The Scottish Experience as a Model for Emerging Economies*. Working Paper No. 1536. Washington, DC: The World Bank

None of these arguments successfully discards the theoretical concept of an international lender of last resort. Experience contradicts Schwartz' claim that markets are always willing to provide creditworthy debtors with additional loans. As the crises in Mexico and East Asia have shown, in times of uncertainty financial markets can be unwilling to extend loans even to fundamentally solvent sovereign debtors. At the same time, domestic central banks struggle to fulfil their role as lender of last resort when large parts of sovereign and private sector debt are denominated in foreign currency. Experience also discards the Free Banking critique as central banks have proved their importance for the stability of the financial sector and the economy at large over and over again. Without central banks, the occurrence of financial crises would have been far more frequent while governments would have lacked their most effective tool of economic policy-making. Finally, regarding public choice reservations, if doing without supranational institutions could be justified on grounds of monitoring and control issues alone, it would be all but impossible to deal with global problems that require multilateral responses.

Consequently, the majority of arguments opposing the creation of an international lender are based on practical considerations. While an international institution providing liquidity assistance to mitigate financial crises in emerging economies is in principle desirable, its creation is often assumed impossible in practice due to several issues ranging from funding constraints to moral hazard considerations. Fundamental differences between the domestic and the international context are widely perceived as too extensive to allow for the creation of an international lender of last resort in practice.

4.3.3 Fundamental Differences between International and Domestic Settings

Although the theoretical concept of both a domestic and an international lender of last resort is similar, there are at least three fundamental differences between the domestic and the international context. The most obvious distinction between an international and a domestic lender of last resort relates to its ability to create high-powered money. While a domestic lender of last resort—usually the central bank—can draw on unlimited resources for providing local currency by issuing notes via the printing press, there is no such thing as an international or world currency[34]. The ability of the IMF to issue SDRs is limited and SDRs are not a common medium of exchange. Although the world's major currencies like dollar, euro, yen, and sterling are utilised globally, their country of origin remains the only place where they can

---

34 During the Bretton Woods Conference in 1944 John Maynard Keynes proposed the creation of an international central bank as well as a common unit of currency named *Bancor*. These proposals were subsequently dropped and instead the International Monetary Fund was created.

be issued. Consequently, there can be no international body with the power to create foreign currency reserves. Indeed, given that the dollar is accepted almost universally, it is often argued that only the Federal Reserve has the ability to act as international lender of last resort. As a result, the access to sufficient liquidity is much more difficult to secure internationally than at the domestic level. For Capie, this lack of money issuing capacity alone renders the concept of an international lender of last resort[35]. Others convincingly caution that the international community would not be willing to provide the resources necessary for an institution to assume the responsibility of an international lender of last resort[36].

Another difficulty arises in terms of authority and discretion in decision-making. Domestic central banks are either independent or controlled by the government. In contrast, international organisations usually have a large number of stakeholders and decisions have to be authorised by all of them; at the IMF most important decisions require a supermajority of 85 percent of the executive board's 25 directors. Institutional arrangements of this kind render decision-making a long and cumbersome process and severely restrict the ability to agree on policy responses as timely as necessary when dealing with financial crises[37]. Furthermore, the higher the resources available to any international institution, the more limited will be institutional discretion over its resources. International stakeholders' unwillingness to delegate decision-making power to unaccountable technocrats naturally increases with the amount of resources involved. As a result, timely and efficient responses to financial crises are far more difficult to reach at an international than at a national level.

Strong supervisory and monitoring capabilities are essential in order to establish rules and regulations that foster financial sector stability. Since a vulnerable banking sector increases the danger of banking panics and financial crises substantially, an adequate regulatory system is a vital building block for effective crisis prevention. Without it, a lender of last resort will fail to effectively mitigate financial panics. Supervision is of vital importance primarily in order to distinguish solvent borrowers facing short-term liquidity constrains from insolvent institutions. This is necessary not only for an efficient allocation of limited funds but also to reduce moral hazard problems. Achieving effective supervision is an ambitious task for national authorities already; at the international level these difficulties multiply and

---

35 Forrest Capie. 2000. "Can There Be an International Lender-of-Last-Resort?" In Charles Goodhart and Gerhard Illing (Eds.). 2000. *Financial Crises, Contagion, and the Lender of Last Resort. A Reader*. Oxford: Oxford University Press: 437

36 See Kenneth Rogoff. 1999. "International Institutions for Reducing Global Financial Instability." *Journal of Economic Perspectives*. No. 13: 14.

37 See Anna Schwartz. 1999. "Is There a Need for an International Lender of Last Resort?" *Cato Journal*. Vol. 19 No. 1

may render the operation of an effective international lender of last resort impossible.

4.3.4 The IMF as International Lender of Last Resort

Another argument suggests that there already is an international lender of last resort for the international monetary system: The IMF, acting as lender of last resort for national governments[38]. At least since 1997, when the Fund created facilities to allow for the disbursements of emergency loans even to countries in arrears, claims that the IMF is moving towards becoming an international lender of last resort can claim some merit[39]. The most prominent representative of this view is Stanley Fischer who argued that

> The IMF, although it is not an international central bank, has undertaken certain important lender-of-last-resort functions within the current system, generally acting in concert with other official agencies, and that this role can be made more effective within a reformed international financial system[40].

The IMF indeed provided at several occasions substantial foreign currency loans to countries facing difficulties in their balance of payments accounts. Moreover, the Fund has lent at times when international capital markets were closed to developing country borrowers and no other institution had the clout to provide liquidity assistance in comparable quantities. The considerable stock in foreign reserves and gold at disposal to the IMF as well as its ability to create Special Drawing Rights is sometimes regarded as sufficient to qualify the IMF as lender of last resort to the global financial system. Despite these similarities, in its current form a number of issues disqualify the Fund as an international lender of last resort. These issues are not specific to the IMF; instead they fundamentally resemble the differences between a lender of last resort at the domestic and at the international level.

First, the IMF is clearly unable to issue international currency. Consequently, its funds in international currency are by definition limited. Its ability to issue Special Drawing Rights is strictly regulated by the Articles of Agreement and only possible under quinquennial quota reviews requiring a supermajority of no less than 85 percent of votes in the executive board. Moreover, SDRs cannot serve the same

---

38 Paul Krugman. 1999. *The Return of Depression Economics*. New York: W. W. Norton & Company: 114
39 Jean Tirole. 2002. *Financial Crises, Liquidity, and the International Monetary System*. Princeton, NJ: Princeton University Press: 30
40 Stanley Fischer. 2000. *On the Need for an International Lender of Last Resort*. Essays in International Economics No. 220. Princeton, NJ: Princeton University: 4

function as international hard currency since its use is restricted to transactions between central banks; SDRs cannot be lent on by a central bank to other institutions and thus are unsuitable to provide liquidity to the financial sector. Although the Fund formally controls over USD 300 billion, its actual commitment capacity is only around a third of this amount. This is due to the fact that a large share of those funds are denominated in internationally not widely accepted currencies and that the majority of funds has already be lent out to emerging market borrowers. Access to additional funds under the New Arrangements to Borrow (NAB) or the Fund's stock of gold add to the Fund's commitment capacity but are still insufficient for the provision of effective lender of last resort services.

Second, in order to mitigate financial crises timely action is essential. The more time a panic has to spread, the harder it is to arrest it; with every day a financial crisis continues, the stability of financial institutions declines and more funds are necessary to prevent even fundamentally solvent entities from bankruptcy. Ideally, a lender of last resort takes action to arrest a crisis as soon as it develops. Due to its multiple stakeholders, the IMF is unable to reach decisions on emergency loans as timely as necessary. Loan agreements have to be authorized by a supermajority of members; they are voted on by 25 executive directors and both the largest members individually as well as coalitions between the three following largest members can veto every emergency package. Decisions are taken after a long process of deliberation, further extended by the fact the executive directors have to consult with their national governments. Finally, when loans are made, they are conditional on a multitude of monetary and fiscal reforms which have to be implemented before individual tranches are dispersed. Instant responses to looming banking or currency crises are thus impossible.

IMF lending policies violate every principle an effective lender of last resort is supposed to follow according to Walter Bagehot. Regarding the recipients of emergency loans, he insisted that loans should be dispersed to illiquid but solvent borrowers only; for reasons of allocative efficiency and to curb moral hazard insolvent institutions should be left to fail. Given the difficulties of distinguishing between illiquid and insolvent institutions, Bagehot advised that loans should be advanced against good collateral only. In contrast to this principle, the IMF forgoes collateral and lends on policy conditions. As a result, at several instances it advanced large scale liquidity assistance to sovereign borrowers that were insolvent rather than illiquid, the latest example being the USD 8 billion rescue package advanced to Argentina in August 2001.

In a similar way, the IMF violated the principle of charging premium interest rates for emergency loans. Bagehot underlined the importance of this principle since only penalty rates can ensure that only borrowers in severe financial difficulties apply for emergency loans; and only when emergency loans are perceived truly the last resort, borrowers' incentives to follow prudent policies in order to prevent liquidity problems remain intact. Penalty rates encourage borrowers to seek every possible alternative and if loans are granted provide motivation to repay them as soon as possible. In contrast to this principle, the majority of IMF loans are advanced at the Fund's cost of capital and thus at subsidized interest rates. As a consequence, IMF loans became a financially attractive source of capital for emerging market countries despite the need to negotiate a stability program. Demand for IMF loans is thus not limited to countries in severe liquidity problems, but comes from all countries willing to accept a certain level of interference in their economy; in addition, subsidized interest rates mean that countries have no incentive to repay loans as early as possible. As a result, a large part of IMF resources are utilised and cannot be used when severe liquidity crises arise.

In resemblance of Bagehot's critique on the Bank of England in 1873, a lack of transparency at the IMF in regard to its lending policies also means that a central function of a lender of last resort cannot be achieved: To create confidence in the market and thereby reduce the likelihood that financial panics develop in the first place. While moral hazard considerations partly justify following a the strategy of creative ambiguity, the fact that markets cannot count on the existence of an international lender of last resort increases the probability of bank runs and violent capital flow reversals. Initially providing extensive emergency loans in Latin America and Southeast Asia, and then refusing to support Russia and eventually Argentina, the Fund proved successful in curbing moral hazard; at the same time it increased uncertainty and thus the fragility of the global financial system.

4.3.5 The Fund's Record as Crisis Manger

Although the IMF does not operate as a lender of last resort to the global financial system, the responsibility of preventing and mitigating financial crises today rests almost exclusively on its shoulders. While other institutions have contributed to many rescue packages, the Fund's prominent role as coordinator and crisis manger has been clearly visible over more than a decade. However, its record as crisis manager has been mixed at best; as a result, the Fund has come increasingly under attack for its handling of financial crises in emerging market economies. In many instances, policy mistakes stem directly from the Fund's deviation from the Bagehot Rules. According to the Meltzer Report

> The frequency and severity of recent crises raises doubts about the
> system of crisis management now in place and the incentives for private
> actions that it encourages and sustains. The IMF has given too little

attention to improving financial structures in developing countries and too much to expensive rescue operations. Its system of short-term crisis-management is too costly, its responses too slow, its advice often incorrect, and its efforts to influence policy and practice too intrusive[41].

Although attention has been drawn to a large number of deficiencies, in regard to the Fund's role during the Asian Crisis three problems stand out[42]. All three are a consequence of the Fund having significantly expanded its traditional role of offering assistance to economies in balance-of-payments difficulties. At the Fund's inception it was restricted to provide financial assistance to help countries coping with temporary liquidity crunches and reversing trade deficits. Conditionality, the policy of making loans conditional on wide ranging economic reforms and the implementation of often pro-cyclical fiscal and monetary policies was no part of the Fund's original mandate. The central policy mistakes in dealing with emerging market crises can thus be attributed to at least two factors: Firstly, the Fund's original structure was based on a system of fixed exchange rates which made effective liquidity assistance under a system of floating rates very difficult. Secondly, by extending its functions the IMF has altered its operational procedures to differ substantially from the principles that should guide an effective lender of last resort.

Originally founded to support a global regime of fixed exchange rates, the collapse of the Bretton Woods Agreement between 1971 and 1973 rendered this role obsolete. Moreover, the Fund's resources became inadequate for easing balance-of-payments problems in an environment of floating exchange rates. As a result, the IMF expanded its mandate into other areas. When Latin American economies found themselves unable to service their foreign debts, it became involved in negotiations between lending banks and debtor governments to restructure unsustainable debt burdens. Subsequently, it began monitoring the tight fiscal and monetary policies Latin American countries had to commit to in order to increase export earnings and complete the rescheduling of their sovereign debt burdens. IMF conditionality policy developed out of this monitoring role. With the fall of the iron curtain the IMF added the mandate of advising former communist countries in the transformation process from planned to market economies and started adding structural economic reforms to its expertise. Dealing with emerging market crises during the 1990s, IMF advice incorporated all those experiences and thereby strongly increased the Fund's interference in national economies with often substandard success.

---

41 International Financial Institution Advisory Commission. 2000. *Report of the International Financial Institution Advisory Commission.* Washington, DC: Senate Committee on Banking, Housing, and Urban Affairs: Executive Summary
42 See Martin Feldstein. 1998. "Refocusing the IMF." *Foreign Affairs.* Vol. 77, No. 2: 20–33

The Asian crisis was the result of a number of different developments and no single reason can explain it satisfactorily. Fixed exchange rate regimes, structural deficiencies, excessive short-term indebtedness and herd behaviour by international investors all had a role. Triggered by a depreciation of the Baht, the crisis spread from Thailand to the whole East Asian region and eventually infected both Russia and Brazil. The IMF was not the culprit, but its handling of the crisis contained aspects clearly counterproductive at least from an aftermath perspective. Although the reforms proposed were in principle desirable, the Fund excessively micro-managed the process by insisting not only on pro-cyclical adjustments to economic policy but also on numerous structural reforms[43]. In its original role the Fund would have restricted its actions to provide temporary liquidity support to weather inevitable balance-of-payments adjustments and to build confidence in the markets. In practice, it made its help conditional on the implementation of structural reforms in the individual economies reaching from issues of foreign trade to banking require-ments as well as industrial and financial liberalisation. Many conditions put excessive burdens on governments, hampered growth and cost precious time through lengthy negotiations. Often they commenced to late and further reduced investor confidence by drawing attention to economies' weaknesses.

Similarly, insisting on drastic fiscal and monetary tightening proved counter-productive in the cases of Thailand, Korea and Indonesia by exacerbating economic contraction[44]. At the outset of the crisis, most economies were in a relatively healthy shape: Government deficits and most current account deficits were in acceptable ranges and did not urgently require raising taxes and cutting expenditures. The resulting economic decline and falling export earnings increased their difficulties in servicing foreign-denominated debt obligations. The expanded role of the IMF was the root cause of these misguided policies; a more restricted role similar to that of an international lender of last resort might have mitigated the severe effects these crises had on the region's economies and via contagion on economies all over the world.

Insisting on structural reforms and fiscal and monetary tightening as one-size-fits-all approach may have proved most harmful to Korea. While Korea faced a tem-porary liquidity crunch due to imprudent debt structures and insufficient inter-national reserves, economic fundamentals were basically sound. Total external debt was at an acceptable 30 percent of GDP[45]. In contrast to Thailand, in Korea the cur-rent account deficit was below three percent and falling. Despite structural problems, Korea's was a case of short-term illiquidity rather than of fundamental solvency. What was needed most was the restoration of confidence and encouragement for

---

43 See Stiglitz (2002): 113–118
44 See Krugman (1999): 115
45 Feldstein (1998): 25

international creditors to roll-over short-term loans. Putting strong emphasis on structural problems and highlighting the issue of incestuous corporate relations proved unsuccessful in restoring confidence in the markets. By underlining the shortcomings of the Korean economy, the IMF strengthened and encouraged investor fears instead of facilitating the extension of short-term loans by international creditors.

The policies proposed by the IMF in response to the Asian Crisis were based on experiences made in crisis management over a period of several decades. The reasoning behind these policies was often sound and by no means as fundamentally flawed as suggested by critics like Stiglitz or Krugman. While the negative impact IMF programs had on Southeast Asian economies can be traced to a variety of causes, a central factor has surely been the Fund's deviation from the Bagehot Rules in its efforts to provide liquidity assistance. One the one hand, it failed to provide liquidity assistance freely and against good collateral only. On the other, its insistence on excessive conditionality requirements meant that liquidity assistance was not disbursed as timely as necessary and therefore failed to increase investors' confidence in the region.

5. The Lender of Last Resort: The Concept in Practice

In past financial crises the responsibility for providing emergency loans during liquidity crunches has been assumed by a variety of actors and institutions; very often their eventual resolution was a combined effort of several institutions working together in order to raise the necessary funds. To explore the viability of an international lender of last resort, it is necessary to analyse the resolution of past financial crises and the strategies embarked on to provide liquidity assistance to distressed borrowers.

Out of a large number of crisis episodes identified, three haven been chosen to highlight typical problems during periods of financial distress and to draw lessons on the effective provision of liquidity assistance: The Panic of 1907 in the United States, the 1960s Sterling Crisis and the Asian Financial Crisis in 1997–98. On the one hand, these episodes' relevance stems from their international character. On the other, each crisis took place in a specific period in international monetary history: During the Panic of 1907 most countries were on a well functioning gold standard. In 1960 the Bretton Woods system of fixed exchange rates and capital controls had just started operating. And the Asian Crisis in 1997–98 erupted in the post-Bretton Woods environment where some countries choose flexible exchange rate regimes and others opt for adjustable pegs. Despite these different monetary settings, the task for the institution assuming the responsibility of a lender of last resort has been the same: To prevent a collapse of the financial system by providing emergency loans to distressed institutions.

The crisis episodes selected also add real world examples to the theoretical discussion in chapters 2 and 4. While 1907 exemplifies a typical banking crisis, the Sterling Crisis provides an example for a pure currency crisis as described in first generation models. The twin crises in Asia and Latin America shared aspects of both banking and currency crises and provide particularly relevant lessons regarding the Fund's capacity as crisis manager.

5.1 The Panic of 1907

The Panic of 1907 is of particular relevance to this analysis in several ways: First, it was the last and—although short—one of the most severe financial panics in the United States during the Era of National Banking that lasted from 1863 to 1914[1].

---

1 Under the National Banking System private banks were permitted to issue bank notes which were collateralized by government bonds deposited at the U.S. Treasury. They were thus explicitly guaranteed by the government. These notes could be exchanged at par against gold or

Second, it was in the aftermath of this crisis that steps were taken that eventually led to the creation in 1914 of the Federal Reserve System, a central bank controlling the money supply and taking on the responsibilities of a lender of last resort. The crisis of 1907 serves as a showcase not only how financial crises can develop from bank runs but also illustrates that occasionally liquidity crunches can be overcome even without the existence of a formal lender of last resort. Although the contemporary debate on the creation of an international lender of last resort is focussed on emerging market currency crises and the banking crisis of 1907 was restricted to the United States, no episode is better suited to provide an example of a typical banking crisis involving panicking depositors and contagious bank runs.

5.1.1 The Setting

The Crisis of 1907 is a classic case of financial panic turning into a fully-fledged banking crisis and a lack of liquidity endangering the stability of the whole financial system. Liquidity crunches arise due to excessive demand for currency generally caused by depositors loosing confidence in their own bank or the banking system as a whole. A loss of confidence can be triggered by a variety of different shocks including war, bad harvests or the failure of a big financial institution. In 1907 the shock came in form of the downfall of a prominent speculator, named F. Augustus Heinze. However, the setting for the crisis was already in place on October 16 when Heinze and his brother went bankrupt.

Under regular circumstances the collapse of a single speculator would not necessarily have led to severe a crisis as erupted in 1907. But New York money markets had already been under strain during October given seasonal characteristics and a generally weak state of the domestic economy. After a strong cyclical expansion until 1905 and a short but contained crisis in 1906, the American economy was in decline. Stock markets recorded losses and a tightening of credit markets had led to a rise in interest rates. In addition to the failure of a number of companies during the summer, in fall the seasonal pattern of liquidity outflows into the interior of the United States further fuelled already high demands for cash.

In the early twentieth century agriculture still accounted for a considerable part of the U.S. economy: between 15 and 18 percent of GDP were created in the rural economy. Agricultural production took place in the Southern and Middle Western parts of the country and the produce was shipped to both East Coast and Europe; New York acted as middle man for trades in agricultural goods like cotton or grain. Immediately after harvest in autumn, the agricultural producers in the interior of the

---

greenback and consequently served as perfect substitutes to species. The era of National Banking was established with the National Banking Act in 1863 and lasted until 1914.

United States shipped their crops to the East Coast creating a trade surplus with New York. New York's trade deficit with the interior during these months led to large outflows of cash to mid-western banks where it was needed to finance the harvest and to transport the produce. In contrast, during the summer months banks in the interior of the United States were in possession of unused cash surpluses that were transferred to New York money markets to earn higher interest. These seasonal variations of liquidity were mirrored by low interest rates in the summer and high interest rates in fall when liquidity became scarce[2].

Interest differentials between New York and Europe usually led to inflows of gold and currency from European money markets, predominantly from London where interest rates where lower and the influence of harvest time on rates weaker. But in the fall of 1907 scarcity of cash and high interest rates in European money markets caused the typical flow of money to the United States to subside and turned England from a net exporter to a net importer of gold. Not only was the Bank of England unwilling to see gold leaving for the United States, but according to Sayers it actually *was fighting New York speculation*[3]. O.M.W. Sprague attributes the scarcity of cash in London and Paris to high gold exports to the United States of USD 50 million in spring and USD 80 million in the fall of 1906. These exports to New York threatened the fixed exchange rate between sterling and the dollar of USD 4.867, and the Bank of England initiated several measures to stem the outflow of specie: In October it aggressively raised interest rates 200 basis points within less than two weeks; later it introduced penalty rates on U.K. banks discounting finance bills from the United States[4]. According to this reasoning, the Bank of England's actions to defend its exchange rate were responsible for the weak financial condition of New York's money market in which the collapse of a single speculator could trigger one of the most severe banking crises ever experienced in the United States[5].

Another explanation put forward to explain tight money markets in Europe and London relates to the San Francisco Earthquake on April 18, 1906. The damage to San Francisco by both earthquake and the following fires were estimated at between USD 350 and USD 500 million. Since U.K. insurance companies had a market share of nearly 40 percent in California and even more in San Francisco, insurance claims related to the earthquake had a considerable impact on the flow of specie between both countries. Around 40 percent of gold exports worth over USD 70 million from

---

2 See Charles Goodhart. 1969. *The New York Money Market and the Finance of Trade 1900–1913*. Cambridge, MA: Harvard University Press

3 Richard S. Sayers. 1976. *The Bank of England 1891–1944*. Cambridge, UK: Cambridge University Press: 55

4 Oliver M. W. Sprague. 1910. *History of Crises under the National Banking System*. Washington, DC: National Monetary Commission: 241

5 See Milton Friedman and Anna Schwartz. 1963. *A Monetary History of the United States 1867–1969*. Princeton, NJ: Princeton University Press

London to New York are estimated to have been related to insurance claims for the year 1906; the flows accounted for a 14 percent stock loss of gold in the United Kingdom[6]. In this view, the protective behaviour by the Bank of England was initiated to counter pressure on the sterling exchange rate caused by British payments of insurance claims to California. Regardless of what explanation has more merit, distressed New York money markets made the financial system of the United States far more vulnerable to external shocks that it would have usually been.

5.1.2 The Run on Banks and Trust Companies

F. Augustus Heinze had interests in several New York banks and engaged in a wide range of speculative activities on the New York Stock Exchange. On October 16, 1907 Heinze went bankrupt when his attempt to corner the shares of United Copper Company failed. In the advent of his collapse Heinze had aggressively built up positions in United Copper stock, which peaked at USD 62 on October 14 but dropped to USD 15 the following day, resulting in the defaults of his brother's brokerage Otto Heinze & Co as well as his own Montana Savings Bank. A day later Heinze resigned his post as President of the Mercantile National Bank, but depositors already lost confidence and started to withdraw their deposits from Mercantile National[7].

One of Heinze's closest banking associates in New York, C.F. Morse, a director of Mercantile National and four other New York banks, got dragged into the scandal and had to renounce his directorships and ties to these banks as depositors began running on all financial institutions Morse and Heinze were affiliated with. When the New York Clearinghouse announced its intention to support all member banks under pressure provided both Heinze and Morse would retire from banking on October 21, the run on New York's clearinghouse banks subsided, but continued on other institutions lacking New York clearinghouse support. Those institutions were predominantly New York's trust companies, financial institutions less strictly regulated than banks and thus not eligible for clearinghouse membership.

While bank runs on all banks with ties to either Heinze or Morse could be contained by guarantees from the New York clearinghouse, the run on New York's trust companies is often credited with being the real cause of the 1907 crisis. The run by depositors on Knickerbocker Trust Company started on October 18 when an affiliation of its president Charles Barney to Heinze's copper scheme was made

---

6 See Kerry Odell and Marc D. Weidenmeier. 2001. *Real Shock, Monetary Aftershocks: The San Francisco Earthquake and the Panic of 1907.* Working Papers in Economics. Claremont, CA: Claremont Colleges

7 See Jon Moen. 2001. *Panic of 1907.* EH.Net Encyclopedia, edited by Robert Whaples. August 15, 2001. http://www.eh.net/graphics/encyclopedia/rawdata.backup.12162003/moen.panic.1907

public. It increased in severity as the National Bank of Commerce resigned as clearing agent of Knickerbocker Trust three days later. On October 22, Knickerbocker Trust closed for business after depositors had withdrawn over USD 8 million within three hours[8]. Other trust companies under pressure were Lincoln Trust and Trust Company of America which was claimed to have lent in large amounts to Heinze and Morse. On October 23, depositors withdrew USD 13 million of the company's USD 60 million deposits, a day later a further USD 8 million and during the whole run on Trust Company of America allegedly nearly USD 48 million[9].

When it became apparent that the failure of one or more trust companies would endanger the whole New York money market, support strategies were deliberated by various actors. Executives of five healthy trust companies collectively started supporting trust companies under pressure but failed to halt the runs due to a lack of resources. For help they turned to John Pierpont Morgan who formed a consortium of leading bankers to assess the situation and provide support. Although Morgan and his counsel refused to support Knickerbocker Trust Company as it could not ascertain its long-term solvency, support was forwarded to the Trust Company of America which was found to be financially healthy. In a similar manner J. D. Rockefeller deposited USD 10 million with Union Trust. After meeting with J. P. Morgan on October 23, George Cortelyou, Secretary of the Treasury, announced a deposit of USD 25 million by the Treasury into the national banks of New York. When the support by Morgan enabled Trust Company of America to survive another run on its reserves on October 24, pressure on the trust companies decreased only to put focus on the call loan market of the New York stock exchange. A further loan of USD 25 million was eventually necessary to stave off runs on trust companies for good: Again Morgan organised the loan as well as the creation of a trust fund consortium to handle future runs more effectively.

5.1.3 Pressure on Money, Stock and Call Loan Markets

From the trust companies financial distress spread to both call loan and stock markets. Since the most liquid assets trust companies could sell were call loans, the excessive demand for cash by depositors forced trust companies to stop extending call loans needed by investors to buy equity[10]. By October 24, the call loan market at the New York stock Exchange had all but dried up. Interest rates for call money which had opened at 6 percent rose up to 60 percent on the same day and reached

---

8 Sprague (1910): 252
9 See Moen (2001)
10 Call loans are loans redeemable on call and collaterized by the value of the underlying stock. There is no connection to call options as traded in derivative exchanges.

100 percent only hours later, but even at those rates no loans were supplied. By October 25, J. P. Morgan put together another consortium of lenders and was able to support the stock market by the injection of a further USD 12.5 million. USD 10 million came from Morgan's own group while USD 2 million were put up by First National and USD 500 thousand by Kuhn, Loeb, and Company. In order to achieve an efficient distribution of the limited funds available for loans, money was provided at market interest rates of nearly 50 percent while the use of funds was restricted to cash investments in securities.

Although pressure was strongest on trust fund companies and stock and call loan markets, banks also saw their cash reserves diminishing rapidly. However, due to their preferential legal position and particularly through the existence of the New York Clearing House Association, New York's banks were in a position to evade collapse without external help. Most important was the issuance of loan certificates by the clearinghouse association. Clearinghouse loan certificates were used by banks to settle obligations between each other; freeing up cash reserves in banks for depositor withdrawal, certificates were valid only in inter-bank clearing operations and based on informal agreements. By creating artificial substitutes for cash, the clearinghouse association informally increased the money supply by up to USD 256 million, despite the fact that the United States lacked a central bank. Over the whole panic nearly 500 million of currency substitutes were in circulation[11].

New York Banks also economised on their reserves by suspending the convertibility of deposits into cash. Despite the illegality of such suspensions, the practice was hardly sanctioned by public authorities and copied by country banks all over the United States. Restrictions on deposit convertibility shrank the money supply and scarcity of cash led to further hoarding of currency and a premium of 400 basis points of cash over deposits. Both premium on cash and high interest rates were partly responsible for the inflow of USD 100 million in gold from Europe in November and December 1907; the money supply was further increased by the Treasury's issuance of nearly USD 140 million in notes[12]. Although the danger of immediate failure had been reduced by increasing the stock of high-powered money, it was not before February 1908 that cash reserves at banks started to increase and the panic subsided for good.

---

11 See Moen (2001)
12 Friedman and Schwartz (1963): 162

5.1.4 Lessons of 1907

The panic of 1907 can serve as a prime example for a typical financial crisis: it shows how panic can develop into crisis in a vulnerable financial system as a consequence of various shocks to the economy. Although it was a domestic rather than an international crisis, it followed the pattern observed in emerging market crises during the 1990s. An already strained financial environment provided the setting, but the crisis itself was triggered by the collapse of Heinze's copper scheme. Without the scarcity of cash in New York money markets, the event itself might not have been severe enough to set off the crisis; a panic among depositors might still have occurred, but in a situation where there would be ample liquidity in the money markets, it would have been arrested quickly since depositors at other banks would have maintained confidence.

1907 also underlines that the provision of sufficient amounts of liquidity is the only way to resolve a financial crisis once it has emerged. The crisis was eventually resolved when the money stock was increased through the provision of emergency loans. However, emergency loans were not provided by a lender of last resort, but by a variety of actors which began to cooperate only after the panic had developed into a liquidity crisis threatening the whole financial system. As the panic took place in the Era of National Banking and the Federal Reserve System was yet to be founded, when panic developed there was no institution with clear responsibility or a mandate to initiate appropriate action. Liquidity was provided in a coordinated effort by private individuals like J. P. Morgan and J. D. Rockefeller, by consortia of National Banks, other trust companies, the New York Clearing House and the Treasury.

The crisis of 1907 also highlights the importance of clearly assigned lender of last resort responsibilities to maintain the stability of the financial system. While the panic was finally controlled, the injection of liquidity took place in ad-hoc initiatives coordinated by J. P. Morgan. Although the effort proved successful, the lack of a responsible institution endangered the stability of the financial system considerably. Action took place only after the crisis had bloated into a threatening dimension. By acting earlier, less funds would have been necessary to arrest the panic and many bankruptcies could have been prevented. Furthermore, arguably J. P. Morgan was— due to his standing in the markets and his widespread net of interests and associations—the only individual able to bring together the coalition of interested parties which provided the necessary funds. Without an individual of this stature, the attempt could have failed by a lack of co-ordination, a lack of funds and asymmetric information. It therefore is not surprising that the lessons of 1907 led to the creation of the Federal Reserve System by 1913.

5.2 The 1960s Sterling Crisis

When the currencies of major industrialised economies came under pressure in the 1960s, it was again a consortium of several actors which made the provision of liquidity possible by assuming the responsibility of a lender of last resort. In contrast to the ad-hoc effort by a coalition of private individuals, banks, trust funds, clearing-houses, and the treasury in 1907, in the 1960s co-operation between national central banks allowed for restoring stability to the international monetary system.

5.2.1 The Setting

Following World War II the U.S. Dollar had emerged as the world's leading currency in terms of international transactions and use as reserve asset; already in the Bretton Woods agreements of 1944 it had been formally embraced as principal reserve currency. Exchange rates of other currencies were fixed to the dollar and their governments obliged to maintain their currency's value within bounds of one percent of the fixed rate. Adjustments of the fixed exchange rate were possible under specific conditions only. The dollar was convertible to gold at a fixed rate of USD 35 per ounce and the Federal Reserve obliged to sell and buy gold at that rate without limitations.

In 1971 the Bretton Woods System broke down and two years later exchange rates of the world's major currencies were allowed to float freely. When John Maynard Keynes and Harry Dexter White drafted the agreement in 1944 in order to replace the pre-war system of an international gold standard with a more flexible set of rules, the dollar was the sole freely convertible currency. By 1958 currencies of most major industrial countries became fully convertible in gold and dollars on the current account[13]– except for Japan which established convertibility in 1964.

When foreign economies strengthened considerably during the 1950s, U.S. balance of payments deficits rose rapidly; at the same time foreign economies like Germany and Japan were building up vast stocks of dollar reserves causing a drain on the United States' gold stock. After the war economic recovery in Europe was the core objective of U.S. economic policy and the corresponding effects in form of current account deficits and a redistribution of the gold stock were viewed favourable. Indeed, under the Marshall Plan between 1948 and 1952 the United States encouraged foreign countries to build-up reserves in order to reach convertibility of

---

13 Current account convertibility implies unhindered access to foreign exchange for current account transactions, in essence for the import and export of goods and services. In contrast to capital account convertibility, current account convertibility does not allow for exchanging foreign currency to make investments.

their currencies. By the early 1960s, concerns about the competitiveness of the U.S. economy and excessive balance of payments deficits started to grow. As Alan Meltzer argues, these problems did not stem from deficits in the current account or the trade balance, but from the fact that U.S. current account surpluses in the 1960s were not sufficient for financing both rising government expenditures—particularly foreign aid and defence spending—and increasing net private investment abroad simultaneously[14]. The drain on gold reserves and the build-up of large dollar holdings abroad nurtured fears for the sustainability of dollar convertibility as the ratio of dollar liabilities abroad to gold reserves in the U.S. increased steadily. Similarly, widespread believes that the fixed rates of the dollar to European currencies were overvalued and the main culprit for decreasing competitiveness in the United States further fostered a climate of uncertainty in the capital markets. Doubts about the sustainability of fixed exchange rates and the ability of the U.S. to maintain convertibility at USD 35 per ounce of gold provided the setting for the multiple speculative attacks on currencies which were to follow. A visible sign of market concerns was the rise in the price of gold above the fixed rate: On 27 October 1960 the price of gold reached USD 40 per ounce in London as the Bank of England refused to sell gold for dollars. By the end of the decade, the system created at Bretton Woods had become unsustainable; it formally ended in 1971 when President Nixon officially abolished convertibility of the dollar.

5.2.2 The Crisis

Like the dollar, the British pound was severely overvalued long before its eventual devaluation in 1967. Overvaluation had been the consequence of a clash of internal and external policy objectives since the early 1960s. In order to maintain low unemployment the U.K. government had followed expansive fiscal and monetary policies even before Labour took office in 1964. Corresponding inflation, increasing current account deficits and a drain on international reserves induced speculation in the capital markets on the sustainability of sterling's fixed rate at USD 2.80. Fear of devaluation increased as due to sterling's role as secondary official reserve currency there was a large overhang in the form of holdings of foreign central banks. That latter point is of particular importance since many countries holding large sterling reserves, like Australia or Hong Kong, were politically dependent or closely connected to the United Kingdom.

Although devaluation seemed inevitable long before 1967, the British government strictly opposed an adjustment of the fixed exchange rate. Neither was there

---

14 Allan Meltzer. 1991. *U.S. Policy in the Bretton Woods Era*. Homer Jones Lecture. St. Louis, MO: Federal Reserve Bank of St Louis: 56

international pressure on Britain to do so given the political sensitivity of the subject and considerable level of national pride involved. Furthermore, it was widely feared that a British devaluation would lead to a domino effect on the French Franc and other European currencies. Accordingly, the Bank of England embarked on a variety of measures to maintain the exchange rate within the permissible boundaries of one percent. As fellow reserve currency, sterling was supported also by the United States who feared repercussions on the dollar should Britain devalue its currency. The incoming Labour government endorsed Britain's negative stance on devaluation and responded to the current account deterioration by introducing a tax on imports and raising central bank interest rates.

British attempts to evade devaluation by monetary and fiscal restraints were insufficient and forced the government to arrange for funds to meet balance of payments requirements. Already before the general election, balance of payments difficulties had led the conservatives to negotiate a stand-by agreement of USD 1 billion with the IMF. A month later, swap lines in a volume of USD 500 million were arranged with several foreign central banks adding to the USD 500 million available through swap agreements with the Federal Reserve Bank of New York[15]. In the second half of November, a month after Labour assumed office, the Bank of England had to arrange additional credit agreements of USD 3 billion with foreign central banks in order to support the sterling within its fixed bands. USD 500 million were put up by the United States, USD 2.5 billion by European central banks, Canada, Japan and the Bank of International Settlements. A further billion dollars was drawn from the IMF in December[16], which on this occasion for the first time invoked its General Agreements to Borrow. The massive injection of liquidity enabled the Bank of England to defend the pound; for a short period between the end of 1964 and the first quarter of 1965 pressure subsided.

While sterling's fixed rate was initially defended, pressure on the pound started rebuilding in March 1965. After drawing on available swap lines, the Bank of England used up its quota at the IMF by drawing the remaining USD 1.4 billion in May to repay obligations from the swap agreements. Again, the IMF invoked the GAB in the process. In September the Group of Ten supported the pound by buying in a co-ordinated operation around USD 1 billion thereby causing a severe short squeeze in the foreign exchange markets. The pain felt by speculators during the squeeze combined with more aggressive attempts to reign in on excessive wage expansion were sufficient to relieve sterling for the remainder of 1965. Due to

---

15 Robert Solomon. 1977. *The International Monetary System, 1945–1976: An Insider's View.* New York, NY: Harper & Row: 87
16 Harold James. 1996. *International Monetary Cooperation Since Bretton Woods.* Oxford: Oxford University Press: 187

capital inflows in the following months the Bank of England was even able to repay large parts of its debt obligations.

In 1966 wage increases as well as attractive interest rates in both Germany and the United States again put pressure on the pound. Coupled with labour action in the shipping industry in July, the Bank of England made use of its swap agreements with foreign central banks in order to support its currency. Its swap facility with the New York Fed was extended to USD 1.4 billion from USD 750 million before[17] as were facilities with other central banks. In turn, the Federal Reserve increased its credit lines in the swap network. Critique on expensive stabilisation policies in order to maintain the fixed rate of sterling increased, but both Wilson and Callaghan firmly resisted calls for floating the pound and instead introduced a severe austerity program. Stabilisation policies and falling interest rates in Germany and the United States led to a gradual recovery of the pound and allowed the Bank of England once again to repay its obligations to swap counterparts, the Treasury and the IMF.

In 1967 rising unemployment and a fall in output enticed the Labour government to expand the money supply by reducing interest rates rapidly. The balance of payments account worsened in the process. Triggered by expectations on the effects on sterling of the Six-Day War and of a close-down of the Suez Canal on shipping costs, pressure on the pound again started building and recession in Germany and the U.S. and the United Kingdom's failed attempt to join the European Common Market strengthened this trend. Between May and July the Bank of England spent USD 800 million to support the pound, in September further USD 345 million were used up. According to Salomon, between May and September USD 1.7 billion were borrowed for intervention in the currency markets while additional obligations arose from forward contracts[18]. After incurring the largest trade deficit in the country's history in October, confidence in the ability to sustain sterling parity began to worsen in government and even Wilson and Callaghan's convictions began to crumble. While still negotiating with IMF officials on a further stand-by agreement, cabinet decided to devalue sterling by 14.3 percent to USD 2.40 on November 15 and officially announced the move two days later.

Although the British pound was eventually forced into devaluation, its par value was defended successfully several times. Some of its rescues were due to IMF stand-by agreements, but to a large extent rescues were made possible by international cooperation in form of the *central banker's club*[19], consisting of the Group of Ten meeting at the Bank for International Settlements in Basel. The Basel agreement

17 Michael D. Bordo. 1999. "International Bailouts versus Rescues: A Historical Perspective." *Cato Journal.* Vol. 18, No. 3: 369
18 Solomon (1977): 93
19 Kindleberger (1978): 197

initiated in 1961 to support Great Britain allowed coordinating multilateral co-operation between the central banks of the major industrial countries. Most importantly, an agreement was made to install a swap network to make quick responses to short-term balance of payments difficulties possible.

The network was led by the Federal Reserve Bank of New York which arranged a system of short-term credit facilities between foreign central banks. Central banks provided liquidity in form of temporary currency swaps to be reversed when pressure subsided. In case of inability to reverse the agreement after a specified period, the initiating counterpart would draw on its IMF quota to meet its obligations. The swap network proved to be an efficient mechanism for the provision of lender of last resort services and grew rapidly in volume from around USD 900 million in 1962 to nearly USD 30 billion by 1978[20]. The United Kingdom was not the only country to benefit from this method of liquidity provision. Although initially sceptical regarding the swap arrangements, claiming this form of co-operation to be an extension of American financial hegemony, during the Franc Crisis in 1968 France drew its USD 100 million swap facility with the Federal Reserve and subsequently expanded the credit line to USD 700 million[21]. However, although this form of multilateral co-operation is sometimes hailed as a breakthrough in international post-war finance, the swap network was unlikely to be sufficient to mitigate the impact of several speculative attacks at once. Moreover, it included only member countries of the G-10.

5.2.3 Lessons of the Sterling Crisis

In contrast to the crisis of 1907, the Sterling Crisis was of truly international character. It took place under the system of fixed exchange rates established at Bretton Woods in 1944 and its resolution was essential in order for this system of monetary relations to survive. The sterling episode was a fundamentally different type of financial crisis: While in 1907 a lack of liquidity endangered the domestic financial system and underlined the need for a domestic institution to act as lender of last resort, the Sterling Crisis came as a pure breed of currency crisis. Liquidity assistance was not required to prevent the failure of individual financial institutions but to enable the Bank of England to maintain its currency peg to the dollar. As the crisis of 1907 exemplifies how external shocks can create financial panics in a vulnerable financial environment, pressure on the sterling in the 1960s provides a showcase of the difficulties in maintaining a currency peg without unlimited foreign currency reserves.

---

20 James (1996): 160
21 Solomon (1977): 153

As in 1907, the Sterling Crisis could be resolved only through the cooperation between various actors. And as in 1907, this cooperation came not in an institutionalized form, but was executed in an ad-hoc manner. But given its character as currency crisis, the resolution of the Sterling Crisis required cooperation not on a national, but at an international level. The 1960s can thus be interpreted as *the beginning of efforts to solve international monetary or economic problems by coordinating policy actions*[22]. International actors were willing to cooperate since a failure of the Bank of England to maintain its fixed exchange rate would have meant the end of Bretton Woods. While eventually devaluation could not be averted, by acting collectively international central banks were able to defend Britain's exchange rate against numerous speculative attacks.

The Sterling crisis also indicates that fixed exchange rates are almost impossible to defend with limited foreign currency reserves, even for advanced industrial economies. Successful intervention in the currency markets is a costly undertaking and requires access to vast amounts of international currency. Both Britain's eventual devaluation and the collapse of the Bretton Woods system half a decade later suggest that in the long-term fundamentally overvalued exchange rates cannot be upheld against consecutive speculative attacks. If a currency peg has to finally be given up, funds employed on currency market interventions have been consumed to no avail; in case they were borrowed, the government is left with an even higher debt burden than before.

5.3 Emerging Market Crises in the 1990s

The financial crises in emerging market economies that have occurred since 1995 share characteristics with both the Crisis of 1907 as well as the Sterling Crisis. They involved domestic banking crises as in 1907 and currency crises of the type experienced by the U.K. in the 1960s and thus were twin crises by nature: Currency crises in combination with either a debt or a banking crisis and very often both. Although currency depreciations took most public interest, Kazuo Ueda of the Bank of Japan concurs that financial turmoil in Asia followed the typical pattern of a *domestic banking crisis arising from boom and bust cycles in bank lending and capital investment*[23]. However, in contrast to 1907 and the 1960s, the International Monetary Fund emerged as the central institution to respond to the new breed of financial crisis. While various institutions contributed financial resources, the IMF coordinated all rescue efforts and put together the rescue packages by drawing on own

---

22 Meltzer (1991): 82
23 Kazuo Ueda. 1998. "The East Asian Economic Crisis: A Japanese Perspective." *International Finance.* Vol. 1 No. 2: 327

resources and loans by international development banks and bilateral sources. It set the terms of support, negotiated stability packages and determined the size of emergency loans.

5.3.1 The Mexican Peso Crisis

The Mexican Peso Crisis was the result of a misalignment between fiscal and monetary policy on the one hand and exchange rate policy on the other[24]. In early 1994 the Mexican economy was in good shape and investors expected further improvements from the recent admission to NAFTA and the OECD. Government deficits had fallen to zero, and capital inflows reached 5 percent of GDP. Between 1989 and 1994 the economy had grown on average by 3.1 percent. However, the deregulation of the financial sector, a reduction of public indebtedness and excessive availability of securitised debt in combination with booming stock and real estate markets led to a vast expansion of credit[25], most of which came in form of debt and equity portfolio investments. As part of stabilisation efforts Mexico issued so-called *tesobonos* to replace conventional short-term debt. These securities, whose principal was indexed to the dollar, allowed to retain funds which otherwise would have fled the country due to fears for devaluation. The danger of this strategy consisted in the threat that devaluation would vastly expand the levels of Mexico's public debt.

In addition, Mexico still faced domestic inflation, although far less than during the 1980s, and was burdened by an overvalued fixed exchange rate with the dollar that reduced competitiveness and led to a contraction of the economy in the third quarter of 1994. Investor confidence started crumbling with rising political instability due to the Chiapas uprising in January, the assassination of PRI presidential candidate Luis Donaldo Colosio on March 23 and rising interest rates in the U.S. that increased pressure on the peso[26]. After reserves had shrunk from around USD 30 billion in March to USD 5 billion by December, the government opted for devaluation. On December 20, the peso's trading range was first expanded to 15 percent; a day later the currency was floated completely[27]. In response, instead of an

---

24 See United States General Accounting Office. 1996. *Mexico's Financial Crisis: Origins, Awareness, Assistance, and Initial Efforts to Recover*. Report to the Chairman, Committee on Banking and Financial Services. Washington, DC: House of Representatives: 40–73

25 See Francisco Gil-Diaz. 1998. "The Origin of Mexico's 1994 Financial Crisis." *Cato Journal*. Vol. 17, No. 3

26 Douglas W. Arner. 1996. *The Mexican Peso Crisis: Implications for the Regulation of Financial Markets*. Essays in International Financial & Economic Law 4. London: The London Institute of International Banking, Finance & Development Law: 12

27 In 1989 the fixed exchange rate system in Mexico was replaced by a so-called *crawling peg* mechanism: the exchange rate between peso and dollar was adjusted daily to allow for a slow adjustment of the nominal rate.

expected decline in the range of 15 to 20 percent, the peso fell by 50 percent igniting severe financial panic and collapsing stock markets. Fears of hyperinflation, further devaluation and potential default led to a credit crunch. When investors refused to roll-over *tesobono* debts of nearly USD 30 billion, Mexico found itself temporarily unable to service its debt obligations. Regarding the long-term, however, the Mexican economy appeared solvent rather than insolvent: Debt-to-GDP had fallen to an acceptable level of 34.7 percent compared to well over 80 percent in 1980. There were no fundamental reasons to doubt the continuity of Mexican fiscal responsibility; indeed, the following year Mexico recorded a trade surplus of USD 7.4 billion.

Mexico was saved from default by pledges for financial support totalling around USD 50 billion, provided mostly by the United States and the International Monetary Fund. Despite initial agreement in the Senate, congress opposed the funding plans for the U.S. share of the package. Eventually the Clinton administration drew on funds of the Treasury's Exchange Stabilisation Fund (ESF), effectively by-passing congressional consent. The ESF facility accounted for USD 20 billion and was collateralized with export revenues from state-owned oil producer PEMEX. Further USD 17.8 billion were provided by the IMF, USD 10 billion by European central banks and USD 5 billion by World and Inter-American Development Bank. In turn, the Mexican government committed to several sets of policy conditions. Despite intense criticism the U.S.-led bailout operation proved effective: By averting default Mexico evaded being shut out from international capital markets and eventually proved able to service its debt obligations in full.

5.3.2 The Asian Financial Crisis

As in the case of Mexico, the economies of Thailand, Indonesia, South Korea, Malaysia and the Philippines seemed to be relatively healthy regarding most macro-economic indicators when crisis struck in 1997. The debate on the factors which caused the crisis to erupt remains controversial: Given the relatively healthy state of most Southeast Asian economies' fundamentals, advocators of *multiple equilibria* approaches explain the crisis in terms of self-fulfilling panics[28]. Others argue that as in past cases of financial panic it are fundamental reasons nevertheless which best explain the Asian Crisis, only that those fundamental problems were not exhibited in the set of macroeconomic indicators followed at the time[29]. According to Krugman

---

28 See Chang and Velasco (1998) and Radelet and Sachs (1998)
29 See Craig Burnside, Martin Eichenbaum, and Sergio Rebelo. 1999. "What Caused the Recent Asian Currency Crises?" In Hunter et al. 1999. *The Asian Financial Crisis: Origins, Implications, and Solutions.* Boston, MA: Kluwer Academic Publishers

the Asian financial crisis is best understood in terms of financial excess rather than by applying first and second generation crisis models[30].

First and foremost, the crises in Thailand, Indonesia, South Korea, Malaysia and the Philippines resulted from investors' reluctance to continue providing credit to highly indebted banks, financial institutions and other commercial enterprises in the region. A rising number of missed debt service obligations and bankruptcies reversed the massive inflow of capital by international investors originally attracted by high yields and implicit government guarantees[31]. While in 1996 the region experienced capital inflows of USD 93 billion, the following year saw a net outflow of USD 12 billion. Due to the USD 105 billion capital flow reversal financial distress within East Asian economies increased and put heavy pressure on local currencies. Investor uncertainty was fuelled by political fragility in the region: Elections in South Korea and Thailand as well as a lack of clarity on the succession of Suharto in Indonesia hurt sentiment towards the whole region. Local central banks tried to mitigate these *twin crises* by aggressively raising interest rates and publicly confirming the sustainability of their currency pegs. Despite heavy intervention in the currency markets most countries were eventually forced to abandon their pegs and apply to the IMF for liquidity support.

Thailand, South Korea and Indonesia all followed a similar path during the crisis. Central banks pushed up interest rates in order to stem capital outflows and introduced drastic austerity programs, both monetary and fiscal, to meet the conditions set by the IMF in exchange for liquidity assistance. The programs contributed to the sharp contraction of the economy in terms of private sector bankruptcies and public suffering. At the same time, even the vast rescue packages by IMF, World Bank, Asian Development Bank and bilateral agreements which amounted to a total of USD 118 billion failed to restore confidence. IMF lending rules, which determined maximum lending amounts in terms of borrowers' quota, were surpassed significantly with financial support for Indonesia amounting to 490 percent, for Thailand 505 percent and in the case of South Korea to 1939 percent of each country's respective quota[32].

Malaysia stands out of the economies hurt by the Asian Crisis as it followed an individual and drastically different path than its neighbours. Faced with similar problems of indebtedness, stock market declines and heavy currency depreciation, Mahathir refused to accept the conditions established by the IMF when negotiating a

30 See Krugmann (1998)
31 Michael Dooley. 1999. "Origins of the Crisis in Asia." In Hunter et al. 1999. *The Asian Financial Crisis: Origins, Implications, and Solutions.* Boston, MA: Kluwer Academic Publishers: 29
32 Padma Desai. 2003. *Financial Crisis, Contagion and Containment: From Asia to Argentina.* Princeton, NJ: Princeton University Press: 214

potential rescue package. Instead of the austerity programs imposed by the IMF on Thailand, South Korea and Indonesia, the Malaysian prime minister increased public infrastructure projects and lowered interest rates in order to foster economic growth. To stem capital outflows he introduced strict exchange controls that aimed at controlling short-term capital or *hot money* flows. Malaysia succeeded in re-gaining stability without drawing on the IMF as lender of last resort. Nevertheless, the success of this alternative approach was based on Mahatir's powerful autocratic position within the country which enabled him to push through his strategy without having to make concessions to a domestic political opposition.

5.3.2.1 Crisis in Thailand

The financial crisis in Thailand outshines those of South Korea, Indonesia, Malaysia and the Philippines as it triggered the Asian financial crisis that eventually spread to Russia and even Brazil. As in all crises various factors contributed to its outbreak and it is controversial which factors had the largest impact. When pressure built on the baht in summer 1997, export growth had been already slowing for a year. An increasing number of bankruptcies in South Korea and debt defaults in other Southeast Asian economies during early 1997 had increased fears of further corporate failures and fuelled insecurity within the economy. The corresponding loss of confidence in the economy by international investors led to a sharp decline in capital inflows. This decline exposed the vulnerable state of Thailand's financial and real estate sectors, and more specifically widespread insolvency among Thailand's now infamous finance companies, banks and real estate developers[33]. Each of those factors was reinforcing the other, transforming panic into crisis and resulting in a sharp contraction of the economy.

Financial authorities in the region tried to contain the developing crisis by imposing laws to reign in on excessive lending correctly identified as the root of solvency problems in Thailand's financial institutions and corporations. These measures proved insufficient to alleviate fears in the financial community; instead, a speculative attack on the Thai baht was launched which cost the central bank around USD 10 billion in foreign currency reserves in its effort to defend the baht's fixed exchange rate of 24.7 to the dollar[34]. In addition, financial authorities imposed stricter currency controls, closed down several financial institutions and tried to reduce capital outflows by raising interest rates. Despite continuous pledges by Prime Minister Yonchaiyudh to defend the currency peg, the baht was floated on

---

33 See Malcolm Falkus. 1999. *Historical Perspectives of the Thai Financial Crisis.* UNEAC Asia
    Papers No. 1. Armidale, Australia: University of New England
34 See Desai (2003): 120

July 2 when the Bank of Thailand had almost run out of foreign currency reserves. Its value instantly dropped by 18 percent.

Despite strong resentments against conditionality policy intruding into its sovereignty, Thailand's government finally turned to the IMF having unsuccessfully pursued all alternatives. By August, the Fund arranged a rescue package worth USD 18 billion: USD 4 billion were provided by the IMF in form of a three-year Stand-By Agreement; World Bank and Asian Development Bank together put up USD 2.7 billion and an additional USD 10 billion came from other interested parties including Japan which contributed USD 4 billion[35]. The package was conditional on commitment by Thai authorities to an IMF-designed adjustment program aimed at restoring investor confidence by a reduction of the current account deficit, re-building of currency reserves and limiting inflation. The program called for efforts to restructure the financial sector, fiscal adjustments amounting to 3 percent of GDP and controlling domestic credit by interest rate increases. These measures further exacerbated economic contraction and rapidly rising unemployment. Subsequently the IMF reversed its policies, softening the austerity program at each quarterly review and corresponding to weak economic conditions. When the crisis came to an end in October 1998, USD 12.2 billion of the pledged rescue package of USD 17.2[36] billion had been disbursed, the IMF accounting for USD 3 billion and World Bank, Asian Development Bank, Japan and other participants for the remainder of USD 9.2 billion. As a consequence of the crisis, unemployment had tripled and the economy contracted by 10.8 percent[37].

5.3.2.2   Crisis in South Korea

More than in any other of Southeast Asia's financial crises, turmoil in South Korea was the result of a vulnerable financial system. While the crisis erupted due to investor panic causing a violent capital flow reversal, Korea's financial sector had been vulnerable for a long time as a consequence of the country's development strategy. During the 1960s and 1970s, when Korea's rapid development took off, bank management was dominated by government intervention which ensured that credits where allocated according to official development strategies and Korean banks were lagging international best practice in credit allocation ever since. When

---

35 Despite obviously strong interest in Thailand due to its geographic proximity, Japan also took the opportunity to underline its role as leading economic power in the region as in Japan's perception the U.S. intervention had done during the Mexican crisis in 1994–95.

36 See Timothy Lane, Atish Gosh, Javier Hamann, Steven Phillips, Marianne Schulze-Ghattas, and Tsidi Tsikata. 1999. *IMF-supported Programs in Indonesia, Korea, and Thailand: A Preliminary Assessment*. IMF Occasional Paper. Washington, DC: International Monetary Fund: 3

37 Stiglitz (2001): 97

government intervention subsided in the 1990s, banks were so closely intertwined with large Korean conglomerates that credit allocation in Korea continued to lack the fundamental principles of scrutiny and prudence. As D. W. Nam, former Korean Prime Minister, asserted:

> Korea's financial system is characterized by a lack of independence from the business conglomerates as well as from the government. For example, I have never seen a bank request that any chaebol (the Korean word for a business conglomerate) prepare a consolidated financial statement combining its member companies to asses the financial standing of the business group as a whole; banks have taken no serious look—let alone a formal feasibility study or risk analysis—into the large-scale investment project for which bank credit was requested by a chaebol. The banks did not bother to check misuse of loans by the borrower to make financial contributions to politicians and the political parties. Something like risk analysis is confined to the powerless small and medium-sized companies[38].

Despite a large number of distressed commercial institutions, banks, and chaebols, and bankruptcies of prominent companies like Hanbo, Sammy Steel and Kia early in the year, a speculative attack on the South Korean won did not occur until October 1997. Caused by a sell-off of South Korean equities, growing pressure on the won forced the central bank to raise interest rates and intervene in the currency markets to defend its currency peg with the dollar. Both actions failed to stop the attack on the won as did an attempt to ease pressure by initiating a restructuring of the excessively indebted banking sector. Of South Korea's 26 commercial banks, 12 failing Basel I capital adequacy standards were obliged to submit restructuring plans. The government, which subsequently invoked the licence of 5 of them, expected the rest to be taken over by more healthy rivals. Two commercial banks, Korea First and the Seoul Bank, were nationalised. In addition, 12 merchant banks were forced to close down[39].

South Korea abandoned its fixed exchange rate on October 17, followed by a heavy slide in the won's exchange rate to the dollar. On November 21, the government applied for help to the IMF which arranged the largest rescue package of all the Crisis Five. Its combined worth of USD 58.2 billion consisted of USD 21 billion by the IMF, USD 14 billion by World and Asian Development banks as well as

---

38 D. W. Nam. 1999. *The Distinct Nature of the Korean Crisis.* Paper prepared for presentation at the 11th Conference of the Korea U.S. Business Council at the Maui Prince Hotel. January 19, 1998. Maui, Hawaii. http://www.dwnam.pe.kr/6imf02.html
39 See Hunter (1999): 128–129

additional bilateral backups amounting to further USD 23 billion. The adjustment program imposed by the IMF mission resembled the programs designed for Thailand and Indonesia: It demanded financial sector restructuring, tight monetary policy, and current account adjustments via fiscal austerity.

Even the substantial rescue package proved inadequate and failed to end the crisis. Missing transparency on the true state of South Korea's financial position, where initial estimates of short-term public debt were raised from USD 65 billion to USD 100 billion in September 1998, and the massive debt burden on the private sector did not allow for a restoration of investor confidence despite rescheduling agreements with private creditors in January 1998. When pressure on the won and capital flight came to a halt, the adjustment program had been altered several times and South Korea had spent USD 27.2 billion of the total package, USD 18.2 billion of which provided by the IMF. Although in Korea the crisis had less severe effects than in Thailand or Indonesia, in 1998 Korean GDP declined by 6.7 percent while unemployment quadrupled[40].

5.3.2.3   Crisis in Indonesia

The Indonesian economy was similar to other economies in the region; like Korea and Thailand, it had an impressive record of economic development and was widely regarded as a model for successful development policy. While the country shared the problems of a vulnerable financial sector, a contrasting feature of Indonesia was the problem of widespread corruption. Indeed, in the aftermath of the crisis, many commentators identified the KKN problem, *korupsi, kolusi, dan nepotisme* (corruption, collusion, and nepotism), as the core reason for Indonesia's downfall. But as in Thailand and Korea a problem of similar importance was that the private sector had accumulated excessive foreign currency debt, generally without hedging against currency depreciation.

When the authorities raised interest rates aggressively in response to baht-induced pressure on the rupiah, they fuelled balance sheet difficulties at domestic banks, financial institutions and other commercial enterprises and nurtured the number of bankruptcies and defaults. On July 11, 1997 the government widened the floating band of the rupiah to 12 percent, and by August 17 further depreciation forced the Bank of Indonesia to abandon its system of managed floating and release its currency entirely. As pressure on the rupiah eased in October 1997, government caused further declines by reducing interest rates in order to lessen credit scarcity. In November, a rescue package was arranged consisting of a USD 10 billion loan by the IMF, an USD 8 billion facility provided by the World and Asian Development

---

40 Stiglitz (2001): 97

Banks and bilateral agreements with other interested parties accounting for further USD 18 billion. In the corresponding letter of intent the Indonesian government promised policies to restore market confidence, turn around the current account and limit the impact of exchange rate devaluation on domestic inflation. As in other IMF-supported programs, measures resembled those in Thailand and Korea: tight monetary policy, fiscal austerity and restructuring efforts to strengthen the financial sector and increase general transparency and governance[41].

However, the stability program failed to restore confidence in the Indonesian economy. While the closure of 16 Banks in November was expected to boost confidence in the banking system, it had the opposite effect on Indonesian citizens who lost confidence in their financial system and their economy at large[42]. Despite weak execution and—according to the IMF—a lack of commitment to a strengthened adjustment program, a large part of this failure was due to political instability, including riots, student demonstrations and large-scale corruption scandals, surpassing uncertainty about electoral outcomes in both Thailand and South Korea by far. Political quarrels within the country and between government and the IMF on whether to peg the rupiah or install a currency board delayed inevitable restructuring efforts of the economy and the financial sector in particular.

In June 1998, an agreement on debt restructuring was reached with private creditors covering both inter-bank and commercial private debt. In August, an extended arrangement worth USD 6.4 billion and backed up by further USD 3 billion from World Bank, ADB and other participants was established to replace the former Stand-By Agreement. Liquidity support was conditional on the implementation of a stability program crafted by the IMF: It included the closure of insolvent banks, several measures to restructure the financial system and strengthen institutional, legal and regulatory frameworks[43]. By October 1998, USD 9.5 billion from the total package of USD 42 billion had been disbursed to Indonesia, comprising USD 6.8 billion by the IMF, USD 1.3 billion from World Bank and ADB and USD 1.4 billion from additional sources. As a result of the crisis, Indonesia's economy contracted by 13.1 percent in 1998 while unemployment increased substantially[44].

---

41 Lane et al. (1999): 4
42 J. Soedradjad Djiwandono, 1999. "Causes and Implications of the Asian Crisis: An Indonesian View." In Hunter et al. 1999. *The Asian Financial Crisis: Origins, Implications, and Solutions.* Boston, MA: Kluwer Academic Publishers: 120
43 Jjiwandono (1999): 123
44 Stiglitz (2001): 97

5.3.3 The Asian Crisis' Aftermath

The 1990s emerging market crises did not end with the Asian Crisis. While the crises in Russia and Brazil were clearly triggered by events in East Asia, the crisis and eventual default of Argentina happened over a year after Brazil's devaluation of the real and was due to unsustainable sovereign indebtedness rather than contagion.

5.3.3.1 The Rouble Crisis

Unlike economies in Southeast Asia, the Russian economy was in a dismal state when the Rouble Crisis erupted in 1998. Having started the process of reforming a communist planning economy into a capitalist market economy only in 1992, Russia's institutions lacked both the strength and the stability to fend off speculative attacks on the rouble in August 1998. When prices were freed in 1992, vital institutions like a central bank, an effective tax system or currency exchange markets were either not functioning or non-existent. Despite these institutional deficiencies, Russia had liberalised its financial system radically over a very short period of time[45].

When Russia started the process of restructuring its economy, it faced budget deficits of up to 20 percent of GDP and inflation rates reaching 2500 percent. The stabilisation program devised by the IMF consequently put curbing inflation at the top of its agenda and insisted on strict monetary tightening. The exchange rate of the rouble was submitted to a system of managed floating. After painful stabilisation efforts and a 40 percent decline in output between 1992 and 1997, the Russian economy began showing signs of stabilisation. By 1997 inflation was down while substantial advances were made in terms of liberalisation and privatisations.

At the same time, success in containing the budget deficit was limited. Although deficits had been reduced from a range between 17 and 21 percent in 1991 to 7–8 percent by 1997, they remained at an unhealthily high level. Lacking tax revenues, the government continuously struggled to keep budget deficits from exploding. Fiscal targets could only be met by taking on large amounts of debt—to a great extent foreign denominated and of short maturity. The growing issuance of both short-term GKOs and long-term OFZs[46] to foreign investors added to the economy's vulnerability, particularly in case of a potential devaluation of the exchange rate.

---

45 For an overview of Russia's financial liberalization see Akira Uegaki. 2000. *Russia as a New-comer to the International Financial Market: 1992–2000*. Acta Slavica Iaponica. Tomus 21: 23–46

46 GKO refers to *Gosudarstvennye Kratkosrochnye Obligatsii*, short-term bonds issued by Russian states; OFZ refers to *Obligatsii Federal'nykh Zaemov*, longer-term bonds issued by the federal government.

GKO and OFZ debt rose from 4.5 percent of GDP at the end of 1995 to 18 percent by the first quarter of 1998; 30 to 40 percent were held by foreign investors[47]. This increase put further pressure on the budget: Monthly interest payments as part of the budget grew from 23 percent of revenues in January to 51 percent by July 1998[48]. Regarding the banking sector, the balance sheets of Russian banks swung from a surplus of USD 3.7 billion in foreign assets over foreign liabilities in January 1996 to net foreign liabilities of USD 8.1 billion by July 1998.

The rouble's collapse in August 1998 was triggered by exogenous shocks hitting a fragile economy. A sharp decline in the oil price, to USD 11 per barrel, and falling prices for nonferrous metals reduced Russia's export earnings, hurt its balance of trade and increased the budget deficit. Investors were pulling out funds after having been burned in Southeast Asia, loosing confidence in emerging markets generally and in politically unstable Russia in particular. As the rouble came under selling pressure, the central bank raised interest rates to 150 percent and spent large amounts of currency reserves on interventions in the currency markets to maintain the fixed exchange rate. The IMF supported Russia's efforts to maintain the over-valued exchange rate as it feared devaluation would lead to a resurgence of infla-tionary pressures[49].

The first USD 4.8 billion tranche[50] of a rescue package negotiated in late July proved insufficient to successfully fend of speculative attacks on the rouble. Under the program arranged by the IMF under strong pressure from the Treasury[51], a con-sortium including IMF, the World Bank, Japan and other international lenders was to provide loans worth a total of USD 22.5 billion in several instalments and con-ditional upon economic reforms. Although Russia called on the Fund for further loans as their reserves were running out, unprecedentedly this demand was flatly denied. Prime motivation for the refusal was to curb moral hazard and refute market perceptions that some countries were too big to fail or as in the case of Russia to nuclear to fail. Furthermore, IMF finances were strained to the limit. On August 17 in 1998 Sergei Kiriyenko announced the devaluation of the rouble, a restructuring of USD 40 billion GKOs into securities with 3–5 year maturity and a 90-day mora-torium on debt servicing by Russian commercial banks and other private sector

---

47 William Tompson. 1999. "The Bank of Russia and the 1998 Rouble Crisis." In Vladimir Tikhomirov (Ed.). 1999. *Anatomy of the 1998 Russian Crisis.* Contemporary Europe Research Centre. Carlton, Australia: University of Melbourne: 5
48 See Desai (2003): 142–144
49 See Stiglitz (2001): 146
50 Originally the IMF pledged $5.6 billion as first instalment, but the amount was reduced to $4.8 billion when the Duma reject key reform legislature proposed by Yeltsin.
51 See Michael R. Gordon and David E. Sanger. 1998. "Bailout of the Kremlin: How U.S. Pressed the IMF." *New York Times.* July 17, 1998

entities[52]. The rouble's fluctuation band was widened to a range between 6.0 to 9.5 roubles per dollar. The devaluation decision has been interpreted as representing the Bank of Russia's preference for saving the banking sector from breakdown over the goal of maintaining exchange rate stability[53]. At the same time, The Fund's unwillingness and inability to provide additional credit made further interventions to prop up the rouble impossible.

5.3.3.2 Crisis in Brazil

When the *Real Plan* was initiated by then finance minister Henrique Cardoso in July 1994, Brazil looked back on several years of political fragmentation, corruption, and economic instability including inflation of up to 2000 percent since the military regime ceded power to civil authorities in 1985. The Real Plan attempted to achieve economic stability by limiting the federal fiscal deficit, reducing the flow of funds from the federal government to the provinces and municipalities and increasing federal income taxes. In addition to a large-scale privatisation program, the economy was opened to international trade and capital flows. To arrest inflation, the central bank tightened monetary policy and fixed Brazil's currency to the dollar in a crawling peg system. The Real Plan proved successful, reduced inflation to single digits by 1997 and yielded the presidency for its architect Henrique Cardoso.

While the austerity measures reduced economic growth only slightly and did not result in a rise in unemployment, fiscal balances started deteriorating again during the program's final phase. By 1998, the government deficit had reached 7.4 percent of GDP. The central cause of Brazil's budget problems was the federal government's failure to control spending by the provinces, particularly regarding wages, pensions and social security payments to public employees. Despite annual devaluation under the crawling peg system, inflation differentials between the United States and Brazil caused an overvaluation of the real, hurting exports and adding to current account difficulties. Moreover, rising interest rates and increasing indebtedness resulted in a sharp expansion of the portion of debt servicing costs within the budget.

Fears by international investors regarding budget and current account deficits led to capital outflows and increased pressure on the real by late 1997 while uncertainty was strengthened by the meltdown in Southeast Asia. In response, the central bank raised the lending rate to 43.5 percent and cut government spending by 2.5 percent of GDP. Following a short-term easing of speculative pressures on the real during the Rouble Crisis in August 1998, pressure on the real resumed shortly after. The

---

52 See Desai (2003): 137
53 See Tompson (1999)

central bank attempted to maintain the real within its fluctuation bands by massive intervention in the currency markets which cost the country over USD 30 billion in currency reserves between July and December 1998 alone[54]. Notwithstanding further fiscal tightening, renewed restructuring efforts and an IMF rescue package worth USD 41.5 billion approved in November, efforts to stabilize the currency were finally abandoned on January 15, 1999. A week earlier, on January 6, a provincial governor had declared a 3-month moratorium on debt service to the federal government. As a result of letting go the dollar peg, the exchange rate fell nearly 40 percent by the end of the month[55].

The USD 41.5 billion rescue package arranged in November 1998 was a novelty having been arranged before Brazil experienced severe financial difficulties. Drawing on lessons provided by the Asian Crisis, the package was designed to help Brazil counter problems caused by contagion from turmoil in Southeast Asia and Russia. It consisted of USD 18 billion in IMF funds and of USD 23 billion put up by the World and Inter-American Development Banks; USD 4.5 billion of the package were released immediately in a first instalment. The conditions imposed by the Fund demanded a further increase in interest rates and Brazilian authorities committed to primary budget surplus targets for the years 1998 to 2001. A stability program was devised in March 1999 after the real's floatation in January. Inflation, which since 1997 had again risen to over 40 percent, was to be brought back to single digits by year end via further fiscal and monetary tightening. Budget surplus targets were revised upwards by 50 basis points to a range between 3.0 and 3.5 percent of GDP for the period between 1999 and 2001. The Government further agreed to implement measures in order to reduce public debt as percentage of GDP to a level below the 46.5 percent initially agreed upon. Adjustment efforts to reduce government expenditure and increase revenues were concentrated at the federal level while state and local governments were expected to support this process by restructuring their debt obligations to the federal government. These measures were successful in achieving an unexpectedly high budget surplus in 2000, but structural reforms of both tax and pension systems were moving slowly, necessitating a further USD 15 billion in IMF assistance by August 2001. In contrast to the economies in East Asia, which generally saw quick improvements after debt restructuring and structural reforms, Brazil continued to suffer from fiscal difficulties for a considerable period after the crisis had ended.

---

54 See Desai (2003): 160
55 See Brett D. Schaefer and John P. Sweeney. 1999. *The IMF Strikes out on Brazil.* Executive Memorandum No. 569. Washington, DC: The Heritage Foundation.

5.3.3.3 Crisis in Argentina

Argentina's financial crisis resulted from excessive indebtedness and weak fundamentals. Despite abundant natural resources, during the twentieth century Argentina has been characterised by continuous political instability and economic crises. Argentina lived beyond her means ever since the populist rule of Juan Peron in the 1940s when government expenditures were expanded excessively by providing the public with vast amounts of entitlements ranging from high unemployment to health benefits and pension payments. On the income side, high taxes and an ineffective system of tax-collection limited government revenues. The country's long history of military coups and economic turmoil was expected to finally end with reform efforts initiated by finance minister Domingo Cavallo in the early 1990s. Cavallo's reforms implemented the Washington Consensus in its purest form: He opened Argentina for international capital flows, introduced privatisation initiatives and liberalised the overly regulated economy. Most importantly, he effectively fought excessive inflation by creating a currency board linking the peso to the dollar on parity by 1991. Despite the initial success of these measures on economic growth, efforts to curb excessive public spending were largely unsuccessful.

While the currency board pushed down inflation from 3000 percent in 1991 to negative rates by 1999, the resulting overvaluation of the peso hurt the current account by making Argentina's exports prohibitively expensive. This trend was strengthened by the real's devaluation in 1999. By banning discretionary monetary policy the currency board contributed to rising public indebtedness as the government increased its borrowing abroad to finance the budget deficits run every year since 1994. Inability to increase the money supply and the resulting liquidity crunch hampered investment, hurt economic growth and led to shrinking tax revenues. With a range of between 17 and 19 percent, both saving and investment rates were considerably lower than in Southeast Asia where economies recorded rates in the high 30s[56]. Continuous current account and budget deficits led to increased borrowing by the public sector, at both federal and provincial levels. Although the level of short-term debt seemed acceptable compared to economies in Southeast Asia and the ratio of foreign exchange reserves to short-term debt was actually increasing, the sheer size of overall indebtedness reaching USD 130 billion at its peak hurt investor sentiment and caused heavy pressure on the peso.

In December 2000 a rescue package of USD 40 billion was arranged by the IMF enabling Argentina to postpone a default on its debt obligations and to continue supporting the peso and maintain dollar parity. In return, the Argentine government in its *Memorandum of Economic Policies* committed to reforms aimed at achieving a

---

56 See Desai (2003): 177–178

balanced budget by 2005 which included reductions in public sector wages and pension payments as well as the introduction of fiscal responsibility laws and a reform of the revenue sharing system in the provinces; in addition, it involved the simplification of the tax system by reducing exceptions, special treatments and loopholes. In order to evade default the government also arranged swap agreements with local banks on USD 60 billion of short-term debt but markets remained concerned with the remaining amount of USD 35 billion in foreign debt maturing in the short-term. The IMF package temporarily enabled the government to fend off default and maintain the peg to the dollar. Continuing recession and the swelling of Argentine debt increased pressure in 2001 and led to a further USD 8 billion of IMF support. When the government failed to secure full disbursement conditional on a zero budget deficit for the year, it officially announced default on December 23 2001. The corresponding freeze on bank deposits led to political turmoil and the resignation of several cabinets in a rapid sequence. The peso was floated in February 2002 and immediately fell to 3.5 per dollar from initial parity. It took Argentina's creditors until March 2005 to agree on a restructuring of the defaulted debt; eventually, they received 30 cents for the dollar.

5.3.4 Lessons from Emerging Market Crises

The crisis episodes discussed above highlight the international community's difficulties in responding to the breed of financial crises experienced since the Mexican Crisis in 1995. While stability programs arranged by the IMF were by no means as counterproductive as often claimed, as argued at the end of the previous chapter, the Fund's lending policies in many instances failed to produce the desired results. Although some economies fared better than others under the Fund's one-size-fits-all approach, the negative effects it had on the majority of crisis countries adds further weight to claims that the Fund's current procedures to mitigate and manage financial crises are lacking. Exploring more effective ways of dealing with financial crises in emerging market economies thus requires to analyse policy mistakes and to draw the appropriate lessons.

Two lessons surpass all others in importance: The first regards the effectiveness of liquidity assistance by the IMF. While the Fund provided extensive foreign currency loans to all economies discussed above, its assistance's effectiveness has varied greatly. In Mexico and South Korea liquidity assistance prevented sovereign default and averted a collapse of the financial sector. Consequently, both countries recorded economic growth relatively quickly after their problems' peak. Other economies in Southeast Asia also managed to prevent sovereign default, but the crises' impact proved deeper and economic growth took longer to resume. In Russia and Argentina international liquidity support failed to prevent the countries from defaulting on parts of their foreign debt; as a consequence, negative effects on economic growth and public welfare were substantial. Levels of public indebtedness in Mexico and Korea suggest that these countries faced liquidity crises, but were fundamentally solvent; in contrast, the defaults of Argentina and Russia indicate that both countries were not only illiquid, but –given the failure to reign in on rapidly increasing fiscal deficits[57] and the billions of dollars spent on currency market interventions—also close to insolvency. Moreover, in all instances international liquidity assistance failed to prevent the government from devaluing its currency. During the futile attempts to do so, vast amounts of foreign currency were consumed in currency market interventions and ended up bailing-out international investors. This experience suggests that an improved procedure to deal with twin crises in emerging economies should follow at least two principles: First, emergency loans should be granted to illiquid, but fundamentally solvent economies only; insolvent economies should be assisted in restructuring their unsustainable debt burdens. Secondly, international emergency loans should not be provided to bolster countries' efforts to defend a fixed exchange rate regime as in the majority of emerging market crises these efforts proved costly and eventually failed[58].

The second lesson these episodes provide regards the Fund's policy of conditionality: As indicated in the previous chapter, IMF conditionality policy had a number of negative effects. Due to its pro-cyclical nature, in Thailand, Indonesia and South Korea it exacerbated economic contraction. As a consequence, populations suffered and governments were destabilized. Political unrest not only in Russia and Argentina, but also in Thailand, Korea and Indonesia overthrew governments and made the process of crisis management even more difficult[59]. In many instances, the negative effects of conditionality requirements were due to attempts by the Fund to excessively micromanage the crisis country's economy: In Korea it went as far as prescribing an increase in bus fares since fares were subsidized by the government. Conditionality requirements also proved costly in terms of time spent on negotiations; a more timely provision of liquidity assistance would have required less IMF funds, prevented more bankruptcies and reduced contagious effects on other

---

57 See Guillermo Ortiz. 2002. *Recent Emerging Market Crises: What Have We Learned?* The 2002 Per Jacobsson Lecture. Basel, Switzerland: Per Jacobsson Foundation: 14

58 However, currency market interventions are not ineffective per se: Particularly in the short-term intervening in foreign exchange markets can be an effective strategy to reduce exchange rate volatility or soften currency realignments, as Bundesbank, Federal Reserve and the Bank of Japan have shown in several instances. Due to inevitably limited foreign currency reserves, interventions to soften an appreciation of domestic against foreign currency are generally more successful than interventions to prevent currency depreciation.

59 Jeffrey E. Garten. 1999. "Lessons for the Next Financial Crisis." *Foreign Affairs.* Vol. 78 No. 2: 80

economies. Moreover, in order to evade intrusions into their sovereign right to determine their country's economic policy, most crisis countries turned to the IMF only at the very last minute. Had the Fund been approached earlier, assistance might have been more effective and surely less costly. Consequently, the second major lesson of emerging market crises in the 1990s underlines the problems aligned with conditionality policy and suggests that improving the Fund's capability to manage financial crises requires an effort to substitute conditionality by a more effective policy instrument.

6. The Principle of Lending Freely

The Bagehot Rules prescribe that in times of crisis a lender of last resort should lend freely, at penalty rates and on good collateral. While his rules have been abided by central banks all over the world, compliance would be far more difficult for an international lender of last resort. The discussion below attempts to explore various issues regarding the principle of lending freely in an international context: It attempts to answer the question of how much resources would be necessary for an international lender of last resort to fulfil its role and whether resources currently available to the IMF would be sufficient. Arguing that lending freely must not be understood literally, the chapter further explores for what purpose emergency loans should be made available and whether assistance should be granted to every country in need of liquidity.

The question of funding is the most important among the issues indicated above. If funding needs for an international lender of last resort were to be unlimited, its creation would be practically and politically unfeasible. Not surprisingly, the funding question also constitutes a central argument advanced by the concept's opponents[1]. Eichengreen, for example, argues that due to limited funding *the Fund will never be in a position to lend freely even to its most creditworthy members*[2]. Indeed, during the Rouble Crisis in 1998 resources available to the IMF were under considerable strain given the large rescue packages it had previously advanced in support of East Asian economies. Although the Fund's decision not to increase the amount of emergency loans to Russia above the USD 4.8 billion already dispersed was a correct one, financial realities did not allow for an alternative course of action: The IMF had depleted its resources leaving it unable to avert Russian default and devaluation.

Although requests for increasing the Fund's resources have been voiced at several occasions, arriving at a specific amount that would be sufficient for the Fund to fulfil its mandate is all but impossible. The only agreement there is appears to be that considerably more funds are necessary than currently available, both to continue operating in its current manner and particularly in case of assuming the responsibilities of an international lender of last resort.

---

1 For examples see Capie (2000), Rogoff (1999) or Schwartz (1999)
2 Barry Eichengreen. 1999. *Towards a New Financial Architecture.* Washington, DC: Institute for International Economics: 102

6.1 The Fund's Resources

Resources available to the IMF consist of members' currencies, gold, and Special Drawing Rights (SDRs). At year end 2004, total resources amounted to SDR 220 billion, roughly USD 339 billion. The vast majority, 96.5 percent, is held in form of members' currencies. However, the Fund's usable resources amount to only USD 167.9 (SDR 109.2) billion as USD 85.2 billion are lent out to member countries and a large number of currencies is unsuitable for IMF operations due to reasons of illiquidity. Accounting for resources undrawn but already committed and for an internal reserve requirement, the Fund's one-year forward commitment capacity (FCC) in December 2004 stood at USD 112.0 (SDR 71.9) billion.

Table 6.1
IMF Financial Resources 2002–2004 (SDR/USD billion)

	2002 SDR	2003 SDR	2004 SDR	2004 USD
Total Resources	218,1	219,1	220,6	343,0
Members' currencies	210,3	211,3	213,1	331,0
SDR holdings	1,2	1,1	0,8	1,0
Gold holdings	5,9	5,9	5,9	9,0
Other assets	0,8	0,9	0,8	1,0
Non-Useable Resources	117,9	118,4	109,2	17,0
of which: credit outstanding	63,6	65,0	55,4	86,0
Usable Resources	100,2	100,7	111,4	173,0
Undrawn balances	31,9	22,8	19,4	30,0
Uncommited usable resources	68,3	77,9	91,9	143,0
Repurchases one year forward	19,0	9,2	12,9	20,0
Prudential balance	32,6	32,8	32,8	51,0
One-year forward commitment capacity	54,7	54,2	71,9	112,0
Potential GAB/NAB facilities	34,0	34,0	34,0	53,0

Source: IMF's Financial Resources and Liquidity Position, 2002–December 2004: http://www.imf.org/external/np/tre/liquid/2004/1204.htm

IMF financial resources are generated by quota subscriptions originally allocated by the United States and the United Kingdom taking into account members' share in the world economy. A member's quota subscription determines the amount a country must contribute to Fund resources as well as the maximum amount it is permitted to borrow in a single year. In addition, the quota represents member's voting share at both Board of Governors and Executive Board. As largest member the United States commands a quota of SDR 37.1 billion, while Palau's quota subscription stands SDR 3.1 million. Members have to contribute at least 25 percent of their quota in SDR's or other hard currency; the remaining 75 percent can be contributed in local currency. Changes in members' quotas are determined by several indicators including GDP, current account position and the level of reserves. Quotas are reviewed by the Board of Directors generally every five years and a change demands consent by no less than 85 percent of votes. In contrast to the 11th quota review in 1999 which decided on a 45 percent quota increase, the most recent review in January 2001 did not recommend a further increase in IMF resources. Since 1946 eight reviews recommended quota increases averaging 44.2 percent.

Table 6.2
General Quota Reviews

Quota Review	Date Resolution Adopted	Overall Quota Increase (5)
First Quinquennial	No Increase	–
Second Quinquennial	No Increase	–
1958/1959	February and April 1959	60.7
Third Quinquennial	No Increase	–
Fourth Quinquennial	March 1965	30.7
Fifth General	February 1970	35.4
Sixth General	March 1976	33.6
Seventh General	December 1978	50.9
Eigth General	March 1983	47.5
Ninth General	June 1990	50.0
Tenth General	No Increase	–
Eleventh General	January 1998	45.0
Twelfth General	No Increase	–

Source: IMF Quotas: http://www.imf.org/external/np/exr/facts/quotas.htm

In addition, the IMF under certain circumstances can draw on further SDR 34 billion via the *General Agreement to Borrow* (GAB) and the *New Arrangements to Borrow* (NAB). The GAB was created in 1962 for an amount of SDR 6 billion in order to provide additional funds in case quota subscriptions would prove insufficient to satisfy borrowers' needs. As reaction to increased demand the agreement was expanded to SDR 17 billion in 1982 with an additional facility of SDR 1.5 billion by Saudi Arabia. Although initially funds were exclusively available to contributors to the agreement, a subsequent amendment allows for GAB funds to be lent to non-participating countries as well. Interest rates applicable to loans made under the GAB equal the SDR rate of currently 2.43 percent. The GAB has been renewed several times and is next due for renewal in 2008.

Table 6.3
GAB Participants and Credit Amounts (SDR millions)

United States	4.250
Deutsche Bundesbank	2.380
Japan	2.125
France	1.700
United Kingdom	1.700
Italy	1.105
Swiss National Bank	1020
Canada	892,5
Netherlands	850
Belgium	595
Sveriges Riksbank	382,5
Total	17.000
Associated Arrangement with Saudi Arabia	1.500

Source: IMF Borrowing Arrangements: GAB and NAB:
http://www.imf.org/external/np/exr/facts/gabnab.htm

Table 6.4
NAB Participants and Credit Amounts (SDR million)

Australia	801	Kuwait	341
Austria	408	Luxembourg	340
Banco Central de Chile	340	Malaysia	340
Belgium	957	Netherlands	1302
Canada	1381	Norway	379
Denmark	367	Saudi Arabia	1761
Deutsche Bundesbank	3519	Singapore	340
Finland	340	Spain	665
France	2549	Sveriges Riksbank	850
Hong Kong Monetary Authority	340	Swiss National Bank	1540
Italy	1753	Thailand	340
Japan	3519	United Kingdom	2549
Korea	340	United States	6640
		Total	**16955**

Source: IMF Borrowing Arrangements: GAB and NAB:
http://www.imf.org/external/np/ exr/facts/gabnab.htm

Following the Mexican crisis in 1994, the New Arrangements to borrow were created at a G-7 summit in Halifax. The new arrangements expanded the number of participants to 26 countries and doubled the amount of financing available to the IMF to SDR 34 billion. The NAB became effective in 1998 and has been renewed for further five years in 2003. New participants can be accepted by majority consent of 80 percent of participants. While still relying on the GAB, addressing exceptional threats to global financial stability the IMF would first draw on the New Arrangements to Borrow before resorting to the GAB.

GAB and NAB can be activated at the request of the IMF managing director and requires agreement by both participants and the Executive Board; approval is thus essentially double-locked[3]. This mechanism was mainly responsible for the fact that the IMF did not draw on GAB facilities during most emerging market crises in the 1980s and 1990s although lending to non-participants had been possible since 1983. The GAB had its largest impact in 1977 and 1978 when the Fund borrowed around SDR 4 billion to finance claims by Italy, Great Britain and the United States. So far the facility has been activated ten times; the latest activation took place in 1998 providing resources for the Fund's loan to Russia worth SDR 6.3 billion of which SDR 1.4 billion where effectively disbursed. The NAB has been activated once to provide assistance to Brazil at an amount of SDR 9.1 billion of which SDR 2.9 billion was actually drawn. In March 1999 both activations were cancelled when the IMF secured additional funds by the 11th General Quota Review.

6.1.1 Current Funding Needs of the IMF

A total of SDR 34 billion under GAB and NAB in addition to current IMF one-year forward commitment capacity of SDR 71.9 billion leaves the Fund with SDR 105.9 billion or around USD 165 billion of reserves to draw on in case of a major financial crisis. This may seem hardly sufficient considering that recent rescue packages arranged by the IMF involved USD 118 billion in East Asia, USD 41 billion in Brazil and USD 40 billion in Argentina. However, several qualifications and a clear distinction between the IMF in its current form and its potential role as international lender of last resort have to be made. While an amount USD 165 billion is sufficient for the IMF to continue operating according to its current lending policies, assuming the responsibilities of an international lender of last resort is likely to require additional resources.

---

3 See Curzio Giannini. 1999. *Enemy of None but a Common Friend of All? An International Perspective on the Lender-of-Last-Resort Function.* IMF Working Paper WP 99/10. Washington, DC: International Monetary Fund: 19

Continuing its current lending policy, the Fund's total commitment capacity of USD 165 billion is more adequate than claimed by proponents of further quota increases. This is due to the fact that the IMF does not follow the principles Bagehot defined for an effective lender of last resort. Most importantly, the Fund does not lend freely. While it provided liquidity assistance to countries in capital account crises, the amounts it lent often proved insufficient to restore confidence in the markets. The size of loan packages appeared to be an outcome of negotiations between mission staff and the country's authorities as much as of considerations on how much funds would be necessary to arrest the crisis. Despite substantial improvements in transparency, the Fund still declines to provide detailed information on how the size of individual rescue packages is determined; nor is there information on what the borrowing countries have spent these funds on[4].

The IMF bases neither its access criteria nor the credit limits in terms of members' quotas on actual balance-of-payments needs. As acknowledged by the Executive Board at several occasions *there are several reasons that quotas may not be correlated with the size of members' economies, their potential balance of payments need or their capacity to service debt to Fund*[5]. In fact, the quotas of most emerging economies are substantially below their share in the world economy, and the perceived unfairness of the allocation process is a source of growing discontent in the developing world[6]. Even if IMF quotas would be allocated to accurately reflect the size of members' economies or their share in world trade, in today's global financial system IMF quotas fail as an indicator of potential balance of payment needs of the Fund's members. In capital account crises, balance of payment needs depend on previous inflows and potential outflows of capital; both are determined by investors' asset allocations. The estimation of balance of payments needs thus requires accurate information on the external indebtedness of both public and private sector entities, debt service obligations and potential capital outflows; quotas are irrelevant in this context. The IMF takes account of this fact by projecting so-called *gross financing needs* (GFN) defined as the sum of current account deficits net of official transfers, amortization payments on debt in excess of one year's maturity, repurchases and repayments to the IMF, accumulation official reserves and clearance of arrears[7]. Access limits applicable for regular lending facilities are set at

4 See Anna Schwartz. 1999. "Is There a Need for an International Lender of Last Resort?" *Cato Journal.* Vol. 19 No. 1: 3

5 See IMF. 2003. *Access Policy in Capital Account Crises – Modifications to the Supplemental Reserve Facility (SRF) and Follow-up Issues Related to Exceptional Access Policy.* January 14, 2003. Washington, DC: International Monetary Fund: 9

6 The issue of quota allocation is addressed at greater detail in chapter 10.

7 See IMF. 2003. Review of *Access Policy Under the Credit Tranches and the Extended Fund Facility.* Report prepared by the Policy Development and Review and Treasurer's Departments. January 14, 2003. Washington, DC: International Monetary Fund: 13

100 percent of a member's quota annually and a maximum of 300 percent in total. In case of exceptional balance of payments difficulties due to violent capital flow reversals, members can apply for additional resources under the Supplemental Reserve Facility (SRF). For the SRF no access limits are defined. The amounts lent under this facility are determined by taking into account

> (i) the financing needs of a member; (ii) its capacity to repay, including the strength of its program, its outstanding use of Fund credit, and its record in using Fund resources in the past and in cooperating with the Fund in surveillance, as well as (iii) the Fund's liquidity[8].

As such, the size of additional facilities provided under the SRF is not primarily determined by a member's funding needs, but by ad-hoc assessments through IMF staff. As IMF staff takes into account the Fund's liquidity position, for its current lending policies IMF resources and indeed any level of funding are theoretically sufficient. However, resources are not necessarily sufficient to arrest a member's capital account crisis.

Indeed, in the cases of Mexico, Thailand, Korea and Brazil, IMF resources made up only a share of the USD 200 billion in emergency loans pledged by the international community. Large contributions were also made through bilateral agreements, by the World Bank and other multilateral agencies: Of the USD 18 billion package to Thailand, the IMF put up USD 4 billion only, in case of Indonesia it contributed USD 10 billion of a package worth USD 36 billion and in Korea's USD 58 billion package its USD 21 billion share amounted to less than 50 percent. For all three crisis episodes combined, the Fund's share amounted to USD 35 billion of a total USD 118 billion commitment by various sources.

The effectiveness of official sector liquidity assistance in arresting capital account crises further depends on the degree to which international investors are willing to roll-over maturing loans and to retain the crisis country's assets. As the IMF acknowledges, even when exceptional access was approved, the Fund provided only a share of members' gross financing needs—the remainder stemming from private and additional official sector sources[9]. IMF resources are therefore sufficient for effectively responding to members' capital account crises only when additional support is forthcoming and the Fund has to put up only a fraction of gross financing needs; without additional contributions from both the private and the official sector, its programs are unlikely to succeed.

Given its one-year forward commitment capacity of USD 165 billion and the shares of gross financing needs the Fund has stemmed so far, current quota sub-

---

8 See IMF (2003): 12
9 See IMF (2003): 8

scriptions are fully adequate for the IMF to continue its current approach to crisis management. Nevertheless, the effectiveness of this approach to manage financial crises is controversial and crucially depends on the continuing willingness and ability of other official sector actors to contribute to these efforts. If the international community intends to increase the stability of the global financial system more effectively and to arrest a larger share of financial crises, its approach to crisis management needs to be improved.

6.2 Funding Needs of an International Lender of Last Resort

Operating as international lender of last resort, the IMF would require resources substantially above its current commitment capacity. While it does not have to lend in unlimited amounts as Bagehot's advice is often misinterpreted, its capacity to provide liquidity assistance must be sufficient to restore confidence in the markets. Confidence will only be restored if market participants are ensured that their sovereign and private sector debtors will not default due to a lack of liquidity. How many resources are required to achieve this goal is impossible to determine in absolute numbers. It depends upon many factors not known before a crisis actually occurs: how severe the panic is going to be, how many countries would be affected at the same time and how capital flows will develop over the coming months. The obnoxiousness to accurately determine the funding requirement for an international lender of last resort is resembled by the fact that in the academic debate there exist no estimates on the amount required. Questioning the willingness of member countries to provide the increase in funding necessary for the IMF to assume the responsibilities of an international lender of last resort, without any further clarification Kenneth Rogoff mentions an amount of *1 trillion or more*[10]. Arguing in favour of an IMF role as international lender of last resort Stanley Fisher points out that if

> the IMF were today the same size relative to the output of its member states as it was in 1945, it would be more than three times larger than it will be when the present quota increase is completed; if the quota formula applied in 1945 were used to calculate actual quotas today, the Fund would be five times its size; and if the size of the Fund had been maintained relative to the volume of world trade, it would be more than

---

10 Kenneth Rogoff. 1999. *International Institutions for Reducing Global Financial Instability.* NBER Working Paper 7265. Cambridge, MA: National Bureau of Economic Research: 14

nine times larger—that is, the size of the Fund would be over 2.5 trillion dollars[11].

The intuition behind estimating the funding needs for the IMF to function as international lender of last resort relative to the size of either the world economy or world trade is questionable. The international financial system has changed considerably since the time of Bretton Woods and so have IMF lending practices. Full dollar convertibility and the fixed exchange rate system have been abolished since 1971 and 1973 and most currencies today are floating either dirty or fully. In the process of European integration a number of the world's largest economies have introduced a common currency. In addition, the type of borrower has changed. In 1945 nearly all members but the United States were potential borrowers of IMF funds; today the Fund lends almost exclusively to developing countries and emerging market economies, while industrial countries have become net creditors. More importantly, capital controls have been abolished in most industrial economies, while the volume of capital transactions has multiplied several times over. As a result, since the mid 1990s most financial crises have been triggered by problems in the capital account, not by current account imbalances as in the post-war era.

Funding requirements of any institution should rationally be based on the means required for the institution to achieve its mandate. While a member's share in world trade might allow drawing conclusions on the funds necessary to mitigate a current account crisis, in case of capital account crises the share in world trade is an indicator of limited suitability. The central mandate of an international lender of last resort in the twentyfirst century is to prevent or mitigate capital account crises in developing countries and emerging economies by restoring confidence in international capital markets. To restore confidence, it must credibly commit to prevent the default or bankruptcy of solvent borrowers due to a lack of liquidity. The financial means necessary to do so depend on the strategy an international lender of last resort pursues in order to achieve this objective.

There are three strategies for an international lender of last resort to prevent a shortage of liquidity from causing sovereign default and private sector bankruptcy. Each is ideally implemented by the crisis country's domestic central bank; the role of an international lender of last resort would be to provide central banks with the necessary funds to pursue the appropriate strategy. The first option is to intervene in the currency markets to maintain the exchange rate at a fixed level; this would prevent currency depreciation from increasing foreign currency denominated debt

---

11 Stanley Fischer. 1999. *On the Need of an International Lender of Last Resort.* Paper prepared for delivery at the joint luncheon of the American Economic Association and the American Finance Association. New York: January 3, 1999: 10–11

burdens to excessive levels. Goodfried and King term this approach *lending-in-last-resort as an input in monetary policy*[12]. The alternative strategy is to mitigate the effect of exchange rate depreciation on the real economy by providing foreign currency to the sovereign and the banking sector; short-term loans in foreign currency would enable both the sovereign and the private sector to meet debt service payments and avoid default and bankruptcy until the liquidity crunch has subsided. As such, this approach can be understood as *lending-in-last-resort as an input in banking policy*. The third option, chosen by the majority of emerging economies during the 1990s, is to combine both policies. Each approach requires a different level of resources to contain financial crises.

In industrial economies domestic central banks are generally well equipped to pursue either strategy without external assistance. Both sovereign and private sector debt is mainly denominated in the domestic currency. In case of liquidity problems, the central bank can increase the money supply until the liquidity problem is overcome. Its commitment to do so is credible since it has the authority to issue hard currency. Moreover, in case foreign currency is required, central banks in industrial countries can raise foreign currency with relative ease in both capital markets and from fellow central banks. In contrast, central banks in developing countries and emerging market economies are often unable to function as effective lender of last resort. In developing countries usually a large portion of both public and private sector debt is denominated in foreign currency. To be effective, liquidity support must be provided in foreign currency as well. As foreign currency reserves are inevitably limited, developing country central banks often lack the credibility to restore confidence during financial panics. Credibility can be enhanced by ensured access to external sources of foreign currency. An international lender of last resort's mandate would thus be to provide foreign currency loans to developing country central banks enabling them to function as effective lender of last resort for their economies.

6.2.1 Lending-in-last-resort as Input in Monetary Policy

When providing liquidity support as input to monetary policy an international lender of last resort would insert foreign currency into the market either directly or indirectly via the local central bank. Generally this would be done by a sterilized foreign exchange intervention, i.e. by buying local currency denominated bonds and

---

12 See Marvin Goodfriend and Robert King. 1988. "Financial Deregulation, Monetary Policy and Central Banking." (1988). In Haraf, W. and R. M. Kushmeider (Eds.). 1988. *Restructuring Banking and Financial Services in America.* Lanham, MD: American Enterprise Institute and UPA

selling foreign currency for domestic currency at the same amount. However, this approach is based on a high confidence in market forces and the sophistication of modern financial systems. The market is expected to bring liquidity efficiently to its best uses by allocating it to illiquid but solvent banks, based on the assumption that markets have more accurate and timely information than public authorities. Market forces are expected to ensure efficiency by refraining from bailing-out insolvent institutions since they are less prone to principal agent conflicts, crony capitalism, and re-election strategies than public institutions.

For a lender of last resort at the international level this approach poses two problems: The first is that in emerging market economies, which have been the key focus of IMF intervention in recent years and would be the main recipients of international emergency loans, financial systems often are not sufficiently advanced and sophisticated to effectively allocate liquidity to its best uses. This shortcoming of financial systems in emerging market economies is widely accepted. Nearly every policy prescription by international agencies calls for emerging market authorities to improve their financial systems and the regulation of banking sectors specifically. Due to their communist heritage transition economies of Eastern and Central Europe initially lacked a minimum level of financial infrastructure including central banks or regulatory bodies[13]. In Southeast Asia and Korea the fundamental institutions required for a healthy financial system existed but often failed to discharge their duties as a consequence of excessive governmental intervention, corruption or inefficiency. Similar problems are present in many economies of both Latin America and Africa.

Furthermore, the injection of funds as input in monetary policy requires vast resources in form of foreign currency reserves. In case of perfectly integrated international capital markets and lacking exchange controls foreign currency resources needed would be almost unlimited. Jeanne and Wyolosz, among others, have shown that in an open economy and given uncovered interest parity *sterilized foreign exchange interventions have no impact on the interest rate, the exchange rate or the depositors' actions*[14]. Given free capital mobility and a lack of exchange controls foreign currency injected into the domestic economy is likely to leave the country instead of being deposited at local banks as foreign currency deposits to allow for preventing default and bankruptcy.

In order to maintain the exchange rate fixed at a level inconsistent with uncovered interest parity, an international lender of last resort would have to inject foreign cur-

---

13 See Desai (2003)
14 Olivier Jeanne and Charles Wyplosz. 2001. *The International Lender of Last Resort: How Large Is Large Enough?* Paper presented at the NBER conference on Management of Currency Crises, Monterey, CA: March 28–31, 2001: 19

rency into the domestic financial system until the demand for short positions in local currency ceases as a consequence of external constraints on investors such as leverage restrictions or margin requirements. If interpreting last resort lending at the international level as the provision of foreign currency as input in monetary policy for the sake of maintaining a fixed exchange rate, the funding argument put forward by Schwartz, Capie, Eichengreen or Rogoff is valid. To maintain an overvalued exchange rate by intervention in the currency markets alone, indeed almost unlimited amounts of foreign currency would be necessary; without the ability to issue international currency, no institution could provide liquidity assistance in such magnitudes.

6.2.2 Lending-in-last-resort as Input in Banking Policy

An alternative approach, lending-in-last-resort as input in banking policy, allows for an international lender of last resort to assume its stabilizing role without the need for unlimited amounts of foreign currency. Under this approach, an international lender of last resort directly addresses the impact exchange rate depreciation can have on developing economies: In developing economies both financial and public sectors are often exposed to large foreign currency liabilities. When these liabilities are not matched by foreign currency income streams, a depreciation of the exchange rate—increasing the debt burden in domestic currency terms—can cause liquidity crunches and potential default. By forcing banks into bankruptcy and hindering the banking system's efficient channelling of funds, exchange rate depreciation can hurt economic growth and thus reinforce the pressure on local currencies in a circular pattern. The Asian Crisis has shown that economies exhibiting large currency and maturity mismatches in the banking sector are particularly prone to the eruption of financial crises[15]. In contrast to industrial countries, developing country central banks are often unable to intervene due to a lack of foreign currency reserves. An international lender of last resort would address this problem by providing developing country central banks with hard currency loans. In countries like Thailand, Indonesia or South Korea initial pressure and eventual devaluation of exchange rates caused the high level of foreign-currency denominated debt to increase further in terms of local currency. As a result, a wave of bankruptcies was triggered that led to a fall in output and reinforced the downward pressure on local currencies.

To prevent widespread bank failures as a consequence of currency depreciation, an international lender of last resort would provide foreign currency loans to solvent but illiquid banks, enabling them to meet their foreign currency denominated debt obligations to both international and domestic creditors: This approach to last-resort-

---

15 See Chang and Velasco (1998)

lending aims to cut the link between bank runs and a decline in output. By safe-guarding the functioning of the financial system, an international lender of last resort thus mitigates the negative effects of exchange rate depreciations on economic growth; as a result, the self-enforcing circularity of exchange rate depreciation can be broken. Following this approach, an international lender of last resort would need adequate funding to meet net short-term foreign-currency denominated liabilities of emerging market banking institutions, but not to prop up fixed exchange rates until demand for short positions in the currency is satisfied.

Figure 6.1
The Currency Depreciation Cycle

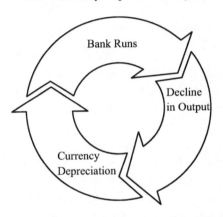

Source: Author; Jeanne and Wyplozs (2001)

In contrast to lending-in-last-resort as input in monetary policy, an international lender of last resort would provide liquidity to solvent financial institutions via domestic central banks. The most common way of targeted liquidity provision is for central banks to lend foreign currency via the discount window. The decision whether to consider a bank insolvent or fundamentally solvent but merely tem-porarily illiquid would rest on domestic regulatory authorities, which should be generally better informed about local banks than an international agency. Solvency would be assessed by valuing borrowing banks' assets at non-crisis market prices and in accordance to the Bagehot Rules. Valuing the borrower's assets at non-crisis market value is of central importance because it is in situations of depressed asset prices that the need for a lender of last resort arises. Since during periods of financial turmoil international currency is scarce, private financial institutions are often unable to shoulder the risk and unwilling to value assets on a basis other than current market prices. A public institution can facilitate the process of restoring stability by filling the gap arising from the private sector's failure to provide short-term liquidity to the market.

In addition, lending-in-last-resort as input in banking policy would enable domestic monetary authorities to offer guarantees to domestic depositors' on foreign-currency denominated deposits. The international lender of last resort would provide foreign currency to the domestic central bank which then could credibly commit to a guarantee on foreign currency deposits. Guarantees on foreign currency deposits would cut the link between currency depreciation and bank runs since depositor uncertainty would be alleviated and incentives to run on banks reduced[16]. To be effective, an international lender would thus need sufficient funding to match the difference between short-term foreign currency reserves and foreign currency deposits withdrawable in the short-term. However, this approach would also require a way of signalling to depositors which banks are solvent and which are not since depositors would not be halted from running at banks if they doubt their institution's eligibility to public guarantees. While contributing to a reduction of vulnerability to bank runs, deposit insurance alone would be insufficient in preventing a collapse of the banking sector: in most emerging economies foreign currency denominated loans owed to international investors by local banks far outweigh foreign currency denominated deposits owed to domestic depositors.

For reasons of effectiveness and for the sake of limiting moral hazard, domestic central banks would need to restrict liquidity assistance to illiquid but fundamentally solvent borrowers. Despite the negative effects every bank failure has on the economy, insolvent banks should be left to fail for two reasons: Firstly, if banks are insolvent, emergency loans will not restore solvency, but merely defer bankruptcy. Funds spent on prolongation of insolvent banks' survival are not available to support fundamentally solvent institutions with short-term liquidity problems. Bailing-out insolvent financial institutions would also increase moral hazard problems and undermine banks' incentives for responsible and prudent lending policies. Consequently, liquidity support should be advanced to domestic central banks on the condition that funds will be used to lend exclusively to illiquid, but fundamentally solvent institutions as recommended by Bagehot. Spending international assistance on bailing-out insolvent entities or market interventions to uphold unsustainable exchange rate pegs would have to be strictly excluded and violations sanctioned. Close scrutiny on domestic central banks' uses of international liquidity assistance would therefore have to rank high among the Fund's supervisory responsibilities.

---

16 See Jeanne and Wyplosz (2001): 22

6.2.3 Necessary Funding for an International Lender of Last Resort

Neither in its current form nor restructured into an international lender of last resort is the IMF likely to have access to unlimited funding. But to defend a currency peg the market perceives as overvalued, unlimited resources are necessary. In practice, resources required to maintain a fixed exchange rate against market pressure may not be unlimited, but still far above the amount G-7 countries would be willing to put up for any international organisation. This implies that an international lender of last resort would lack the clout to defend overvalued exchange rates at least for the medium to long-term. The only responsibility an international lender of last resort could thus effectively assume is to enable central banks of developing countries to act as effective lender of last resort to their governments and financial sectors. For this task, required funds may still be substantial, but by no means unlimited.

To meet this objective, an international lender of last resort requires the means necessary to enable developing country central banks to provide liquidity assistance if solvent banks are threatened by default due to currency or maturity mismatches in their debt structures. In addition, resources must allow for short-term assistance if sustainably indebted governments struggle to meet short-term debt service obligations as international investors assess economies' stabilities by their ability to service both sovereign and banking sector external debt obligations[17]; if the ability to meet either is in doubt, the likelihood of investor panic and violent capital outflows increases considerably.

Following Bagehot's principles, to minimize the number of bank failures in a distressed economy, central banks have to *lend freely* to all solvent banks in need of hard currency. To rebuild confidence in the financial system, markets must be convinced that the central bank is not only willing, but also able to do so. An international lender of last resort must thus control enough foreign currency reserves to realistically commit to providing central banks with sufficient foreign currency loans to prevent a collapse of their financial systems due to a lack of liquidity. To credibly do so, an international lender of last resort must be perceived as having access to enough resources for providing emergency assistance to every emerging market central bank in need of foreign currency loans even if several economies require international assistance simultaneously.

Publications by the Bank of International Settlements and Joint BIS-IMF-OECD-World Bank statistics on external debt for the year ended December 2004 provide selected financial data on both industrial and over 175 developing economies. To approximate the funding needs for an international lender of last resort, only the debt figures for developing countries are relevant. In line with contemporary IMF prac-

---

17 See Paul Stiglitz. 2003. *The Roaring Nineties.* New York, NY: W. W. Norton & Company: 224

tice, an international lender of last would provide liquidity assistance primarily to developing countries and emerging economies, although monitoring and statistical work would continue to focus on all members equally. The focus on developing countries and emerging economies is warranted on multiple grounds: First, in times of crisis, industrialised economies can help themselves; their central banks can independently act as lender of last resort given the ability to issues hard currency. Second, as most industrialised countries today refrain from operating fixed exchange rate systems, currency crises are far less likely to occur than during the Bretton Woods era or the early years of the European Monetary System. Third, due to advanced financial regulation and banking practices, and given comparably limited maturity and currency mismatches in industrial countries' public and private sector debt structures, currency depreciations are less likely to cause the banking and debt crises they caused in Developing Asia and Latin America. Moreover, providing liquidity support to industrial economies would be financially unfeasible as funding needs for an international lender of last resort would inevitably be gargantuan. As a consequence, an effective international lender of last resort would need to restrict its mandate to providing liquidity assistance to developing countries and emerging economies; the same conclusion was reached by the Meltzer Commission in early 2000[18].

6.2.4 Estimating Short-term External Obligations in the Developing World

Funding requirements for an international lender of last resort to be effective thus require an estimate of short-term external debt owed by developing countries and emerging economies, particularly by their public and financial sectors. Financial statistics collected by IMF, BIS, the World Bank and OECD provide a rough indication of the amounts involved. They indicate that the amount of funds necessary to enable developing country central banks to act as lender of last resort may be far less than the notorious amount of at least $1 trillion.

The Bank for International Settlements (BIS) provides data on the consolidated claims of reporting banks on individual countries. These figures provide both long and short-term external liabilities. While developing countries' total external liabilities to BIS reporting banks amount to nearly USD 1100 billion, those maturing within one year amount to merely USD 534 billion. Widening the definition of short-term debt to include liabilities maturing within two years yields a similar amount of close to USD 590 billion in external short-term liabilities to BIS reporting banks.

---

18 See International Financial Institution Advisory Commission 2000. *Report of the International Financial Advisory Commission.* Washington, DC: House of Representatives: 24–51

Table 6.5 presents external liabilities in individual countries owed to BIS reporting banks. They fail to include external liabilities owed to the non-bank and official sectors. At the same time they exaggerate external liabilities of the banking and public sectors to foreign banks as they include the claims of international banks on the non-bank private sector. Although the majority of external borrowing generally originates in the banking sector or is undertaken by the sovereign, as the case of Korea has shown external obligations owed by the corporate sector can also be substantial. While the over 30 BIS reporting banks represent the central source of developing countries' foreign creditors—making up the majority of world wide capital—the amount of USD 533 billion fails to include liabilities not only to non-bank institutions like multinationals or investment funds but also liabilities owed to the official sector, either to multilateral development banks and other international institutions or bilaterally. Regarding non-bank private creditors, liabilities to investment funds are highly relevant while, due to their marginal size, liabilities to multinationals can be neglected. Data on debt securities outstanding is available at BIS for both domestic and international issues.

Table 6.5
Consolidated Claims of Reporting Banks on Individual Countries
(USD millions)

December 2004	Total External Liabilities to Banks	Maturity of up to one year	Maturity between one and two years
Developed Countries	11.125.197	6.034.793	448.242
Europe	8.338.409	4.747.748	329.064
United States	1.880.720	771.094	94.663
Japan	523.745	343.183	9.541
Developing Countries	1.130.314	533.478	55.098
Africa & Middle East	182.076	83.399	10.932
Asia & Pacific	386.730	219.691	12.364
Europe	344.946	137.587	21.214
Latin America & Carribean	216.562	92.801	10.588

Source BIS Quarterly Banking Review June 2005: A54.

To estimate funding needs for an international lender of last resort, the amount of international issues outstanding is central as the vast majority of international borrowing by developing countries is undertaken in foreign currency: 97 percent of all debt issues in international markets between 1997 and 2001 were issued in dollar, euro, yen, sterling or the Swiss franc[19]. In contrast, domestic issues are often de-nominated in local currency and to provide short-term loans in domestic currency, external assistance is not required. However, data on international debt security issues is not disaggregated in terms of maturity. Consequently, the combined amount of USD 737 billion in international debt securities issued by both the public and the private sector substantially overstates the short-term obligations to inter-national investors in marketable debt. Assuming no more than 25 percent of international issues outstanding are likely to mature within one year leaves an amount of USD 185 billion. Adding total external debt to BIS reporting banks due within one year yields an estimate of USD 718 billion of short-term external debt owed by developing countries' public and private sectors.

Table 6.6
International Debt Securities by Nationality of Issuers (USD billion)

December 2004	Financial Institutions	Corporate Issuers	Governments
Developed Countries	10.051	1.463	944
Europe	6.544	876	829
United States	2.944	406	3
Japan	229	64	3
Developing Countries	219	128	390
Africa & Middle East	15	12	26
Asia & Pacific	108	64	42
Europe	33	12	102
Latin America & Carribean	63	40	220

Source BIS Quarterly Banking Review June 2005: A54

A similar amount of short-term external debt owed by developing countries is suggested by the Joint Debt Statistics provided by the Inter-Agency Task Force on Finance Statistics[20]. Although the joint BIS-IMF-OECD-World statistics on external debt is the most comprehensive source of data available, it lacks information on several additional external debt obligations: For one, debt arising from non-officially guaranteed suppliers' credit not channelled through banks is excluded. Second, the

---

19 See Martin Wolf. 2004. "We Need a Global Currency." *Financial Times.* August 4, 2004
20 Originally set up in 1992 by the UN Statistical Commission, the Inter-Agency Task Force on Finance Statistics aims at enhancing timeliness, quality, transparency and availability of data on external debt and international reserves. It is chaired by the IMF and includes repre-sentatives of the BIS, World Bank, OECD, European Central Bank, European Statistical Office and the United Nations.

statistics fail to account for private placements of debt securities, domestically issued debt held by non-resident investors and deposits held by non-residents in domestic banks. Bearing in mind these caveats, Joint BIS-IMF-OECD-World Bank Statistics imply external short-term bank liabilities owed by developing countries to international banks amount to USD 770 billion. Adding short-term securities of USD 202 billion and short-term trade credits yields an estimated USD 1030 billion short-term external debt[21]. Drawing on both sources indicates an estimated maximum range of combined short-term external debt for 175 developing countries and emerging economies of between USD 700 and USD 1000 billion.

Both estimates exclude external debt owed by developing countries to the official sector. Debt owed to multilateral organisations, predominantly the IMF and multilateral development banks amounts to roughly USD 450 billion. Bilateral loans would add a further USD 220 billion. However, the majority of these loans represent development assistance supplied by industrial countries; as such they involve highly concessional terms, both regarding maturity and interest rates. Most countries with significant multilateral or bilateral obligations lack access to international capital markets and are unlikely to experience violent capital outflows. Nevertheless, a number of emerging economies that experienced financial crises over the last decade also carry substantial bi- and multilaterally debt on their balance sheets. In case of financial panic and liquidity problems, the official sector could extend these loans maturity for a limited period; given this possibility, funding requirements for an international lender of last resort need not to include resources to meet debt service obligations to multinational or other official sector creditors.

An estimate of combined short-term external debt between USD 700 and USD 1000 billion substantially overestimates the resources an international lender of last resort would require to prevent or mitigate financial crises: Since the primary responsibility of developing country central banks would lie in providing liquidity assistance to the sovereign and the financial sector, debt owed by the non-bank private sector could be subtracted[22]. Moreover, the estimate represents external debt owed by all developing economies, while an effective international lender of last resort should provide liquidity only to countries with sustainable levels of external

---

21 International issues maturing within one year and held by BIS reporting banks are represented twice as they appear both in short-term external liabilities to banks and in international debt securities outstanding. As such they exaggerate the amount owed by developing countries to holders of debt securities. The same applies to the estimate derived by relying on BIS data only.

22 Given that defaults of large non-financial institutions can have severe consequences on lending banks, it may be argued that international debt issues by the non-bank corporate sector should be included. However, if liquidity assistance ensures the liquidity of fundamentally solvent banks, the latter are in a position to lend to fundamentally solvent non-financial private sector entities.

debt and a healthy financial sector. In addition, central banks receiving short-term loans by the IMF would provide liquidity assistance only to solvent financial institutions against good collateral, not to all financial sector entities in need of liquidity. Most importantly, not all developing countries are equally likely to experience liquidity problems as a result of problems in the capital account: In fact, only countries with access to international capital markets are vulnerable to violent capital flow reversals. Countries like Palau, Antigua & Barbuda or Benin hardly receive speculative inflows of capital and consequently are unlikely to be hurt by international investors fleeing the country. The vast majority of those countries obligations' are to multilateral development institutions; when they struggle to repay their debts, the problem is usually one of solvency and not of liquidity. However, countries with access to international capital markets account for the majority of developing countries' short-term external debt. Of nearly USD 700 in short-term debt owed to BIS reporting banks, their obligations make up 90 percent of the combined total. Eliminating distortions by offshore financial centres like the Cayman Islands leaves short-term debt owed to BIS reporting banks at USD 533 billion, short-term bonds outstanding at USD 85 billion and trade credits at USD 45 billion, totalling USD 663 billion[23]. When approximating the actual funding needs of an international lender of last resort the USD 600 to USD 700 billion in short-term external debt owed by potential crisis countries appears a more accurate estimate than the USD 700 to USD 1000 billion owed by all developing countries together, regardless whether integrated in international capital markets or not.

Two additional considerations suggest that resources required to enable developing country central banks to function as lender of last resort are substantially below USD 600 to USD 700 billion. First, international liquidity assistance has catalytic effects[24]. When the official sector engages in liquidity support, a share of the private sector will follow suit; the more banks and investors roll-over their loans and continue to hold securities, the less international liquidity assistance is required to arrest a crisis. Second, developing countries themselves hold foreign currency reserves against their external liabilities. Predominantly, these reserves are held by central banks as foreign currency reserves. But even commercial banks operating in developing countries will either hold a fraction of external liabilities in hard currency or at least be repaid a share of foreign currency claims. Particularly the former consideration suggests that necessary funding for an international lender of last resort to be effective will be far below the total amount of developing country short-term, foreign-currency denominated debt.

---

23 Countries excluded as offshore financial centres are the Bahamas, Bermuda, Cayman Islands, Netherlands Antilles and the British West Indies.
24 For a more detailed discussion on catalytic finance see Chapter 9 on moral hazard.

The more currency reserves a developing country holds, the less vulnerable it is to liquidity problems as a consequence of large scale capital outflows. In addition, the higher their central banks' foreign currency reserves, the less liquidity assistance by the official sector is required during liquidity crunches. As a result, the ratio of short-term debt to international reserves is widely perceived the central indicator of international liquidity. At the end of December 2004 total international reserves excluding gold held by developing countries and emerging economies amounted to over USD 2400 billion, more than twice the amount of external short-term liabilities outstanding. Similarly, developing countries with access to international capital markets hold currency reserves worth over USD 1700 billion against USD 600 to USD 700 billion in short-term external debt[25]. However, the distribution of international currency reserves is heavily skewed. China, Taiwan and Hong Kong alone held USD 980 billion at year end 2004. But as China's currency reserves are not available to finance liquidity gaps in countries like Argentina, the large amount of currency reserves only increases the stability of those countries holding them. At the same time, the existence of substantial international reserves implies that not all countries with substantial short-term external liabilities would be dependent on international assistance in case financial panic develops. The resources necessary for an international lender of last resort to credibly commit to enabling developing country central banks to act as lender of last resort are thus considerably below the combined short-term external debt outstanding of potentially vulnerable emerging economies. An international lender of last resort only needs enough foreign currency reserves to bridge the gap between distressed economies' short-term liabilities and international reserves; it does not require funding to meet all vulnerable economies' short-term external debt positions.

6.2.5 Liquidity Gaps in the Past

Given the unequal distribution of international reserves, aggregated estimates do not allow for the documentation of individual countries' liquidity gaps. While there are nearly 200 developing countries, most of which are members of the IMF, the number of developing countries affecting the international monetary system is much smaller. Since an international lender of last resort's responsibility lies in fostering global financial stability, its core objective must be to provide liquidity assistance to emerging market economies able to destabilize the international monetary system[26].

---

25 See IMF. 2005. *World Economic Outlook 2005*. Washington, DC: International Monetary Fund and the Joint BIS-IMF-OECD-WB Statistics on External Debt
26 See Robert Litan. 1999. "Does the IMF Have a Future. What Should It Be?" In Hunter et al. 1999. *The Asian Financial Crisis: Origins, Implications, and Solutions*. Boston, MA: Kluwer Academic Publishers

As argued above, violent capital flow reversals only occur in countries with access to international capital markets. In practice, most often they occur in larger and more developed emerging economies, a subset of the around 50 countries that have been able to place debt securities with international investors. To improve global financial stability, an international lender of last resort will have to concentrate on preventing financial crises in emerging economies that are large enough to have repercussions on a global scale. Consequently, funding requirements must primarily suffice to prevent these countries from defaulting on their international obligations and their financial sectors from collapsing due to widespread bankruptcies.

The group of emerging economies most relevant for global financial stability makes up the greater part of international capital flows to emerging markets: Argentina, Brazil and Mexico for Latin America; China, India, Thailand, Malaysia, South Korea, Indonesia, Vietnam and the Philippines for Asia as well as Russia, South Africa and Turkey. Together these countries constitute the group of the ten largest emerging economies by GDP, trade and capital flows; most belong to the leading economies in their geographical region. Except for China, India, Vietnam, and South Africa, all have experienced large gaps in international liquidity over the past decade. The financial crises they experienced provide for up-to-date case studies and lessons drawn from these episodes are more applicable than those drawn from current account crises during the Bretton Woods era. If the creation of an international lender of last resort would contribute to reduce the risk of financial crisis for those economies alone, stability of the global financial system would be considerably enhanced.

A gap in international liquidity is generally defined as the excess of external liabilities due within one year over international reserve assets excluding gold. Short-term external debt is made up of short-term liabilities to banks, debt securities issued abroad maturing within one year and the short-term portion of non-bank trade credits. International reserves exclude the gold stock and are based on IMF estimates. Table 6.7 below is draws on an analysis of the Joint BIS-IMF-OECD-World Bank Statistics on External Debt and identifies each economy's largest gap in international liquidity on a quarterly basis since 1995. This period is the longest for which coherent data is available and includes the major financial crises of the recent past.

The largest mismatch between external short-term debt and international reserves over the last decade occurred in South Korea: Its international liquidity gap during the fourth quarter of 1997 amounted to USD 58.8 billions. However, except in the case of Argentina in late 2000 no other gaps in international liquidity have exceeded USD 20 billion since. The sum total of maximum gaps in international liquidity in each of the ten emerging economies over the past decade amounts to USD 196 billion. Since the Asian Crisis, most economies have improved their policies and built-up their currency reserves thereby reducing their vulnerability to external shocks. At present, none of the ten economies is facing a substantial gap in international liquidity. But even if liquidity positions would deteriorate to the levels experienced during the Asian financial crisis, USD 200 billion would suffice for an international lender of last resort to provide effective liquidity assistance to all affected emerging economies at once.

Table 6.7
International Liquidity of Crisis Economies
(USD millions)

Country	Period	Maximum Liquidity Gap
Argentina	2000-Q4	34.280
Brazil	2000-Q4	9.743
Mexico	1995-Q4	16.565
Philippines	1997-Q4	5.556
Indonesia	1997-Q4	19.519
Thailand	1997-Q4	12.795
Korea	1997-Q4	58.795
Malaysia	1997-Q4	n.a.
Russia	1997-Q4	19.969
Turkey	2000-Q4	7.768

Source: Own Calculations based on IMF-BIS-OECD-
World Bank Debt Statistics Data

However, one qualification is in order: the USD 200 billion estimate does not include a potential international liquidity gap in China; nor does it account for India since the 1990s emerging market crises did expose neither to violent capital flow reversals. Today, their vulnerability appears still limited: Both have amassed a large and growing stock of foreign currency reserves: In the case of China reserves amount to well over USD 600 billion and substantially more when adding those of Hong Kong while India's reserves stood over USD 120 billion at year end 2004. Given strong growth and its currency peg to the dollar, pressure on the renminbi continues to be upwards—the high level of international reserves is a direct consequence. While China is of great importance to the world economy, controls on capital flows and currency exchange combined with the high level of foreign currency reserves imply limited vulnerability to violent capital flow reversals in the medium term. In the long run, both China and India will join the group of industrialised economies.

Examining past gaps in international liquidity suggests that the funding requirement for an effective international lender of last resort may lie significantly below the level of developing countries' short-term external public and financial sector debt. Resources necessary are not only far less than USD 1 trillion, but also significantly below the USD 600 to USD 700 billion external short-term liabilities of developing countries with access to international capital markets. Providing sufficient liquidity assistance to fully meet the largest gaps in international liquidity of the ten major crisis economies at once would have required less than USD 200 billion in hard currency. To restore confidence and increase the credibility of international support, the IMF should have access to resources above this level. But even accounting for the potential needs of emerging economies other than the ten above, USD 250 to USD 350 billion appears a far more reasonable estimate of funding required for an international lender of last resort than the amount of *at least one trillion*.

Moreover, as indicated earlier, past episodes have shown that an international lender of last resort would rarely have to finance gaps in international liquidity in full. Generally, at least a minority of international investors are prepared to roll-over short-term loans in a coordinated effort. Their contribution will increase if international assistance is forthcoming and the government commits to policy reforms. Corsetti, Guimaraes and Roubini show that due to *catalytic effects* liquidity provision by the IMF does not need to cover shortages in international liquidity completely. Instead, liquidity support at a fraction of the funding gap may prove sufficient to end a liquidity crisis in case official sector intervention induces international investors to roll over some of their claims by sending signals suggesting the debtor country's solvency[27].

Under normal circumstances an international lender of last resort would very seldom be forced to commit resources above USD 200 billion, even if financial crises in emerging economies are often related and can occur within a relatively short time span. Despite contagious effects having spread financial distress from Southeast Asia to Russia and Latin America, crises have never occurred all over the world at once. Assuming financial crises will continue to be mostly linked regionally, increasing the Fund's commitment capacity to USD 250 billion would significantly enhance its credibility as a crisis manager. To provide for extraordinary systemic threats, swap agreements over additional USD 100 billion could be nego-

---

27 See Giancarlo Corsetti, Bernardo Guimaraes and Nouriel Roubini. 2003. *International Lending of Last Resort and Moral Hazard: A Model of IMF's Catalytic Finance*. NBER Working Paper 10125. Cambridge, MA: National Bureau of Economic Research

tiated with major industrial countries' central banks, resembling the monetary arrangements between European central banks during the 1960s and 1970s.

6.3 Conclusion and Implications

This chapter argued that Bagehot's principle of *lending freely* does not imply that an international lender of last resort must make available unlimited amounts of foreign currency to every distressed government or central bank in order to effectively address the problem of global financial instability. As industrial economies are less vulnerable to twin currency and debt crises and given inevitable funding constraints, an international lender of last resort should focus its efforts on preventing and arresting crises in emerging economies. Neither does *lending freely* imply providing liquidity assistance for every purpose. An international lender of last resort should provide foreign currency loans to enable local central banks to prevent a collapse of their financial systems, not to manipulate their currency's exchange rate since the latter is not only ineffective but also impossible due to funding constraints. Finally, *lending freely* does not imply that domestic central banks should lend to every financial institution in need for foreign currency; instead they should restrict liquidity assistance to fundamentally solvent institutions as discussed in the following chapter.

In addition, the chapter argued that for an international lender of last resort to be effective it has to be adequately funded. Adequate funding can only be realised, if its mandate is restricted to enable domestic central banks to function as lender of last resort to their economies. As the majority of emerging market central banks would be unable to do so due to a lack of foreign currency reserves, pursuing this objective would go a long way in enhancing global financial stability. To be effective an international lender of last resort also requires a clear framework of lending rules. The discussion above implies two of them:

> *Rule I:* Short-term loans by an international lender of last resort should be provided exclusively to enable domestic central banks acting as lenders of last resort for their economies. In doing so, they must adhere to the Bagehot rules: lending to illiquid but solvent institutions only, at penalty interest rates and against good collateral. Central banks must not employ international funds in efforts to bail-out insolvent banks or service preferred creditors of bankrupt entities. And neither must international funds be employed in market interventions to halt exchange rate depreciation or to prop-up pegs to other currencies.

Using international liquidity assistance to intervene in the currency markets would be a misappropriation of funds due to reasons of ineffectiveness. Lending of last resort as input to monetary policy requires essentially unlimited international funds. No institution can provide unlimited international liquidity unless it can issue international currency. Markets are aware that international funds are limited and their own resources dwarf any funding available to a domestic central bank. The futile attempts by central banks in Latin America and East Asia to maintain their currency pegs by intervention are just one example: Given eventual devaluation, the funds employed in market intervention proved ineffective and were essentially spent in vain. Even if effective, the competence of domestic central banks in determining its currency's optimal exchange rate is at least questionable. Experience has shown that fixed exchange rates often increase instability, attract speculative attacks and increase the probability of financial crises. While the choice of exchange rate regime is a matter of national sovereignty, the official sector can legitimately determine how its funds are employed by borrowers. As such, currency market intervention should be excluded from the permissible uses of international liquidity assistance.

Banning central banks from using international funds to bail out insolvent entities and servicing creditors of bankrupted entities is warranted on two counts: Both practices increase moral hazard and are ineffective. A lender of last resort provides liquidity support to banks because bank failures can have severe effects on the whole economy. Providing emergency loans to insolvent banks just postpones an institution's inevitable bankruptcy; good money would be thrown after bad without fundamentally eliminating the problem. Bailing-out insolvent banks is a questionable redistribution of taxpayers' money. A stellar example for the futility of such approaches is the case of Credit Lyonnais in France. More importantly, bailing out insolvent institutions increases moral hazard, both at financial institutions themselves and for these institutions' creditors; financial institutions might be discouraged from following responsible and prudent banking practices. Incentives to take on excessive risks increase if success is enjoyed exclusively but the costs of failure will be born by the taxpayer. Therefore insolvent banks should be closed down or taken over. Similar reasoning applies to international creditors of emerging market banks. A practice of unselective bail-outs encourages imprudent lending as international creditors would rationally aim at receiving the high interest premiums paid by emerging market banks while running little risk as credits are implicitly guaranteed by the domestic government.

Rule II: Liquidity assistance should be provided on a strictly short-term basis which is warranted for two reasons: Lacking the ability to issue its own currency, funds available to an international lender of last resort for liquidity assistance are inevitably limited: In order to fulfil its responsibility an international lender of last resort must be adequately capitalised at all times. By making medium or long-term loans an international lender of last resort would bind its resources and so considerably reduce its flexibility. Consequently, as soon as the immediate liquidity mismatch is resolved and default prevented, funds should flow back to become available for the next crisis.

If a crisis is the result of liquidity and not of solvency problems, information asymmetry and panic behaviour in the market should subside within a relatively short period of time. Otherwise the crisis would appear more fundamental and a debt restructuring the preferable alternative. Longer maturity loans are a feature of development policy and not of emergency liquidity assistance. While developing countries benefit from development aid and support for structural reforms, the World Bank and similar development agencies are the institutions best suited to provide such services. The IMF lacks mandate, funds, skills and experience to plan and execute development policy.

Liquidity crises develop in different forms and last for varying periods of time. In the majority of liquidity crises, six months provided enough time for solvent borrowers to originate new funds or restructure mal-aligned debt burdens. When they take longer, usually factors pointing to fundamental problems are at play. The maturity of emergency loans by an international lender of last resort should thus be restricted to six months. Under exceptional circumstances loans could be renewed once if a supermajority of 85 percent in the executive board supports an extension. Such circumstances would include natural disasters, severe cases of contagion by distress in other economies or substantial external shocks. Penalty interest rates should then be raised to a level ensuring that even under exceptional circumstances international funds remain an unattractive source for any other than emergency purposes.

7. The Collateral Question

The Bagehot Rules insist that emergency loans should be made against good collateral only. In Bagehot's framework for an effective lender of last resort the collateral requirement serves a twofold purpose: First, it ensures that the lender will be repaid in case the borrower defaults. Second, and more importantly, the borrower's ability to put up collateral can be utilized as a rough indicator of solvency. In addition, collateral requirements reduce moral hazard by providing disincentives for holding risky assets that would be unacceptable as collateral for loans during potential liquidity crunches. Both Thornton and Bagehot went to great lengths to delineate the rationale for restricting emergency loans to solvent borrowers. As argued in the previous chapter, they assert that emergency loans should prevent fundamentally solvent banks from bankruptcy as a consequence of short-term liquidity crunches but should not be employed to bail-out insolvent banks and their shareholders. Insolvent banks should instead be allowed to fail for reasons of moral hazard and effectiveness: Hence a lender of last resort should lend around a crisis, not into a crisis.

To be effective, an international lender of last resort must follow the same principle and restrict liquidity assistance to illiquid, but fundamentally solvent economies. Insolvent economies should not receive liquidity assistance but enter the inevitable process of debt restructuring. Providing insolvent countries with further liquidity does not constitute emergency lending but a bail-out, and bailing-out insolvent borrowers is not only ineffective but also reduces incentives for governments and financial sector institutions to pursue prudent economic and lending policies respectively. The official sector might still support countries entering a debt restructuring, but support would have to facilitate a restructuring process and not help to evade or postpone it. Support could take the form of providing limited amounts of hard currency to be used as up-front incentive for international investors to agree on a sustainable restructuring plan. A more innovative approach would be for an international lender of last resort to offer buying all debt owed by the government to private investors at significant discounts. This would allow to prevent contagion and to bail-in the private sector by increasing liquidity in the market for defaulted debt securities[1].

Restricting liquidity assistance to solvent borrowers is difficult to implement in practice: Distinguishing between illiquid, but fundamentally solvent institutions and

---

1 See Allan H. Meltzer and Adam Lerrick. 2001. *Beyond IMF Bailouts: Default without Disruption.* Quarterly International Economics Report May 2001. Pittsburgh, PA: Carnegie Mellon University

insolvent entities in the financial sector is not easy. Accurately determining the solvency status of sovereign borrowers and whole financial sectors is all but impossible. Given these difficulties and the fact that during financial panics timely decisions are essential, assessments of a borrower's solvency status can be no more than approximations. There are essentially three approaches to form an opinion on whether a country and its financial sector are solvent or not. The first is to advance emergency loans exclusively against good collateral as suggested by Bagehot. The collateral then functions as rough indicator of a country's solvency position. The viability of this approach in an international context will be discussed below. An alternative approach is to make liquidity assistance dependent on borrowers' willingness to commit to policy reforms that aim at ensuring that borrowers' solvency will be restored in the short to medium-term. However, conditionality policy as practiced by the IMF makes timely assistance almost impossible and often proved counterproductive during recent crisis episodes. The third strategy is to define a set of conditions whose satisfaction would be accepted as indicator of solvency. Under this approach an international lender of last resort would restrict the provision of liquidity assistance to countries which meet a set of pre-defined qualification criteria as suggested in the Meltzer Report and analysed in the following chapter.

7.1 The Concept of Collateral

Recommending the Bank of England to *advance freely and vigorously to the public* in times of crisis, Bagehot emphasised the importance of lending freely on *good banking securities* and to refuse lending to insolvent entities unable put up good collateral:

> The reason is plain. The object is to stay alarm, and nothing therefore should be done to cause alarm. But the way to cause alarm is to refuse someone who has good security on offer. The news of this will spread in an instant through all the money market at a moment of terror; no one can say exactly who carries it, but in half an hour it will be carried on all sides, and will intensify the terror everywhere. No advances indeed need to be made by which the Bank will ultimately loose ... That in a panic the bank, or banks, holding the ultimate reserve should refuse bad bills or bad securities will not make the panic really worse...[2]

The rationale for insisting on good collateral as non-negotiable condition for liquidity assistance applies to domestic and international settings alike. Of all the

---

2 Bagehot (1999): 197–198

functions a collateral requirement serves, facilitating the decision whether a potential borrower is temporarily illiquid but fundamentally solvent or whether it is essentially insolvent is the most important. Deciding on an applicant's solvency status requires thorough analysis which is almost impossible to undertake in the short time span a successful lender of last resort operation requires. Indeed, the key challenge for a lender of last resort is precisely to *make quick decisions on the basis of only partial, and possibly faulty, information*[3]. To assess the solvency status of a whole economy is far more complicated for an international lender of last resort than it is for a central bank to discriminate between solvent and insolvent banks. Lending against good collateral allows circumventing this tedious and time-consuming process through the assumption that availability of good collateral indicates funda- mental solvency; it can therefore serve as *a rough but robust test of whether the institution in trouble is likely to be solvent in normal times*[4]. Using collateral as indicator for fundamental solvency thus allows the lender to reach decisions timely enough for liquidity assistance to be effective in arresting financial panics. Con- sequently, Calomiris and Meltzer advocate that the IMF should start to provide emergency loans exclusively against good collateral not only to ensure repayment but also to indicate a borrower's solvency status[5].

Moreover, collateral requirements ensure that the creditor will be repaid and so safeguard creditor solvency. If the borrower defaults, the creditor can sell the collateral at market value to satisfy its outstanding demands. This is important not only financially but as well in terms of legitimacy for unless repaid emergency loans funded by the official sector entail re-distributive elements. Loans advanced by central banks or the IMF are funded by taxpayers' money. Support by the public for this type of intervention depends on the likelihood that funds lent to distressed banks or foreign sovereigns can be recouped at least via collateral in case of default. In 1995, despite by-passing Congress by using funds of the Exchange Stabilization Fund to provide USD 20 billion as part of the Mexican rescue package, the Clinton administration insisted on the provision of good collateral by the Mexican govern- ment: Revenues from the export of oil pledged by the Mexican government were essential for the administration to demonstrate that American taxpayers' money was safe and would be repaid.

Basing lending decisions on the availability of good collateral can also have beneficial effects on potential borrowers in terms of moral hazard as incentives for investing in excessively risky assets are reduced. In order to qualify as collateral,

---

3 Giannini (1999): 10
4 Fischer (1999): 6
5 See Charles Calomiris and Alan Meltzer. 1999. "Fixing the IMF – Reforming the International Monetary Fund." *The National Interest* 56: 93

assets must be liquid and safe. In Thailand, banks and other financial institutions lent their foreign borrowed funds to finance real estate projects whose real value and marketability in case of crisis was limited. Facing short-term liquidity gaps these assets were rarely accepted as collateral and thus could be sold at fire-sale prices only. By insisting on good collateral the central bank can create incentives for financial institutions to hold in their portfolios safe and liquid assets that qualify as collateral at other lending institutions or the central bank. Similarly, at the international level, insisting on good collateral by an international lender of last resort would provide incentives for local central banks to restructure their holdings with a clear focus on internationally tradable assets acceptable as collateral to an international lender of last resort[6]. For governments in an ongoing process of privatisation this could imply the need for keeping assets that are either easily marketable or produce stable foreign currency earnings.

7.2 Assets Acceptable as Collateral

Making use of collateral pledges is already possible under current IMF statutes. The Articles of Agreement explicitly mention the possibility of taking into account the willingness of a potential borrower to pledge good collateral in exchange for the advancement of IMF funds. Regarding a potential weaver of limitations on IMF transactions Article 5 states that

> The Fund may in its discretion, and on the terms which safeguard its interests, waive any of the conditions prescribed in Section 3 (b) (iii) and (iv) of this Article, especially in the case of members with a record of avoiding large or continuous use of the Fund's general resources. In making a waiver it shall take into consideration periodic or exceptional requirements of the member requesting the waiver. The Fund shall take also into consideration a member's willingness to pledge as collateral security acceptable assets having a value sufficient in the opinion of the Fund to protect its interests and may require as a condition of waiver the pledge of such collateral security[7].

The fact that no definition is provided of what constitutes acceptability of assets as collateral allows for a wide range of possibilities. Indeed, a generous definition of what assets qualify as good collateral is explicitly demanded by Bagehot when dis-

---

6 See Allan Meltzer. 1998. *What's Wrong with the IMF? What Would Be Better?* Paper prepared at the "Asia: An Analysis of Financial Crisis" conference. October 8–10, 1998. Chicago, IL: Federal Reserve Bank of Chicago: 23
7 See IMF Articles of Agreement: Article V, Section 4

cussing the collateral issue in a domestic context. Applauding the Bank of England on the complete adoption of right principles when dealing with the banking panic of 1825, Bagehot quotes Sir Robert Peel describing the Bank's directors' lending practice:

> We lent money by every possible means, and in modes which we had never adopted before; we took in stock on security, we purchased Exchequer Bills, we not only discounted outright, but we made advances on deposits of bills of Exchange to an immense amount—in short, by every possible means consistent with the safety of the Bank[8].

Although Peel praised the generous way in which the Bank of England lent in 1825, assets accepted as collateral consisted exclusively of financial securities— although of varying risk and maturity. As Bagehot's recommendations to the Bank of England regard a domestic lender of last resort, or rather a lender of last resort for the City of London's bill brokers, joint-stock and private banks, this focus is not surprising. An international lender of last resort dealing with countries and central banks would have to endorse a broader view on assets' acceptability as collateral. According to Article 5 quoted above any asset having a value sufficient in the opinion of the Fund to protect its interests could be acceptable. Thus apart from financial securities both other internationally tradable assets as well as any secure and continuous stream of export earnings could in theory serve as acceptable security. In practice, apart from financial securities, earnings from commodity exports, particularly revenues derived from the export of oil, are the assets most suitable to serve as good collateral. Nevertheless, other possibilities exist.

7.2.1 Financial Assets

Financial securities are the assets most commonly pledged as collateral due to reasons of liquidity. This holds not only for central banks lending to local financial institutions but also for an international lender of last resort advancing short-term liquidity support to countries' central banks. Indeed, a year before the Meltzer Report was drafted, Calomiris and Meltzer suggested that at least a portion of the collateral should consist of negotiable foreign bonds while the balance could be made up of other assets[9].

In its Revised Framework on the International Convergence of Capital Measurement and Capital Standards, generally referred to as Basel II, the Basel Committee on Banking Supervision lists a variety of assets eligible as financial collateral.

---

8 Cited in Bagehot (1999): 202
9 See Calomiris and Meltzer (1999): 93

Although in Basel II financial collateral is considered in respect to the possibility of reducing credit exposure when calculating capital requirements for banks, financial assets acceptable under Basel II should also qualify as collateral to be pledged by borrowers to an international lender of last resort. It may even be argued that an international lender of last resort should accept more assets than those identified by Basel II as its aim is to restore confidence while the latter merely introduces security

---

Box 7.1
Assets Eligible as Collateral under Basel II

1 Cash (as well as certificates of deposit or comparable instruments issued by the lending bank) on deposit with the bank which is incurring the counterparty exposure
2 Gold
3 Debt securities rated by a recognised external credit assessment institution where these are either:
   - at least BB- when issued by sovereigns or PSEs that are treated as sovereigns by the national supervisor; or
   - at least BBB- when issued by other entities (including banks and security firms); or
   - at least A-3/P-3 for short-term debt instruments
4 Debt securities not rated by a recognised external credit assessment institution where these are:
   - issued by a bank; and
   - listed on a recognised exchange; and
   - classified as senior debt; and
   - all rated issues of the same seniority by the issuing bank that are rated at least BBB- or A-3/P-3 by recognised external credit assessment institution; and
   - the bank holding the securities as collateral has no information to suggest that the issue justifies a rating below BBB- or A-3/P-3 (as applicable); and
   - the supervisor is sufficiently confident about the market liquidity of the security.
5 Equities (including convertible bonds) that are included in a main index
6 Undertakings for Collective Investments in Transferable securities (UCITS) and mutual funds where:
   - a price for the units is publicly quoted daily; and
   - the UCITS/mutual fund is limited to investing in the instruments listed in this paragraph
7 Equities (including convertible bonds) which are not included in a main index but which are listed on a recognised exchange;
8 UCITS/mutual funds which include those Equities

standards. Box 7.1 lists the financial assets mentioned as eligible collateral instruments for banks under Basel II[10].

While negotiable foreign bonds issued by strong borrowers are surely a prime asset to pledge as collateral, countries facing liquidity problems and applying for emergency assistance are likely to have sold off the bulk of potential foreign sovereign bond holdings. AAA rated sovereign bonds are the asset easiest to monetise and therefore likely to be sold early on in a liquidity crisis. Foreign currency reserves of central banks are already generally held in form of industrial countries' sovereign bonds and not in cash; facing a liquidity crisis, by definition a country will have run out of most of its reserves in either cash or foreign sovereign bonds. But both industrial and developing country central banks often hold considerable quantities of debt securities issued by their own governments; in addition, governments often retain interests in domestic industries that are not vital considering aspects of national security and could therefore be sold if necessary. Even in countries having pursued strong privatisation agendas, governments often retain at least minority stakes in publicly quoted companies. These types of local securities could under certain circumstances be acceptable as collateral in exchange for foreign currency loans not only for official institutions but also for foreign commercial banks.

7.2.1.1 Argentina's Contingent Repurchase Facility

The contingent credit line arranged by Argentina with a consortium of initially 13— and later more—international commercial banks provides an example of collateralising financial securities on a sovereign level. The Contingent Repurchase Facility was put in place in December 1996 as part of Argentina's official liquidity policy. It stipulated the possibility for the Argentine central bank (BCRA) to sell specific financial assets to a group of banks in exchange for foreign currency: Subject to a repurchase agreement, the BCRA thus acquired a put option to sell USD 6.2 billion dollar-denominated Argentine bonds plus an additional USD 500 million in dollar-denominated mortgages in exchange for U.S. dollars. The option was priced via a commitment fee at 32 basis points while interest payable averaged around 205 basis points above LIBOR[11].

The contingent repurchase agreement's maturity was set at 3 years, extendable by 3 months and subsequently renewed every quarter depending on Argentina servicing

---

10 Basel Committee for Banking Supervision (BCBS). 2004. *International Convergence of Capital Measurement and Capital Standards*. Basel, Switzerland: Bank for International Settlements: 31–32

11 See Steve H. Hanke and Kurt Schuler. 1999. *A Dollarization Blueprint for Argentina*. Foreign Policy Briefing 52. Washington, DC: Cato Institute: 6

its international debt. In case of Argentina defaulting on any of its international debt service obligations, the agreement was to be instantly invalidated. The contingent repurchase facility offered modestly priced liquidity protection by allowing the Banco Central de la Republica Argentina instant access at its own convenience to USD 6.7 billion to stabilise its financial system in times of crisis. To increase lender protection the facility was considerably over-collateralised: The market value of Argentine bonds and mortgages pledged as collateral were 125 percent of the amount accessible by the BCRA[12]. In addition, a margin call in form of further bonds was required in case the market value of the collateral declined by more than 5 percent.

The possibility of securing liquidity protection without resorting to the official sector is often cited as point invalidating the case for an international lender of last resort. Commercial banks are willing, it is argued, to provide emergency funds given the borrower's ability to pledge sufficient collateral thus rendering the creation of an international lender of last resort unnecessary[13]. However, the willingness of international banks to offer this modestly priced contingent repurchase facility has to be viewed in context: Firstly, an amount of around USD 7 billion dollar is not sufficient to provide genuine liquidity protection. The Argentine facility does not imply willingness by banks to provide similar arrangements in a range five to ten times that amount. Secondly, at the time the agreement was reached in December 1996, Argentina had risen to become a role model and poster child for successful reform efforts in emerging market economies[14]. Following the passage of the convertibility law (Law 23, 928) by Congress in March 1991, Argentina's unorthodox currency board led to a period of financial stability and stellar growth. Inflation declined from a peak above 3000 percent per year to single digits in 1992 and seemed effectively eliminated by 1996. Under these positive conditions the private sector was willing to offer a contingent credit line given the strict security provisions it entailed. In less prosperous times, commercial banks have proven much less generous and it is an environment where the private sector is generally not prepared to lend even on good collateral that the need for an international lender of last resort arises. Nevertheless, collateralization of locally issued, dollar-denominated bonds and mortgages is one possibility for the official sector to provide liquidity support in line with Bagehot's principles.

---

12 Maintenance of the 25 percent over-collateralization requirement was secured by the obligation to raise the amount of bonds pledged in accordance with any decline in the collateral's market value.

13 See Steve Hanke. 2000. "Please, No More 'New' IMFs." *The Wall Street Journal.* March 21, 2000

14 Stiglitz (2003): 219

7.2.2 Collateralising Equity

Another financial asset to be pledged as collateral by countries facing liquidity problems is equity in state-owned enterprises. During the 1960s and 1970s many emerging economies took on entrepreneurial roles in order to develop their economies and foster economic growth. As part of their development strategies, the state often owned and operated industries lacking strategic relevance for national security interests. State-owned enterprises were active in the provision of goods of public interest like gas, water and electricity, were operating buses, railroads and airlines and offered phone and postal services. Beside involvement in utilities, transport, and communications, governments built up considerable interests in finance, construction, large-scale manufacturing, agricultural goods and natural resources. In Senegal, Tanzania, Bangladesh, Myanmar, India, Mexico, and Nicaragua state-owned enterprises accounted for 75 percent of natural resource output. In Syria, Tunisia, Egypt and Ethiopia 60 percent of manufacturing value added was created by entities belonging to the state[15].

Growing support for neo-classical economics led to a reversal of these tendencies by the early 1980s when a rapidly growing process of privatisation started developing. Privatisation efforts in emerging economies were further pushed by international financial institutions which often made financial support conditional on privatisation goals and were well received by financial markets. Privatisation programs were also attractive for the governments of less developed economies themselves: Apart from reasons of efficiency and competitiveness gains in order to increase future tax receipts, additional motivation came in form of fiscal pressures. Selling off state-owned companies not only provides initial windfall revenues, but also cuts continuous fiscal burdens in case of loss-making entities. As a consequence of increasing privatisation programs since the 1990s many emerging economies have sold off the majority of state-owned industry holdings. Nevertheless, in some countries specific industries remain in state ownership; alternatively, governments often retain minority stakes in publicly quoted companies. For some countries these equity interests can provide a potential source for pledging collateral in exchange for foreign currency loans. However, a large disparity exists between individual economies and geographical regions: while some are still in possession of substantial interests in large industries, the majority of developing countries almost completely sold off most of its state-owned enterprises over the last two decades.

---

15 See Michael Todaro and Stephen Smith. 2003. *Economic Development*. Eighth Edition. Boston, MA: Addison-Wesley: 759

7.2.2.1   Privatisation in Latin America

Having entered important industries in order to promote economic growth in the 1960s, by the late 1970s Brazilian state-owned enterprises had risen to dominant roles in petrochemicals, telecommunications, steel and electricity[16]. While privatisation remained subdued in the 1980s when 38 state-owned enterprises were sold for a total USD 723 million, efforts increased drastically under the administration of Fernando Collor de Mello. From 1990 onwards Brazil embarked on a major privatisation process as part of the National Privatisation Program. Selling off assets worth USD 2 billion in 1992, privatisation receipts peaked in 1997 and 1998 reaching USD 27.7 and USD 37.5 billion respectively. Of the USD 105 billion generated by privatisation efforts between 1990 and 2002, almost two thirds involved the sale of state-owned enterprises in the energy and telecommunication industries, each generating 31 percent of privatisation receipts; interests sold in mining, petroleum, gas and petrochemical sectors accounted for 8, 7 and 4 percent of revenues respectively[17].

As a consequence, today the vast majority of commercial entities in Brazil is either publicly owned or has been acquired by foreign multinationals. Of Brazil's 10 largest companies, the government retained a controlling stake in only one; however, it is by far the largest in terms of revenues: Petrobras has a market capitalisation of USD 30 to 40 billion and annual revenues of over USD 38 billion; the federal government holds 55.7 percent of voting shares. It also controls 52.5 percent of publicly quoted BRL and USD 22 billion worth Eletrobras, an energy holding controlling several generation companies. In addition, the government remains owner of airport operator Infraero which operates all 67 airports of Brazil. Government interests further include the ownership of Banco do Brasil offering both retail banking through over 5000 branches as well as wholesale banking services via fully owned subsidiary BB Securites. 2003 revenues for the Bank amounted to USD 15.9 billion. While limited in number, Brazil's remaining stakes in formerly state-owned enterprises could serve as part of a collateral pledge in exchange for liquidity support in case a liquidity crisis were to occur in the future.

In Argentina and Mexico privatisation efforts have been even stronger. Argentina's privatisation program was initiated in 1989 as part of the new administration's attempt to end hyperinflation and return to stability and growth. Beside an ambitious privatisation program among other initiatives the stabilisation strategy included

---

16 See Thomas Trebat. 1983. *Brazil's State-Owned Enterprises*. Cambridge: Cambridge University Press

17 See Banco Nacional de Desenvolvimento Economico e Social. 2002. *Privatization in Brazil 1990–2002*. Rio de Janeiro, Brasil: Banco Nacional de Desenvolvimento Economico e Social

trade liberalisation and the introduction of a currency board. In the stabilisation program privatisation efforts were to signal sound economic policy while at the same time providing a source of fiscal revenue. Despite the fact that the Argentine government once owned a circus[18], contrasting other economies in the region state-owned enterprises in Argentina were generally few in number and consisted mainly of large, monopolistic entities that accounted for a large part of Argentina's economy[19].

The first wave of privatisation from 1989 to 1992 was focused on the telecommunications sector but also included the national flag operator in the airline industry. In 1990 the government sold a majority stake in Aerolineas Argentina for USD 1.87 billion to an Iberia-led consortium and 50 percent of Telecom SA to an Italian-Franco consortium raising USD 2.4 billion; a further 30 percent was sold in the market for USD 1.2 billion in 1992. A 60 percent stake in Argentina's other large telecommunications operator, Telefonica de Argentina, fetched USD 2.8 billion by a consortium led by Citibank and Spain's Telefonica; additional 30 percent were offered to the public a year later raising a total of USD 830 million. The second wave—more focussed on efficiency—began in 1992 and included the sale of public utilities providing gas, water, electricity and oil. In 1993 Argentina sold 45.3 percent in oil and gas company Yacimientos Petroliferos Fiscales (YPF) for over USD 3 billion while retaining majority control. In 1999 a 15 percent stake in YPF fetched USD 15.4 billion by Spain's Repsol. Further USD 3.1 billion were generated by the sale of Argentina's postal service Encotesa to a local consortium. In addition, over a hundred other entities spanning a variety of different sectors were sold for amounts below USD 500 million, including the national airport operator in 1997. Privatisation has left Argentina without significant ownership interests in businesses that could be pledged as collateral during future liquidity crunches.

Government involvement in the economy was higher in Mexico, where in contrast to Argentina state-owned enterprises did not dominate only a few selected industries but were operating in a wide array of sectors and institutional forms. Accordingly, Mexico's privatisation program involved the sale of considerably more entities than in any other Latin American country. In 1982 1155 state-owned enterprises accounting for 14 percent of GDP were operating in Mexico. Privatisation began in 1983 and pace was increasing continuously up to 1992 where the number of state-owned enterprises had fallen to 225; 96 percent of the sales were negotiated

---

18 See Daniel Yergin and Joseph Stanislaw. 1998. *The Commanding Heights: The Battle for the World Economy*. New York, NY: Touchstone
19 See Sebastián Galiani, Paul Gertler, Ernesto Schargrodsky and Frederico Sturzenegger. 2003. *The Benefits and Costs of Privatization in Argentina: A Microeconomic Analysis*. Research Network Working Paper #R–454. Washington, DC: Inter-American Development Bank

between 1989 and 1992 under the administration of President Salinas[20]. In spite of this massive privatisation program the Mexican government retained ownership interests in oil, petrochemicals and gas as well as in utilities providing water and electricity. In addition, the state remains involved in the transportation sector by owning most highways, railways and port authorities.

Mexico's prime asset is its ownership of Petroleos Mexicanos (Pemex), the world's 8th largest oil producer with exclusive rights to drill, refine and sell the country's oil reserves. Pemex produces 3.2 billion of barrels crude a day and its revenues account for roughly one third of the Mexican budget. The government also maintains control of the energy sector owning Comisión Federal de Electricidad (CFE) and Luz y Fuerza Centro (LCF) which account for over 85 percent of Mexican electrical generation capacity. In addition, around 30 airports, the airlines Mexicana de Aviacion and Aeromexico as well as Banco de Mexico remain state-owned. Furthermore, the government retains interests in pharmacies, department stores and telecommunication providers.

Privatisation efforts during the 1980s and 1990s have left Latin America's largest economies with limited government ownership in valuable industries. The exception is the oil sector, where the governments of Brazil and Mexico still retain large and valuable stakes. Remaining state-owned enterprises in the utility sector are far less valuable and thus less useful in terms of collateral provision. Argentina in contrast lacks major assets in the oil sector since formerly national petroleum company YPF has already been sold off. While of limited importance in the case of Argentina, Mexico's and Brazil's remaining stakes in formerly fully state-owned enterprises could form part of potential collateral agreements. By themselves, however, those equity stakes are not sufficient to collateralize the liquidity needs in case substantial liquidity gaps would arise.

7.2.2.2   Privatisation in East Asia

Despite strong privatisation efforts Thailand still owns over 60 state enterprises as well as three state-owned banks. Two further businesses are owned by the government, but are fully independent. Combined these businesses possess assets worth THB 5.6 trillion (against 5.1 trillion in liabilities) and generate over THB 1.3 trillion in revenues per year. Most profitable businesses include oil and gas producer/refiner PTT which has been floated but in which government still holds 68 percent, the Electricity Generating Authority of Thailand and the Telephone Organisation of

---

20 See Rafael La Porta and Florencio Lopez-de-Silanes. 1997. *The Benefits of Privatization: Evidence from Mexico.* NBER Working Paper 6215. Cambridge, MA: National Bureau of Economic Research

Thailand. State Railway, Bangkok Mass Transit Authority and Bangchak Petroleum were the state-owned enterprises generating the largest losses in recent years. Thailand's government is also active in the production of electronic consumer goods like television and radio sets, automotive parts, iron and steel and provides telecom services through the Telephone Organisation of Thailand and the Communications Authority of Thailand.

As part of wide ranging economic reforms following the Asian Crisis, South Korea also embarked on an ambitious privatisation program. By 2002 six of Korea's largest state-owned enterprises had be privatised, including Korea Tobacco and Ginseng Corporation, Korea Telecommunications Corporation, Korea Electric Power Corporation (KEPCO) and the monopolistic Korea Gas Corporation (KOGAS). Korea Heavy Industries Corporation has been sold off and the country's largest steelmaker POSCO was floated on the stock exchange. Nevertheless, according to Korea's Finance and Economy Ministry the value of assets still owned by the government surpassed KRW 200 trillion (USD 170 billion) in 2003. While more than 60 percent of this amount is attributable to real estate interest and intellectual property rights, the value of state-owned equity stakes increased as the government took control of the Korea Airport Corporation for KRW 1.6 billion and Korea Highway Corporation for KRW 905 billion[21].

In Malaysia privatisation efforts were guided by the so-called Privatization Master Plan as part of a broader development program. Between 1996 and 2000, 98 state-owned entities were in the process of being transformed into corporations or fully privatised. 51 of those were new projects, almost entirely in transportation, construction, gas and electricity. In most privatisation projects improvements in efficiency and productivity could be realised. Privatisation is continuing in the 8th Plan period lasting from 2001 to 2005. Major projects principally marked for privatisation include a number of expressways, Kuala Lumpur central station, the Southern International Gateway and National Solid Waste Management. However, the state's involvement in the economy remains large. Oil and gas producer Petroliam Nasional (Petronas), the country's most valuable asset is owned and operated by the state. Other state-owned companies of international significance include power distributor Tenega Nasional, Telecom Malaysia, Malaysia International Shipping Corporation and Malaysia Banking Berhad.

---

21 See Chosun. 2004. "South Korea's State Assets Exceed W200 Trillion in 2003." *The Chosun Journal.* May 6, 2004

7.2.2.3 Privatisation in China

In the Chinese economy about 300,000 enterprises are owned by the state. In spite of privatisation programs many corporatised entities are in fact still controlled and owned by the state despite their huge inefficiency. Consuming around 70 percent of China's capital and labour resources, their share of total GDP amounts to merely 40 percent. Particularly the largest state-owned enterprises are often heavily loss-making but continue to be subsidised due to their importance as provider of essential goods and services and employer to an estimated 75 million employees. Further-more, state-owned enterprises account for 60 percent of tax revenues. Public enter-prises are controlled and managed by the State-owned Assets Supervision and Administration Commission (SASAC). The Chinese government continues to hasten privatisation efforts and due to the attractiveness of the Chinese market international interest remains high despite overwhelming problems of inefficiency.

Table 7.1
Chinese SOEs in 2004 Global Fortune 500

Company	Rank	2003 Sales USD billion
State Grid Corporation of China	46	58.348
China National Petroleum Corporation	52	56.384
China Petroleum & Chemical Corporation	54	55.062
China Mobile Communications Corporation	242	20.760
China Telecommunications Corporation	257	19.460
Sinochem Corporation	270	18.250
Shanghai Bao Steel Group Corporation	372	15.448
China National Cereals, Oils and Foodstuffs Import & Export Corporation	415	13.290

Source: Fortune Magazine; SASAC

Consequently, government ownership of the largest parts of the Chinese economy indicates the country's ability to pledge equity stakes in state-owned enterprises in case collateral would be needed to access short-term foreign currency loans during liquidity crunches. Indeed, China may be the only country in possession of an amount of industry ownership sufficient to serve as collateral alone—without the need to find different sources in order to provide security for potential liquidity sup-port. The fact that of China's larger state-owned enterprises supervised by SASAC eight feature in the 2004 Fortune 500 list of global companies may give a rough indication of the wealth the Chinese state holds in industry equity. According to the

Economist, provinces, cities and the central government in China hold shares worth over USD 240 billion in formerly state-owned enterprises[22].

7.2.2.4 Privatisation in Russia

Despite several waves of privatisation since the early 1990s, the Russian state remains majority owner of over 20 000 enterprises as of the year 2002. 15 000 are fully state-owned, while a further 5000 are joint-stock companies in which the Russian state retains a majority stake. Many of those enterprises were formerly part of Russian ministries and are today autonomously managed[23]. The largest remaining state-owned enterprises are operating in the energy, pipelines, armaments, telecommunications, railway, and banking sectors. The government officially aims to conclude its privatisation program by 2008 with state-owned enterprises to be sold-off by 2006 already. Expected receipts for government stakes are in the range of RUR 35–40 billion, highlighting the relatively limited market value of remaining ownership. However, recent developments suggest that the pace of privatisation efforts may be slowing as the Russian government seems interested in retaining and even increasing its involvement in the energy sector[24]. On September 14, 2004 Russia announced its intention to merge fully owned gas producer Rosneft into Gazprom, the world's largest gas producer; the transaction would leave the government in majority control of the combined entity.

Currently, Russia's most valuable equity stake is its USD 10 billion 38.4 percent interest in Gazprom. The company accounts for 90 percent of Russia's gas production and controls 60 percent of gas reserves; its revenues make up around 8 percent of Russia's GDP. It also holds a majority stake of 52.7 percent of RAO UES, the world's largest energy holding valued at over USD 5 billion. In the oil industry Rosneft, the largest state-owned oil producer, and Transneft, the joint-stock oil transportation company, are both fully owned by Russia's federal government. Substantial interests also remain in the banking sector, 80 percent of which is under state control; the four largest state-owned banks together control 55 percent of total deposits and 45 percent of total loans. The state's prime banking asset is USD 5 billion worth Sberbank holding around 70 percent of Russia's retail deposits. The state also owns Vneshcononbank which handles the country's foreign currency oper-

---

22 See "Hangover Cure: China Is Finally Dealing with the Share Overhang Depressing Its Stock-markets." *The Economist.* May 5, 2005

23 See Canadian Team for the Russian Public Expenditure Project. 2002. *A Taxonomy for Budgetary Control of Stated-owned Enterprises.* February 2002. http://www.globalcentres.org/html/docs/PER%20Taxonomy%20FINAL%20Feb%2028.pdf

24 See Anders Aslund. 2004. "Putin's Quest for Power is Harming Russia." *The Financial Times.* August 24, 2004

ations. However, due to weak capitalization, the market value of most other state-owned banking assets is limited.

7.2.3 Securitisation of Future Flow Receivables

Aside from pledging financial assets like sovereign bonds or equity in state-owned enterprises, a further possibility to put up collateral is the securitisation of future flow receivables. Securitisation denotes the process of repackaging cash flows from pools of assets into marketable securities. By pledging secure future cash flows, securitisation allows entities lacking collaterizable assets to nevertheless provide additional security in order to obtain loans or reduce borrowing costs. Assuming perfect capital markets, this form of financing would be of limited relevance. But given information asymmetries—particular regarding credit risk in emerging economies—securitisation of future flow receivables can help to offer borrowers in distress access to international capital[25]. The practice of securitisation was developed during the 1970s when home mortgages were pooled and structured into tradable securities which could be sold by original lenders. Key to this practice is the segregation of the cash flow generating assets from the originator in order to protect investors from any events which might impair the originator's ability to meet its debt service obligations.

Today securitisation is widely used and not restricted to cash flows from financial assets; instead, a large number of future cash flow receivables generated by a variety of different assets is being securitised. Given high credit ratings due to the stability of future cash flows and yield premia for investing in developing economies, future flow transactions are an attractive proposition for investors and can allow governments to access private capital even during liquidity crunches and periods of financial distress. However, the IMF has been highly critical of securitised future flow transactions: Their negative stance builds on possible breaches of negative pledge clauses, potential increases in future borrowing costs and an erosion in the flexibility of both future debt management and fiscal flexibility[26]. While valid regarding their use in general budget financing, these issues do not disqualify future flow transactions as one among several possibilities of pledging collateral in order to obtain emergency loans during liquidity crises.

---

25 See Chalk, Nigel. 2002. *The Potential Role for Securitizing Public Sector Revenue Flows: An Application to the Philippines*. IMF Working Paper. Washington, DC: International Monetary Fund
26 See International Monetary Fund. 2003. *Assessing Public Sector Borrowing Collaterized on Future Flow Receivables*. Paper prepared by FAD, ICM, LEG, and PDR. June 11, 2003. Washington, DC: International Monetary Fund

Securitisation of future flow receivables can be undertaken both directly and indirectly. In a typical indirect future flow securitisation, the originator, the borrowing entity, sells a pool of cash flow generating assets to a special purpose vehicle (SPV) to provide for segregation between originator and assets. The SPV then issues securities based on the cash flows generated by the pool of assets. These securities are sold to investors (the obligors) in the market and the proceeds then lent on to the originator. The SPV collects the cash flows generated by the pool of assets and services debt obligations to the obligors. Any remaining proceeds are returned to the originator. In a direct securitisation, instead of selling assets to a SPV, the originator provides an alternative guarantee to creditors that ensures preferential access to the collateralized assets. Guarantees can take several forms including pledge, charge, assignment, title retention or lien. In order to enhance security and mitigate risk, transactions involving the securitisation of future flow receivables are usual over-collateralized, sometimes several times.

A similar procedure applies when countries securitise future flow receivables to provide collateral for official sector assistance. Most commonly, future flows consist of the payments made by foreign importers in exchange for goods exported by the securitising country. In theory, all exports paid for in foreign currency and for which stable demand and pricing can be assumed are acceptable: Due to their demand characteristics natural resources like oil, gas, minerals and individual agricultural produce are particularly suited. But securitised income streams can also include receipts from the sale of airline tickets, telephone or even credit card receivables.

Trying to identify potential resources of foreign-denominated future flow receivables, national export statistics are the obvious source of information. However, in the case of a country securitising future flow receivables in order to obtain emergency loans, a limiting constraint arises in form of ownership issues. Advocating the importance of property rights for economic development, no international agency can accept any type of collateral connected with a violation of property rights. Similarly, as a country can only pledge as collateral equity stakes in state-owned enterprises, future flow export receipts eligible for securitisation can only come from state-owned assets. As a result, a large number of potential sources for export earnings securitisation cannot be utilised.

7.2.3.1 Securitising Natural Resources

As indicated above, natural resources like oil and gas but also metals and minerals are ideal commodities for the securitisation of future flow receivables due to their stable demand characteristics. However, certain agricultural produce shares these characteristics. Export earnings generated by the sale of oil and gas products serve particularly well as repayment guarantee for loans since their demand comes from a large and dispersed group of international buyers which not only ensures stable demand but also reduces buyers' pricing power. To a lesser extent the same applies to metals like gold and silver, iron, copper or nickel ores but also to minerals like fertilisers, stone and gravel, sulphur, natural abrasives. A further advantage of revenues generated by mining natural resources is the relative profitability of these enterprises. In contrast to many other industries, only a small share of export earnings received from natural resources is needed as working capital; consequently, delays in payment or potential reduction of revenues to pay for government loans do not necessary harm the operations of the enterprise.

Nevertheless, the usefulness of foreign currency earnings derived from exporting natural resources as collateral is limited by two major constraints. First, the volume of natural resource exports needs to be of considerable size, since loans to be securitised in case of financial crises often amount to several billion of U.S. dollars. Consequently, in practice volume consideration restrict the usefulness of a large number of natural resources for future flow transactions. In addition, the state must have large interests in the industries involved since it cannot pledge the export earnings of private enterprises as collateral for emergency loans. Both issues make oil and gas products the predominant commodities for use in future flow transactions.

7.2.3.1.1 The US-Mexican Framework Agreement

In contrast to the 1982 debt crisis, in 1995 Mexico recovered relatively quickly from the liquidity problems in connection with the peso's devaluation in December 1994. This outcome is widely attributed to the fast and efficient response by IMF, BIS and particularly the United States which provided massive liquidity support and so enabled Mexico to service its short-term debt obligations. In February 1995 an emergency package was arranged which consisted of a USD 17.8 billion IMF facility, USD 10 billion committed by the G-10 through the BIS and a further USD 20 billion put up unilaterally by the United States through its Exchange Stabilisation Fund. While liquidity support was conditional on a stabilisation program agreed with the IMF, the United States imposed further conditions and insisted on repayment guarantees for ESF funds.

Negotiations between the United States and Mexico led to four separate accords: The Framework Agreement provided the umbrella, outlining terms and conditions for US loans to support economic stabilisation in Mexico and included provisions for the 90-day swap arrangements between both countries. The Medium-Term Exchange Stabilization Agreement detailed terms and conditions regarding the new medium-term swap arrangements between the United States and Mexico. When buying dollars, the Mexican government had to deposit the corresponding amount of pesos into a specially created account at the Bank of Mexico. To compensate the U.S. for the risks taken, interest payments applicable were increasing with the size of swaps executed. Interest rates started at the 90-day Treasury bill rate to which a premium between 225 and 375 or more basis points could be added. The Guarantee Agreement specified the terms and conditions applicable for guarantees by the United States for debt securities issued by the Mexican government. Securities to be guaranteed by the United States had to have a maturity of under 10 years after the agreement was signed. As in the swap agreement, guarantees were subject to interest payments that increased with the amounts guaranteed. Finally, the Oil Proceeds Facility Agreement laid out in detail terms and conditions regarding the provision of repayment security in form of export receipts by state-owned oil producer Pemex which were channelled through secure U.S. accounts. Under the contract, the Mexican government agreed for Pemex to instruct its international customers to make all foreign currency payments for crude oil, petroleum products and derivatives into an account at a bank based in the United States. The U.S. bank in turn was instructed to transfer all proceeds to a specially created account in the name of the Mexican Government at the Federal Reserve Bank of New York. Instructions were non-negotiable and irrevocable. As long as debt service obligations to the United States were met, the Mexican government could freely access its account at the FRBNY. In case it missed any debt repayments, the outstanding amount could be drawn by the Treasury before any payments would be made to either Pemex or the Mexican government.

Table 7.2
Government Shares in Selected Oil & Gas Producers

Country	Company	2003 Revenues (US$ million)	Ownership (%)
Brazil	Petroleo Brasilea	38.411	55.7
Mexico	Pemex	45.240	100.0
Malaysia	Petroleam Nasional	21.430	100.0
China	China National Petroleum Corp.	56.384	100.0
China	China Petroleum & Chemical Corp.	55.062	100.0
Indonesia	Pertamina	21.780	100.0
Russia	Gazprom	12.800	38.37

Source: Company Information

The Oil Proceeds Facility Agreement can serve as a useful blue-print for future securitisation transactions by sovereign borrowers. However, in most countries circumstances are less ideal for structuring similar trans-actions. In contrast to the Mexican government, which retains 100 percent interest in oil producer Pemex, most economies have privatised the majority of assets generating large and stable foreign currency income. Even when retaining majority stakes in formerly state-owned enterprises, governments' ability to pledge cash-flows as collateral is constrained as hurting minority shareholders' interests would incur high costs in terms of reputation. Nevertheless, regarding fully state-owned enterprises, a securitisation of future flow receivables modelled along the U.S.-Mexican Framework Agreement is a realistic option. Table 7.2 provides an overview of selected sovereign stakes in oil-producing enterprises.

7.2.3.2 Securitising Alternative Foreign Currency Receivables

While securitisation transactions of future flow receivables by sovereign governments have been limited so far, future flow transactions by both public and private enterprises have been more numerous—especially in Latin America. Only 4 of 37 developing countries' future flow transactions analysed by the IMF involved a sovereign originator; all others were undertaken by state-owned enterprises[27]. Future flow securitisation is particularly attractive when enterprises have difficulties obtaining regular loans during liquidity crises. Asset-backed securitisation enables enterprises to obtain loans by allowing for higher credit ratings; given adequate securities corporate borrowers can even surpass the sovereign rating of their country of operation thereby opening access to more funds and better lending terms. Since the first transaction by Mexico's telecommunications operator in 1987, over 200 future flow transaction have been rated by major rating agencies[28]. While also possible at the sovereign level, these types of transactions are usually too small in value to provide sufficient collateral for large emergency loans. However, in combination with other collateral sources, some transactions might be of interest for governments in need to pledge collateral in order to qualify for liquidity assistance.

Again, most private sector transactions so far involved the securitisation of oil, mineral and metal receivables like Argentinean YPF's three oil-backed issues, comprising USD 400 million and rated BBB-, Brazilian Alcoa's aluminium backed placement worth also USD 400 million and rated BB- or Mexicican Grupo Mineiro's several metals-based placements involving amounts between USD 75 and

---

27 See IMF (2003): 7
28 Suhas Ketkar and Dilip Ratha. 2001. *Development Financing During a Crisis: Securitization of Future Receivables*. WB Working Paper 2582. Washington, DC: The World Bank: 13

USD 375 million rated at BB-. However, an increasing number of smaller private sector transactions involve the securitisation of alternative receivables like foreign denominated telephone and credit card receivables or workers' remittances. Securitisation of the latter appears of particular attractiveness for economies in South East Asia that lack the vast amount of natural resources available in Latin America, Central Europe and Central Asia. Instead, as countries like India, Thailand, Korea, Indonesia and the Philippines are densely populated, securitising foreign currency denominated telephone and credit card receivables may be more rewarding. But even airline ticket receipts, construction receivables, tax receipts, personal loans and mortgages have been securitised in various transactions.

Table 7.3
Collateral Preferences

Rank	Collateral
1.	Heavy Crude Oil Receivables
2.	Airline ticket receivables; telephone receivables; credit card receivables; electronic remittances
3.	Oil and gas royalties; export receivables
4.	Paper remittances
5.	Tax revenue receivables

Source: S&P; Fitch

Although almost all types of future flow receivables can be securitised, receivables generated by certain assets are preferable given specific risk characteristics. Preferences can be observed by analysing spread differentials between issues of asset backed securities. According to Ketkar and Ratha, both Standard & Poor's and Fitch rank receivables from the export of heavy crude oil highest and tax revenues at the bottom of international investors' collateral preferences[29].

7.2.3.2.1 Telephone Receivables

One of the earliest future flow receivables transactions in a developing country rated was the securitisation of Telmex telephone receivables in 1987. The transaction was structured by Citibank and allowed the Mexican telecommunication services provider to access international capital at a time when capital markets were closed to Mexican corporations as Mexico was restructuring its foreign debts. By securitising its future net international settlement receivables, Telmex was able to place an issue

---

29 See Ketkar and Ratha (2001)

of investment grade bonds with international investors. Net international settlements occur to a telephone operator when the amount of calls originating abroad but ending in its network surpasses the number of outgoing calls completed in other carriers' networks. In the case of Telmex, calls involved where primarily those between Mexico and AT&T's network in the U.S. where home calls by Mexican expatriates substantially exceeded calls into the U.S. from Mexico. In order to provide for segregation of originator and receivables, a U.S. trust was created while AT&T was notified of the transaction and instructed to pay Telmex settlement revenues into the trust's account. Further security was provided by considerable over-collateralisation[30].

In 1999 Telefonica de Peru was able to realise a similar transaction by securitizing 88 percent of its future international settlement revenues generated mostly in Japan and the United States. To provide for potential bankruptcy, foreign operators were instructed to pay invoices into a Cayman account opened by an agreed trustee who became the effective creditor. The issue was rated A- by Duff & Phelps while the credit rating of Peruvian sovereign debt did not surpass BB and that of the local currency not BBB-. However, a transaction involving receivables of Pakistans's PCTL worth USD 250 million was rated at CCC+ only. But although the Government of Pakistan was forced to reschedule its Paris Club debt, PCTL's securitised bonds performed. Due to reasons of competition, the stability of international settlement receivables is negatively related to the number of operators in the originator's economy. Consequently, securitising foreign denominated future settlement receivables is especially attractive for countries where a state-owned telecommunications company operates in a relatively monopolistic market.

7.2.3.2.2 Workers' Remittances

Next to foreign direct investment, remittances by migrant workers are the second largest source of foreign currency inflows to developing countries. In recipient countries they are a source of both direct consumption and local investment, the former being the more stable part. Compared to other capital inflows, workers' remittances have proven very stable and steadily increased—even during the Asian financial crisis when other private capital inflows fell sharply or even reversed[31]. Given increasing international mobility and migration, workers' remittances are likely to

---

30 See Stone, Charles and Anne Zissu. 1999. *Engeneering a Way around the Sovereign Ceiling*. The Securitization Conduit. Vol. 2, No. 2 & 3
31 See Dilip Ratha. 2003. *Workers' Remittances: An Important and Stable Source of Development Finance*. Global Development Finance 2003. Washington, DC: The World Bank

continue their rise. With annual workers' remittances over USD 10 billion, India is the largest developing country recipient, followed by Mexico and the Philippines.

Table 7.4
Top 10 Developing Country Receipients of
Workers' Remittances: 2004 Estimates ($ billions)

1.	India	23,0
2.	Mexico	17
3.	Philippines	8,1
4.	China	4,6
5.	Pakistan	4,1
6.	Morroco	3,6
7.	Bangladesh	3,4
8.	Colombia	3,1
9.	Egypt	3,0
10.	Brazil	2,8

Source: Global Development Finance 2005

Future flow remittances by migrant workers into their countries of origin have been securitised by the receiving financial institutions in emerging economies. In 2001 Banco Creditó de Perú was able to raise USD 100 million backed by securitised electronic payment transfer instructions. In light of the political turmoil at the time, political risk was mitigated as J. P. Morgan, Citibank, Standard Chartered and the Banks of New York and America were instructed to redirect electronic money transfers to the Peruvian bank to a trustee account established on the Bahamas. Given that Banco Creditó de Perú receives electronic money transfers from the U.S. surpassing USD 3 billion annually, the transaction led by ING Barings was significantly oversubscribed. It mirrored offerings by Banco Cuscatalan in El Salvador and Banamex in Mexico. Securities issued were awarded ratings of BBB and BBB+ respectively[32]. Also in 2001, Banco do Brazil placed securities worth USD 300 million with international investors. The issue was backed by remittances denominated in Japanese Yen and rated BBB+ by Standard & Poors, above the BB-rating awarded to Brazil's local currency.

---

32 United Nations Development Program. *Worker Remittance as an Instrument for Development* (2003). Comparative Research, December 2003. UNDP El Salvador. http://www.undp.org/surf-panama/referrals.htm

7.2.3.2.3 Credit Card Receivables

Securitisation of credit card receivables is another way of obtaining loans backed by future foreign currency earnings. Following a credit card purchase, the merchant usually presents the receipt to a local bank which pools credit card receipts. The banks acquiring those vouchers are in turn reimbursed in foreign currency by the credit card companies. In credit card receivables transactions, the transfer payments by credit card companies to local voucher-acquiring institutions are securitised. In 1998 Banco de Creditó de Peru issued USD 100 million of bonds backed by future credit card receivables from VISA. In the transaction, VISA transferred dollar payments to the Bahamas-based Banco de Credito Overseas Ltd., a SPV created to serve as trustee. The low risk structure—it included an over-collateralization of 250 percent—was awarded AAA status by S&P, considerably above Peru's sovereign credit rating of BB[33]. Given the high ratings of debt issues securitised by future credit card receivables, several similar issues were placed by Mexican banks Bancomer and Banamex; amounts involved ranged from USD 150 to USD 250 million. Similar transactions include South Africa's First Rand offering worth USD 250 million and the placement USD 100 million by Turkey's Akbank.

7.2.3.2.4 Taxing Export Earnings

If lacking state-owned assets and suitable future receivables, governments can resort to imposing a tax charge on all export earnings generated in their economy. This option appears especially attractive to economies in East Asia: Lacking large reserves of natural resources and well advanced in the process of privatisation, the economies of Korea, Malaysia and Thailand, but also those of Indonesia and the Philippines are among emerging economies' strongest exporters. Lawrence Lau and Joseph Stiglitz suggest that by imposing a surcharge of 5 percent on exports, China alone could earn annual revenues between USD 30 and USD 42 billion[34]. Imposing and securitising a surcharge on export revenues may thus allow economies facing liquidity problems to provide some form collateral in order to obtain foreign currency loans when no other assets are available for collateralisation.

While the WTO does not prohibit export taxes, a number of regional trade agreements including EU, NAFTA, CARICOM, and Mercosur have banned export duties due to efficiency and trade-distorting effects; in the United States they are even

---

33 Dilip Ratha. 2003. *Financing Development through Future-Flow Securitization.* Prem Notes No. 69. Washington, DC: The World Bank
34 Lawrence Lau and Joseph Stiglitz. 2005. "China's Alternative to Revaluation." *The Financial Times.* April 25, 2005

unconstitutional. Nevertheless, particularly in developing countries the practice of imposing export taxes is widespread. Often levies are imposed on agricultural products like on sugar in Brazil, palm oil in Indonesia or vanilla in Madagascar. Argentina earns around USD 1.5 billion per year by levying taxes on export earnings generated by its booming soy bean production[35]. Natural resources like minerals, metals or oil exports as in the case of Russia are further popular targets for imposing export duties. Nevertheless, the taxation of export earnings entails a number of problems. Most importantly, although providing a source of foreign currency revenues for the government, export taxes reduce exporters' profitability and competitiveness. This leads to a decline in economies' attractiveness to foreign direct investment and may thus entail negative welfare effects. Given the number of actors involved, the process of tax collection may be very difficult and inefficient. Furthermore, often export taxes are imposed by governments not as a short-term emergency measure, but for the long-term; motivations differ and apart from generating foreign currency revenues for the government often include price stabilization, influencing income distribution or altering resource allocation.

When export taxes are levied, trade in the commodity affected is generally reduced. Export taxes increase costs of trade and lead to a fall in supply in the world market and an increase in supply at home. For large exporting nations with pricing power, efficiency loss and reduction in trade can be out-weighted by improving terms-of-trade due to higher prices achieved in the global market. This beneficial effect does not arise for small producers whose supply decisions leave world prices unchanged. While for large exporters with pricing power in their markets the imposition of export taxes may involve both positive and negative effects on national welfare, export duties are predominantly welfare reducing for smaller developing countries. Since effects for importers are solely negative, imposition of export taxes is an extremely unpopular policy in the eyes of trading partners who may retaliate by implementing corresponding beggar-thy-neighbour policies.

The imposition of export taxes can also have strong income distribution effects within the domestic economy. Apart from affecting directly taxed goods' own markets, markets for substitutes and complimentary goods as well as for factors of production can all be influenced. Given this impact on income distribution an imposition of export taxes will generally be opposed by affected interest groups and thus difficult to implement by a democratically accountable government. These arguments apply in both the case when export taxes are imposed on all exporters equally as well as in the case when particular industries are targeted selectively— although opposition is likely to be stronger in the latter case. As argued above, for larger exporters with a dominant position in world markets, export taxes will reduce

---

35 See "Argentina's Soya Boom." *The Economist.* August 28, 2004

production and export volume thus hurting producers; domestic consumers may benefit from lower prices due to purchasing power parity effects[36]. While interest groups representing exporters will lobby against imposition, support by domestic consumers may be limited due to the likelihood of job losses as a consequence of reduced profitability in exporting enterprises.

Although export taxes are bound to have harmful effects on exporting industries in the long-term, they could be a sensible approach if restricted to the short-term. Furthermore, instruments can be devised which soften the negative impact on exporting industries for the limited period in which taxation would be necessary. One possible step in that direction would be for governments to lower domestic taxation on exporting enterprises to soften the fall of profitability a sudden introduction of export duties can entail. In this case, taxation could remain constant at the bottom line as duties normally payable in domestic currency would be substituted by duties payable in foreign currency. However, as soon as this change in the type of taxation would impede exporters' access to foreign currency funds required to continue operations, effects would be equally harmful.

Table 7.5
Potential Export Tax Revenues of Selected Exporting Nations (USD billions)

Country	2004 Merchandise Exports	Tax Rate 2.5%	Tax Rate 5%	Tax Rate 7.5%	Tax Rate 10%
China	593.3	14.8	29.7	44.5	59.3
Korea	253.8	6.3	12.7	19.0	25.4
Mexico	189.1	4.7	9.5	14.2	18.9
Russia	183.5	4.6	9.2	13.8	18.4
Malaysia	126.5	3.2	6.3	9.5	12.7
Thailand	97.4	2.4	4.9	7.3	9.7
Brazil	96.5	2.4	4.8	7.2	9.7
India	75.6	1.9	3.8	5.7	7.6
Indonesia	72.3	1.8	3.6	5.4	7.2
Philippines	39.7	1.0	2.0	3.0	4.0

Source: International Trade Statistics 2005; Own Calculations

On the other hand, a limited level of export taxes that doesn't lead to a sharp reduction of profitability in the export sector is unlikely to be sufficient. Export duties in the single-digit range will not suffice even in the case of large exporting countries for the size of emergency loans to be collateralized is usually far larger

---

36 See Roberta Piermartini. 2004. *The Role of Export Taxes in the Field of Primary Commodities.* Geneva: World Trade Organization

than the revenues generated by short-term export duties. For emerging economies like Korea or Mexico, a 2.5 percent export levy would generate foreign currency revenues of under USD 5 billion annually. At a rate of 5 percent, revenues would double, but still be less than USD 10 billion dollars. Compared to the rescue packages negotiated by the IMF during the 1990s which involved amounts in the range of USD 50 to 60 billion, these amounts seem insufficient. To match these amounts, export duties would have to be up to 50 percent or spread over several years. Both would mean at least significant cost disadvantages and more likely a destruction of large parts of countries' exporting industries. While in highly monopolistic sectors it may be possible to set very high levies, like the 500 percent duties on raw/split rattan in the case of Indonesia, in the majority of developing countries such rates are unthinkable. In the Philippines even the 6 and 4 percent levied on copra and other coconut products respectively proved excessive[37].

As in the case of alternative future flow transactions, if prudently devised, securitisation of export taxes can be a conceivable approach for the short-term. But although generating substantially more foreign currency revenues than the securitisation of future-flow receivables by state-owned enterprises, they would suffice to collateralize only a fraction of the liquidity necessary to effectively contain a crisis in the capital account. Even at tax rates of 10 percent or more, the largest emerging market exporters could provide collateral for no more than one third of the amounts required during financial crises in the last decade.

7.3 Problems Arising from the Imposition of Strict Collateral Requirements

The analysis above suggests that there are many countries which lack the type of assets that could be pledged as collateral in exchange for liquidity support. In addition, the need to provide collateral in order to access liquidity support can create incentives for countries to halt privatisation efforts widely perceived as important part of any strategy to reform developing country economies; a collateral requirement would thus contradict the policies the IMF has preached over the last decades. Countries that followed successful privatisation strategies today lack substantial collateralisable assets and would disqualify for liquidity support in case strict collateral requirements would be introduced.

Moreover, the collateralisation of state-owned assets and income streams is a complicated and cumbersome process as argued by the Meltzer Commission[38] since the procedures of how collateral pledged by sovereign borrowers could be realised remain unclear. There are neither precedents nor any provisions in international law

---

37 See Piermartini (2004): 16
38 IFIAC (2000): 44

for forcing sovereign borrowers to hand over the pledged collateral—a problem encountered not only recently. During the League of Nations' efforts to stabilise the financial system and restructure ailing economies in Central and Eastern Europe after World War I, it found itself confronted by similar problems. As Royall Tyler, representative of the League's Financial Committee in Budapest remarked:

> In particular the words pledge, security, mortgage, and guarantee may create the wrong impression ... in the mind of the holder. A moment's reflection makes it clear that the implementation of such pledges cannot be achieved in the same conditions ... as in a domestic loan, unless the pledged assets or revenues are situated outside the national territory of the borrower[39].

Given these difficulties, the introduction of a collateral requirement for international emergency loans has found limited support in contemporary debates regarding IMF reform. Stanley Fischer argued that the Fund's preferred creditor status does in practice serve the collateral function of securing repayment[40]. On similar grounds, although both Alan Meltzer and Charles Calomiris originally argued in favour of collateral requirements, the Meltzer Report did not endorse them and settled with the demand that borrowers must *give the IMF explicit legal priority with respect to all other creditors, secured and unsecured. Member countries that default on their IMF debts would not be eligible for loans or grants from other multilateral agencies or other member countries.* Negative pledge clauses without strict exclusion of the IMF would not be permitted[41]. In a hearing on the final report of the Meltzer Commission in March 2000, Charles Calomiris declared that

> The Commission considered the costs and benefits of requiring physical collateral and determined that this was too limiting a requirement. For many countries, collateral would be hard to pledge, and requiring such collateral might even discourage privatization of important exporting sectors. Furthermore, what is really essential is that IMF claims be senior, which the Commission was able to ascertain could be accom-

---

39 Cited in Marc Flandreau (Ed.). 2003. *Money Doctors. The Experience of International Financial Advising 1850–2000.* New York, NY: Routledge

40 See Stanley Fischer. 2000. *Presentation to the International Financial Institution Advisory Commission.* February 2, 2000. Washington, DC: International Monetary Fund http://www.imf.org/external/np/speeches/2000/020200.htm

41 IFIAC (2000): 44–45

plished without the pledging of collateral, so long as loan amounts were limited and legal protections were in place[42].

The analysis above supports this view. At the international level, Bagehot's collateral requirement for a lender of last resort seems impossible to satisfy. Although there is a wide variety of potential sources for providing some sort of collateral in exchange for foreign currency loans, the amounts necessary for effective liquidity assistance are too large to be fully collateralized by most developing economies, even if all potential sources would be tapped simultaneously. Only countries in possession of substantial reserves of valuable natural resources, almost predominantly oil and gas, could possibly provide enough collateral to qualify for sufficient amounts of international liquidity assistance. If strict collateral requirements would be imposed by an international lender of last resort, less than a handful of emerging economies would be able to access international liquidity assistance in times of crisis. Hence a strict collateral requirement could exclude even fundamentally solvent countries from international assistance in case they lack suitable assets to pledge as collateral. Moreover, as argued by Anna Schwartz[43], countries that own assets suitable for collateralization should often be able to obtain loans from commercial sources as the function of providing loans against adequate collateral is generally satisfactorily filled by the private sector: Based on this premise involvement by the official sector may at best be unnecessary while potentially crowding out private sector solutions.

7.4 Implications for the Viability of an International Lender of Last Resort

The fact that strict collateral requirements are not feasible when dealing with developing country borrowers in balance-of-payment crises does not render the concept of an international lender of last resort unviable. The collateral requirement's most central function, to serve as quick solvency test in order to ensure that emergency loans are only advanced to fundamentally solvent institutions, can be provided by alternative instruments. Its second function, the security function, is less relevant when dealing with sovereign borrowers:

For one, if able to repay official sector loans, sovereign debtors in the vast majority of cases will choose to do so. Moreover, the effectiveness of collateral to ensure loan repayment at the international level is limited. As argued earlier, the

---

42 See Calomiris, Charles. 2000. *Prepared Testimony of Dr. Charles W. Calomiris*. Hearing on the Final Report of the International Financial Institution Advisory Commission. March 9, 2000. Washington, DC: Senate Banking Committee

43 See Anna J. Schwartz. 1999. "Is There a Need for an International Lender of Last Resort?" *Cato Journal*. Vol. 19, No. 1: 6

sovereignty of states poses difficulties for the realisation of collateral in case of default. Countries are neither likely nor should they be desired to resume the practice of going to war on debt issues not uncommon a century earlier. Securitisation transactions could circumvent this problem but were shown to be insufficient in terms of quantity. As such, repayment of sovereign debt ultimately depends on the willingness of the sovereign borrower. Several reasons account for the general willingness of sovereign debtors to meet their debt service obligations. The two most important are the aversion of states to become a pariah to the international community and the fear of loosing access to international capital markets. These motivations provide strong enough incentives for the vast majority of countries to do everything in their means to repay their debts, particularly to the official sector. That they are able to repay their debts can be ensured by a solvency test that does not require the existence of collateral.

In contrast, the collateral's function as instrument facilitating assessments of borrowers' solvency status is essential since an effective lender of last resort should restrict its assistance to illiquid, but fundamentally solvent economies. While the ability to put up collateral can be no more than a rough indicator since it does not necessarily imply solvency, it allows for timely lending decisions. However, collateral requirements are not the only instrument to provide a rough indication of borrowers' solvency. Two alternative approaches can achieve similar results: The first is the conditionality approach currently employed by the IMF. Experiences made in a number of emerging economies have shown that this approach involves severe costs in terms of institutional effectiveness and legitimacy. The second approach is pre-qualification and will be discussed in the following chapter.

8. Pre-qualification

Pre-qualification or ex-ante conditionality aims at determining whether liquidity assistance would be an effective instrument to address individual financial crises ex-ante. It entails the definition of a set of conditions which if met are taken as indicator that a country faces a liquidity rather than a solvency crisis. Regarding the lending practice of an international lender of last resort a pre-qualification or ex-ante conditionality approach implies that only countries meeting pre-qualification requirements would be eligible for large-scale liquidity assistance by the official sector. Countries that fail to meet these requirements would be refused exceptional access to official sector funds; instead, they would be assisted in restructuring their debts to sustainable levels and in reforming their financial sectors. In this respect pre-qualification can serve as a substitute for the regulatory powers central banks or supervisory authorities hold over the financial sector in national economies that are lacking at an international level.

8.1 Advantages of Pre-qualification

For deciding under what circumstances large-scale liquidity assistance by the official sector is an effective instrument, pre-qualification is preferable to both strict collateral requirements and to the Fund's current policy of ex-post conditionality. Strict collateral requirements are on grounds of practicability infeasible as argued in the previous chapter. While providing incentives for economic and financial reform, ex-post conditionality renders effective liquidity assistance to crisis countries very difficult. Since Fund-approved stability programs require lengthy negotiations between IMF and the crisis country, a timely disbursal of liquidity assistance is almost impossible. In addition, insofar as the Fund insists on specific conditions opposed by the crisis country, conditionality can severely undermine the ownership felt by national authorities regarding corresponding stability programs.

Pre-qualification or ex-ante conditionality has several advantages over the Fund's ex-post conditionality approach: For one, it provides stronger incentives for countries to pursue prudent economic and financial policies than current IMF lending policy. Moreover, countries are not more likely to reverse their policies after receiving assistance under a pre-qualification approach than under ex-post conditionality. In contrast to the latter, ex-ante conditionality provides countries with incentives for reform and sustainable policies not only when they experience liquidity problems, but also before. Being aware that unless meeting pre-qualification criteria no international support would be forthcoming, countries are more likely to aim at achieving minimum standards of financial stability which in turn reduce the likelihood of financial crises developing in the first place. Additional incentives come from financial markets since countries qualifying for international liquidity assistance would be able to borrow at better terms than those failing to meet pre-qualification requirements. Most likely, private sector capital flows would concentrate on those countries which qualify and so reduce the likelihood of violent capital flow reversals in more vulnerable economies.

In contrast to the terms and conditions imposed by the IMF during negotiations on stability packages, pre-qualification would be voluntary. Countries would be free to opt against qualification and for more risky or costly economic and financial policies. This is important as it is unlikely that emerging economies will continue to accept the Fund's intrusion into their sovereign right of economic policy-making. Since 1998 most Asian economies have amassed large amounts of foreign currency reserves with the explicit aim of evading dependence on IMF funds should financial difficulties arise in the future[1].

Moreover, it is hard to imagine that sovereignty-conscious countries like China, whose importance for global financial stability increases by the day, would put up with being seen as bowing to foreign pressure even if liquidity assistance by the official sector should be required at some point in the future. When trying to persuade Chinese leaders to implement reforms that would increase the stability of their financial system, a tactic of embarrassment and bullying as utilized on Japan in the 1990s is bound to prove ineffective[2]. The soft-power approach employed by John Snow to persuade China to abandon its currency's peg with the dollar underlines that this finding has already gained entrance into policy-maker circles in the Treasury[3]. By opting to meet pre-qualification requirements, countries could implement policy reforms to ensure access to official sector liquidity assistance without having to accept intrusions into their sovereignty or being seen as conforming to foreign demands.

---

1 An alternative explanation of the strong increase in international reserves suggests they are best explained as by-product of mercantilist trade policies. According to this view countries do not voluntarily hoard reserves to self-insure against sudden stops but inevitably accumulate them in their efforts to promote exports by slowing the domestic currency's appreciation against other currencies. See Michael Dooley, David Folkerts-Landau and Peter Garber. 2003. *An Essay on the Revised Bretton Woods System.* NBER Working Paper No. 9971. Cambridge, MA: National Bureau of Economic Research. However, empirical evidence clearly supports an explanation in terms of precautionary self-insurance. See Joshua Aizenman and Jaewoo Lee. 2005. *International Reserves: Precautionary vs. Mercantilist Views, Theory and Evidence.* IMF Working Paper WP/05/198. Washington, DC: International Monetary Fund

2 Discussing China's cooperation during the Asian Crisis, former Secretary of Treasury Robert Rubin concurs with this assessment by arguing that putting pressure on Chinese leaders would have proved ineffective. See Rubin (2004): 227

3 See Andrew Balls. 2005. "The US Diplomacy behind China's Revaluation." *Financial Times.* July 24, 2005

Abandoning ex-post conditionality would also increase the Fund's standing in many other parts of the world. Resentments have focussed particularly on the contractionary fiscal and monetary policies that were imposed by the IMF and perceived as causing excessive hardship in the countries concerned. Indeed, during the Asian Crisis, countries like Thailand, Indonesia and South Korea had weak bargaining positions when negotiating stability programs with the IMF. Being dependent on quick IMF assistance to evade default, they agreed on many policy conditions they deeply resented; under different circumstances these countries' governments would have rejected external involvement into their sovereign prerogative to formulate economic policy. It is indicative of the sentiment at the time that Korea's minister of finance Lim Chang Yuel, after agreeing to the terms proposed by the IMF in exchange for the USD 58 billion rescue package, stepped to the cameras and stated:

> I have come here to beg the forgiveness of the Korean people... Please understand the necessity of the economic pain we must bear and over-come... These pains and burdens are the cost our economy has inevitably to pay to revive and to recover our lowered credibility in the world financial society[4].

Furthermore, the Fund has been widely perceived as fostering U.S. foreign policy objectives and representing the interests of U.S. financial institutions. The strong pressure the Treasury exerted on IMF staff to include in its policy conditions financial sector opening—particularly for foreign brokerages—has fuelled this sentiment considerably[5] as did the rumours that strict austerity measures imposed on Indonesia at least partially served the purpose of creating political instability and remove Suharto from power. Legitimacy of the IMF, essential to discharge its monitoring and supervisory responsibilities, would strongly benefit from an end to the intrusions in the sovereign prerogatives of its members. The less distrust there is regarding the Fund's legitimacy, the more transparent will countries be regarding the economic and financial state of their economies.

Most importantly, and in contrast to conditionality lending, pre-qualification would allow for timely decisions and an immediate payout of emergency loans; both would considerably increase the efficiency and effectiveness of international liquidity assistance. Rescue programs during the Asian Crisis were agreed following long and cumbersome negotiations. While IMF and borrowing countries argued over

---

4 See Andrew Pollack. 1997. "Package of Loans Worth $55 Billion Is Set for Korea." *The New York Times.* December 4, 1997 and Paul Blustein and Sandra Sugawara. 1997. "Seoul Accepts $55 Billion Bailout Terms." *The Washington Post.* December 4, 1997
5 See Blustein (2001): 145

policy conditions, exchange rates continued to fall, making it even harder for resident banks to meet foreign-currency denominated debt service obligations without external assistance. And since emergency loans were paid out in tranches upon meeting specific mile-stones of reform, rescue efforts and emergency loans were slow in mitigating panic and uncertainty. Ex-ante conditionality would allow for emergency loans to be provided to eligible countries instantly and upfront; lengthy negotiations would become unnecessary. Calomiris concurs that

> The current IMF formula of taking weeks or months to negotiate terms and conditions for liquidity assistance, and then offering that assistance in stages over a long period of time, simply is a non-starter if the goal is to mitigate or prevent liquidity crises … If the IMF is to focus on liquidity assistance, and if liquidity assistance is to be effective, there is no viable alternative to having countries prequalify for lines of credit[6].

8.2 Pre-qualification Criteria

For liquidity assistance to be effective, economies must be fundamentally healthy during non-crisis times. Otherwise, liquidity assistance by the international community would at best postpone financial crises and more likely prevent an inevitable restructuring from being undertaken on time. If sovereign debt is at unsustainable levels, short-term liquidity assistance cannot prevent an eventual default but only prolong the period until the necessary process of debt restructuring commences. Similarly, unless financial institutions are fundamentally solvent in spite of liquidity problems, short-term loans would not prevent an eventual default but only bail-out banks' creditors. Finally, if the financial sector lacks fundamental regulatory and data dissemination standards, national central banks cannot ensure that loans are advanced to solvent institutions only. International funds could instead be misappropriated by bailing-out creditors of insolvent banks thereby increasing incentives for both creditors and debtors to resort to irresponsible lending and borrowing practices. As a consequence, the likelihood of a collapse of the financial sector would not be reduced but heightened.

Pre-qualification or ex-ante conditionality as approach to determine which countries should receive liquidity assistance requires the definition of clear and concise pre-qualification criteria. This is essential not only for the official sector to reach its lending decisions on time but also for countries to introduce reforms in order to become eligible. To allow for monitoring and transparency, requirements for pre-

---

6 See Charles Calomiris. 2000. "When Will Economics Guide IMF and World Bank Reforms?" *Cato Journal.* Vol. 20, No. 1: 87

qualification should be few and easy to assess not only by IMF staff but also by international investors. Due to reasons of legitimacy and acceptance, pre-qualification criteria must also refrain from excessively infringing on sovereign prerogatives on economic policy. As a consequence of the latter, pre-qualification requirements suggested below exclude a requirement to refrain from fixed currency regimes. Likewise, pre-qualification requirements do not include demands regarding budget deficits as suggested by the Meltzer Commission. Instead, they concentrate on financial transparency, the stability of the banking sector and the sustainability of sovereign indebtedness.

8.2.1 Transparency Criteria

The existence of accurate, detailed and timely financial and economic information is of vital importance for the functioning of international capital markets. Almost every proposal to reform the international financial architecture stresses the importance of increasing transparency and disclosure of the financial position of both the financial sector and government finances. Requests for improved data dissemination feature prominently in financial reform reports issued by both G-10 and G-22. Following the Asian Crisis the IMF introduced a number of initiatives regarding standards of transparency and data dissemination: As of 2004, 380 Reports on the Observance of Standards and Codes (ROCS) have been filed by 79 countries. 57 out of 184 IMF member countries have subscribed to Special Data Dissemination Standards (SDDS)[7]. In addition to IMF, OECD and the World Bank, issuing bodies include the International Accounting Standards Committee (IASC), the Basle Committee on Banking Supervision (BCBS), the Financial Action Task Force (FATF) and the International Organisation of Securities Commissions.

   Detailed and accurate financial information alone cannot prevent financial crises, but it facilitates monitoring efforts by regulators, financial sector watchdogs and other government agencies; as a consequence, destabilizing developments can be determined at an early stage and addressed more effectively. Regarding the private sector, financial transparency allows for more informed decision-making by both local and international investors. For emerging economies increased financial transparency is necessary to attract capital inflows from abroad to finance investment. For individual institutions an increase in accuracy and timeliness of financial information allows for better assessment of portfolio risk. The need for improved financial information applies not only to government finances and financial institu-

---

7   Benu Schneider. 2004. *The Road to International Financial Stability: Are Key Financial Standards the Answer?* Presentation held at the IMF Book Forum "Standards and Codes: Can they Prevent Financial Crises?" May 27, 2004. Washington, DC: International Monetary Fund

tions, but also entails the adherence to internationally acceptable standards of accounting and auditing as well as quarterly reporting by public companies in general[8].

Increased transparency and disclosure regarding the financial sector is of particular importance given banks' close linkages with the real economy. In order to effectively provide liquidity assistance to the banking sector, central banks require detailed and accurate information regarding the capitalisation of financial institutions. A lack of transparency poses difficulties for discriminating between solvent and insolvent institutions, often enabling insolvent banks to survive and weaken both healthier competitors and the banking systems as a whole. The success of the international community in providing emergency assistance to countries facing liquidity crises also depends on the availability of detailed and timely financial information. Because it cannot advance liquidity support and monitor emerging market banks directly, it has to rely on national central banks' ability to responsibly discharge their function as lender of last resort in adherence to Bagehot's principles.

However, the quest for increased transparency and accuracy in financial reporting, particularly regarding the financial sector, is not a novelty and numerous attempts and declarations of intent have been passed with limited effect. Sufficient levels of transparency are difficult to achieve and even industrial economies face a continuous struggle in this respect. In developing countries a high level of corruption often further exacerbates the problem making efforts to increase financial transparency even harder. Matching Moody's Bank Financial Strength Ratings (BFSR) with Transparency International's Corruption Perceptions Index (CPI) yields a positive correlation: The more corrupt a country is according to the CPI, the less stable are its banks and thus its whole financial sector[9].

To assess the degree of financial sector stability detailed information regarding debt obligations of the financial sector and the sovereign itself is essential. Dissemination of financial data must thus entail the provision of accurate information on bank debt's maturity structure and currency exposure. Regarding governments, financial transparency requires full disclosure of both sovereign and publicly guaranteed debt, both on and off the balance sheet. Two additional issues are important in this respect: The first regards the question whether disclosure by banks and financial institutions provides adequate information on non-performing loans within individual banks' portfolios since undisclosed non-performing loans were a key factor contributing to the Asian Crisis. Reported capital in financial statements

---

8 Eichengreen (1999): 80
9 See Jerome Fons. 1999. "Improving Transparency in Asian Banking Systems." In Hunter et al. 1999. *The Asian Financial Crisis: Origins, Implications, and Solutions.* Boston, MA: Kluwer Academic Publishers

should further resemble economic capital closely: if accounting rules allow the use of book instead of market values to measure asset values, the meaningfulness of financial statements is severely curtailed[10].

The more information and the higher transparency regarding financial and economic conditions of private and public sector borrowers, the more efficient markets can function and regulators discharge their monitoring responsibilities. In this respect, there can never be enough transparency. But there are minimum standards of transparency and disclosure that are essential for the international monetary system to function at all. Providing this necessary level of information regarding financial and economic conditions should be required for countries to qualify for large-scale liquidity assistance during capital account crises. However, as transparency highlights weaknesses and vulnerabilities, increasing it during confidence crises may prove fatal. Instead, efforts to increase transparency should be implemented in periods of stability. Establishing adequate standards of data dissemination as pre-qualification requirement creates incentives for countries to improve transparency before a crisis develops. A minimum level of data dissemination must allow national authorities, international investors and the international community to assess the stability of a country's economy. It must allow for painting a realistic picture of the financial sector's vulnerability to external shocks and of the sustainability of sovereign indebtedness.

Regarding the financial sector, a minimum level of disclosure needs to include accurate information on the following areas: non-performing loans as a portion of total assets and corresponding provisions, capitalisation and solvency ratios, country-by-country asset breakdowns, external liabilities, and banking sector profitability. These disclosure requirements correspond with the set of indicators deemed most important by the G-22 Working Group on Transparency and Accountability to assess financial sector vulnerability to external and internal shocks[11]. National monetary or supervisory authorities should gather the information from individual banks and other financial institutions and timely publish the data aggregated for the whole financial sector. In addition, national authorities should demand resident banks to contribute to the Bank of International Settlements' *International Banking Statistics*.

Data dissemination requirements for the public sector must provide comprehensive information on sovereign indebtedness and foreign currency reserves with particular emphasis on the short-term. Consequently, national authorities

---

10   Eric Rosengreen. 1999. "Will Greater Disclosure and Transparency Prevent the Next Banking Crisis?" In Hunter et al. 1999. *The Asian Financial Crisis: Origins, Implications, and Solutions*. Boston, MA: Kluwer Academic Publishers: 371
11   See Group of 22 (1998): 9

should be required to disseminate on time reserve statements on a monthly basis as suggested by the G-22 Working Group[12]. Reserve statements should include two sets of information: First, foreign currency assets of immediate availability to national authorities excluding any reserves pledged as collateral or tied up in hedging transactions. Second, they must provide comprehensive data on the full amount of short-term foreign currency obligations owned by the government, the central bank or other public entities able to draw on the country's stock of foreign currency reserves. Public external debt figures must include off-balance sheet items like forward contract obligations or foreign currency credit line commitments to private sector institutions. Despite the relevance of short-term data, adequate transparency also requires the dissemination of a country's overall level of external indebtedness; otherwise, an assessment on the sustainability of a country's total external obligations is impossible. Consequently, the dissemination of a country's international investment position should be made compulsory[13].

To a large extent, these transparency requirements are comprised in the Special Data Dissemination Standard devised in 1996 by the IMF as a guidance regarding the adequate provision to the public of economic and financial information by countries seeking to access international capital markets. Since 1996, it has been revised several times with the fifth and last review completed in July 2003. The SDDS provides financial and economic information on a country's real economy as well as on the public, financial and external sectors. It defines 18 data categories and prescribes best practice regarding coverage, timeliness and periodicity of as well as public access to financial and economic data; in addition, it defines provisions for both integrity and quality of the disseminated data. Although commitment to the standard is voluntary, over 60 countries have already subscribed. Apart from OECD countries, subscribers include the vast majority of larger emerging economies. With technical assistance by the World Bank and regional development banks, most developing countries should be able to fulfil the standard's transparency requirements following a transitional period. Eligibility to international liquidity assistance should therefore require countries to subscribe to the Fund's Special Data Dissemination Standards.

---

12 See Group of 22 (1998): 16
13 An IIP functions as a country's balance sheet regarding external assets and liabilities. It includes full information on a country's claims and liabilities on non-residents as well as monetary gold and SDRs. In combination with a record of balance of payment transactions, it comprises the set of an economy's international accounts.

8.2.2 Criteria Ensuring Financial Sector Stability

The importance of effective financial sector regulation stems from the impact that bank failures can have on the real economy. Countries with fundamentally healthy financial sectors are far less likely to suffer economic contraction as a consequence of significant currency depreciation. The reason is that in a healthy banking sector the majority of banks is not excessively vulnerable to sudden stops or currency deprecation due to prudent debt structures and limited foreign currency exposure[14]. As pre-qualification requirement, adequate financial sector regulation aims at ensuring that large-scale liquidity assistance will not be disbursed to sovereign borrowers with excessively vulnerable financial sectors. Banks' compliance with regulatory standards indicates that in spite of short-term liquidity problems the financial sector is fundamentally healthy while the existence of regulatory requirements enhances the capacity of central banks to distinguish between solvent and insolvent financial institutions.

Liquidity assistance is an effective instrument only if financial sectors are fundamentally healthy during non-crisis periods. If banks hold too risky loan portfolios and exhibit unsustainable debt structures, they are excessively vulnerable to external shocks. A limited number of creditors refusing to roll-over loans or a few borrowers defaulting on their debt service obligations may be enough to cause insolvency. Debt structures involving high currency and maturity mismatches heighten this risk. To reduce the banking sector's vulnerability to external shocks, national regulators and central banks utilize various instruments. Three are essential to safeguard that banks operating in the domestic financial sector are fundamentally healthy: Capital adequacy requirements, cash reserve requirements and the existence of a deposit insurance scheme. Empirical evidence further suggests that opening financial sectors to foreign competition leads to an increase in banking sector stability.

Designing an effective system of financial sector regulation is a task for specialists and beyond the scope of this analysis. Furthermore, financial sectors in emerging economies differ widely in their stage of development and depth of their capital markets. As a result, one-size-fits-all approaches to financial sector regulation are unlikely to be effective in the case of developing countries and emerging economies.

---

14 See Piti Disyatat. 2001. *Currency Crises and the Real Economy: The Role of Banks.* IMF Working Paper WP/01/49. Washington, DC: International Monetary Fund

8.2.2.1 Capital Adequacy Requirements

Capital adequacy requirements are essential to ensure that financial institutions are strong enough to survive short-term liquidity crunches in the money market. They do so by establishing minimum ratios of capital to total assets. Risk-based capital standards limit banks' ability to allocate too large a part of their deposits in risky investments by defining a minimum capital requirement in terms of risk-weighted assets. At the same time capital adequacy requirements ensure a certain degree of private sector monitoring via the control exerted by the owners of equity capital. Definition and implementation of adequate capital requirements and regulation of banks' asset composition are therefore of central importance to limit financial sector vulnerability. Eligibility to international liquidity assistance should require domestic banking regulators to define and enforce credible and transparent capital adequacy standards for banks operating in their financial sectors.

Defining appropriate capital adequacy standards is a complex task in industrial countries; it is even more complex in developing countries and emerging market economies. When implemented in 2006, the Basel Committee on Banking Supervision's regulatory framework will go a long way to increase financial sector stability in the G-10+, the world's major industrial countries. However, the framework is designed to address primarily the regulatory needs in advanced industrial economies. Implementation of the revised framework for *International Convergence of Capital Measurement and Capital Standards* requires a high degree of financial sector development, and in particular strong supervisory and regulatory capacities. While industrialised countries generally meet these requirements, the majority of developing countries do not. On average, industrial countries meet around 19 of the 30 Basel Core Principles on Effective Banking Supervision (BCP)[15]; the corresponding number for developing countries is just 7.

In order to increase financial sector stability in developing countries, an adequate capital framework must take into account the specific characteristics of developing countries' financial systems. Consequently, a universal implementation of Basel II is problematic. Instead, the Basel framework should be adapted to allow for implementation in less developed financial systems and specific counterproductive aspects of the framework eliminated.

In contrast to the capital adequacy standard of 8 percent suggested in Basel II, adequate minimum capital requirements for developing countries should be considerably higher, ideally in a range of 10 to 15 percent. Higher capital requirements are justified on two accounts: One the one hand the volatility of returns is much

---

15 Andrew Powell. 2004. *Basel II and Developing Countries: Sailing through a Sea of Standards.* World Bank Policy Research Working Paper 3387. Washington, DC: The World Bank

higher in developing than in industrial countries. On the other, supervisory capabilities in developing countries are generally lower than in advanced industrial economies. IMF research suggests that the less effective supervisory authorities, the higher capital requirements are necessary to increase financial sector stability[16]. The application of Basel II to banks in developing countries and emerging economies would thus result in less bank protection than in industrial countries. Majnoni, Miller and Powell have shown that protection resulting from applying the Basel II internal ratings based approach (IRB) to a sample of non-G10 economies is in a range between 95 and 99 percent while the level of protection advised by the Basel Committee is at 99.9 percent[17]. Partly, the divergence is due to differences in loan portfolio quality between advanced and less advanced economies; this implies that the IRB approach struggles to correctly model default risks in loan portfolios held by emerging market banks. In order to achieve a protection level of 99.9 percent while maintaining the IRB approach would require minimum capital requirements of around 15 percent for a sample of Latin American economies[18]. Given the various degrees of economic and financial development in Latin America, this finding is likely to also apply to developing countries in other parts of the world.

An alternative to higher capital requirements than suggested by the Basel Committee is to modify the IRB foundational approach to resemble default risk inherent in developing country banks' loan portfolios more closely. But even when adjusting the IRB foundational approach, for developing countries a higher minimum capital requirement may still be advisable. Beneficial effects of signalling prudent bank regulation alone might render higher capital requirements a sensible proposition. As financial sectors develop and deepen, capital requirements could be reviewed and set closer to the level suitable for developed countries. Indeed, before its default in 2001 Argentina had a minimum capital requirement of 11.5 percent that in combination with additional requirements effectively approached 15 percent. Although higher capital requirements reduce banks' profitability, financial sector regulation in Argentina was widely hailed as exemplary at the time.

Regulation must provide clear guidelines on how banks should estimate their capital adequacy requirements. Basel II allows for two methodologies: The Standardised Approach and the Internal Ratings-Based Approach. The latter allows international banks to use their own system of risk management subject to certain

---

16 See Elina Ribakova. 2005. *Liberalization, Prudential Supervision, and Capital Requirements: The Policy Trade-Offs.* IMF Working Paper WP/05/136. Washington, DC: International Monetary Fund

17 Giovanni Majnoni, Margaret Miller and Andrew Powell. 2004. *Bank Capital and Loan Loss Reserves under Basel II: Implications for Latin America and Carribbean Countries.* World Bank Policy Research Working Paper 3437. Washington, DC: The World Bank: 11

18 Majnoni, Miller and Powell (2004): 12

minimum conditions and disclosure requirements. It can be applied in two forms: A foundational and an advanced IRB approach[19]. The Standardised Approach instead provides specific rules on the calculation of credit risk[20]. Given generally limited supervisory capabilities in emerging markets, a standardized approach similar to the one laid out in Basel II may be preferable for most developing country financial institutions. Indeed, the majority of banks operating in emerging economies are unlikely to qualify for the use of either IRB approach.

The Basel II Standardised Approach is unsuitable for emerging economies due to a number of reasons. One relates to the valuation of risk arising from loans to the government. By attaching a zero risk weighting on loans to the government, Basel II encourages banks to concentrate lending activities on the sovereign to the detriment of the private sector. While sovereign debt of industrial countries can usually be assumed safe, in developing countries government debt is often more risky, even if denominated in local currency. The Basel Standardized Approach further relies heavily on risk estimates by external rating agencies. But the coverage of private sector institutions by major external rating agencies is limited for most developing economies; moreover, the fact that external rating agencies receive fees by the institutions they rank naturally entails conflicts of interest. These problems are exacerbated at rating agencies operating solely in their domestic market since the pressure to provide positive ratings in order to stay in business is even higher.

An adequate approach to estimate capital requirements must address such problems and be designed to suit the specific risks faced by banks operating in developing or emerging economies. As such, particularly exchange-rate related credit risks should be incorporated in risk assessments. In addition, strict rules regarding adequate loan-loss provisions are necessary since insufficient loan-loss provisioning severely constrains the protective capabilities of capital requirements[21]. Exchange rate risks from foreign-denominated loans to the non-tradable sector are an additional source of vulnerability, particularly in case of lacking adequate loan-loss provisioning: When a borrower defaults as a consequence of currency depreciation, bank capital has to absorb the loss which further reduces the buffer necessary to ward of market risks[22].

Given the various degrees of financial sector depth and liquidity in developing economies, it is impossible to define a one-size-fits-all standard for capital adequacy

---

19 See Basel Committee on Banking Supervision (2004): 48–112
20 See Basel Committee on Banking Supervision (2004): 12–47
21 See Michelle Cavallo and Giovanni Majnoni. 2001. *Do Banks Provision for Bad Loans in Good Times? Empirical Evidence and Policy Implications.* World Bank Policy Research Working Paper 2619. Washington, DC: The World Bank
22 See Liliana Rojas-Suarez. 2001. *Can International Capital Standards Strengthen Banks in Emerging Markets?* Washington, DC: Institute for International Economics: 33

requirements. A one size-fits-all approach cannot account for the different degrees of financial sector development in developing countries and emerging economies. Hence capital adequacy requirements should be tailored to countries as close as possible. While the minimum capital requirement of 10 to 15 percent would be the same for all, the approach employed to determine capital requirements would depend on the degree of financial sector development. Following Powell's framework[23], the degree of a country's compliance with Basel Core Principles would be the central factor determining the adequate method of capital measurement. Other factors would include the development of the external rating sector, the depth of domestic capital markets and the level of loan-loss provisioning.

For countries failing to comply with a minimum of BCPs adopting Basel II capital standards would be ineffective. Such countries could be required to comply with the original Basel I standard while concentrating their efforts on improving their financial sectors and fulfilling the requirements of Pillar 2 and 3 of the revised Basel framework. Countries in compliance with more BCPs and working towards full Pillar 2 and Pillar 3 compliance would derive appropriate capital requirements by applying a Simplified Standardized Approach. Countries in compliance with even more BCPs and Pillars 2 and 3, would adopt a standard close to Basel II's Standardized approach. Finally, emerging economies with more advanced financial sectors could apply a Centralized-Ratings-Based Standard that would give banks a certain degree of freedom while not requiring regulatory and supervisory capabilities necessary for monitoring Basel II IRB standards. Both foundational and advanced IRB standards are appropriate for countries with effective systems of supervision and regulation only and thus of limited relevance for most developing countries. Applicable standards could be determined under annual Article IV consultations with the IMF.

The Basle Committee attached particular importance to market discipline as an instrument to increase financial sector stability. The issuance of uninsured and subordinated debt securities by financial institutions could enhance private sector monitoring of banks' lending policies significantly. The recommendations made by the Meltzer Commission[24] explicitly highlight the subordinated debt requirement as a core building block of adequate minimum capital standards as did an earlier proposal by Calomiris[25]. While markets can play an important role in identifying and highlighting irresponsible banking practices, market discipline requires a certain depth of capital markets to operate. Given this depth, a subordinated debt requirement is an effective regulatory instrument. If a minimum level of depth is lacking,

---

23 See Powell (2004): 28–29
24 See International Financial Institutions Advisory Commission (2000): 47
25 See Calomiris (1998): 8–10

subordinated debt requirements are ineffective. Accordingly, the issuance of subordinated debt seems unsuitable as universal pre-qualification criterion for all developing economies. However, it may be made compulsory for countries adopting more advanced capital standards like CRB or IRB approaches.

8.2.2.2 Minimum Reserve Requirements

In contrast to capital adequacy requirements which attempt to ensure responsible lending practices and improve banks' resilience to external shocks, minimum reserve requirements address liquidity problems specifically. The need for minimum reserves is a consequence of fractional reserve banking. Every bank operating under a system of fractional reserves holds a certain amount of cash reserves to repay depositors and transact daily operations. The higher the cash reserve, the longer a bank can repay depositors in case of a bank run. While strengthening a banks' liquidity position, minimum reserve requirements have no effect on medium and long-term solvency. A bank can be faced with more liabilities than assets while maintaining sufficient cash reserves in the short run. While higher cash reserves increase the protection of banks against liquidity problems, at the same time they carry the opportunity costs of business foregone. Hence banks have incentives to maintain as low a level of cash reserves as possible. Minimum reserve requirements specify a mandatory amount of reserves to be laid aside by banks to protect against unexpected liquidity problems. To evade tedious supervisory efforts minimum reserve requirements are usually held in accounts at the central bank.

In order to improve the capacity of financial institutions to cope with sudden bank runs, the implementation of a minimum cash reserve requirement of 15 percent should be required to qualify for large-scale liquidity assistance by the official sector. This minimum reserve would not necessarily have to be kept at the domestic central bank in full, but could be held partially at foreign commercial banks thereby allowing to keep a portion of reserves at arms length from the government while earning market interest. Alternatively, a portion of reserve requirements could be secured by standby agreements allowing domestic banks to make use of their deposits in exchange for a fee paid to foreign providers of standby credit.

In a well functioning and effectively regulated financial system minimum reserves have become dispensable as central banks can fully provide for most liquidity needs. While the United States still maintain a minimum reserve requirement of 10 percent of transaction deposits, the majority of G-7 countries over time reduced minimum reserve requirements to a range between 1.0 and 2.5 percent. However, other countries operate with substantially higher ratios such as Argentina with an up to 20 or Russia with an up to 14 percent minimum reserve requirement.

Only Canada has abolished minimum reserve requirements entirely. Given high economic and financial volatility, minimum reserve requirements are a sensible regulatory tool to increase the stability of banks operating in emerging economies, specifically of those accepting foreign currency deposits.

The main justification for demanding minimum reserve requirements in addition to minimum capital requirements lies in the differences among developing countries' financial systems. The less developed the domestic financial system and especially accounting, reporting and supervisory capabilities, the less effective capital adequacy standards will be in strengthening the stability of financial institutions[26]. Accordingly, advanced industrial economies can afford to forego minimum reserve requirements as capital standards are usually sufficient to ensure the domestic financial system's stability. To a lesser degree this reasoning applies to the major emerging economies where over the past decade strong improvements in financial sector development have increased the effectiveness of capital adequacy ratios. Minimum reserve requirements primarily target those developing countries with the least mature financial sectors. In such economies capital adequacy requirements are unlikely to be effective while reserve requirements can increase the capacity of local banks to weather the volatility of international capital flows.

8.2.2.3 Internationalisation of the Financial Sector

In addition to the existence of capital adequacy and reserve requirements, modern financial sectors are typically characterised by their openness to international competition. Claessens and Glaessner report that experiences in Southeast Asia indicate that—notwithstanding the degree of financial sector development—the internationalisation of the banking sector *can help in the process of building more robust and efficient financial systems by introducing international practices and standards, by improving the quality, efficiency and breadth of financial services and by allowing more stable sources of funds*[27]. A 2001 World Bank study on bank regulation and supervision concurs that fewer barriers to entry for foreign competitors increase financial sector stability[28].

Allowing international investors to compete in the banking sector fosters financial sector development primarily via the spread international banking expertise

---

26 See Liliana Rojas-Suarez. 2004. *Domestic Financial Regulations in Developing Countries: Can They Effectively Limit the Impact of Capital Account Volatility?* Washington, DC: Centre for Global Development: 23

27 Stijn Claessens and Tom Glaessner. 1998. *Internationalization of Financial Services in Asia.* Paper presented at the conference "Investment Liberalisation and Financial Reform in the Asia-Pacific Region." August 29–31, 1998. Sidney, Australia: 2

28 See James Barth, Gerard Caprio and Ross Levine. 2001a. *Bank Regulation and Supervision: What Works Best?* Working Paper. Washington, DC: The World Bank: 40

and best practices. Imported financial sector know-how can enhance banking sophistication in several fields: It may improve resource allocation and the functioning of payments systems, introduce state-of-the-art techniques of portfolio diversification, risk control and internal monitoring as well as facilitate the mobilization of domestic savings[29]. Financial sector development is not only vital for economic growth in general but also necessary for regulatory efforts to be effective in increasing financial sector stability. Particularly capital adequacy standards are usually less effective in developing countries with limited financial sector development[30].

Additional benefits from allowing international banks to enter domestic markets stem from the competitive pressure that foreign banks exert on domestic financial institutions. Competition from international banks forces local institutions to improve their performance and can reduce the degree of corruption in the relationship between corporations, financial institutions and the government. There is empirical evidence that a larger share in foreign ownership of banks indeed increases efficiency by cost reductions at domestic financial institutions[31]. These welfare gains were correlated not with the market share but with the number of foreign-owned banks active in the economy which implies that the impact of opening the banking sector to international competition may show gains in efficiency faster than widely assumed. Similar findings come from cross-country evidence on Asian economies where a positive correlation between profitability and openness of the banking sector could be established[32]. In the same way, gains in financial sector efficiency were observed to be associated with increasing regulatory and supervisory effectiveness. Similar findings are reported by Levine in a study undertaken shortly after the 1995 Tequila Crisis: Entry of foreign banks was found not only to improve financial services and broaden access to international capital for developing countries, but also to contribute to an increase in supervisory and regulatory capabilities in the domestic financial system[33].

Allowing foreign banks to operate in domestic markets further raises the share of locally denominated loans held by international banks that otherwise almost

---

29 See Ross Levine. 1996. "Foreign Banks, Financial Development, and Economic Growth." In Claude E. Barfield (Ed.). 1996. *International Financial Markets: Harmonization versus Competition.* Washington, DC: American Enterprise Institute
30 See Rojas-Suarez (2004): 23
31 See Stijn Claessens, Asli Demirgüc-Kunt and Harry Huizinga. 1998. *How Does Foreign Entry Affect the Domestic Banking Market.* World Bank Working Paper. Washington, DC: The World Bank: 18
32 See Claessens and Glaessner (1998): 31
33 See Ross Levine. 1996. "Foreign Banks, Financial Development and Economic Growth." In Claude E. Barfied (Ed.). 1996. *International Financial Markets.* Washington, DC: American Enterprise Institute

exclusively lend in dollar, yen or euro[34]. In addition, the entrance of foreign banks often increases the inflow of foreign direct investments into the banking sector: By taking shares in local banks foreign financial institutions inject external capital which may be vital for local banks to meet the capital requirements suggested above. By taking over and investing in state-owned financial institutions, international investors also contribute to an increase in the share of private banks operating in developing country financial sectors. This should be welcomed as state-ownership of financial institutions was found to frequently be *associated with significant short-comings in the preconditions for an effective banking system*[35]. Compared to private sector entities, public-sector performance was identified as particularly poor in terms profitability, capitalisation, non-performing loans and administrative expenses. According to a conference report regarding state-owned financial institutions, non-performing loans of China's largest financial institutions amounted to RMB 2440 billion at the end of 2003, an equivalent of 21 percent of GDP[36]. By directing loans—often at subsidised interest rate—to industries deemed of particular importance by the government, lending by state-owned banks often leads to significant distortions within the economy. Furthermore, government finances may be exposed to large off-balance sheet liabilities via implicit guarantees for deposits at state-owned banks.

At the same time, a number of concerns have been raised regarding the beneficial effects of foreign banks entering developing country financial sectors. First, there is the fear that the existence of a large number of foreign banks in the domestic banking sector may exacerbate the violence of capital outflows in times of financial distress. In the case of Chile, foreign banks increased their portfolio share of foreign assets more and faster than domestic banks when the economy experienced a credit crunch in the late 1990s[37]. Due to their expertise foreign banks may also crowd out domestic banks and thus hamper domestic banking expertise from developing. If foreign banks concentrate their efforts on the most profitable clients, usually a country's largest corporations, a decline in domestic banks may also lead to a reduction in access to capital for small and medium enterprises. Therefore, at times, liberal-

---

34 See Allan Meltzer. 1999. "What's Wrong with the IMF? What Would Be Better?" In Hunter et al. 1999. *The Asian Financial Crisis: Origins, Implications, and Solutions.* Boston, MA: Kluwer Academic Publishers

35 A. Michael Andrews. 2005. *State-Owned Banks, Stability Privatisation and Growth: Practical Policy Decisions in a World without Empirical Proof* (2005). IMF Working Paper 05/10. Washington, DC: International Monetary Fund: 289

36 See Gerard Caprio, Jonathan Fiechter, Robert E. Litan, and Michael Pomerleano. 2004. *The Future of State-Owned Financial Institutions.* Policy Brief No. 18 – 2004. Washington, DC: The Brookings Institution

37 See Ricardo J. Caballero. 1996. "Coping with Chile's External Vulnerability: A Financial Problem." In Norman Loayza and Raimundo Soto. 1996. *Economic Growth: Sources, Trends, and Cycles.* Santiago de Chile: Central Bank of Chile: 389–390

ising developing country financial sectors can be counterproductive to financial sector development in developing countries.

While not to be dismissed out of hand, empirical evidence for most of these points is weak. Claessens and Glaessner argue that many of the allegations resemble those typically cited by vested sector interests in any process of trade reform[38]. Loosing parties, in this case domestic financial service providers, are naturally opposed to an opening of their markets to foreign competition. The most pervasive argument opposing internationalisation is that foreign banks tend to concentrate their activities on servicing only the most profitable sectors by providing credit exclusively to a country's largest institutions. As the flow of credit to small enterprises is important for increasing living standards in developing countries, a reduction in credit to small and medium enterprises would indeed be detrimental. However, it does not seem obvious that entrance of foreign banks necessarily reduces the availability of credit to small businesses. Local banks are unlikely to reduce their lending activities to small and medium-sized enterprises just because foreign banks may neglect this line of business. In contrast, it seems far more likely that increased competition in wholesale banking services to larger companies provides incentives for competitors to concentrate on less crowded segments like that of small businesses. While more research is necessary to gain a deeper understanding of the relationship between foreign competition and service provision to less profitable clients, most studies point to positive effects of financial sector internationalisation. As a consequence, eligibility to large-scale liquidity assistance should require countries to open their financial sectors for international competition—although phased over an adequate period of transition.

8.2.2.4 Deposit Insurance

The creation of a system of deposit insurance for bank debt—excluding subordinated debt requirements if imposed—can increase the stability of the financial system by eliminating depositors' incentives to run at banks and create financial panics. Diamond and Dybvig have shown that some form of deposit insurance can be desirable to prevent bank runs from occurring in the first place[39]. Today, most modern financial systems operate some form of deposit insurance scheme that insures depositors on either a fraction or all of their deposits if their bank becomes insolvent. In this respect deposit insurance is a complementary instrument to a lender of last resort. While the latter provides liquidity assistance to fundamentally solvent banks facing liquidity crunches, deposit insurance repays depositors in case

---

38 Claessens and Glaessner (1998): 11
39 See Diamond and Dybvig (1983)

of insolvent entities. Consequently, the existence of a deposit insurance scheme can reduce the likelihood that depositors attempt to withdraw all their deposits at once due to concerns that their bank may be unable to repay all of its depositors.

Like a lender of last resort, the existence of deposit insurance can increase problems of moral hazard and adverse selection. Depositors may loose incentives to carefully choose the institution they deposit their funds at since in case of default deposits would be repaid anyway. Similarly, banks may have more incentives to engage in risky investments and imprudent lending decisions if they expect to be bailed-out via a deposit insurance scheme. The effects of moral hazard problems can be substantial as badly designed schemes are not only ineffective but even may facilitate the emergence of banking crises. Problems of adverse selection arise if membership in official deposit insurance schemes is not binding. If membership is voluntary, only unhealthy banks would have incentives to join the scheme. Depositors would prefer to deposit their funds at insured banks and fragility of the banking sector would increase since unhealthy banks would attract more deposits than healthy institutions.

Even if properly designed, the effectiveness of deposit insurance schemes is determined by a country's ability to ensure that its stabilizing effects outweigh destabilizing effects caused by moral hazard and adverse selection. In general, this ability is found in advanced industrial economies rather than in developing countries. Analysing empirical evidence from a country panel for the years between 1980 and 1997, Demirgüc-Kunt and Detragiache found even explicit deposit insurance schemes to be negatively associated with banking sector stability. The negative relationship was strongest for countries with underdeveloped regulatory and supervisory systems[40]. This finding implies that for the majority of developing economies moral hazard problems neutralise the stabilizing effects of reducing the likelihood of bank runs. Given the uncertainty about deposit insurance schemes' ability to increase financial sector stability and the technical know-how required for their implementation, qualification for international liquidity assistance should not require countries to operate a system of deposit insurance.

However, countries should be free to design a scheme that fits their economy's and financial sector's characteristics. To minimize moral hazard problems, an adequately designed deposit insurance scheme should adhere to a number of principles. Experience suggests that systems should be explicit rather than implicit and limited instead of unlimited although limited coverage inevitably discriminates

---

40 See Asli Demirguc-Kunt and Enrica Detragiache. 1999. *Does Deposit Insurance Increase Banking System Stability? An Empirical Investigation.* World Bank Policy Research Working Paper 2247. Washington, DC: The World Bank: 22

between depositors[41]. If there is ambiguity, banks and depositors are likely to assume that they will be implicitly insured by the government and as a result lack incentives to follow prudent lending policies. Furthermore, implicit insurance is understood to cover all types of bank debts in case of insolvency. Explicit deposit insurance instead allows defining clear and transparent rules and procedures regarding repayment in case of bank failures.

In order to minimize moral hazard and simultaneously reduce incentives for bank runs, effective deposit insurance should define limited maximum amounts and restrict eligibility to individuals rather than including corporate and banking sector depositors. As a general rule, deposit insurance should aim at reaching as many depositors as possible while covering as little of total deposits as viable. In the United States the Federal Deposit Insurance Corporation Protection Act limits coverage to USD 100.000 per account; in the United Kingdom all accounts up to GBP 20.000 are insured to 90 percent. Notwithstanding, higher insurance may be an option when additional instruments like subordinated debt requirements exist to reduce moral hazard. An alternative would be to introduce co-insurance, leaving deposits insured up to a pre-specified percentage only. Depositors would loose in case of their bank's insolvency, but losses would be limited while incentives for careful analysis and prudent lending decisions would be retained.

8.2.3 Criteria Indicating Sustainable Sovereign Indebtedness

Pre-qualification requirements for international liquidity assistance should further include restrictions on the level of sovereign indebtedness. Excessive levels of sovereign debt increase financial instability and can trigger violent capital flow reversals. Although financial crises can occur even in countries with sustainable levels of sovereign debt, unsustainable indebtedness increases the likelihood that financial crises occur substantially. Recent crises have shown the importance of particularly short-term indebtedness since high levels of short-term debt can force countries to default even if overall debt levels are at sustainable levels. Mexico's financial crisis in 1994–95 is a prime example: Although at around 37 percent of GDP Mexico's total sovereign debt burden was by no means excessive, international investors were unwilling to roll over short-term loans as they questioned the government's ability to meet its short-term commitments. The resulting capital outflows put pressure on the peso which in turn destabilized the financial sector and exacerbated the crisis.

---

41 See George Benston. 1999. "Banking Fragility, Effectiveness, and Regulation in Less-Developed Countries." In Hunter et al. 1999. *The Asian Financial Crisis: Origins, Implications, and Solutions.* Boston, MA: Kluwer Academic Publishers

The danger of excessive levels of government indebtedness may be best under-stood as providing a crisis zone as suggested by Cole and Kehoe[42]. While high levels of sovereign and particular short-term debt may not necessarily result in a crisis, they create an environment of instability and uncertainty in which any kind of shock can cause financial panic and massive capital flight. For developing countries this problem is particularly severe as the difficulties in issuing local currency denomi-nated debt with long maturities often contributes to imbalances in debt structures, particularly in terms of short-term and foreign currency denominated debt[43]. If capital outflows cause the local currency's exchange rate to depreciate, the burden of foreign denominated debt becomes even harder to service in terms of local currency thereby further fuelling investor uncertainty. Moreover, as the value of sovereign debt declines, capital structures of local banks that hold large parts of their assets in domestic sovereign debt securities are weakened and vulnerability increases. Hence even relatively healthy financial sectors can be destabilized by excessive levels of sovereign indebtedness, especially if denominated in foreign currency or of short-term maturity.

If levels of foreign debt are fundamentally unsustainable, short-term liquidity assistance by the international community will not prevent a financial crisis from developing, at least in the medium to long-term. At best, it can extend the period until default becomes inevitable. While in the meantime international investors in sovereign debt are repaid, debt levels of the country in crisis will not only remain at unsustainable levels but even increase. The only lasting solution for dealing with un-sustainable sovereign debt in this case is to enter a restructuring process to which both private investors and sovereign creditors will have to contribute. Without a restructuring and the participation of international creditors, losses from default will be born solely by the official sector and both domestic and international taxpayers.

Consequently, eligibility to international liquidity assistance must require sover-eign indebtedness to be at sustainable levels. Analysing the effects of recent IMF rescue packages Roubini and Setser report that *the most successful bailouts were provided to countries that had comparatively small debt levels*[44]. To ensure sustain-able levels of indebtedness, clear debt ceilings should be imposed. Given the vulner-ability caused by high levels of short-term debt, debt ceilings should not only address the overall debt burden but also impose restrictions on the share of short-term maturity and foreign currency denominated debt in the overall debt structure.

---

42 See Cole and Kehoe (1996)
43 See Eduardo Borensztein, Marcos Chamo, Olivier Jeanne, Paolo Mauro and Jeromin Zettel-meyer. 2004. *Sovereign Debt Structure for Crisis Prevention*. IMF Research Paper. Washing-ton, DC: International Monetary Fund
44 See Nouriel Roubini and Brad Setser. 2004. *Bailouts or Bail-Ins? Responding to Financial Crises in Emerging Economies*. Washington, DC: Institute for International Economics: 120

8.2.3.1 Solvency Ratios

While it is impossible to define optimal one-size-fits-all debt ratios, countries should indicate fundamental solvency and a sustainable debt structure in order to qualify for international liquidity assistance. Budget deficits fail to allow for objective conclusions on fiscal sustainability as running consecutive budget deficits during recession may be a sensible policy for countries with limited levels of public debt. Consequently, a budget deficit ceiling as provided in the European Stability Pact and suggested by the Meltzer Commission is unsuitable as criterion for pre-qualification. Public or sovereign debt as percentage of GDP is more indicative. According to Wyplosz, *the only valid definition of fiscal sustainability is that the public debt—as a share of gross domestic product—does not grow without limits*[45].

As shown by Kray and Nehru, different countries can service different levels of sovereign debt—the quality of a country's institutions and economic policies being the decisive factor[46]. Eligibility to large-scale liquidity assistance by the official sector should thus require borrowers to strictly abide to three-year average maximum debt ratios depending on the quality of their institutions and economic policies. Maximum debt ratios suggested here are based on the *Debt Sustainability Framework* developed jointly by IMF staff and the World Bank's International Development Association[47]. The framework lists different maximum thresholds of external indebtedness subject to Country Policy and Institutional Assessments (CIPA) devised by the World Bank[48]. Debt levels below these maximum thresholds can thus be interpreted as indicating sustainability and fundamental solvency. Employing three-year-average ratios instead of setting strict annual ceilings serves two purposes: First, it allows determining trends in countries' fiscal policy—a deteriorating trend indicates the need for reform and austerity measures. Second, it allows the market to adjust expectations in accordance with perceived trends regarding the sustainability of fiscal policies which would help to avoid panic reactions in case a country unexpectedly overshoots its maximum ceiling.

---

45 See Charles Wyplosz. 2005. "How to Rebuild the Stability Pact." *Financial Times*. January 31, 2005

46 See Aart Kraay and Vikram Nehru. 2004. *When is External Debt Sustainable?* World Bank Policy Research Working Paper 3200. Washington, DC: The World Bank: 31

47 See IDA and IMF. 2004. *Debt Sustainability in Low-Income Countries – Proposal for an Operational Framework and Policy Implications*. February 3, 2004. Washington, DC: International Monetary Fund

48 World Bank Country Policy and Institutional Assessments rate countries on 20 indicators of 4 broad categories: economic management, structural policies, policies for structural inclusion and equity, and institutions and public sector management. In each category scores from 1 to 6 are awarded and updated annually.

Table 8.1
Thresholds for Sustainable Levels of External Indebtedness (%)

	Country Institutional and Policy Assessment		
	Poor	Medium	Strong
NPV of debt-to-GDP	30	45	60
NPV of debt-to-exports	100	200	300
NPV of debt-to-revenue	150	200	250
Debt service-to-exports	15	25	35
Debt-servive-to-revenue	20	30	40

Source: World Bank

A large number of economic variables are employed by financial market participants to analyse the solvency status of sovereign debtors and their vulnerability to
short-term liquidity problems. Most of them make effective indicators to determine
whether sovereign borrowers should qualify as fundamentally solvent and thus be
eligible for large-scale liquidity assistance by the official sector. For the sake of
designing simple pre-qualification criteria, only the most indicative solvency and
liquidity ratios should be chosen as compulsory qualification criteria. A number of
studies provide indications which ratios market participants judge most effective in
determining sovereign borrowers' solvency status. Using panel data from a sample
of 16 emerging economies for the period between 1998 and 2002, Rowland and
Torres identified the key determinants explaining yield differentials between
emerging market sovereign bonds and U.S. Treasuries: GDP growth, both debt-to-
GDP and debt-to-exports ratios as well as foreign reserves, exports-to-GDP and debt
service-to-GDP ratios[49]. Regarding yield spreads, further significant variables were
found to be the share of exports in GDP and the ratio of debt service to GDP. These
findings were backed by a follow-up study employing OLS regressions on an
expanded country set[50]; they closely resemble the 1996 findings of Cantor and
Packer whose data set consisted of 49 economies the majority of which were industrialised[51].

While empirical findings regarding the most significant debt indicators are relatively coherent, the actual maximum ceilings of the debt ratios suggested are more
debatable. They are rough approximations and draw on lessons from empirical

---

49 See Peter Rowland and José Torres. 2004. *Determinants of Spreads and Creditworthiness for
    Emerging Market Sovereign Debt: A Panel Data Study.* Working Paper. La Paz, Bolivia:
    Banco de la Republica
50 See Peter Rowland. 2004. *Determinants of Spread, Credit Ratings and Creditworthiness for
    Emerging Market Sovereign Debt: A Follow-Up Study Using Pooled Data Analysis.* Working
    Paper. La Paz, Bolivia: Banco de la Republica
51 See Richard Cantor, Richard and Frank Packer. 1996. "Determinants and Impacts of Sovereign
    Credit Ratings." *The Journal of Fixed Income.* Vol. 6, No. 3

evidence regarding developing countries' indebtedness. A number of studies have found that from a certain level of national indebtedness further debt increases have negative, non-linear effects on economic growth. In terms of solvency variables, in 1997 Patillo, Ricci and Poirson identified the turning point between positive and negative effects on GDP growth at debt levels above 160 to 170 percent of exports or 35 to 40 percent of GDP[52]. Analysing the impact of external debt on growth in developing countries in Africa and Latin America, Cohen suggests the critical levels are above 200 percent in terms of debt-to-exports and around 50 percent in debt-to-GDP[53]. At the Paris Club, a debt-to-exports ratio above 150 percent qualifies developing countries for the Heavily Indebted Poor Country (HIPC) initiative. As a qualification criterion for determining the sustainability of sovereign indebtedness the ceilings defined in the Debt Sustainability Framework appear the most suggestive.

8.2.3.2   Liquidity Ratios

Liquidity problems often arise as a consequence of currency or maturity mismatches in the debt structure. Rodrik and Velasco have shown that high levels of short-term debt are associated with more severe financial crises in case international capital flows dry up or reverse[54]. Compared to advanced economies, debt structures in emerging economies often contain very large portions of both foreign-currency denominated and short-term maturity debt[55]. Such debt structures increase the likelihood of financial crises, destabilize the economy and amplify economic fluctuations of the business cycle. In order to qualify for international liquidity assistance, not only the level but also the structure of sovereign debt should be sustainable.

To evade liquidity problems arising from excessive levels of short-term debt within the overall debt structure, pre-qualification must require adherence to a maximum ceiling on short-term debt as a share of total debt. To reduce the risk of liquidity crunches arising from currency mismatches a country should maintain an adequate ratio of foreign currency reserves over short-term external debt. Both ratios are among the financial indicators most widely followed by participants in the

---

52 See Catherine Patillo, Hélène Poirson and Luca Ricci. 2002. *External Debt and Growth.* IMF Working Paper WP/02/69. Washington, DC: International Monetary Fund: 19

53 See Daniel Cohen. 1997. *Growth and External Debt: A New Perspective on the African and Latin American Tragedies.* Discussion Paper No. 1753. London: Centre for Economic Policy Research

54 See Dani Rodrik and Andrés Velasco. 1999. *Short-term Capital Flows.* NBER Working Paper 7364. Cambridge, MA: National Bureau of Economic Research

55 International Monetary Fund. 2004. *Sovereign Debt Structure for Crisis Prevention.* Paper prepared by the Research Department. Washington, DC: International Monetary Fund: 19

markets for foreign currency and sovereign debt. In addition, they can be easily reported on a monthly basis and monitored by both the public and the private sector.

To ensure that countries' debt structures are not excessively tilted towards short-term obligations, eligibility to large-scale liquidity assistance should require countries to adhere to a short-term debt to total debt ceiling of 25 percent. A 25 percent ceiling on short-term debt indicates a sustainable debt structure and minimises the risk of default as a result of maturity mismatches. By adhering to a maximum ceiling of 25 percent of total debt, countries can signal that potential capital account problems are not the result of imprudent debt structures but of short-term market distortions due to asymmetric information, irrational panic or herd behaviour.

To reduce the risk of default as a consequence of currency mismatches, pre-qualification should require central banks to maintain a unity ratio of foreign-currency reserves to total short-term foreign-currency denominated debt. The IMF's Policy Development and Review Department determined the ratio of reserves to short-term external debt the single most important indicator for reserve adequacy and prudent liquidity management[56]. Consequently, it is a central variable in the early warning model for financial crises developed by the Fund's Developing Country Studies Division[57]. The indicator's importance is based on the fact that fundamentally solvent countries are in danger of default if their liquidity is insufficient to service debt obligations in the short-term. A prudent level of reserves-to-short-term external debt is a strong indicator that the borrower is unlikely to default because of maturity or currency mismatches. Empirical evidence suggests a unity ratio of reserves to short-term external debt as suitable requirement, although—as in the case of solvency ratios—an optimal level is impossible to define. In a testimony before congress, Alan Greenspan supported this assessment arguing that *usable foreign exchange reserves should exceed scheduled amortizations of foreign currency debts (assuming no rollovers) during the following year*[58]. Bussiére and Mulder qualify this view by arguing that a unity in reserves to short-term debt protects against contagion only given modest current account deficits and a lack of

---

56 See International Monetary Fund. 2000. *Debt- and Reserve-Related Indicators of External Vulnerability*. Paper Prepared by the Policy Development and Review Department. March 23, 2000. Washington, DC: International Monetary Fund. http://www.imf.org/external/np/pdr/debtres/#summary

57 See International Monetary Fund. 2002. *Global Financial Stability Report: A Quarterly Report on Market Developments and Issues*. March 2002. Washington, DC: International Monetary Fund: 49–50

58 See Alan Greenspan. 1999. *Efforts to Improve the "Architecture" of the International Financial System*. Testimony given before the Committee on Banking and Financial Services. May 20, 1999. Washington, DC: House of Representatives

severe exchange rate distortion[59]. Despite the differences between individual countries' economic situation an appropriate reserves to short-term external debt requirement will reduce the vulnerability to liquidity problems resulting from maturity or currency mismatches within sovereign debt structures.

8.3 Conclusion: Pre-qualification Is the Way Forward

By meeting the pre-qualification criteria suggested above, a country can signal that large-scale liquidity assistance would likely be effective in solving its financial crisis. Their fulfilment indicates that the crisis is likely to be a temporary liquidity problem rather than a solvency crisis. Implementation of capital adequacy and reserve requirements and the internationalisation of the financial sector signal that liquidity assistance would not be employed to bail-out insolvent financial institutions. By abiding to the maximum ceilings of sovereign indebtedness, governments would signal that their indebtedness is at sustainable levels. Likewise, by keeping a unity level of foreign currency reserves to short-term external debt and restricting the portion of short-term obligations to 25 percent of total public debt countries could indicate that their vulnerability to external shocks as a result of currency or maturity mismatches in their debt structures is limited. Subscription to the Fund's Special Data Dissemination Standards allows both official sector and international investors to assess countries' financial position and base their lending decisions on accurate information. Box 8.1 below summarizes the seven pre-qualification requirements suggested above.

By monitoring countries' adherence to these requirements the official sector can determine the appropriate response to potential balance-of-payments problems in advance: For countries meeting pre-qualification requirements short-term liquidity assistance would be advanced given a high probability that emergency loans would be effective in arresting the crisis. Countries in violation of the criteria would have to restructure their debts as liquidity assistance by the official sector would likely be ineffective in addressing the underlying economic problems. Providing a decision rule to determine whether liquidity assistance would be effective in restoring stability and confidence in a crisis economy is the central objective of pre-qualification as approach to the management of financial crises.

---

59 See Matthieu Bussiére and Christian Mulder. 1999. *External Vulnerability in Emerging Market Economies: How High Liquidity Can Offset Weak Fundamentals and Effects of Contagion.* IMF Working Paper 99/88. Washington, DC: International Monetary Fund

Box 8.1
Pre-qualification requirements for Liquidity Assistance

Condition 1	To qualify for liquidity assistance by the official sector, countries must subscribe to IMF Special Data Dissemination Standard.
Condition 2	Members must not surpass more than one of the four applicable three-year average maximum sustainability thresholds of sovereign indebtedness as defined in Table 8.1. Applicable thresholds are determined by a member's CIPA rating.
Condition 3	Short-term sovereign debt, defined as debt maturing within the period of three months, must not surpass 25 percent of a member's total sovereign indebtedness.
Condition 4	Members must maintain a prudent level of foreign currency reserves; the minimum level is an amount sufficient to meet three months of external debt service obligations
Condition 5	Members have to implement effective financial sector regulation ensuring that banks maintain a 15 percent capital adequacy ratio. Capital requirements are determined by a standardized approach based on Basel II, but altered to fit the characteristics of developing country financial sectors.
Condition 6	Members must implement a cash reserve requirements demanding financial institutions to keep 15 percent of deposits in cash or cash equivalents
Condition 7	Member countries have to ensure their financial sectors are open to the entry of foreign competitors and allow for foreign investment into local financial institutions.

Ex-ante conditionality not only offers clear advantages in terms of crisis management, it is also preferable regarding crisis prevention: One the one hand, it would provide incentives for countries to reform their economies and adhere to sound economic policies well in advance of potential balance-of-payments problems. By qualifying for official sector assistance countries could increase their economies' resilience to external shocks and enhance their attractiveness for international investors. As a result, access to international capital would be widened and borrowing terms improved for those countries resilient enough to receive and benefit from additional capital flows. On the other, ex-ante conditionality would enable financial market participants to reach more accurate investment decisions as it would yield additional information on countries' financial positions while the official sector's response to capital account crises would become rules-based and thus more transparent.

9. Moral Hazard

A central reason why the IMF continues to abide by ex-post conditionality, despite the difficulties it poses for providing effective liquidity assistance, is to address moral hazard problems. Issues of moral hazard and adverse incentives have been at the core of critique on IMF lending practices ever since it arranged the then largest rescue package worth USD 48.8 billion to prevent a Mexican default during the Tequila Crisis in 1995. Indeed, it has been argued that by exacerbating moral hazard problems IMF interventions during the 1990s have actually increased both number and scale of financial crises in emerging market economies[1].

While moral hazard problems resulting from IMF interventions can be identified in many areas, the most important relate to subsequent changes in the behaviour of developing country borrowers on the one hand, and the providers of short-term financing on the other. IMF critics argue that the prospect of IMF bailouts generates incentives for debtor countries to take on large amounts of short-term foreign-currency denominated debt and to pursue irresponsible fiscal and monetary policies as they expect to be bailed-out by the official sector in case of a crisis. Similarly, international creditors as the providers of short-term finance to emerging economies are claimed to be encouraged to expand lending activities imprudently and to assume excessive risks by betting on a rescue in case the borrowing country would threaten default.

Moral hazard problems relating to liquidity assistance by the international community follow the same dynamics as in the area in which the concept was first identified—the insurance industry. An insurance provider underwriting an insurance contract will find itself exposed to two types of different hazards: *real* and *moral* hazard. Real hazard refers to all risks arising from factors outside the control of the insured party, in the case of home insurance to risks like blizzards, tornadoes or tsunamis. Moral hazards stem from the behaviour of the insured party which may change after insurance has been taken out. Being insured she might expose herself to higher risks and spend less efforts on prevention, a typical example being to build dangerously close to a river when flooding damage is insured. Problems of asymmetric information are the root cause of moral hazard problems: Were insurers able to gather perfect information on policy holders' actions once a contract has been signed, the insurance contract could be adequately priced to include premiums for

---

1 See Michael Mussa. 2002. *Reflections on Moral Hazard and Private Sector Involvement in the Resolution of Emerging Market Financial Crises*. Paper presented at the Bank of England Conference on the Role of the Official and Private Sectors in Resolving International Financial Crises, July 23–24, 2002. London: Bank of England

additional moral hazard risks. Given problems of imperfect information the industry's rational response is to engage in efforts to reduce moral hazard until the costs of doing so exceed the benefits.

9.1 IMF Induced Moral Hazard

The concept of moral hazard can easily be transferred to the case of a national central bank acting as lender of last resort to the domestic financial system. Like an insurance company, a lender of last resort provides banks with the benefit of liquidity insurance in case its reserves become strained by a bank run. As a consequence, the bank can keep its level of cash reserves below the level it would need in case no central bank existed thereby reducing returns foregone by not investing cash in more productive uses. However, the existence of liquidity insurance by the central bank may induce banks to keep reserves even below the minimum level necessary to reduce the vulnerability to liquidity crunches to an acceptable level. On the creditor side, the existence of a central bank may induce depositors to analyse deposit banks less carefully. As a result, they may deposit their funds at banks engaging in excessively risky activities they would avoid without the expectation of liquidity support by a lender of last resort.

The IMF provides comparable services for emerging markets and developing economies. International creditors who lend their funds to either the sovereign or private sector entities in developing countries may regard the possibility of IMF bailouts as implicit insurance against investment loss in case a financial crisis develops. Moral hazard can therefore arise in form of the willingness by international investors to advance larger loans and take on higher risks than they would without the existence of the IMF. In case of the borrower, the possibility of IMF support can function as implicit insurance against the negative effects a default has on the real economy. Assuming that the IMF would intervene to prevent default, borrowers may feel incentives to pursue policies that increase default risk. Such policies include increased foreign borrowing at short maturities or unsustainable fiscal and monetary policies in the case of the sovereign and risky investments and unsustainable capital ratios for financial institutions. The former behaviour is referred to as *direct moral hazard* since it involves a change in behaviour by the recipients of IMF support; *indirect moral hazard* is attributed to private creditors initiating the capital flows whose reversal might put a debtor country into liquidity problems in the first place[2].

---

2 Axel Dreher. 2004. *Does the IMF Cause Moral Hazard? A Critical Oeview of the Evidence.* Working Paper. Exeter: University of Exeter: 2

Moral hazard problems are impossible to fully eliminate without foregoing the benefits of insurance; however, it is possible to reduce the scale of moral hazard problems to a more acceptable level. Compared to an insurance company, central banks and regulatory authorities are in possession of extensive monitoring rights that allow for reducing moral hazard via regulation, supervision and the ability to close down vulnerable entities. The IMF lacks most of these essential tools. Although endowed with large and relatively strong monitoring and surveillance capabilities, it lacks authority for supranational regulation and the ability to shut down particular destabilising institutions.

An even more important distinction between insurance companies and IMF or national central banks arises in terms of benefit dispersion: in contrast to insurance companies, neither national central banks nor the IMF hand out payouts but advance emergency loans that have to be repaid. These loans are usually senior to all other claims on the borrower and carry short to medium-term maturities; in addition, they are subject to interest charges, even if often at subsidised levels. Since loans by the official sector extend recipient countries' debt positions rather than taking the form of non-refundable grants, moral hazard problems may appear less severe regarding debtor countries than international creditors. International investors in short-term, foreign-currency denominated, both sovereign and private sector debt often receive principal and interest charges in full once an IMF loan has been disbursed. At the same time IMF resources are inevitably limited and thus fail to provide unlimited insurance. Following this line of reasoning, moral hazard effects on international creditors may also be less severe than widely claimed since the existence of official sector liquidity assistance cannot eliminate the risk of at least some losses on investments. Moreover, the common underperformance of asset markets prior to the announcement of IMF stability programs may eradicate any following gains[3].

Jeanne and Zettelmeyer suggest that under certain conditions IMF interventions do not create adverse incentives at all. They show that if the IMF lends at a fair interest rate and debtor governments act to maximise taxpayers' welfare, all effects of IMF liquidity assistance are efficient: this includes changes in economic policies by the government, a reduction in the borrowing costs for recipient countries as well as an increase in capital inflows. Jeanne and Zettelmeyer's *Mussa's Theorem* suggests that given the lending takes place at an actuarially fair interest rate and the borrowing government aims at maximising the welfare of its taxpaying citizens,

> the anticipation of IMF crisis lending increases the volume of capital
> flows to emerging market countries and reduces the cost of borrowing for

---

3 See Richard Brealey and Evi Kaplanis. 2002. *The Impact of IMF Programs on Asset Values.* Working Paper. London: London Business School

these countries. In addition the anticipation of crisis lending may decrease the domestic efforts to avoid a crisis. However, the IMF does not generate Moral Hazard stricto sensu. The expectation of IMF lending unambiguously increases the welfare of recipient countries at no cost to the rest of the world[4].

9.2 Empirical Evidence on Moral Hazard Issues

While moral hazard problems arising from IMF arranged rescue packages may be persuasive conceptually for both the debtor and the creditor-side, empirical evidence is less conclusive. This is despite a growing number of studies testing for either creditor-side moral hazard, debtor-side moral hazard or both. Although a number of studies claim to identify empirical evidence in favour of moral hazard, conclusions of many other papers fail to find solid proof for changes in lending and borrowing behaviour by either debtors or creditors as a result of IMF liquidity assistance.

One reason for this conflicting evidence lies in methodological difficulties when testing for moral hazard. In case of debtor-side or direct moral hazard a key problem is the difficulty of specifying the counterfactual[5]. Identifying a change in recipients' borrowing behaviour resulting from IMF intervention would require information on the course of action the debtor would have taken in case there would be no IMF; but this can only be speculated on. Even without IMF support a debtor country can still choose from several alternatives to default including a devaluation of its currency in order to improve the balance of trade. There is no way to know what kind of fiscal and monetary policies a government would pursue without any form of external liquidity assistance. A government could resort to irresponsible policies by betting on rescue by the IMF but a lack of IMF support might also encourage it to opt for short-term gains over responsible policies when costly reform efforts would be wasted as soon as liquidity problems arise.

Testing for creditor-side moral hazard is less problematic due to the information provided by the market in emerging market securities, primarily by yield spreads of sovereign, but also of corporate debt securities. Yet a change in yield spreads does not necessarily imply the existence of moral hazard: International capital markets daily price in numerous events and various pieces of information and in the process generate a large amount of noise. As a consequence, changes in security prices are very difficult to trace to specific events such as a change in expectations regarding

---

4 Jeanne, Olivier and Jeromin Zettelmeyer. 2004. *The Mussa Theorem (and other results on IMF induced moral hazard)*. Paper written for the IMF Conference in Honour of Michael Mussa. June 4–5, 2004. Washington, DC: International Monetary Fund: 13

5 Timothy Lane and Steven Phillips. 2000. *Does IMF Financing Result in Moral Hazard?* IMF Working Paper 00/168. Washington, DC: International Monetary Fund: 6

the likelihood of IMF intervention. Notwithstanding, the analysis of yield spreads allows to draw conclusions regarding creditor moral hazard that seem more conclusive than most findings in relation to debtor-side moral hazard.

9.2.1 Evidence on Creditor-side Moral Hazard

Tests for creditor-side moral hazard by drawing on pricing information on emerging market securities have been undertaken in several studies. Empirical evidence has been sought by observing the change in security prices after events assumed to alter the probability of future bailouts. From the outset the mere existence of credit spread differentials can be interpreted as excluding the possibility that investors view the existence of IMF programs as eliminating risk entirely[6]; otherwise, emerging market bonds would trade at the same yields as Treasuries or other risk-free securities. When the market perceives IMF support as conditional and perhaps insufficient to eliminate risk entirely, the likelihood of intervention should influence investment decisions of rational investors. In case of emerging market bonds any event or announcement providing new information on the likelihood of future IMF interventions should influence yield spreads above publicly traded risk-free securities of the same maturity. Specifically, an increase in the probability of future IMF interventions should narrow the risk premium of emerging market bonds over Treasuries. Information suggesting an increased likelihood of IMF intervention can further be expected to foster an increase of capital flows into emerging economies, facilitate borrowing, reduce interest charges and lengthen maturity for economies likely to receive liquidity support in case of crisis[7].

In an early empirical study on the topic, Zhang analysed the effects on bond yield spreads arising from the Mexican bailout in 1995. While the observed reduction in spreads following the rescue package has been widely interpreted as evidence for moral hazard effects, Zhang questions this thesis and identifies other explanations[8]. His sample covers the period between 1992 and 1997 and is based on regressions of average quarterly spreads between eurobonds and Brady bonds issued by eight emerging economies. The sample yields no significant statistical correlation between a reduction in yield spreads and the 1995 rescue package for Mexico. Indeed, instead of indicating a negative correlation, the dummies included for both the time during crisis as well as the following period until 1997 were found to be completely insignificant. Zhang consequently reports a lack of evidence for moral hazard and

---

6 See Lane and Phillips (2000): 8
7 See Dreher (2004)
8 See Xiaoming Zhang. 1999. *Testing for "Moral Hazard" in Emerging Markets Lending.* IIF Research Papers No. 99–1. Washington, DC: Institute for International Economics

attributes the reduction in yield spreads to other influences, primarily increased liquidity in international capital markets and a change in economies' fundamentals.

At best limited influence of moral hazard in the international capital markets has been reported by Kamin[9]. Based on the assumption that reasonable expectations of IMF intervention have developed only after the Mexican Crisis, he identifies the period before 1995 as representative for a lack of moral hazard. Consequently, emerging market spreads before 1995 are used as benchmark. A comparison of EMBI spreads before and after the Mexican bailout shows a considerable increase of an average of 700 basis points ever since the Russian Crisis in July 1998. Only for the period between Q2 1996 and Q2 1998 a narrowing of yield spreads is observed; other evidence for a significant impact of moral hazard is scare. These findings are not altered when analysing potential factors which might have pushed up spreads since the second half of 1998, therefore potentially cancelling out or hiding any significant moral hazard effects. Neither a change in average Treasury yields or those of corporate high-yield bonds, nor a change on the perceived risk of emerging market assets, represented by a weighted average of major credit ratings for EMBI countries' sovereign bonds, suggest that post 1998 EMBI yields are artificially depressed and may include a reduction in yield spreads caused by heightened moral hazard problems.

Kamin further analyses the effects of differences in creditworthiness on bond spreads, reasoning that an increase in moral hazard since 1995 would have reduced the responsiveness of yield spreads to perceived credit risk as identified by rating agencies. Instead of observing a reduction in sensitivity, a substantial increase in the correlation between yield spreads and credit ratings is reported. Kamin also fails to identify a reduction in the dispersion of spreads between different countries which could have indicated a significant increase in moral hazard. The development of capital flows into emerging economies seems to further suggest that moral hazard effects may be vastly overstated. Although rapidly increasing after 1995, financial flows peaked in the fourth quarter of 1997 and appear to have converged since the Asian Crisis to a level similar to the period before the Mexican rescue. The same conclusion can be drawn when searching for discriminatory decision-making by investors among emerging economies. Existence of strong moral hazard should result in a beneficial impact on lending conditions for countries most likely to be recipients of IMF interventions. In contrast, countries which appear of high importance to the global financial system's stability or of strategic geo-political

---

9 See Steven Kamin. 2002. *Identifying the Role of Moral Hazard in International Financial Markets*. International Finance Discussion Paper 736. Washington, DC: Board of Governors of the Federal Reserve System

interest to the largest IMF members have neither faced substantially different borrowing costs nor received more capital inflows than other economies.

A similar method of testing for the scale of change in moral hazard is to employ news-based approaches. When identifying specific events which changed the likelihood of future IMF interventions, short-term market responses on news releases can yield further conclusions on the severity of moral hazard effects. Phillips and Lane analysed the changes for both EMBI and other specific economies' yield spreads to two event categories: Announcements regarding the provision of IMF rescue packages in connection with events like the 1995 Tequila Crisis, the 1997 Asian Crisis or financial support for Russia in 1998 form the first. The second includes releases of new information on the amount of financial resources available to the IMF to provide emergency loans to distressed members: Events chosen were the decision to raise access limits in 1994, the introduction of the Supplemental Reserve Facility in 1997 and the 1999 quota increase. The vast majority of the sample's 22 cases fail to provide evidence for substantial changes in the degree of moral hazard: Yield spreads generally changed insignificantly or even increased[10]; in case of severe moral hazard implications these events should have been followed by a substantial narrowing of spreads. An exception is the case of Russia in 1998, where perceived changes in yield spreads do indeed point to an impact on moral hazard.

McBrady and Seasholes examined the effect of the 1999 decision by the Paris Club to bail-in international investors in Pakistani debt. Their study analyses the movements in yield spreads of bonds outstanding for 41 emerging economies between February 24 and February 26. Unlike their predecessors, the authors report significant evidence for moral hazard effects which—given the short time-frame of three days only—is unlikely to be the result of a change in fundamentals. Depending on instrument and country, price movements in the 400+ emerging markets bonds sample varied considerably. For countries with large and yet undrawn Standby and Extended Fund Facilities[11], the refusal to bail-out Pakistan's creditors increased yield spreads considerably; for countries with undrawn Enhanced Structural Adjustment Facilities (ESAF), effects on spreads were more limited. One interpretation of this result is that investors judge the risk of being bailed-in to be lower for countries with ESAF arrangements assuming the international community to be unlikely to withhold what essentially amounts to development assistance to least developed

---

10 See Lane and Philipps (2000): 28

11 Stand-By and Extended Fund Facilities are IMF lending arrangements to developing countries facing temporary balance of payment difficulties. As payout is conditional on meeting specific policy requirements, the IMF may refrain from continuing to advance loans to members with undrawn Stand-By and EFF arrangements if they fail to fulfil agreed policy conditions. Enhanced Structural Adjustment Facilities are advanced to particularly underdeveloped economies and lack conditionality requirements. As such they share similarities with development aid and commitments are less likely to be withdrawn by the Fund.

economies. In contrast, the Paris Club's decision on Pakistan rendered IMF bailouts for more robust developing countries that could be expected to meet policy conditions for liquidity assistance less probable. McBrady and Seasholes argue that *investors lowered their expectations of future bailouts by approximately US$ 20bn*[12].

The effects of the Fund's decision in 1998 to refuse further assistance to Russia have been examined by Dell'Ariccia, Schnabel and Zettelmeyer[13]. In contrast to Zhang, Kamin and Lane & Phillips they identify direct and significant effects on yield spreads. In the study the authors examine the long-run behaviour of emerging market yields by controlling for changes in prices of other international debt securities and a wide range of fundamentals in specific economies. They also draw conclusions from yield spreads' sensitivity to economic fundamentals and cross-country variance. The paper concludes that the Fund's decision to refrain from providing additional liquidity assistance to Russia had substantial effects on long-term investor behaviour: Spreads for most countries increased significantly after the Russian crisis indicating that international financial markets priced in an increase in default risk particularly for debt instruments issued by emerging economies with relatively weak fundamentals. Dell'Ariccia, Schnabel and Zettelmeyer also discovered a rise in the dispersion of spreads between different economies suggesting that investors attributed more weight to fundamentals after the too-big-to-fail doctrine proved flawed in the case of Russia.

In order to assess the viability of various proposals to reign in on the dangers posed by violent short-term capital flows, Eichengreen and Mody analysed the impact of IMF rescue packages on accessibility and costs of borrowing for emerging market issuers of tradable debt[14]. Their sample assesses effects on emerging market debt securities issued by either sovereign or other public or private sector borrowers between Q1 1991 and the end of 1999. The analysis yields a positive correlation between IMF interventions and market access and a negative correlation with borrowing costs, overall supporting the hypothesis that IMF programs increase moral hazard. The authors further report that the impact of IMF programs differs widely between individual emerging market borrowers. Differences in creditworthiness seem to be mirrored by the distinct effects that rescue programs have on yield spreads at the date of issuance. Impact on spreads and accessibility seems highest for countries in need of modest macroeconomic and structural reforms, while countries

---

12 See Matthew McBrady and Mark Seasholes. 2001. "Bailing In." *Journal of Restructuring Finance.* Vol. 1, No. 1: 21

13 See Giovanni Dell'Ariccia, Isabel Schnabel & Jeromine Zettelmeyer. 2002. *Moral Hazard and International Crisis Lending: A Test.* IMF Working Paper 02/181. Washington, DC: International Monetary Fund

14 See Barry Eichengreen and Ashoka Mody. 2000. *Bail-Ins, Bailouts and Borrowing Costs.* Paper prepared for the First Annual IMF Research Conference, November 9–10, 2000. Washington, DC: International Monetary Fund

in severe difficulties appear not to profit in a comparable way. The same applies to countries with strong fundamentals suggesting that IMF involvement is not judged as necessarily leading to substantial improvements[15].

In their argument, Eichengreen & Mody distinguish between two interpretations of IMF-induced changes in yield spreads. *Commitment explanations* expect IMF intervention to be interpreted by the market as indicating that governments have committed themselves to more prudent policies. The rational consequence of this reading would be to increase lending and lower borrowing costs. *Signalling explanations* in contrast imply that IMF interventions indicate severe problems within the specific economy: Here it is argued that only in case of severe liquidity problems would a country call on the IMF for support. The consequent market reaction would be an increase in yield spreads and a reduction in the volume possible to place with investors. The authors detect more evidence for the latter, supporting the view that IMF involvement indeed influences creditor decision-making. In addition, differences between different types of IMF support are reported to have distinct effects on borrowing arrangements: While the announcement of Standby Arrangements and Extended Fund Facilities had a negative impact on yield spreads, for Enhanced Structural Facilities no significant impact could be discovered. These findings seem plausible when SBAs, EFFs and ESAFs are associated with a rising degree of structural problems as suggested by Goldstein[16]: While Standby Arrangements point to predominantly easily adjustable macroeconomic imbalances, the acceptance of Extended Fund Facilities would imply a higher degree of structural problems suggesting a need for more difficult reforms. Consequently, resorting to Enhanced Structural Adjustment Facilities would be associated with even larger and more severe structural problems.

Mina and Martinez-Vasquez have argued that an alteration in foreign loan maturity as consequence of changed expectations regarding IMF interventions would constitute a strong indicator of moral hazard[17]. Based on the assumption that a perceived increase in risk will reduce both volume and maturity structure of foreign loans and vice versa, they analysed a sample of over 70 economies for the period between 1992 and 1997. Market expectations on IMF intervention are represented by the percentage of loans to GDP a year ahead of program announcement, while countries' commitment to IMF stability programs is approximated by the amount of credit drawn one year after the announcement. Assumption here is the

---

15 See Eichengreen and Mody (2000): 25
16 See Morris Goldstein. 2000. *IMF Structural Programs.* Paper prepared for NBER conference "Economic and Financial Crises in Emerging Economies." Woodstock, VT. October 19–21, 2000
17 See Wasseem Mina and Jorge Martinez-Vasquez. 2002. *IMF Lending, Maturity of International Debt and Moral Hazard.* Working Paper. Atlanta, GA: Georgia State University

expectation that due to low IMF interest charges a country would rationally draw the maximum allowable of resources pledged by the IMF in a stability program, while allowances are conditional on the country meeting agreed milestones. The results show that the fraction of short-term to total flows of international capital decreases when markets expect IMF support to be forthcoming. Breaking down the type of Fund programs yields the result that this effect holds for Standby and Extended Fund Facilities while in the case of ESAF programs no such reaction could be observed.

Testing for creditor moral hazard in Korea and Indonesia during the Asian Crisis, Evresel and Kutan have analysed bond spread movements to announcements on IMF programs in the period between 1996 and 2003[18]. Their findings suggest IMF programs can increase moral hazard as yield spreads for both countries' sovereign bonds were found to narrow in response to announcements on IMF programs. While bond markets quickly priced in news regarding Indonesia's and Korea's fundamentals and their progress in negotiations with the IMF, no significant reactions to similar news regarding other Asian economies could be observed. Yield reactions were strongest for news regarding the start of negotiations and program approval, while the period in between and after implementation did not exhibit significant movements. The fact that sovereign bond spreads narrowed only temporarily suggests that moral hazard effects caused by news on IMF programs are merely a short-term phenomenon.

In two related papers, Evresel and Kutan further analyse effects of IMF- related news on other asset classes, namely equity markets and financial sector stocks. Regarding equities, they analyse the influence of news of program negotiations, approval, and implementation for stock returns in the period between 1992 and 2002. As in the case of sovereign bonds, findings point to the existence of moral hazard effects: Particularly for Korea news on program negotiation and approval were found to increase stock returns. The same applies for Thailand and Indonesia, although stock price movements here were less dramatic[19]. Examining the effects on IMF-related news on stock returns in Indonesia, Korea, Argentina, Brazil, Pakistan and Russia for the period between July 1997 and year end 1999, Hayo and Kutan arrive at similar results. The sample considered all news on interactions between IMF and the six emerging economies, grouped into 11 distinct categories and additionally classified *negative* or *positive*. As result of their analysis, the authors

18 See Ayse Evrensel and Ali Kutan. 2004. *Testing for Creditor Moral Hazard in Sovereign Bond Markets: A Unified Theoretical Approach and Empirical Evidence.* Working Paper. Portland, OR: Portland State University

19 See Ayse Evrensel and Ali Kutan. 2004. *Creditor Moral Hazard in Equity Markets: A Theoretical Framework and Evidence from Indonesia and Korea.* Working Paper. Portland, OR: Portland State University

report a correlation between IMF news and changes in equity values, arguing that in a period of uncertainty and volatility the *IMF can be viewed as a lender of last resort and investors trading in these markets form their actions based on their anticipation of the actions of the IMF in the near future*[20]. On average, IMF-related news were found to go along with a one percentage change in stock prices either up or down while market reaction appeared most sensitive for news regarding a delay in the payout of IMF funds.

To analyse moral hazard effects of IMF-related news on the financial sector, Evresel and Kutan examined a sample of stock returns for banks, insurance companies and other financial institutions including real estate, asset management, mortgage and investment banking service providers between 1992 and 2002. Reasoning that IMF programs—when credible—imply painful economic and structural reforms for the economy and a loss of governmental support for financial sector entities specifically, returns are expected to decrease with announcements indicating forthcoming IMF intervention[21]. In case the market judges reform efforts incredible, an increase in financial sector returns would be the likely consequence since painful adjustments would not be executed and IMF resources used to strengthen implicit government guarantees. Positive stock returns were observed as response to news regarding IMF program negotiations and approval particularly in the case of Korea and Indonesia.

An earlier study with focus on the financial sector arrives at the same verdict by analysing movements in the market capitalisation of international banks with significant loans outstanding to emerging market entities. News indicating an increased probability of IMF approval for a stability program should rationally improve the market value of banks with significant emerging market exposure as repayment of outstanding loans would become more likely. The sample examined draws on Bank of England data on country exposure of the seven largest U.K. banks with significant emerging market involvement. The period analysed ranges from January 1995, when Michel Camdessus issued a letter of support for Mexico, to the Fund's approval of the USD 30 billion rescue package to Brazil in December 2002. Market capitalisation of U.K. banks was found to have increased as consequence of news which rendered IMF intervention more likely—even controlling for the overall market movement on the day of announcement. For the period between 1995 and 2002, banks' combined rise in market value surpassed USD 4 billion. In addition,

---

20 Bernd Hayo and Ali Kutan. 2001. *Investor Panic, IMF Actions, and Emerging Stock Market Returns and Volatility: A Panel Investigation.* Working Paper B27. Bonn: Centre for European Integration Studies: 12

21 See Ayse Evrensel and Ali Kutan. 2004. *Financial Sector Returns and Creditor Moral Hazard: Evidence from Indonesia, Korea and Thailand.* Working Paper. Portland, OR: Portland State University: 10

there was a positive correlation between the size of the rescue package and the increase in banks' market value. According to Haldane and Scheibe this *response of market prices is consistent with increased incentives to take emerging market risks*[22].

Considering not only equity, but also sovereign debt and currency prices, Brealey and Kaplanis assessed the wealth effect produced by news regarding IMF interventions[23]. Following Hayo and Kutan, IMF press releases were split into *positive* and *negative* news, stock price movements observed via IFC equity indices and bond prices via EMBI+ data; the period sampled spans the 10 years between 1989 and 1999 with the number of news-induced price responses observed totalling 1383. In order to assess the impact of program news on specific financial institutions, banks were selected according to emerging market exposure. The study's key finding is a significant decline in assets prices in the weeks prior a price sensitive announcement while at the time of announcement a potential positive price reaction failed to materialise. These results suggest that the gains resulting from IMF liquidity support are insignificant compared to the reduction in wealth during the weeks before an announcement and imply that signalling effects of IMF intervention are miniscule.

9.2.2 Evidence on Debtor-side Moral Hazard

Compared to creditor-side moral hazard, debtor-side moral hazard effects have been analysed far less empirically. In spite of the lack of substitutes for pricing information available to study creditor-side moral hazard, there are a limited number of empirical studies that illuminate the issue of debtor-side moral hazard. As indicated before, debtor-side moral hazard refers primarily to irresponsible behaviour by borrowing countries' governments pursuing imprudent monetary and fiscal policies due to the availability of IMF liquidity assistance. Proponents of debtor-side moral hazard argue that the expectation by governments of receiving emergency loans by the IMF in times of crisis encourages authorities to ease the money supply and run large budget deficits financed by increasing sovereign indebtedness to unsustainable levels.

Dreher and Vaubel test for this assertion by analysing panel data from 106 recipients of IMF loans during the period between 1971 and 1997. Running regressions for the correlation between budget deficit (as percentage of GDP) and the amount of

---

22 Andrew Haldane and Jörg Scheibe. 2003. *IMF Lending and Creditor Moral Hazard.* Working Paper 216. London: Bank of England: 7

23 See Richard Brealey and Evi Kaplanis. 2002. *The Impact of IMF Programs on Asset Values.* Working Paper. London: London Business School

credit outstanding at year end (as percentage of a country's IMF quota), previous LIBOR, and dummies representing existence or lack of access to Structural Adjustment or Enhanced Structural Adjustment Facilities, the authors test for both dimensions of moral hazard and price incentives provided by subsidised interest rates[24]. Regarding the former, the motivation for running large budget deficits is rationally expected to decline the closer a borrower gets to his IMF quota borrowing limit. Regarding the latter, a rising interest differential between the rates charged for SAF and ESAF facilities and the market rate should raise incentives to receive IMF funds and reduce efforts to undertake wide ranging reforms.

The results support these expectations: Budget deficits decline the closer a borrower gets to his IMF quota. Furthermore, countries qualifying for SAF or ESAF facilities run relatively larger budget deficits than countries with programs involving less subsidised access to foreign-currency loans. Consequently, an increase in LIBOR is positively correlated to budget deficits as is net new credit[25]. Regressions on monetary expansion also identify a positive correlation with an exhaustion of credit as well as new net credits. According to these results, IMF loans can indeed cause moral hazard problems on the debtor-side as countries expecting IMF intervention behave less responsibly than those for whom IMF funds appear less accessible. A related finding is evidence of a correlation between IMF support and political business cycles: For democracies IMF loans were found to be larger in pre-election years than in the period following an election[26].

The impact of interest rate differentials on moral hazard is called into question by empirical work on the borrowing costs of IMF debtor countries. Analysing interest charges on IMF loans, Jeanne and Zettelmeyer argue that real benefits involved in IMF rescue packages are smaller than widely believed[27]. Except when a borrower is unable to access any other source of financing, the real financial gain of IMF loans to recipients is the interest differential between IMF and comparable market rates. IMF loans are almost always the most senior claims in countries' debt structures and are rarely defaulted on since borrowers fear a pariah status in international capital markets. Due to low default risk the IMF can provide loans at interest rates considerably below the market level. Given the Fund's preferred creditor status, the authors compare interest charged by the IMF to yields on U.S. Treasuries. They suggest that the actual redistribution of international funds to the borrowing country

---

24 See Axel Dreher and Roland Vaubel. 2001. *Does the IMF Cause Moral Hazard and Political Business Cycles? Evidence from Panel Data*. Beiträge zur angewandten Wirtschaftsforschung No. 598-01. Mannheim: Universität Mannheim

25 Net new credit refers to additional IMF loans less repayment on older loans.

26 Dreher and Vaubel (2001): 11–13

27 See Jeanne, Olivier and Jeromin Zettelmeyer. 2001. "International Bailouts, Moral Hazard and Conditionality." *Economic Policy* 30: 407–432.

is usually very limited in size. As a consequence, the financial benefit incurred by the borrower appears too small to be a persuasive factor for debtor-side moral hazard.

Reasoning in a similar way, Gai and Taylor examine whether the decision to introduce the New Arrangements to Borrow and the Supplemental Reserve Facility in 1997 has contributed to debtor-side moral hazard by providing incentives for systemically important borrowing countries to access IMF finance more often or at higher volumes[28]. Given that both NAB and SRF were created to stabilise predominantly those emerging economies whose failure would have de-stabilising effects on the global financial system, the authors construct an *index of systemic importance*. The index serves as indicator for the likelihood of countries being of systemic importance and thus more likely to access IMF funds. It is constructed by variables representing the amount of foreign-denominated debt outstanding and countries' volume of international trade, both positively correlated with potentially contagious effects on the world economy. To test for moral hazard the authors examine a sample consisting of 19 emerging market countries selected by their importance to the stability of the international monetary system; the period analysed spans from January 1995 to December 2001 on a quarterly basis and covers 176 program enrolments. By constructing a binary dependent variable to represent a country's participation or abstention in IMF programs, actually observable actions are included in the model. Unconditional factors explaining program participation to be controlled for are identified as foreign currency reserves over short-term external debt, the real exchange rate and a measure relating to countries' sovereign credit ratings. This allows for testing for the effects of NAB and SRF introduction on the demand for IMF programs, which however still depend, on the fundamental factors specified above.

The findings suggest that the introduction of NAB and SRF has indeed increased the participation of borrowing countries in IMF programs. The effect was found to be particularly significant for countries of high systemic importance as defined by the systemic importance index. Results appear plausible since those countries whose failure is most risky to the global financial system were most likely to receive IMF support. While the results can be interpreted as suggesting the existence of debtor-side moral hazard, Gai and Taylor are unable to exclude the possibility that the observed effects are not a consequence of demand but of supply. As in most empirical studies the results suggest the existence of moral hazard problems but due to methodological difficulties fail to provide hard evidence.

---

28 See Prasanna Gai and Ashley Tailor. 2004. *International Financial Rescues and Debtor Moral Hazard*. Working Paper No. 217. London: Bank of England

In another empirical analysis Evrensel focused on governmental policies during inter-program periods[29]. In case of significant debtor-side moral hazard, countries' fiscal and monetary policies should deteriorate after the conclusion and before the enrolment in new IMF stabilisation programs as countries have to face financial difficulties to qualify for liquidity assistance by the official sector. Examining fiscal and monetary policies of 42 economies during the years 1971 to 1997, Evresel reports a significant deterioration in economic policy from the first to the second inter-program period observed. These results would only indicate debtor-side moral hazard if worsening macroeconomic policies are a consequence of attempts to qualify for subsidised IMF loans. However, policy deterioration could equally be a consequence of other factors like external shocks to the economy.

9.3 Catalytic Finance

The fact that IMF intervention may have effects on both lending decisions by international investors and economic policies pursued by debtor country governments is not necessarily detrimental. IMF-induced moral hazard can have negative effects when leading international creditors to refrain from a thorough process of risk assessment and instead engage in purely speculative investment strategies. Similarly, it would be detrimental to the stability of the international financial system when governments are induced to pursue irresponsible fiscal and monetary policies. However, IMF interventions can also positively influence creditor decision-making in case the Fund's approval of a stabilisation program has *catalytic effects*; indeed, the existence of catalytic effects is one of the core arguments in favour of the Fund's current intervention practice.

The concept of catalytic finance rests on the belief that official liquidity assistance can induce other actors to take actions that mitigate the severity of financial crises. More specifically, its proponents argue that IMF stabilisation programs provide incentives for international investors to roll over maturing loans. Under certain circumstances IMF intervention and private sector provision of funds can thus be *strategic complements*[30]. Since some private investors will be willing to extend their loans in response, partial bailouts by the IMF may end a liquidity crisis even if official funds alone would be insufficient to prevent default. Extending loans may be a rational strategy for investors either because fears of default are reduced due the mere existence of official assistance or as IMF approval for a stabilisation

---

29 See Evrensel, Ayse. 2002. "Effectiveness of IMF-supported Stabilization Programs in Developing Countries." *Journal of International Money and Finance* 21: 565–578

30 See Stephen Morris and Hyun Song Shin. 2003. *Catalytic Finance: When Does It Work?* Cowles Foundation Discussion Paper No. 1400. New Haven, CT: Cowles Foundation for Research in Economics at Yale University: 5

program renders debtor countries' reform efforts more credible. Morris and Shin draw attention to the important role played by private investors arguing that *the active players that generate the greatest degree of spillover effects on other players are the short-term creditors*[31] since their decisions determine the funding gap. Catalytic finance will work best if economic fundamentals are not excessively weak; however, if an economy is fundamentally healthy, the impact of policy reforms by the government might be too small to significantly affect rollover decisions by private investors.

The concept of *catalytic finance* became prominent in the aftermath of the 1980s debt crises when it was advanced as argument in favour of the Treasury's 1985 *Program for Sustained Growth*. In what was to become known as the Baker Plan, catalytic effects were expected to induce international investors to put up private funds adding to the USD 16 to 18 billion provided in official assistance. Gianinni and Cotarelli trace back the concept to the 1970s when the recycling of oil-surplus funds laid the foundations for the following decade's debt crises. Accordingly, already in 1977 the argument was made that countries' eligibility to draw on IMF funds was being interpreted by markets as *a kind of Good Houskeeping* seal[32]. However, as private sector funds were not forthcoming in the Brady Plan's aftermath, the number of catalytic finance advocates declined and the concept lost support. This process culminated in October 1988 when yields of developing country debt shot up as a reaction to the USD 3 billion loss provision on emerging market loans made by Citibank. As the debt crisis subsided in the early 1990s and lending to emerging economies accelerated, arguments of catalytic finance were not invoked; in contrast, the Mexican rescue package in 1995 suggested that the international community rather subscribed to a doctrine of full bailouts.

Corsetti, Guimaraes and Roubini show how IMF intervention can generate catalytic effects as a rational response by several actors whose actions are endogenously determined[33]. As such, international liquidity assistance can end financial

---

31 Morris and Shin (2003): 18
32 See Carlo Cottarelli and Curzio Giannini. 2002. *Bedfellows, Hostages, or Perfect Strangers? Global Capital Markets and the Catalytic Effect of IMF Crisis Lending.* IMF Working Paper WP/02/193. Washington, DC: International Monetary Fund: 8
33 See Giancarlo Corsetti, Bernardo Guimaraes and Nouriel Roubini. 2003. *International Lending of Last Resort and Moral Hazard: A Model of IMF'S Catalytic Finance.* NBER Working Paper 10125. Washington, DC: National Bureau of Economic Research. The model is set in an environment where financial crises can arise of either fundamental shocks or self-fulfilling panics. Three actors try to optimise their strategies in a three-period horizon: The IMF, international investors and the debtor country government which invests a specified endowment in the first period and has the ability to borrow from international investors. In case of liquidity problems in period two, international investors decide whether to extend maturing loans while the IMF considers whether it should offer financial support. Its objective is to lend to illiquid, but solvent and not to insolvent countries. The government in turn bases its decisions on the

panics and prevent liquidity crunches even without unlimited resources. It can do so as any amount of official liquidity support widens the range of economic fundamentals for which it is rational for international investors to extend instead of calling maturing loans. IMF intervention can therefore catalyse liquidity support by the private sector. The higher the amount of funds provided by the IMF the more rational it becomes for international investors to roll-over their loans. Similarly— due to signalling effects—a high level of information at the IMF also widens the range of fundamentals at which private investors are willing to refrain from calling loans.

In Corsetti, Guimares and Roubini's model, signalling effects of superior information at the IMF do not influence decisions by private investors as all actors are assumed to move simultaneously. In practice, unless markets believe IMF actions are solely determined by the political interests of the largest creditor countries, signalling effects are likely to serve as a further channel for catalytic effects. In the model, catalytic finance works via two distinct channels: In the direct channel an injection of funds reduces investment losses by lowering the number of investments being liquidated prematurely. The indirect effect reduces the number of investors willing to position themselves against a currency given a certain state of economic fundamentals: *In other words, the presence of the IMF means that, over a crucial range of fundamentals, private investors are more likely to rollover their positions than roll them off—this is the essence of catalytic finance*[34]. Catalytic effects of IMF interventions can also counter moral hazard problems on the debtor-side. Governments, unwilling to undertake costly longer-term reforms because of the costs incurred in case a financial crisis erupts nevertheless, may be encouraged to implement prudent economic policies when IMF support increases the likelihood that reform measures will eventually be met by success.

9.3.1 Empirical Evidence on Catalytic Finance

Empirical evidence on catalytic finance overlaps with evidence on moral hazard effects of official liquidity assistance. In their comprehensive literature review regarding the topic Giannini and Cotarelli classify empirical work into three categories: case studies, studies analysing capital flows and studies examining the development of yield spreads[35]. Overall, case studies fail to identify evidence for signifi-

---

other actors' strategies. If the government fails to obtain sufficient funds to service debt obligations, liquidation costs occur to all actors.

34 Corsetti, Guimares and Roubini (2002): 4

35 See Cotarelli and Giannini (2002): 18–26. All empirical studies are subject to a number of caveats including the counterfactual problem, difficulties to differentiate between demand and

cant catalytic effects of IMF interventions. In a study based on 17 emerging economies Bird, Mori and Rowlands identify credible commitments by a country's government to pursue sound economic policies as the key factor inducing private capital inflows; official liquidity assistance, in contrast, was not found to be significantly correlated to inflows of private funds[36]. Results by Killick also fail to establish evidence of catalytic effects resulting from IMF interventions[37]. An IMF report came to the same conclusion when analysing the effects of IMF-supported programs during the 1990s emerging market crises. The authors concede that at least in the short-term IMF programs appear to have little impact on international capital inflows[38]. Bird and Rowlands subsequently conclude that not only *the theoretical basis for catalysis in unconvincing* but also, *and unsurprisingly given these theoretical priors, the empirical evidence fails to identify a strong and reliable catalytic effect*[39].

Examining capital flows following the introduction of IMF stabilisation programs also fails to discover persuasive evidence for catalytic effects, but studies analysing demand side factors arrive at the opposite result: while Marchesi finds significant effects of IMF programs on the rescheduling of debt by international creditors[40], others report insignificant positive or even negative correlation between IMF intervention and capital inflows[41]. Similarly, when analysing capital inflows before and after the inception of IMF programs, the majority of studies fail to identify a significant increase in capital inflows after enrolment. Most often, results are insignificant but pointing to an increase rather than decrease in inflows. An exception is the study by Killick, Malik and Manuel that identifies a small negative impact on capital inflows during a two-year period[42].

---

supply factors and the fact that changes in bond prices are hard to pin down to specific events and causes.

36 See Graham Bird, Antonella Mori and Dane Rowlands. 2000. "Do the Multilaterals Catalyize Other Capital Flows?" *Third World Quarterly* Vol. 21, No. 3: 483–503

37 See Tony Killick. 1995. *IMF Programmes in Developing Countries – Design and Impact.* London: Routledge

38 See Atish Ghosh, Timothy Lane, Marianne Schulze-Ghattas, Ales Bulír, Javier Hamman and Alex Mourmouras. 2002. *IMF-Supported Programs in Capital Account Crises.* Washington, DC: International Monetary Fund

39 Graham Bird and Dane Rowlands. 2003. *Financing Balance of Payments Adjustments: Options in the Light of the Illusory Catalytic Effect of IMF Lending.* Working Paper. Guilford: University of Surrey: 21–22

40 See Silvia Marchesi. 2002. *Adoption of an IMF Programme and Debt Rescheduling. An Empirical Analysis.* Working Paper. Siena: Universitá di Siena

41 See Dani Rodrick. 1996. *Why is There Multilateral Lending?* Annual World Bank Conference on Development Economics. Washington, DC: The World Bank

42 See Tony Killick, Tony, Moazzam Malik and Marcus Manuel. 1991. *What Can We Know about the Effects of IMF Programmes?* Working Paper 47. London: Overseas Development Institute

Empirical evidence from an examination of yield spreads as indicators of catalytic finance effects is similarly inconclusive. Work by Eichengreen and Mody supports the existence of catalytic effects as the introduction of IMF programs was found to reduce yield spreads on emerging market bonds at their time of issuance. The fall in spreads was observed strongest for IMF programs involving EFFs, but could also be identified for Standby Arrangement programs. However, in absolute terms the change in spreads was found to be relatively small, averaging between 9 and 24 basis points[43]. Mody and Saravia argue that for an increase in capital inflows and a reduction in borrowing costs credible policy reforms are the most important factor. According to their analysis the signalling effect of IMF programs is comparatively small, although the size of IMF funds lent did show a correlation to a reduction in yield spreads[44]. Similar results appear when analysing the development of yield spreads for Brazil, Argentina, Mexico, Russia, Indonesia, Thailand and Korea. Haldane shows that the yield premium of countries implementing a Fund-supported stability program over a syndicate rate of countries with the same credit rating does not fall as a consequence of program announcement. In the immediate aftermath of introduction, yield spreads were widening rather than narrowing. In the period before the announcement of IMF intervention spreads increased significantly, by 200 basis points in the case of Indonesia and 300 basis points in the case of Mexico[45].

As evidence for moral hazard, evidence on the existence of catalytic finance is not conclusive. Neither case studies on selected countries, nor the analysis of capital inflows before and after program announcement, nor examination of emerging market yield spreads at the time around IMF intervention leads to clear results. Catalytic finance effects appear to be present at times, but their importance seems limited. The concept of catalytic finance points out that at a certain level moral hazard effects might be beneficial; however, their limited scope questions their effectiveness as instrument for crisis prevention. Giannini and Cotarelli suggest five channels how IMF interventions can nevertheless influence private sector capital inflows. First, IMF programs may signal that due to IMF advice economic reform and policies will improve significantly. Second, by employing extensive research capacities IMF support may increase the level of economic information in the market. Thirdly, IMF conditionality increases the credibility of countries' reform efforts. In addition, enrolment in IMF programs may allow international investors to screen countries for responsible fiscal and monetary policies as participation in IMF

---

43 See Eichengreen and Mody (2000)
44 See Ashoka Mody and Diego Saravia. 2003. *IMF Doctor: Better at Prevention than Cure?* Working Paper. Washington, DC: International Monetary Fund
45 See Andy Haldane, Andy. 1999. "Private Sector Involvement in Financial Crises: Analytics and Public Policy Approaches." *Financial Stability Review.* London: Bank of England: 193

programs entails large costs particularly for countries pursuing irresponsible economic policies. And finally, moral hazard effects given implicit IMF insurance are likely to have some impact on private sector lending decisions[46].

9.4 Instruments Mitigating Moral Hazard Problems

While several empirical studies fail to identify evidence for significant moral hazard effects, other regressions yield a correlation between IMF lending and movements in related asset prices. As such, it seems likely that IMF lending can increase moral hazard problems at least to some degree. However, the difficulties in gathering empirical evidence to prove its existence suggest that the size of IMF-related moral hazard problems may be exaggerated[47]. The existence of a limited level of moral hazard does not undermine the case for liquidity assistance by the official sector. Every kind of insurance contract inevitably raises some form of moral hazard problems. So does the IMF and so it would do if restructured into an international lender of last resort. The rational response to these problems is not to abolish the concept of insurance, but to devise an institutional design that reduces these problems to acceptable levels at both the debtor and the creditor side.

Moral hazard at the creditor side seems less of a problem than it used to be. Problems were most severe following the Mexican bail-out in 1995 but the Fund's refusal to extend emergency assistance to Russia in 1998 significantly reduced the problem by invalidating too-big-too-fail, too-strategic-to-fail and too-nuclear-to-fail hypotheses among financial market participants; the *moral hazard play* has thus become a significantly less attractive investment strategy for emerging market investors. Both portfolio investors and lending banks have experienced the dangers of investing in emerging markets without a thorough analysis of the borrower's ability to repay. Sturzenegger and Zettelmeyer found that investor losses as a result of sovereign defaults since 1998 ranged from 13 percent in the case of Uruguay to 73 percent in the case of Argentina with the majority of restructurings involving investor losses of between 25 and 35 percent[48]. The decision to refrain from bailing-out investors in Russia and Argentina has further undermined the perception that investments in major emerging economies are nearly as safe as buying Treasuries. The Fund's policy of constructive ambiguity thus seems sufficient to mitigate creditor-side moral hazard to an acceptable level.

---

46 See Cotarelli and Giannini (2002): 31–35
47 See Kenneth Rogoff. 2002. "Moral Hazard in IMF Loans: How Big a Concern?" *Finance and Development.* Vol. 39, No. 3. Washington, DC: International Monetary Fund
48 See Frederico Sturzenegger and Jeromin Zettelmeyer. 2005. *Haircuts: Estimating Investor Losses in Sovereign Debt Restructurings, 1998–2005.* IMF Working Paper WP/05/137. Washington, DC: International Monetary Fund

Restructuring the IMF into an international lender of last resort would be unlikely to cause an increase creditor-side moral hazard. Countries qualifying for international liquidity assistance would be fundamentally stable and unlikely to threaten default. International investors would lend to these countries based on favourable fundamentals rather than based on dubious too-big-to-fail strategies. Countries not meeting pre-qualification criteria would not be eligible for international liquidity assistance; lending to them would be inevitably riskier and investors would assess their ability to repay more thoroughly. If they invest, they would do so because higher risk entails higher yields and not because they expect to be bailed-out by international taxpayers; in contrast, investors would become aware that in case of default they would have to contribute to a restructuring.

Regarding the debtor-side, moral hazard problems seem more problematic as IMF stability programs have not only painful, but also attractive features for the countries concerned. Although economic reform and fiscal austerity may be painful for the population, IMF liquidity assistance is attractive as interest charges for the funds provided are often below the market rate. To prevent countries from reducing reform efforts after receiving official sector funds, the IMF resorts to its policy of ex-post conditionality. Because loans are disbursed in tranches depending on countries' fulfilment of reform pledges, incentives to deviate from sustainable policies are reduced. Likewise, restructuring the Fund into an international lender of last resort does not imply that moral hazard would be impossible to mitigate. While ex-post conditionality would be abandoned, pre-qualification would ensure that countries have incentives to follow prudent economic policies. Those who not yet qualify have incentives to reform in order to do so in the future since qualification would not only offers access to liquidity assistance in times of crisis, but also enhance countries' capacity of accessing private sector capital at more attractive terms. Countries already qualified would have incentives to maintain economic and fiscal prudence in order to remain qualified and evade a capital re-allocation by international investors.

To ensure that members resort to international funds only as a last resort, liquidity assistance should be available only at interest above the market rate. Countries should not draw on emergency loans from the official sector because they are the cheapest form of financing available. For one, official funds are limited and the official sector must preserve its liquidity to mitigate financial crises and prevent contagion. Moreover, subsidized interest rates are an unwarranted and intransparent market distortion. Under its current practice of lending at rates below the market level, the IMF provides implicit money transfers to borrowing countries via interest subsidies. Zettelmeyer and Priyadarshani have shown that interest charges for emerging economies were subsidized on average by 100 basis points over the period between 1973 and 2003. Subsidies were found substantially higher for low income and HIPC countries at around 400 and 600 basis points below the market rate respectively[49].

By lending at or below the market level of interest, the IMF can crowd out private sector lending. By undercutting market rates in pricing emergency loans, the Fund thus impedes the development of a market for emergency credit lines. Such a market is important not only in light of limited official sector resources but also as a source of information on the health of individual economies. Perceiving the spreads of loans made against comparable collateral to different developing countries, both governments and market participants can draw indications on countries' solvency and liquidity situation. While there is a case to be made for supporting developing countries via interest rate subsidies, the appropriate institution to disperse such aid is the World Bank and not the IMF[50].

To ensure that international funds are requested only as a true last resort, penalty interest rates should be applicable to all forms of short-term liquidity assistance. A sensible penalty rate could be 200 basis points above the market rate as suggested by Calomiris[51]. The market rate would be determined by yield spreads of the borrowing country's publicly traded debt securities. The premium of 200 basis points is no scientific result: It could similarly be set at 150 or 250 basis points; the central objective is to ensure that governments turn to official sector assistance only in case access to capital markets is temporarily cut off. When preference for resorting to capital markets rather than to the official sector is ensured, emergency loans should not impose additional interest costs on the borrower. Neither the IMF nor an international lender of last resort is and should be designed to maximise profits in times of financial crisis[52].

Pre-qualification and penalty interest rates safeguard that moral hazard problems on the debtor-side are kept at an acceptable level. While moral hazard cannot be eliminated, these instruments ensure that costs in terms of moral hazard do not outweigh the benefits of emergency liquidity assistance. In practice, pre-qualification and penalty rates are as likely to mitigate moral hazard problems as the Fund's cur-

---

49 See Jeromin Zettelmeyer and Joshi Priyadarshani. 2005. *Implicit Transfers in IMF Lending, 1973–2000*. IMF Working Paper 05/08. Washington, DC: International Monetary Fund: 31–32

50 However, there are good reasons why even the World Bank might refrain from interest rate subsidies: While middle income countries might be able to pay a market rate, for particularly poor countries outright grants often are a more appropriate instrument to execute development policy. See Jeremy Bulow and Kenneth Rogoff. 2005. *Grants versus Loans for Development Banks*. Paper presented at the American Economic Association Meetings in Philadelphia. January 7, 2005

51 See Calomiris (1998): 20

52 Economically it could even lend at a small discount to the prevailing market rate given its preferred creditor status. The penalty rate is warranted only to mitigate moral hazard problems and economise on the Fund's resources.

rent conditionality policy. But even if ex-post conditionality would be marginally more effective, this effectiveness would not outweigh additional benefits of pre-qualification in terms of timely response, legitimacy and ownership.

10. Principal-Agent Problems

International institutions in general and those created at Bretton Woods in particular are prone to significant principal-agent problems. At the IMF, the most important principal-agent problems arise because the interests of the collective IMF membership and individual member countries are not always aligned. Advanced industrial countries, the Fund's largest creditors, that command a majority of votes in the Executive Board, at times assert policies perceived by the majority of members as detrimental to own interests and advancing individual geo-political interests. As a result, the Fund's legitimacy has declined in large parts of the developing world. Another problem—though not exclusive to IMF or World Bank—stems from the difficulties in aligning the interests of institutions' stakeholders and staff. As budget-maximising and bureau-shaping models of bureaucracies have shown, public servants' private interests can differ from their official mandate. The latter is a management problem and shared by all institutions where ownership is separated from management. Consequently, a discussion on the difficulties in aligning the interests of IMF staff with those of the Fund's shareholders are of limited relevance in the context of this analysis[1]. Instead of management problems, this chapter examines the differences in interest between individual members and the Fund's membership at large.

10.1 The Actors' Interests

Financial crises affect all key participants in international capital markets: hence debtor countries, creditor countries and international investors alike share an interest in maintaining or re-establishing global financial stability. However, while debtor countries and international investors primarily benefit from liquidity assistance by the official sector, for the Fund's creditors international liquidity assistance is beneficial on the one hand, but costly on the other. Because the majority of directors on the Executive Board are nominated by creditor countries that control a majority of votes, G-7 governments exert an overwhelming influence on IMF policies. As a result, they determine what constitutes a threat to global financial stability and under what circumstances IMF resources are to be disbursed to members in balance-of-payments difficulties. The perception of what constitutes a threat to global financial

---

1 For a discussion on principal-agent problems within international institutions see Roland Vaubel. 2003. *Principal-Agent-Probleme in internationalen Organisationen.* HWWA Discussion Paper 219. Hamburg: Hamburgisches Welt-Wirtschafts-Archiv

stability and thus warrants support by the international community often differs between creditor and debtor countries thereby creating severe conflicts of interest.

10.1.1 Interests of Borrowing Countries

Borrowing countries naturally experience the most immediate effects when financial crises erupt in their economies. As access to emergency finance allows mitigating these effects and interest charged by international financial institutions is often subsidised, debtor countries clearly benefit from international liquidity assistance. Although countries have to commit to IMF-supported stability programs in return for emergency loans, conditionality is not necessarily resented by debtor country governments as it can provide a source of support for the government when implementing difficult economic reforms: On the one hand, governments can use IMF conditionality as a scapegoat to prevent disalignment with voters; on the other, it allows to circumvent potential veto powers by the domestic political opposition as governments can unilaterally enter loan arrangements with the IMF, even if conditional on specific policy reforms. Although the domestic opposition could block reform efforts if presented in the legislature, the consequences of breaking off an IMF agreement already in place are dire. Due to the high political and economic costs, the opposition is therefore likely to accept reform proposals it would normally have voted down in parliament. Statistical findings support this reasoning by showing that governments facing large parliamentary opposition are more likely to enter into IMF loan agreements than governments facing a relatively powerless domestic opposition[2].

Compared to creditor countries, the Fund's debtor countries have relatively little direct influence on IMF lending decisions. Although represented in the Executive Board, both voting weights and constituency issues limit their power. The world's major advanced economies control considerably more votes and have a veto power on all significant decisions. The limited influence of developing countries arising from their small voting weights is exacerbated by the constituency system that groups together most countries into unified voting groups. At the same time, developing countries can influence lending decisions indirectly, as there are a number of well-known factors which increase the likelihood of winning support for program approval by the Fund's dominant members. These factors include a country's

---

2 At the same time results found the IMF to be less willing to enter into agreements with countries that face strong domestic opposition to economic policy reforms. This suggests that the Fund realistically perceives powerful political opposition as a threat to the implementation of economic reforms. See James Vreeland. 2002. *Institutional Determinants of IMF Agreements*. Working Paper. Department of Political Science. New Haven, CT: Yale University

importance to global financial stability, its debt owed to industrial countries' commercial banks and its political proximity to dominant members.

10.1.2 Interests of International Investors

For commercial banks and other private financial institutions investing in developing countries the Fund's practice of advancing large bail-out packages to debtor country governments is very attractive. Notwithstanding moral hazard effects in borrowing countries, international liquidity assistance allows private lenders to recoup loans even in situations where borrowers are unable to repay without external assistance. As a result, international investors have been able to lend at high interest rates that incorporated premia for emerging market risk while due to implicit bail-out guarantees the creditworthiness of emerging market borrowers in practice was not far below that of advanced industrial economies. In essence, the existence of IMF rescue programs provides private international lenders with a form of complementary credit insurance. Consequently, international investors are strongly in favour of large-scale liquidity assistance that enhances their profit opportunities.

Financial institutions can influence IMF lending decisions indirectly via lobbying domestic policy makers who control the voting behaviour of their country's representative at the Fund's Executive Board. Nevertheless, financial institutions can also influence IMF lending decisions via more direct channels, particularly via catalytic or *supplementary finance*. Most IMF rescue packages are insufficient to fully cover recipient countries' balance-of-payment gaps. Success of these programs therefore depends on supplementary funds either provided bilaterally by creditor countries, by private financial institutions or other official sector sources. Since the 1980s private sector loans have become the dominant source of supplementary finance and contributed to the success of many stability programs. As provider of supplementary funds the private sector wields influence in the process of structuring IMF assistance programs. Private sector influence is strongest during the formulation of policy conditions attached to IMF programs that financial institutions prefer to be aligned with their commercial interests[3].

10.1.3 Creditor Country Interests

For the Fund's creditor countries, international rescue packages entail both benefits and costs. The Fund's major shareholders have at least three reasons to support large rescue packages by the official sector: For one, as bankruptcies of domestic banks

---

3 See Erica Gould. 2003. "Money Talks: Supplementary Financiers and International Monetary Fund Conditionality." *International Organisation*. Vol. 57, No. 3: 551–586

caused by defaulting borrowers endanger the stability of the domestic financial system, creditor country governments have a rational interest in fostering all efforts to increase global financial stability. Secondly, private sector interest groups exert influence on governments to continue the Fund's current lending practices as commercial banks with large exposure to emerging economies are prime beneficiaries of international balance of payments support; politicians have incentives to promote the interests of domestically powerful interest groups as their funding for electoral campaigns rests on donations[4]. Finally, by influencing IMF lending decisions, powerful member countries can advance national foreign policy objectives.

10.1.3.1 Foreign Policy Objectives

Decisions on approval or rejection of IMF programs are of vital importance for developing countries in financial crisis; therefore they can be utilized to foster dominant members' foreign policy objectives. If financial crises continue and deepen, resulting civil anger and unrest is likely to destabilise incumbent governments. In contrast, by minimising its negative effects or by preventing a crisis in the first place, IMF programs can contribute to stabilise the governments of recipient countries. While Hanke's claim that IMF opposition to his currency board proposal for Indonesia was based on U.S. interests in ousting Suharto appears far-fetched, by influencing size and conditions of IMF rescue programs the Fund's dominant shareholders can indeed effectively stabilise governments of their liking and undermine the standing of those deemed hostile to national interests[5]. Regarding the United States Oatley and Yackee found only limited statistical evidence for this possibility in practice. But their analysis of over 139 lending decisions in the period between 1986 and 1998 indicates that IMF loans tend to be largest when recipient countries are large debtors of U.S. financial institutions and their policies are aligned with U.S. interests[6]. Drawing on an analysis of lending decisions between 1985 and 1994, Thacker identifies significant effects of recipient countries' political alignments on the likelihood of program approval by the Executive Board[7]. Particularly countries

---

4 See Thomas Oatley. 2002. *Commercial Banks and the International Monetary Fund: An Empirical Analysis.* Working Paper. Chapel Hill, NC: University of North Carolina.

5 In February 1998 Professor Steve Hanke advised the Indonesian government to introduce a currency board for arresting the country's financial crisis. His suggestion was strictly opposed both by the U.S. administration and the IMF. The reason, as Hanke claims, was that U.S. policy makers and the IMF were convinced that a currency board would halt the crisis they needed to achieve the ousting of Suharto. See Steve Hanke. 2003. "Iraq, Regime Changes and Currency Boards." *The National Post.* May 28, 2003

6 See Thomas Oatley and Jason Yackee. 2000. *Political Determinants of IMF Balance of Payments Lending: The Curse of Carabosse?.* Working Paper. Chapel Hill, NC: University of North Carolina.

7 See Strom Thacker. 1999. "The High Politics of IMF Lending." *World Politics.* Vol. 52, No. 1

whose policy alignments move towards those of the United States were seen as improving their chances of receiving funding by the IMF, although absolute policy positions were reported to be of limited importance in the decision-making process. Surprisingly, the impact of high politics appears to have increased since the end of the cold war instead of declined as might be expected. While evidence relates to the United States only, lending decisions do not depend on the U.S. alone; the Fund's other dominant members, particularly its partners in the G-7, have an important say on IMF lending policies.

10.1.3.2 Financial Sector Interests

In a micro-level analysis, Broz and Hawes have developed a framework explaining how financial institutions in the United States are able to influence the voting behaviour of the U.S. representative at the Fund' Executive Board. Because Congress has to approve all decisions on U.S. policy regarding the IMF, interests groups can interfere via lobbying efforts at members of congress. Congress wields substantial power over the administration and can so exert pressure on the Secretary of the Treasury who has the final say over voting decisions taken by the U.S. executive director. Analysing data on 120 developing countries between 1983 and 2002, the authors identify a highly significant positive relationship between emerging market exposure of commercial lending banks in the United States and both number and size of IMF rescue packages[8].

In addition, commercial banks were found to wield larger influence over IMF lending decisions than any other private creditor of developing countries, including investors in bonds and other securities. This is not surprising, for in contrast to dispersed security holders, commercial banks have fewer difficulties to overcome collective action problems. This allows for concerted and thus more effective lobbying efforts. Analysing a sample over 140 lending decisions by the IMF between 1985 and 1998, Oatley found that IMF rescue packages were largest for those developing countries with the highest debt obligations to industrialised countries' commercial banks. This finding proved valid not only for commercial banks headquartered in the United States, but also for those of Germany, Switzerland and the United Kingdom; surprisingly, for Japan and France the relationship was significantly weaker[9].

---

8 See Broz, Lawrence and Michael Hawes. 2003. *Domestic Interests of International Monetary Fund Policy*. Paper delivered at the Public Lectures Committee for the UCLA Department of Political Science. June 2, 2003. Los Angeles, CA: University of California: 24

9 See Oatley (2002): 17–18

10.1.3.3 Creditor Country Costs

While benefiting from increased financial stability in the international monetary system, creditor country governments also bear the largest part of costs involved with international liquidity assistance, either through bilateral support or via their funding share at international organisations like the IMF. Unsurprisingly, scepticism regarding the Fund's effectiveness is strongest among those countries that provide the majority of funds required for the provision of emergency loans by the official sector; the opposition of advanced industrial countries to an IMF quota increase at the 12th quinquennial review in 2003 underlines this point. Buira identifies this reluctance as a direct consequence of the fact that industrial countries have become net creditors of the Fund and don't expect to need IMF assistance in the near future[10]. Similarly, the Fund's case-by-case approach and constructive ambiguity can be argued to indicate creditor countries' strong preoccupation with the costs rather than the benefits of reducing instability in the global financial system[11].

Although the Fund's the largest members bear the vast majority of costs arising from IMF liquidity assistance, experiences made since the mid 1990s underline that benefits were often judged to outweigh costs. However, benefits are not necessarily spread equally: Particularly in the case of Mexico, but also at other instances in Latin America and Eastern Asia, U.S. investors appeared to have gained most from IMF bail-outs. This is not surprising as U.S. capital markets are the world's largest. But it highlights that the prime beneficiaries of IMF assistance have often been those countries whose financial sectors were most heavily invested in the respective crisis economies. Regarding the case of Mexico in 1995, former Treasury Secretary Robert Rubin candidly states that

> If our government didn't step in to help, and help quickly, the immediate and long-term-consequences for Mexico could be severe. But the real reason for acting was that critical American interests were at stake[12].

From a rational actor perspective, the Fund's largest and most powerful members should be expected to seek influencing lending decisions in a way ensuring approval for the rescue of countries important to national interests while vetoing assistance to countries that are less relevant to domestic interests. In practice, individual govern-

---

10 See Buira, Ariel. 2004. *Should the Governance of the IMF Be Reformed?* Presentation at the IMF Book Forum on February 5, 2004. Washington, DC: International Monetary Fund: 11

11 See Fernández-Arias, Eduardo and Ricardo Hausmann. 2000. *The Redesign of the International Financial Architecture from a Latin American Perspective: Who Pays the Bill?* Working Paper No. 440. Washington, DC: Inter-American Development Bank: 17

12 Robert E. Rubin and Jacob Weisberg. 2004. *In An Uncertain World: Tough Choices from Wall Street to Washington.* New York, NY: Random House: 3–4

ments, at least by themselves, wield no such universal power. But dominant IMF members clearly influence IMF lending decisions to a great extent. Although individual power is limited by the institutional design of the IMF and thus may be smaller than often claimed, in coalition G-7 countries can block all significant decisions that are taken at both Executive Board and Board of Governors.

10.1.4 Evidence on IMF Lending Arrangements

Although the Fund's mandate as defined in Article 1 of the Fund's Articles of Agreement specifies duties towards all member countries, the IMF has provided liquidity assistance to some members more willingly than to others. Between 1983 and 2001 the Fund provided liquidity support in only 35 percent of the years in which developing countries faced financial distress[13]. Moreover, there are indications that countries of strategic importance to the Fund's largest members received financial assistance faster and more generous than others.

Barro and Lee analysed panel data for 130 countries over five 5-year periods from 1975 to 1999; the sample amounts to 603 observations. They identified a positive correlation between IMF funding arrangements and selected political economy variables[14]. More specifically, they report a positive relationship between IMF lending decisions and the recipient country's political proximity to the Fund's largest members: The United States, Japan, Germany, France and the United Kingdom. Variables representing proximity included similar voting records at the United Nation's General Assembly for political closeness and bilateral trade volumes for the degree of economic involvement. In addition, both number and amount of IMF loans were found to rise with recipient countries' involvement with the institution as measured by countries' quota and number of professional staff at the Fund.

These results are mirrored by Copelovitch's analysis of 34 developing countries that received short–term IMF support between 1984 and 2001. Programs considered were Stand-By Arrangements, Extended Fund and Supplemental Reserve Facilities. The study's key explanatory variable is G-5 commercial banks' exposure to developing countries as recorded by BIS data; trade relations enter the model via variables incorporating data from the IMF *Direction of Trade Statistics*. The findings suggest that states with larger banking or trade relations to the Fund's dominant members are more likely to receive IMF assistance than countries relative-

---

13 See Mark Copelovitch. 2003. *Domestic Interests and the International Lender of Last Resort: The Political Economy of IMF Crisis Lending.* Paper prepared for the Annual Meeting of the American Political Science Association. August 28–31, 2004. Philadelphia, PA: 9
14 See Robert Barro and Jong-Wha Lee. 2002. *IMF Programs: Who Is Chosen and What Are the Effects?* NBER Working Paper W8951. Cambridge, MA: National Bureau of Economic Research

ly less involved with G-5 economies. In addition, loans to countries of high economic interest to the G-5 were found to be larger in size than those to countries of limited importance to the Fund's dominant members[15]. Fears among both developing and smaller industrial countries that IMF decision-making has been hijacked by the world's major industrial countries increased when the Group of Seven decided at the 1999 Cologne Summit to increase their involvement in international monetary affairs. More frequent contact between G-7 representatives and IMF management outside of Board of Governors meetings and the International Monetary and Financial Committee further fuelled this perception undermining the authority of both Managing Director and the Executive Board[16].

Under official decision-making procedures the power wielded by the world's largest industrial countries clearly outweighs that of all other members. Both institutional structure and allocation of voting weights underscores the dominance of G-7 countries at the Board of Governors and the Executive Board. Their lack of influence is clearly felt by developing countries continuously experiencing that their power to take part in decision-making or advance own agendas at the Fund is limited. In an address at the IMF Governance Seminar in October 2004, Li Ruogu, Deputy Governor of the People's Bank of China, complained that

> First, the dominant voting powers of a small group of countries have kept the Fund away from any policy initiative that may benefit the global community as a whole in the long run, but is not in the interest of those countries in the short run...Second, developing countries have had enormous disadvantages in setting rules of games in the Fund, which have weakened their ability to protect their own interests as well as their ownership to implement the Fund's programs...in not few cases, policy decisions were approved without fully engaging all member countries or even regardless of objection or abstention from developing countries[17].

10.2 The Distribution of Voting Power at the IMF

In contrast to other international organisations like WTO or the United Nations' General Assembly where decisions are taken under an one-member-one-vote sys-

---

15 See Copelovitch (2003): 29–31
16 See Leo Van Houtven. 2002. *Governance of the IMF. Decision Making, Institutional Oversight, Transparency, and Accountability.* IMF Pamphlet Series No. 53. Washington, DC: International Monetary Fund
17 Li Ruogu. 2004. *Reform the Governance of the IMF.* Speech given on the Seminar on Governance of the Bretton Woods Institutions. October 1, 2004. Beijing, China: The People's Bank of China

tem, at both Bretton Woods institutions voting power differs between individual members. When the plans for IMF and World Bank were drawn in 1943, a weighted voting structure was chosen to resemble different contributions by individual members. Despite opposition to the inclusion of supermajority requirements by the British delegation under John Maynard Keynes, the United States were able to negotiate what in effect amounted to a national veto on most important decisions. This veto is still present 60 years after, although both membership and Fund resources have increased several-fold; it is also responsible for the difficulties in reforming the Bretton Woods institutions and restructuring the IMF into an institution operating similar to an international lender of last resort.

Decision-making power at the IMF lies with the Board of Governors where each member country is represented directly, usually by the head of the central bank or the minister of finance. The Board of Governors meets biannually and votes on a limited number of strategic and reform proposals. Operational control and day-to-day management is delegated by the Board of Governors to the Executive Board, chaired by the Managing Director. Decisions remaining with the Board of Governors comprise 13 areas including quota adjustments, SDR allocation and other issues of institutional design.

10.2.1 IMF Voting Weights

Quotas at the IMF serve three functions: they determine members' contributions to the Fund's resources, members' access to those resources and members' voting weights in Board of Governors and the Executive Board. Each member country's voting weight is determined by a fixed amount of 250 votes and one additional vote for each SDR million contributed to the Fund's resources as part of the quota. Quotas are allocated according to five formulas based on member's GDP, reserves and current account transactions. The determining variables are official reserves, current account receipts and payments, variability of current accounts and the ratio of current receipts to GDP[18]. The basic 250 votes were granted at the Fund's inception in order to soften the weighted voting system's impact on smaller members. Following twelve quota reviews, the share of basic votes in total votes has shrunk to 2.1 from 11.3 percent in 1944. As a consequence, the voting weights of smaller member states have plummeted to a fraction of one percent, reducing the influence of developing countries at IMF decision-making to a minimum. Table 10.1 exhibits voting weights of selected countries in the Board of Governors.

---

18 See IMF. 2000. *Report to the IMF Executive Board of the Quota Formula Review Group.* April 28, 2000. Washington, DC: International Monetary Fund: 15–16

Table 10.1
Selected Quotas and Voting Shares in the Board of Governors

Countries	Quota (SDR million)	Percentage of Total Quota	Total Votes Cast	Percentage of Total Votes
United States	37149	17.46%	371743	17.14%
Japan	13313	6.26%	133378	6.15%
Germany	13008,2	6.11%	130332	6.01%
France	10738,5	5.05%	107635	4.96%
United Kingdom	10738,5	5.05%	107635	4.96%
Canada	6362,9	2.95%	80636	2.95%
Italy	7055,5	3.32%	90968	3.26%
China	6362,9	2.95%	63942	2.95%
Russia	5945,4	2.79%	59704	2.75%
Brazil	3036,1	1.43%	30611	1.41%
Mexico	2585,8	1.22%	26108	1.20%
Argentina	2117,1	0.99%	21421	0.99%
Korea	1633,6	0.77%	16586	0.76%
Indonesia	2079,3	0.98%	21043	0.97%
India	4158,2	1.95%	41832	1.93%
Philippines	879,9	0.41%	9049	0.42%
Thailand	1081,9	0.51%	11069	0.51%
Chile	856,1	0.40%	8811	0,41%
Egypt	943,7	0.44%	9687	0,45%
Iran	1497,2	0.70%	15222	0,70%
Israel	928,2	0.44%	9532	0,44%
Pakistan	1033,7	0.49%	10587	0,49%
Nigeria	1753,2	0.82%	17782	0,82%
South Africa	1868,5	0.88%	18935	0,87%

Source: IMF Members' Quotas and Voting Power:
http://www.imf.org/external/np/sec/memdir/members.htm

The Executive Board consists of 24 directors, 5 of which are appointed directly by the United States, Japan, Germany, France and the U.K., and 3 by Saudi Arabia, China and Russia. 16 directors are elected biannually by constituent groups consisting of the 176 remaining members. These directors cast both their own as well as the votes of the countries they represent. As votes controlled by these directors cannot be split and have to be cast in unity, the ability of smaller countries unable to appoint their own director to influence day-to-day management decisions is more limited than in the Board of Governors. However, elected directors casting the combined votes of several countries can wield substantial power—far above their country's share of the total.

Table 10.2
Quotas and Voting Shares in the Executive Board

Countries	Quota (SDR million)	Percentage of Total Quota	Votes Cast	Percentage of Total Votes
United States	37149	17.46%	371743	17.08%
Japan	13313	6.26%	133378	6.13%
Germany	13008	6.11%	130332	5.99%
France	10739	5.05%	107635	4.95%
United Kingdom	10739	5.05%	107635	4.95%
China	6369	2.99%	63942	2.94%
Russia	5945	2.79%	59704	2.74%
Saudi Arabia	6986	3.28%	70105	3.22%
Belgium	4605	2.16%	111696	5.13%
Netherlands	5162	2.43%	105412	4.84%
Mexico	2586	1.22%	92989	4.27%
Italy	7056	3.32%	90968	4.18%
Canada	6369	2.99%	80636	3.71%
Norway	1672	0.79%	76276	3.51%
Korea	1634	0.77%	72423	3.33%
Egypt	944	0.44%	70852	3.26%
Malaysia	1487	0.70%	69019	3.17%
Tanzania	199	0.09%	65221	3.00%
Switzerland	3459	1.63%	61827	2.84%
Iran	1497	0.70%	53662	2.47%
Brazil	3036	1.43%	53634	2.46%
India	4158	1.95%	52112	2.39%
Argentina	2117	0.99%	43395	1.99%
Equatorial Guinea	33	0.02%	30749	1.41%

Source: IMF Executive Directors and Voting Power:
http://www.imf.org/external/np/sec/memdir/eds.htm

Ordinary decisions taken in either Board of Governors or the Executive Board require a simple majority of no less than 50 percent of total votes. However, most important decisions require supermajority support of either 70 or 85 percent of total votes. The First Amendment to the Articles of Agreement in 1969 doubled the number of areas requiring supermajority support to 18; since 1978, when the Second Amendment was passed, 13 decisions in the Board of Governors and 40 in the

Executive Board require supermajority support. Of those, 18 require an 85 percent and 21 a 70 percent majority[19]. Supermajorities are necessary for all changes in the Funds structure, including quota increases and allocations, exchange rate arrangements, interest charges, SDRs, gold reserves and access policy. The steady growth of areas requiring supermajority decisions is clearly a consequence of particular country groups' successful lobbying for a veto on certain matters of national interest[20].

10.2.2 Voting Power at the IMF

Analysing *voting power* underscores the dominant position of the United States at the IMF. Voting power differs from voting shares as it considers not only voting weights but also majority requirements and members' power to actually influence decisions. The importance of individual players in making or breaking coalitions was pointed out originally by Shapley & Shubik and Banzhaf in the 1950s and 1960s[21]. Both Shapley-Shubik and Banzhaf power indices attribute power according to player's pivotality in coalition games: Given parties' voting weights and the voting system's majority requirements the number of all possible coalitions is identified. Individual power scores are then derived by the proportion of the number of times each player is pivotal for a coalition to be winning to the total of winning coalitions.

For determining the distribution of voting power at the IMF, the use of a similar Index, termed *Coleman Index* by Dennis Leech, has been suggested as preferable to the classic Shapley-Shubik and Banzhaf Indices[22]. Coleman rejects Banzhaf's assumption of power sharing and the distribution of spoils among winning coalitions as unlikely[23]; instead he argues that the decisions reached by winning coalitions lead *to some action being taken which has a fixed profile of consequences for the*

---

19 See Ariel Buira. 2004. *Should the Governance of the IMF Be Reformed?* Presentation at the IMF Book Forum on February 5, 2004. Washington, DC: International Monetary Fund: 4

20 See Ariel Buira. 2002a. "The Governance of the IMF in a Global Economy." In Inge Kaul, Pedro Conceicao, Katell Le Goulven and Ronald Mendoza. 2002. *Providing Global Public Goods.* Oxford: Oxford University Press: 230

21 See Lloyd Shapley and Martin Shubik. 1954. "A Method for Evaluating the Distribution of Power in a Committee System." *American Political Science Review.* No. 48, 787–792 and also John Banzhaf. 1965. "Weighted Voting Doesn't Work." *Rutgers Law Review.* No. 19, 317–343

22 Both non-normalized Banzhaf and Coleman Indices are very similar; if a simple majority is required, they arrive at identical results. In case of higher majority requirements, results differ at the non-normalized level, but become identical when normalized in order to represent voting shares.

23 See James Coleman. "Loss of Power" (1973). *American Sociological Review.* No. 38, 1–17

Table 10.3
Board of Governors and Voting Power

Member Country	Weight	Absolute Banzhaf Index (Penrose Index)	Normalised Banzhaf Index	Coleman's Power to Prevent Action	Coleman's Power to Initiate Action
		Simple Majority Decisions			
United States	17.14	0.749426	0.240733	0.726652	0.773674
Japan	6.15	0.169209	0.054354	0.164067	0.174684
Germany	6.01	0.165755	0.053244	0.160718	0.171118
France	4.96	0.138401	0.044458	0.134195	0.142879
United Kingdom	4.96	0.138401	0.044458	0.134195	0.142879
Italy	3.32	0.093410	0.030005	0.090571	0.096432
Saudi Arabia	3.23	0.090942	0.029213	0.088178	0.093884
Canada	2.99	0.084226	0.027055	0.081666	0.086951
China	2.95	0.083105	0.026695	0.080580	0.085794
Russia	2.75	0.077499	0.024895	0.075144	0.080007
Netherlands	2.43	0.068517	0.022009	0.066435	0.070734
Belgium	2.16	0.060927	0.019571	0.059075	0.062898
India	1.95	0.055018	0.017673	0.053346	0.056798
Switzerland	1.63	0.046005	0.014778	0.044607	0.047493
Australia	1.52	0.042905	0.013782	0.041601	0.044293
Spain	1.43	0.040367	0.012967	0.039141	0.041673
Brazil	1.43	0.040367	0.012967	0.039141	0.041673
Venezuela	1.25	0.035291	0.011336	0.034219	0.036433
Mexico	1.22	0.034445	0.011064	0.033398	0.035559
Sweden	1.13	0.031906	0.010249	0.030936	0.032938
Argentina	0.99	0.027955	0.008980	0.027106	0.028860
Indonesia	0.98	0.027673	0.008889	0.026832	0.028568
Austria	0.88	0.024851	0.007983	0.024095	0.025655
South Africa	0.88	0.023721	0.007620	0.023001	0.024489
Norway	0.79	0.022310	0.007166	0.021632	0.023032
Denmark	0.77	0.021745	0.006985	0.021085	0.022449
Korea	0.77	0.021745	0.006985	0.021085	0.022449
Iran	0.70	0.019769	0.006350	0.019168	0.020409
Malaysia	0.70	0.019769	0.006350	0.019168	0.020409

Source: Own calculations using ipmme program

members[24]. Hence the Coleman Index takes into account not only members' relative power among each other but also the ease of decision-making given a particular

---

24 Dennis Leech. 2002. "Voting Power in the Governance of the International Monetary Fund." *Annals of Operations Research* 109, 375–397. Amsterdam: Kluwer Academic Publishers: 386

voting structure: *the power to act*. Corresponding power indices derived by Leech and Leech are the average of members' *power to prevent action* (PPA) and *power to initiate action* (PIA)[25].

10.2.2.1 Voting Power at the Board of Governors

In practice, power scores calculated for individual member countries are very similar and lead to identical results. Given a simple majority rule of 50 percent, power scores are identical for both indices. Due to reasons of clarity and higher prominence in the literature, the use of normalised Banzhaf power scores seems preferable over a combined Coleman PPA and PIA index. Table 10.3 comprises both Banzhaf power scores as well as PPA and PIA scores for the Fund's Board of Governors.

The analysis of individual members' voting power yields different results depending on the majority requirement used in the voting process. In case of simple majority requirements of no less than 50 percent, results show that the United States' share in voting power of 24.1 percent is even higher than its share in total votes of 17.1 percent. In contrast, combined voting power of the next four most powerful members Japan, Germany, France and the United Kingdom of 19.6 percent is considerably below these countries' combined share in total voting weights. Similarly, the nine largest emerging economies command a 12.4 percent share of voting power—below their combined voting weight of 13.7 percent of total votes. Accordingly, in simple majority decisions U.S. dominance over all other members of the IMF is even stronger than quotas and voting weights suggest.

Results are different regarding decisions requiring supermajorities of either 70 or 85 percent. Given its share of 17.1 percent of total votes, the United States is the only member with a national veto on both Board of Governors and the Executive Board for all decisions requiring supermajority support of no less than 85 percent of total votes. All other members have to build coalitions in order to block policy decisions. However, policy initiatives can be blocked by relatively small coalitions of other members, particularly when including Japan and Germany with 6.15 and 6.01 percent of total votes and France and the U.K with 4.96 percent each. Similarly, a coalition of developing countries can veto any decisions requiring an 85 percent supermajority. In the year 2000, a coalition of developing country directors blocked a proposal advanced by G-7 directors regarding interest charges on IMF loans and succeeded in achieving an adjusted proposal more aligned to their interests.

---

25 See Dennis Leech and Robert Leech. 2004. *Voting Power in the Bretton Woods Institutions.* Warwick Economic Research Paper. Warwick: University of Warwick

Table 10.4
Differences between Simple and Supermajority Requirements:
Selected Members in the Board of Governors

Member Country	Weight	Normalised Banzhaf Index 50% Simple Majority	Normalised Banzhaf Index 70% Supermajority	Normalised Banzhaf Index 85% Supermajority
United States	17.14	24.07	7.85	3.82
Japan	6.15	5.44	6.30	3.80
Germany	6.01	5.32	6.20	3.79
France	4.96	4.45	5.37	3.74
United Kingdom	4.96	4.45	5.37	3.74
	22.08	19.65	23.24	15.07
China	2.95	2.67	3.35	3.02
Russia	2.75	2.49	3.13	2.99
India	1.95	1.77	2.24	2.55
Brazil	1.43	1.30	1.65	2.03
Mexico	1.22	1.11	1.41	1.78
Argentina	0.99	0.90	1.15	1.47
Indonesia	0.98	0.89	1.13	1.46
Korea	0.77	0.70	0.89	1.17
Malaysia	0.70	0.64	0.81	1.07
	13.74	12.4498	15.76	17.53

Source: Own calculations using ipmme program

The power scores highlight that for all decisions requiring supermajority support, United States' voting power is much weaker than suggested by its share of total votes. With a share of 3.82 percent U.S. voting power is similar to that of Japan at 3.80 percent, Germany at 3.79 percent, and France and the U.K. at 3.74 percent for all decisions depending on the support of 85 percent of total votes. Supermajority requirements disproportionally benefit members with smaller voting weights; they gain in voting power where both U.S. and the Fund's largest members see their voting power reduced. For decisions requiring majorities of at least 70 percent, not only smaller, but also larger member countries benefit in comparison to the strongest member as their combined power share increases to 23.2 percent. Smaller members still benefit, but less than if 85 percent majorities are required, while the U.S. is the only member loosing in both cases.

Nevertheless, as the only single member able to veto decisions requiring 85 percent supermajority support, the United States are very powerful in preventing actions; its power to initiate policies is more limited as differences between PPA and PIA and lower Banzhaf scores indicate. Consequently, in contrast to the common perception, the United States is not as dominant in voting power for all decisions taken at the IMF as widely perceived. While its dominance is obvious in decisions depending on the support of a simple majority of votes, in case of decisions requireing supermajority support of 70 or 85 percent power is more limited.

Table 10.5
Executive Board and Voting Power

Member Country	Weight	Absolute Banzhaf Index (Penrose Index)	Normalised Banzhaf Index	Coleman's Power to Prevent Action	Coleman's Power to Initiate Action
		Simple Majority Decisions			
United States	17.08%	0.64542	0.21480	0.64564	0.64520
Japan	6.13%	0.17504	0.05825	0.17510	0.17498
Germany	5.99%	0.17104	0.05692	0.17110	0.17098
France	4.95%	0.14105	0.04694	0.14110	0.14100
United Kingdom	4.95%	0.14105	0.04694	0.14110	0.14100
Saudi Arabia	2.94%	0.09168	0.03051	0.09171	0.09165
China	2.74%	0.08374	0.02787	0.08377	0.08371
Russia	3.22%	0.07803	0.02597	0.07806	0.07800
Belgium	5.13%	0.14653	0.04877	0.14658	0.14648
Netherlands	4.84%	0.13822	0.04600	0.13827	0.13818
Mexico	4.27%	0.12194	0.04058	0.12198	0.12190
Italy	4.18%	0.11905	0.03962	0.11909	0.11901
Canada	3.71%	0.10568	0.03517	0.10572	0.10565
Norway	3.51%	0.09996	0.03327	0.09999	0.09992
Korea	3.33%	0.09484	0.03156	0.09487	0.09480
Egypt	3.26%	0.09250	0.03079	0.09253	0.09247
Malaysia	3.17%	0.09030	0.03005	0.09033	0.09027
Tanzania	3.00%	0.08535	0.02840	0.08537	0.08532
Switzerland	2.84%	0.08084	0.02690	0.08087	0.08081
Iran	2.47%	0.07009	0.02333	0.07012	0.07007
Brazil	2.46%	0.07009	0.02333	0.07012	0.07007
India	2.39%	0.06812	0.02267	0.06814	0.06810
Argentina	1.99%	0.05671	0.01887	0.05673	0.05669
Equatorial Guinea	1.41%	0.03742	0.01245	0.03744	0.03741

Source: Own calculations using ipdirect program

Table 10.6
Differences between Simple and Supermajority Requirements: Executive Board

Member Country	Weight	Normalised Banzhaf Index 50% Simple Majority	Normalised Banzhaf Index 70% Supermajority	Normalised Banzhaf Index 85% Supermajority
United States	17,1%	21.48	11.26	6.43
Japan	6.1%	5.83	6.47	5.79
Germany	6.0%	5.69	6.34	5.73
France	5.0%	4.69	5.28	5.23
United Kingdom	5.0%	4.69	5.28	5.23
		20.91	**23.36**	**21.97**
China	2.9%	3.05	3.47	3.87
Russia	2.7%	2.79	3.17	3.60
Saudi Arabia	3.2%	2.60	2.96	3.38
		8.44	**9.60**	**10.84**
Belgium	5.13%	4.88	5.47	5.33
Netherlands	4.84%	4.60	5.18	5.17
Mexico	4.27%	4.06	4.59	4.80
Italy	4.18%	3.96	4.48	4.72
Canada	3.71%	3.52	3.99	4.32
Norway	3.51%	3.33	3.78	4.14
Korea	3.33%	3.16	3.59	3.98
Egypt	3.26%	3.08	3.50	3.89
Malaysia	3.17%	3.01	3.42	3.81
Tanzania	3.00%	2.84	3.23	3.68
Switzerland	2.84%	2.69	3.07	3.50
Iran	2.47%	2.33	2.66	3.08
Brazil	2.46%	2.33	2.66	3.08
India	2.39%	2.27	2.59	2.99
Argentina	1.99%	1.89	2.16	2.55
Equatorial Guinea	1.41%	1.25	1.43	1.73

Source: Own calculations using ipmme program

10.2.2.2 Voting Power at the Executive Board

Similar findings apply when analysing the distribution of voting power in the Executive Board. Again, key differences arise from different majority requirements. In case of simple majority requirements of no less than 50 percent of total votes, the United States' 21.5 percent share of total voting power clearly outweighs its 17.1

Table 10.7
Constituencies and Voting Power in the Executive Board

Countries	Represented Countries	Total Votes Cast	Percentage of Total Votes
United States	none	371743	17.1%
Japan	none	133378	6.1%
Germany	none	130332	6.0%
France	none	107635	4.9%
United Kingdom	none	107635	4.9%
China	none	63942	2.9%
Russia	none	59704	2.7%
Saudi Arabia	none	70105	3.2%
	none		0.0%
Belgium	Austria, Belarus, Belgium, Czech Republic, Hungary, Kazakhstan, Luxembourg, Slovak Republic, Slovenia, Turkey	111696	5.1%
Netherlands	Armenia, Bosnia & Herzegovina, Bulgaria, Croatia, Cyprus, Georgia, Israel, Macedonia, Moldova, Netherlands, Romania, Ukraine	105412	4.8%
Mexico	Costa Rica, El Salvador, Guatemala, Hondouras, Mexico, Nicaragua, Spain Venezuela	92989	4.3%
Italy	Albania, Greece, Italy, Malta, Portugal, San Marino, Timor-Leste	90968	4.2%
Canada	Antigua & Barbuda, Bahamas, Barbados, Belize, Canada, Diminica, Grenada, Ireland, Jamaica, St. Kitts and Nevis, St. Lucia, St. Vincent and the Grenadines	80636	3.7%
Norway	Denmark, Estonia, Finland, Iceland, Latvia, Lithuania, Norway, Sweden	76276	3.5%
Korea	Australia, Kiribati, Korea, Marshall Islands, Micronesia, Mongolia, New Zealand, Palau, Papua New Guinea, Philippines, Samoa, Seychelles, Solomon Islands, Vanuatu	72423	3.3%
Egypt	Bahrain, Egypt, Iraq, Jordan, Kuwait, Lebanon, Lybia, Maledives, Oman, Syria, Qatar, United Arab Emirates, Yemen	70852	3.3%
Indonesia	Brunei, Cambodia, Fiji, Indonesia, Laos, Malaysia, Myanmar, Nepal, Singapore, Thailand, Tonga, Vietnam	69019	3.2%
Nigeria	Angola, Botswana, Burundi, Eritrea, Ethiopia, Gambia, Kenia, Lesotho, Malawi, Mozambique, Namibia, Nigeria, Sierra Leone, South Africa, Sudan, Swaziland, Tanzania, Uganda, Zambia	65221	3.0%

Countries	Represented Countries	Total Votes Cast	Percentage of Total Votes
Switzerland	Azerbaijan, Kyrgiztan, Poland, Serbia & Mcnte-negro, Switzerland, Tajikistan, Turkmenistan, Uzbekistan	61827	2.8%
Brazil	Brazil, Colombia, Dominican Republic, Ecuador, Guyana, Haiti, Panama, Suriname, Trinidad & Tobago	53634	2.5%
Iran	Afghanistan, Algeria, Ghana, Iran, Morocco, Pakistan, Tunisia	53662	2.5%
India	Bangladesh, Bhutan, India, Sri Lanka	52112	2.4%
Chile	Argentina, Bolivia, Chile, Paraguay, Peru, Uruguay	43395	2.0%
Equatorial Guinea	Benin, Burkina Faso, Cameroon, Cape Verde, Central African Republic, Chad, Comoros, Congo, DR Congo, Côte d'Ivoire, Djibuti, Equatorial Guinea, Gabon, Guinea, Guinea-Bissau, Mada-gascar, Mali, Mauritania, Mauritius, Niger, Rwanda, Sao Tomé & Principe, Senegal, Togo	30749	1.4%

Source: IMF Executive Directors and Voting Power:
http://www.imf.org/external/np/sec/memdir/eds.htm

percent share of total votes. Given the limited number of players in the Executive Board, the differences between voting weight and voting power are less than at the Board of Governors. Consequently, voting power of the 23 non-U.S. executive directors is higher, although significantly less so than their voting weights may imply.

As in the Board of Governors, in the Executive Board supermajority requirements drastically reduce U.S. dominance given the relative ease coalitions can be formed with to veto initiatives. The increase in voting power of smaller members is higher in the case of 70 than in the case of 85 percent supermajority requirements since countries with smaller voting weights benefit disproportionally. This phenomenon's cut-off point lies at a share of between 4.29 and 4.86 percent of total votes: for Spain and all countries with lower voting weights, power increases linearly with rising majority requirements. But even decisions requiring only 70 percent supermajority support can be blocked by a coalition of only the four largest Fund members.

10.2.2.3 Constituencies at the Executive Board

The Executive Board's composition results in large differences in directors' voting power when compared to their country's share in the Board of Governors. The divergence stems from the constituency principle by which the Executive Board operates. 176 of the Fund's 184 members are grouped into constituencies represented in the Executive Board by a single director. Groupings follow a rough geographic order, while their size ranges from just 4 to 24 members. To facilitate the process of decision-making in the Executive Board, all members except the five largest shareholders as well as China, Russia and Saudi Arabia cast the votes of all their constituency's members. Italy, Canada, Switzerland, India and Brazil control more than half of the votes within their constituency.

As executive directors are elected by simple majority, these countries effectively also possess permanent seats. Belgium and the Netherlands are their constituency's largest members but lack an absolute majority of intra-group voting power; as dominant players within their constituencies these countries are nevertheless also elected on a continuous basis. The remaining constituencies have alternating directors, sometimes alternating only between the constituency's largest members and sometimes between all members of the group.

The Executive Board's constituency structure distorts voting power and undermines legitimacy due to several reasons: As constituencies' combined total of votes can only be cast together, the elected director controls the full amount of voting weight. He cannot account for differences in opinion by selected constituents but has to cast all votes in unity. As a result, Belgium controls a higher share of votes than all other members but the United States, Japan and Germany: It outweighs France and the United Kingdom, as well as China and Mexico. In addition, the diverging size of constituencies leads to substantial under-representation of the developing world in general and Africa in particular: 160 of the Fund's 184 members are developing countries and only 24 are advanced industrialised economies; but 13 of the Executive Board's 24 directors are nominated by industrialised countries. Creditor countries account for 71 percent of total votes[26] and the European Union alone is represented by 8 and sometimes 9 directors in the Executive Board. 44 African states are represented by just two executive directors and control merely 4.4 percent of votes, despite accounting for nearly a quarter of IMF membership: A Tanzanian director currently represents the constituency of 20 Anglophone African states, while a director of Equatorial Guinea casts the combined votes of 24 Franco-

---

26 See Rustomjee, Cyrus. 2004. "Why Developing Countries Need a Stronger Vote." *Finance & Development.* September 2004. Washington, DC: International Monetary Fund: 22

phone African states. The Fund's voting system leaves in effect 41 countries without any voting power at all to influence decisions taken at the Executive Board[27].

10.2.2.4 The Power of Industrialised and Developing Countries at the IMF

The Fund's largest members, the G-5, control 39.6 percent of total votes. Consequently a coalition of these countries can veto any decision or reform proposal that requires either 70 or 85 percent of total votes to pass. Decisions requiring supermajorities of at least 85 percent can be vetoed by the U.S. alone or by a coalition of Japan, Germany, the U.K and France. Including the votes of Belgium, the Netherlands, Italy, Canada and Norway, industrial countries control well over 50 percent of total votes. Accordingly, industrial countries can implement policy preferences in all areas under a simple majority decision-rule.

At the same time, supermajority requirements allow a coalition of developing countries to veto crucial decisions in both Board of Governors and the Executive Board. So while a coalition of G-7 countries can veto all decisions regarding the IMF and its operations, its power to proactively enforce its interests against those of a majority of IMF members is limited to those areas requiring simple majority support: However, the vast majority of decisions taken in the Executive Board, most importantly those regarding approval of loan and stabilization programs fall into this category. A coalition of developing countries can only veto decisions requiring supermajorities of 85 percent. Decisions requiring a majority of 70 percent of total votes can be blocked only when neither Spain nor Australia represents its constituency[28].

In practice this scenario rarely unfolds. The Executive Board has followed a practice of consensus decision-making ever since the Fund's inception. Moreover, executive directors always follow the recommendations proposed by the Fund's staff. Until today, the Executive Board has never voted down a recommendation proposed by the Managing Director; it has been suggested that were this ever to occur, the Managing Director would be expected to resign. If members want to influence IMF decisions, they have to exert their power while recommendations are drafted by IMF staff. When a policy recommendation reaches the Executive Board, the opportunity to achieve substantial changes in its content has passed.

---

27 See Leech and Leech (2004): 2

28 In the constituency of Spain, three countries dominate: Spain with 30739 votes, Mexico with 26108 votes and Bolivia with 26891 votes. As a coalition between two of these countries is sufficient to reach the simple majority required to nominate the group's executive director, the directorship alternates between Spain, Bolivia and Mexico. The same reasoning applies to the constituency of Australia (32614 votes), where a coalition between Korea (16586), New Zealand (9196) and the Philippines (9049) can insist on a rotating directorship.

Initially devised by the United States and the United Kingdom to balance the differing interests of the Fund's diverse membership, the practice of consensus decision-making at the Executive Board has been maintained to this day. IMF Rules and Regulations stipulate that

> The Chairman shall ordinarily ascertain the sense of the meeting in lieu of a formal vote. Any Executive Director may require a formal vote to be taken with votes cast as prescribed in Article XII, Section 3(i), or Article XXI(a)(ii)[29].

According to this guideline, decisions are adopted if supported by the votes necessary to meet majority requirements in case an official vote would have been taken. While consensus and unanimity is wishful, neither is necessary for a decision to be adopted by the chairman. Given relative voting weights, to avert a decision requiring an 85 percent supermajority, directors from developing countries must build almost all-encompassing coalitions. If interests of emerging economies and less developed countries are not fully aligned such efforts are likely to fail. In doubt, a director will refrain from exposing his country by calling for a formal vote without being ensured of support by the necessary number of fellow executive directors. Despite the claim that *consensus decision making ... has provided a particularly valuable protection to the interests of developing countries*[30], it often leaves developing countries supporting G-7 proposals without their concerns being taken into account sufficiently. According to Cyrus Rustomjee, a former director at the Executive Board,

> In the case of sub-Saharan Africa, when an issue is in dispute among the various shareholders, there is no reasonable possibility of forging a consensus that enables the African members' views to prevail. Instead, consensus means joining a creditor-dominated perspective only to see the specific points of objection that were raised slip away[31].

Moreover, developing countries have generally been hesitant to bluntly oppose the interests of stronger players, particularly if a positive outcome appears unlikely. Only when issues are vital and support by fellow developing countries is ensured does it become worthwhile to openly oppose a proposal filed by the world's largest economies. But more often than not developing countries depend on the goodwill of creditor countries rendering cooperative behaviour at international institutions a sensible strategy. By voting through donor countries' proposals, developing coun-

---

29 See *Rules and Regulations of the IMF*: C–10
30 See Leo van Houtven (2002): 37
31 Rustomjee (2004): 22

tries increase their chances of receiving development aid, market access and the likelihood that future loan requests will be considered benevolently.

However, the fact that developing countries rarely reject proposals backed by the Fund's largest shareholders is not exclusively due to the practice of consensus decision making or informal dependencies. Often interests of industrialised and developing countries are aligned rather than opposed. Developed and developing countries benefit alike from efforts to restore market confidence and global financial stability. The consequence of developing countries' limited influence on IMF policy is less that G-7 countries can pass policies detrimental to developing country interests but that developing countries are unable to promote policies more important to themselves than to the Fund's major shareholders.

10.3 The Case for Reforming IMF Governance Structures

Increasing voice and representation of developing countries in the Fund's governance structure appears warranted on several accounts. Firstly, since its inception the IMF has steadily increased its exposure to developing countries and emerging economies. Secondly, the practice of consensus decision-making at the Executive Board has increasingly given way to reaching decisions by simple majority. And finally, a loss of legitimacy in the eyes of developing countries limits the institution's effectiveness as a result of ownership problems. According to Rustomjee

> The current margin of voting share in favour of creditors beyond that required to ensure a simple majority strikes at the foundation of the principles of collaboration and consensus decision–making upon which the IMF operates. It weakens the institution, reduces operational efficiency, gnaws at the institution's legitimacy, erodes ownership of programs and policies by the collective membership, offers no tangible benefit to the collective membership, and has bred understandable resentment in the debtor group[32].

In contrast to its early days the Fund's client base today consists predominantly of developing countries and emerging market economies. IMF lending facilities are almost exclusively utilized by this constituency. Similarly, technical assistance by IMF staff naturally concentrates on the same group of countries. The same applies to the Fund's monitoring activities: Although all members engage in annual Article 4 consultations, surveillance activities to a large extent focus on developing countries and emerging market economies given their higher vulnerability to external shocks. Increasing voice and representation of the institution's core client base seems the

---

32 Rustomejee (2004): 23

logical response to these developments and is necessary to account for the risen importance of emerging markets, transition economies and less developed countries for the global economy.

Another argument for increasing developing countries' voice in IMF decision-making draws on the trend that the principle of consensus decision-making in the Executive Board has given way to an increasing application of simple majority decisions[33]. As Van Houtven asserts *the major industrial countries, the Group of Seven, which command close to one-half of the voting power in the IMF, have exhibited a growing tendency in recent years to act as a self-appointed steering group or "Directoire" of the IMF*[34]. Due to their limited voting weight developing countries' position is hence often neglected when the chairman of the board assesses the sense of a meeting. The result in many instances has been inefficient decision-making. During the Asian Crisis, doubts by developing countries on the effectiveness of IMF-approved stability programs were largely neglected. By having granted developing countries' concerns more attention, many flaws in IMF programs might have been prevented in the first place. Increasing developing countries' voting weights and their number of representative at the Executive Board would enhance these countries' ability to build coalitions. In turn their positions would carry more weight at Executive Board decision-making thereby restoring the credibility of consensus decision-making at least to a certain degree.

Most importantly, a re-allocation of quotas and voting weights in favour of developing countries and emerging economies would contribute to an increase in ownership of the policies approved at the Executive Board. The Fund's least developed members, mostly African states, have little opportunity to add weight to their views on the conditions attached to poverty reduction and growth facilities or the viability of poverty reduction strategies in the context of the HIPC initiative. Furthermore, their representation among IMF staff is insufficient. As a result both motivation and effectiveness in implementing IMF induced policy reforms is lacking among policy makers in many African states. Increasing their say in the decision-making process is likely to improve program design considerably. The effectiveness of stabilisation programs would be enhanced as fairer representation would contribute to higher willingness and motivation in the implementation process on part of national authorities; for without support within the executive, the bureaucracy and the population reform efforts can be easily frustrated. The same reasoning applies to the effecttiveness of IMF monitoring and surveillance activities since cooperation by developing

---

33 See Cyrus Rustomjee. 2005. "Improving Southern Voice on the IMF Board: Quo Vadis Shareholders?" In Barry Carin and Angela Wood. 2005. *Accountability of the International Monetary Fund.* Burlington, VT: Ashgate
34 See Van Houtven (2002): 30

country authorities is likely to increase in line with improving perceptions regarding the Fund's legitimacy.

10.3.1 Governance Reform Proposals

The international community is fully aware of the governance problems at both IMF and the World Bank. Reform commitments were made at the 2002 International Conference on Financing for Development in Monterrey and renewed at the International Monetary and Finance Committee's 12th general review of quotas in early 2003. Following a report by IMF staff on the subject, a majority of directors *saw considerable merit* in a package of measures to be implemented at the 13th general quota review in 2008: the proposed quota increase would contain a relatively large selective component by applying a new allocation formula and implementing a general increase in basic votes[35]. Directors further supported an ad-hoc quota increase for countries whose quotas are most obviously out of line with their position in the world economy[36]. However, as of today quota allocations at the Fund have remained unchanged.

The determination of current quotas was guided by several formulae which took into account GDP, official reserves, current account receipts, payments and volatility as well as the ratio of current receipts to GDP. But ever since the Fund's inception, the actual impact of formulae on quota allocation has been limited as quotas derived have served as a basis for negotiations rather than as authoritative guideline. Given the multiple purposes quotas serve, the re-allocation of quotas is a highly political and sensitive task. However, there is no convincing reason why both access and contribution to IMF resources as well as voting weights should be determined by a single quota. In fact, already 1944 in Bretton Woods it was perceived *both illogical and unnecessary, and this was frequently pointed out during the conference*[37]. A sensible first step would thus be to consider drawing on distinct formulae and quotas to determine different issues and so facilitate an eventual re-allocation of quotas.

All calls for a reform of quota allocations aim at increasing the voting weights of developing countries. Measures to achieve such an outcome include taking into account GDP based on purchasing power parity or letting population figures enter

---

35 See IMF. 2003. *Quota Distribution – Selected Issues.* Report prepared by the Finance Department. Washington, DC: International Monetary Fund

36 See IMF. 2003. *Report of the IMF Executive Board to the International Monetary and Financial Committee on Quotas, Voice and Representation.* Report prepared by the Finance and Secretary's Department. September 12, 2003. Washington, DC: International Monetary Fund. http://www.imf.org/external/np/fin/2003/quota/eng/091203.htm

37 See Raymond Mikesell. 1994. *The Bretton Woods Debates: A Memoir.* Essays in International Finance. No. 192, March 1994. Princeton, NJ: Princeton University: 37

into the calculation of quotas. Prime beneficiaries of both approaches would be China and India, who not only boast the world's largest populations but also some of the world's largest GDP figures if measured in PPP. However, a shift in the Fund's balance of power that eliminates the simple majority of creditor countries is politically unfeasible. Neither is it desirable since effective governance needs to ensure that debtor countries cannot determine the use of IMF resources unilaterally.

A more realistic proposal would be to increase the share of basic votes to its 1944 level of 11.3 percent of the total: Developing countries' voting weights would increase from just below 40 to a little over 47 percent, while a veto for both the U.S. and combined EU members would be maintained[38]. Primary beneficiaries would be small developing countries whose share in total voting weights would increase over-proportionally. Raising the weight of GDP within allocation formulae would benefit larger developing countries and might shore up their support. As both approaches would increase developing countries' share of total votes, they would inevitably involve a reduction in voting weights for industrial countries. Most obvious candidates would be members of the European Union given that the current allocation formulae include intra-EU trade: Excluding those figures would leave EU countries with only 60 percent of their current share.

The last 60 years not only saw considerable changes in the size of individual countries' economies, but also a drastic increase in international capital flows. In order to account for the risen importance of capital account movements, an additional variable to include into a revised allocation formula could be the volatility of capital flows as recommended in a report by the Quota Formula Review Group in April 2000 that above all suggested a simplification of quota determination procedures[39]. Most recommendations of the so-called Cooper Report centre on a simplified linear formula based on members' ability to contribute to IMF resources as well as their economies' vulnerability to external shocks with weights clearly skewed towards the former. To measure a country's ability to contribute the report proposes a three year average of GDP while for measuring vulnerability it suggests the volatility of both a country's current receipts and international capital flows.

Another central aspect of governance reform at the IMF concerns the composition of the Executive Board. Since there is a trade-off between legitimacy and efficiency as an excessively large Executive Board would slow the Fund's decision-making

---

38 Ariel Buira. 2002b. *A New Voting Structure for the IMF*. Working Paper: Washington, DC: Intergovernmental Group of Twenty Four: 6
39 See Quota Formula Review Group. 2000. *Report to the IMF Executive Board of the Quota Formula Review Group*. April 28, 2000. Washington, DC: International Monetary Fund. The eight member commission headed by Richard Cooper of Harvard University included representatives of Ghana, India, Saudi Arabia, Germany, Hungary, Japan and Chile.

process[40], a restructured Executive Board would have to see a drastic reduction in the number of executive directors from Western Europe and redress the over-representation of countries like Belgium, the Netherlands or Switzerland. It would also have to account for the fact that European members have aligned their monetary policy by creating the European Monetary Union.

At the same time and to account for the fact that developing countries make up 160 of the Fund's 184 members, the number of directors from developing countries should be increased considerably. Particular emphasis should be put on increasing the representation of Sub-Saharan Africa which currently is far less represented than Latin America or developing Asia. A strict upper limit should further be set for the number of countries represented by a single executive director, far below the Anglophone African group's current size of 24. Increasing the staff for offices of directors representing the largest constituencies is an improvement, but does not eliminate the need for a drastic reduction of particularly African constituencies' size[41]. In a statement to the International Monetary and Financial Committee, Angolan Finance Minister Jose Pedro de Morais expressed the strong desire for reform on behalf of a group of 22 Sub-Sahara African Countries:

> It is our firm belief that the effectiveness of the sub-Saharan countries' participation in the decision-making process in the BWIs can only be enhanced through additional representation in the board of directors ... We do also think that a decision in this regard does not need to be kept hostage to the conclusion of the current general quota review[42].

10.3.2 Political Difficulties

Reforming the Executive Board and re-allocating quotas and voting weights would mean a change in the balance of power among members, even if vetoes for the United States and members of the European Union would be retained. Members wielding the largest power under the current allocation thus have strong incentives to block any reform proposal that would diminish their influence over IMF policies. Accordingly, reforms can only succeed if parties with the ability to block reform either do not perceive their power to diminish as a consequence of reform or can be persuaded that reforms will benefit all members alike. At a general level, most

---

40 See Carlo Cottareli. 2005. *Efficiency and Legitimacy: Trade-Offs in IMF Governance.* IMF Working Paper WP/05/107. Washington, DC: International Monetary Fund for a detailed discussion on the trade-off issue.
41 See Ariel Buira (2002): 236
42 Webster Malido. 2004. "African Countries Demand for Democracy in IMF, World Bank." Lusaka, Zambia: *The Post.* September 25, 2004

industrialised countries concede that the current distribution of power at the IMF fails to represent today's economic realities. The German government has voiced support for changing the composition of the Executive Board, simplifying the allocation formula and increasing basic votes[43]. According to a Japanese official, Japan's *main interest is not to increase our quota share but to adapt to the actual situation, especially for the Asian Countries*[44]. The fact that neither a re-allocation of quotas nor a reform of the Executive Board has been forthcoming highlights that despite these declarations the Fund's largest shareholders are unwilling to accept any reduction in their own quota allocation and voting weight. In this respect the U.S. position, namely that *the United States is not seeking to increase its own quota share* but *will not accept any decline*[45] is representative for the majority of the Fund's dominant members.

The history of quota determination underlines that the allocation of quotas has always been primarily a political process. Already in 1944 the formula used for determining members' quotas served as nothing more than as a rough guideline; actual quotas were allocated solely on political considerations. Even the formulae used to determine a basis for negotiations were altered several times in order to fulfil specific aspirations. The original formula for negotiating quota shares of the 44 founding members was based on a function of national income, gold and dollar reserves, and external trade. As demanded by Harry Dexter White, Professor Raymond Mikesell had to devise an allocation formula yielding very specific results: The quota share of the United States had to be around a third of the total and around twice that of the United Kingdom and its colonies combined. The U.S.S.R. and China were to be allocated the third and fourth largest quotas respectively as Mikesell recounts in his memoirs:

> In mid-April 1943, shortly after the White Plan was made public, White called me to his office and asked that I prepare a formula for the ISF quotas that would be based on the members' gold and dollar holdings, national incomes, and foreign trade. He gave no instructions on the weights to be used, but I was to give the United States a quota of approximately \$2.9 billion; the United Kingdom (including its colonies) about half the U.S. quota; the Soviet Union, an amount just under that of the United Kingdom; and China, somewhat less. … White's major concern was that our military allies (Roosevelt's Big Four) should have the

---

43 See Bundesministerium der Finanzen. 2004. *60 Jahre Bretton Woods-Institutionen: Standortbestimmung und Ausrichtung.* Berlin: Bundesministerium der Finanzen: 27
44 "The New IMF: Too Many Architects?" *The Banker.* October 2, 2000
45 Timothy Adams. 2005. *The US View on IMF Reform.* Speech presented at the IIE Conference on IMF Reform. September 23, 2005. Washington: Institute for International Economics

largest quotas, with a ranking in which the president and the secretary of state had agreed. I was surprised that White did not mention France...[46]

While the quotas allocated to the United States and the United Kingdom roughly matched the quotas derived by the formula, the greatest deviations to the formula were present at the shares of the U.S.S.R. and China. In order to resemble political order at the time, both countries' share was 57 percent above the quota suggested by the formula, while France initially was allocated a quota 27 percent below the formula's result[47]. A similar discretionary process of quota allocation was used at a selective quota increase in 1959 in order to draw on the strong liquidity positions of recovering economies like Japan and West Germany. At the 9th quota review in 1990 further adjustments were agreed that left Japan and Germany second and third largest members, followed by the United Kingdom and France with identical shares.

10.3.3 Governance Reform and Pre-qualification

As argued above, the reluctance of industrialised countries to embrace a reform of IMF governance rests primarily on political considerations. An altered composition of the Executive Board and a re-allocation of quotas would increase the influence of emerging economies and developing countries on IMF decision-making and curtail the ability of industrial countries to employ IMF funds as foreign policy instrument. Furthermore, creditor countries fear that developing economies would try to tilt IMF policy towards providing ever more loans at continuously less stringent conditions. This would not only put strains on the Fund's limited resources but also reduce incentives for debtor countries to pursue sustainable economic policies. However, particularly the latter argument appears exaggerated All realistic proposals for a re-allocation of quotas explicitly retain a simple majority for the Fund's creditor countries and there is universal agreement that any reform violating this principle is politically unfeasible. But there is no convincing reason why the voting share of creditor countries should be above that required for a simple majority. Consequently, a re-allocation of quotas should increase the combined voting share of developing countries to just below 50 percent. Similarly, the representation of developing countries at the Executive Board should be increased considerably to ensure

---

46 Mikesell (1994): 22
47 The French Delegation was apparently very offended by its allocation and according to Mikesell regarded their quota as a *deliberate insult*. This may be possible given the fact that De Gaulle and Roosevelt were not at good terms; Mikesell describes how Pierre Mendez-France, head of the delegation sent by the exiled government, approached him several times to demand an explanation but was told that quotas were arrived at employing a complicated scientific process.

that at least half of executive directors represent developing countries' and emerging economies' interests.

The case for improving the voice of developing countries at IMF decision-making is overwhelming. The main objective of increasing developing countries' quotas and representation at the Executive Board is to increase the Fund's legitimacy among the majority of its members; it is not to give them the power to highjack IMF decision-making. Increasing the Fund's legitimacy is essential to maintain the institution's effectiveness and capacity in enhancing global financial stability. Improved representation will not only ensure that developing countries' position on IMF policies will be fully taken into account to improve program design, but also increase ownership of IMF programs in the countries that have to implement them. If IMF influence in developing countries continues to decline, the effectiveness of IMF programs, monitoring and surveillance as well as its advice and technical assistance will continue to erode: the losses will be born by advanced industrial economies, developing countries and emerging economies alike.

If the IMF would start operating according to clear and transparent rules as advocated in chapter 8 on pre-qualification, a shift in the balance of power between industrialised and developing countries would be less threatening to creditor countries' interests. As the relevance of voting weights in determining IMF policies, especially regarding approval or rejection of stability programs, would be reduced, creditor countries' insistence on retaining excessive levels of control over IMF decision-making would be likely to decline. Creditor countries would be ensured that IMF policies are determined according to economic principles and could not be hijacked by a coalition of developing countries. While the advantages of increasing the Fund's legitimacy among the vast majority of its members would remain, the primary rationale for resisting pledges for more equal representation at the IMF would be eroded. As a result, opposition by creditor countries to increasing the representation of developing countries at the Executive Board and re-allocating quotas in favour of emerging economies, less developed countries, and transition economies should decline.

11. Sovereign Debt Restructuring

Chapter 6 made the argument that to be effective an international lender of last resort would have to restrict liquidity assistance to illiquid, but fundamentally solvent economies. Chapters 7 and 8 analysed two approaches to decide whether an economy should be perceived temporarily illiquid rather than fundamentally insolvent. This leaves the question of how the official sector should respond in case economies appear fundamentally insolvent.

For fundamentally insolvent economies entering a process of debt restructuring is inevitable since additional loans cannot prevent but merely postpone eventual default. The official sector's role should be to support such countries' restructuring efforts by putting in place an adequate legal framework that allows creditors and debtors to reach a lasting solution to the problem of unsustainable indebtedness. In contrast to national jurisdictions like that of the United States, where Chapter 11 provides clear guidelines on how to deal with distressed or bankrupt private enterprises, the international environment lacks a coherent legal framework for restructuring unsustainable sovereign debt burdens. While even without such a framework sovereign debt burdens have been successfully restructured in countries like Pakistan, Ukraine, Russia, Ecuador or Uruguay, the case of Argentina underlines the difficulties developing countries and emerging economies face when trying to restructure their sovereign debt burdens to sustainable levels.

Opportunities and difficulties regarding the creation of a more effective process of sovereign debt restructuring have been widely discussed. A large number of different approaches has entered the debate since the mid 1990s—the most prominent being the proposal to create a formal Sovereign Debt Restructuring Mechanism (SDRM) as advocated by IMF First Deputy Managing Director Anne Krueger. As in the case of an international lender of last resort, the political and economic feasibility of a potential SDRM is controversial. While there is wide agreement on the benefits a formal process of sovereign debt restructuring could entail, implementational difficulties are generally perceived as prohibitively high. Opponents of the proposal further point out that over the last 20 years a large number of successful debt restructurings have taken place despite the lack of a formal mechanism.

11.1 Debt Restructuring in the Past

Sovereign distress and sovereign defaults are no new phenomena. As financial crises in general, debt crises have occurred regularly over the nineteenth and twentieth century; Standard and Poor's counted 84 sovereign defaults between 1975 and 2002 alone[1]. The 1980s debt crisis provides a particularly extensive range of examples for both sovereign default and debt restructuring: As a consequence of massive petro-dollar-induced lending by commercial banks to developing countries between 1974 and 1979, developing countries' total external debt had doubled to over USD 400 billion by the late 1970s. Suffering from sharply increased U.S. interest rates and foreign commercial banks refusing to grant additional loans, on August 12, 1982 the Mexican finance minister announced that his country would no longer be able to meet its external debt obligations of over USD 80 billion: This was the first in a long series of developing country defaults. By October 1983 no less than 27 developing countries had restructured their debt burdens or defaulted outright; of those, Mexico, Argentina, Brazil and Venezuela accounted for 74 percent of the combined total of USD 239 billion in defaulted external debt.

As a consequence, creditor banks and debtor countries renegotiated the terms of debt outstanding in order to put developing country debt on a sounder footing. These efforts were only partially successful: On the one hand, sovereign debt restructurings under the London Club process prevented a collapse of major commercial banks and the harsh consequences such failures would have had on the stability of the global financial system. But on the other, the agreements negotiated between consortia of private creditors and debtor country representatives addressed short-term liquidity problems only and failed to provide a longer-term solution regarding the problems of debt sustainability and solvency[2]: However, collective action and free rider problems were overcome without the existence of a formal debt restructuring mechanism as the London Club process took the form of ad-hoc committees established at the request of individual debtor countries and resolved after a re-scheduling agreement had been reached.

11.1.1 New Money Approach

The efforts to restructure unsustainable sovereign debt burdens began after Mexico's default in 1982 and lasted until the end of the decade. In what is often referred to as the *New Money Approach* to restructure developing country debt, three distinct periods can be identified. The first period, lasting from 1982 to 1984, saw hastily imposed short-term solutions devised in negotiations between commercial banks and debtor countries to maintain global financial stability by preventing bankruptcies of major international lending banks. Loans re-scheduled where exclusively those

---

1 See Standard and Poor's. 2002. *Sovereign Defaults: Moving Higher Again in 2003?* Research Note published by S&P Sovereigns. New York, NY: Standard and Poor's
2 See Punan Chuhan and Federico Sturzenegger. 2004. *Default Episodes in the 1980s and 1990s: What Have We Learned?* Draft chapter for *Managing Volatility and Crisis: A Practitioner's Guide.* Washington, DC: The World Bank

coming due in the short-term; maturities were usually extended to 8 years with an additional grace period of further 4 years. In order to enable debtor countries to meet their debt service payments, restructuring agreements were dependent on IMF approved adjustment programs, the maintenance of short-term credit lines, and additional loans by commercial banks. In spite of further increasing foreign banks' exposure to developing countries, this approach allowed banks to refrain from writing off the value of outstanding loans in their balance sheets and suffering the corresponding effects on enterprise values. Between 1983 and 1984 the number of agreements negotiated in London Club committees reached 47 and comprised obligations worth over USD 130 billion.

Given the large number of distressed debtor countries and the limitations on loans with short-term maturity, the London Club process of debt restructuring evolved to a continuous effort. As a result, from 1984 onwards re-scheduling efforts were widened from loans coming due within the next one or two years to include loans of medium-term maturity. Restructuring was based on extending maturity from 3 to 5 years to between 9 and 14 years, reducing servicing costs, and eliminating re-scheduling fees. In return, lending banks refrained from providing new money in form of further short-term credit. Until 1985 eight such multiyear restructuring agreements were signed, providing significant cash-flow relief and more time for countries to implement policy adjustments and austerity measures. Nevertheless, the net present value of outstanding loans was not reduced and left debtors with unaltered and hardly sustainable debt burdens for the medium to long term.

Under James Baker's 1985 *Program for Sustained Growth* efforts concentrated on implementing measures to support economic growth and enable indebted countries to break out of the re-scheduling cycle by increasing their capacity to pay off sovereign debt obligations. The Baker Plan focussed on growth-oriented structural reforms such as reducing governments' role in the economy, opening markets to foster international trade, and improving the overall investment climate. In contrast to the second phase of the New Money Approach, economic reforms under the Baker Plan were accompanied not only by debt restructuring but also by strong financial support from the official sector and commercial banks. The scope of financial support was estimated to reach around USD 30 billion, two thirds of which were to be provided by the private sector and the remainder by multilateral development banks. While the terms of existing loans were considerably improved for several middle-income debtors, commercial banks failed to fulfil the program's objective to make available up to USD 4 billion in new loans; as a consequence, many large developing economies refused to join the program. Although over 10 Baker Plan rescheduling agreements were signed, overall the effort had only modest success. But even if fully implemented, it would have involved only 15 middle-income economies while excluding a large number of smaller countries burdened by equally unsustainable levels of sovereign debt.

11.1.2 The Brady Plan

The fact that the cycle of re-scheduling under the New Money Approach implied that many developing countries were insolvent rather than illiquid, began to settle by the late 1980s. Market-based approaches accepted the reality that debt reduction was the only solution to end the vicious circle of re-scheduling sovereign debts and to put the debt burden of developing countries on a sounder footing. A mechanism to restructure defaulted obligations was created with the Brady Plan in 1989, although a similar approach preceded the plan by two years: In 1987 the Mexican government had issued a 20-year sovereign bond in exchange for bank loans stemming from the early 1980s. However, Mexico was able to place only a fraction of the issue, primarily due to the problem that the new bonds involved a 30 percent haircut[3]. The offer's attractiveness was further reduced by the fact that only the principal was collateralised by U.S. Treasuries, but not the interest foregone since default.

Implemented from March 1989 onwards, the Brady Plan aimed at long-term solutions to developing countries' unsustainable debt burdens and was guided by principles common in private sector work-outs. International creditors were to offer debt relief in return for higher repayment security based on collateral and economic adjustment programs. At the same time, the liquidity of restructured debt was to be increased allowing creditors to diversify risk and adjust their emerging market exposures. Consequently, under the Brady Plan syndicated loans were exchanged for sovereign bonds collateralised by U.S. Treasuries. To cater for the diverse interests of international creditors, a variety of instruments were offered to commercial banks allowing them to either exit or retain their exposure to emerging markets and developing economies. Depending on individual interests, syndicated loans were exchanged for either *par* or *discount bonds, front-loaded interest reduction bonds* or *debt conversion* or *new money bonds*. Unpaid interest was capitalised by repackaging it into short-term floating rate bonds termed *Unpaid* or *Interest Due Bonds*. Agreements between creditors and debtors were further encouraged through the provision of additional funds as sweetener by the official sector.

In case creditors decided on exiting developing countries altogether, loans were exchanged for either *par bonds*, issued at below-market fixed rates of interest but at the full principal value, or *discount bonds* which paid market rates but were issued at a discount. U.S. Treasuries served as collateral for both 30-year bonds' principal.

---

3 See Chuhan and Sturzenegger (2004): 14

Commercial banks willing to retain some exposure to emerging markets could exchange their loans for *front-loaded interest reduction bonds* (FLIRB) which paid a below-market rate for the first 5 to 7 years of maturity and were thereafter adjusted to market-based coupons. FLIRBs were collateralised by U.S. Treasuries not only in terms of principal but also in terms of interest payments.

The Brady Plan also addressed the problems of countries that had stopped servicing their debt obligations but were essentially solvent: By exchanging their outstanding loans for uncollateralized *debt conversion bonds* at par and market interest, countries in arrears were offered the opportunity to rehabilitate themselves and re-gain access to capital markets by issuing *new money bonds*. Default risk was minimized since Brady Bonds were issued under New York law and included further provisions like mandatory prepayment, turnover or negative pledge clauses. Under the Brady Plan over USD 200 billion of loans were exchanged for USD 154 billions in bonds; 18 countries participated and saw the net present value of their obligations significantly reduced. The success of the Brady Plan in allowing developing countries renewed access to international capital markets laid the foundations for the lending boom of the 1990s that set the stage for the decade's emerging market crises.

11.2 The Changed Environment

The New Money Approach succeeded in preventing the bankruptcy of major international commercial banks and a collapse of the international financial system. Although it failed in providing a long-term solution to the unsustainable debt burdens of much of the developing world, the London Club process was able to overcome the collective action problems that international creditors face today. The limited role of collective action problems during the 1980s can be attributed to the fact that developing countries borrowed primarily through syndicated loans provided by a relatively small and coherent group of large internationally active commercial banks. The limited number of creditors facilitated negotiations with sovereign debtors and led to generally orderly restructurings of unsustainable debt burdens of developing countries. Syndicated loans often included contractual clauses that excluded the possibility of litigation by minority creditors in the first place. Moreover, commercial banks were interested to uphold good relations with debtor countries in order to secure future business; accordingly, incentives were higher to reach outcomes acceptable to both debtors and creditors. Orderly debt restructurings were further facilitated as national regulatory authorities at times exerted pressure on banks operating within their jurisdiction to reach compromises with their distressed sovereign borrowers[4].

During the 1990s both forms of debt and the composition of international creditors changed considerably. Syndicated loans have largely been replaced by publicly traded securities, predominantly sovereign bonds. Emerging market borrowers have raised funds by issuing a wide variety of debt instruments differing in terms and maturity as well as their place of origination. As a consequence, the composition of international creditors has expanded to comprise a large number of different players ranging from mutual and pension funds to hedge funds, trading desks and retail investors. This diversity greatly complicates the process of debt restructuring in case debtors struggle to meet their debt service obligations. Collective action problems are exacerbated by the large number of different issues outstanding that have to be restructured individually and require the consent of multi-faceted creditor groups pursuing diverse strategies and at the same time demanding creditor equality. Since debt is issued in many different legal jurisdictions, different creditor majorities must be brought together for restructuring different instruments. In the case of bonds issued under U.S. jurisdiction, restructuring requires unanimity. Minority creditor groups can thus veto any agreement and press for the unaltered fulfilment of debt service obligations by seeking litigation in the courts. In contrast to debt issued under the jurisdiction of Germany or the United Kingdom where the consent of a large majority of creditors is sufficient to realize a restructuring transaction, unanimity requirements allow dissenting minority creditors to free-ride and threaten the restructuring process.

11.2.1 Successful Restructurings

Nevertheless, even in the changed environment of the 1990s and without a formal sovereign debt restructuring mechanism, a number of unsustainable debt burdens have been restructured successfully under what is sometimes referred to as a *muddling through approach*[5]. Successful debt restructurings have taken place in Ecuador, Pakistan, the Ukraine, Uruguay and Russia. While Ecuador, the Ukraine and Russia defaulted on their debt, in both Pakistan and Uruguay debt burdens were restructured voluntarily before default became inevitable. In accordance with Paris Club agreements, Pakistan's voluntary bond exchange in November 1999 involved eurobonds worth USD 610 million. In the transaction three issues maturing between

---

4 See Krueger, Anne. 2002. *New Approaches to Sovereign Debt Restructuring: An Update on Our Thinking.* Speech given at Conference on Sovereign Debt Workouts: Hopes and Hazards. Washington, DC: Institute for International Economics
5 Chuhan and Sturzenegger (2004): 18

December 1999 and February 2002 with coupons ranging from 6 to 11.5 percent were restructured into a single USD 623 million bond with 6 year maturity and a 10 percent coupon. The offer's stellar participation rate of nearly 99 percent was facilitated by a relatively small institutional investor base and the fact that the terms offered to creditors included an increase in net present value. An over 90 percent participation rate was also achieved at an exchange operation undertaken by Uruguay in 2003 where both domestic and international bonds were restructured. For USD 3.8 billion in international bonds two options were offered: a fixed coupon dollar-denominated bond for investors primarily concerned with liquidity issues and an additional issue with identical terms but prolonged maturity. Both debt securities included collective action clauses requiring a 75 percent majority to alter the instrument's terms; attractiveness of the offer was enhanced by an up-front cash payment of USD 170 million. In a similar par transaction in February 2000, the Ukraine included a USD 220 million cash pay-out to persuade debt holders to support the proposed exchange. It comprised three dollar-denominated issues worth USD 833 million maturing between March and October 2000, a DEM 1.5 billion bond maturing February 2001 and USD 1.015 billion of Gazprom debt securities. In the transaction, USD 2.3 billion worth of debt, over 85 percent of the eligible issues, were exchanged for two USD 1.13 billion 7-year eurobonds with coupons of 10 and 11 percent respectively.

In Pakistan, Uruguay and the Ukraine debt restructuring efforts succeeded and were backed by a large majority of investors. However, the transactions took place before the countries had to declare default and involved no reduction in the debt burden's net present value. Nevertheless, the cases of Ecuador and Russia show that successful restructurings are also possible under less favourable circumstances. Both transactions took place after the countries had defaulted on its obligations and in both cases investors were exposed to significant haircuts. In Ecuador USD 5.9 billion of Brady bonds and USD 465 million Eurobonds were successfully exchanged for a USD 2.7 billion 30-year multi-coupon bond and USD 1.25 billion 12-year fixed-rate bonds issued at a discount of 35 percent. Combined, investors realized a loss of 40 percent on their outstanding principal. In spite of the unattractive terms offered, 97 percent of bondholders participated[6]. The Ecuadorian effort took a year until completion. Restructuring the obligations Russia defaulted on in 1998 took over 2 years: In the process, a debt volume of USD 31.8 billion was exchanged for USD 21.2 billion in two Eurobond issues maturing in 2010 and 2030. Acceptance for the swap was over 98 percent despite a principal reduction of between 33 and 37.5 percent. A sweetener for investors was that while the original

---

6 Acceptance by investors was facilitated by a limited buy-back promise

securities had been issued by Vneshecomnbank without a corresponding government guarantee, the new bonds issues were offered by the Russian Federation.

On 3 March 2005 Argentina's president Kirchner announced the consent of 76 percent of creditors to the largest debt restructuring ever completed. Under the terms offered by the Republic of Argentina, investors will incur a loss of around 70 percent on their outstanding claims with a nominal value of over USD 100 billion that consists of about USD 80 billion in principal and USD 20 billion in accrued interest. As a result, the government will reduce its debt service payments for the year 2005 to around USD 3 billion from USD 10 billion in the year of default. What the effects of this harsh treatment of investors will be on the ability of emerging economies to borrow from international capital markets remains to be seen. However, the Argentine episode is a showcase for the difficulties the current environment poses for an orderly process of restructuring sovereign debts. While surpassing initial expectations of creditor participation, the acceptance level of 76 percent is far below the threshold of 90 percent expected by the IMF for a successful restructuring transaction[7]. No solution has been found so far on how to deal with the remaining 24 percent of holdout creditors. The large level of abstention highlights that many financial market participants perceive both process and outcome of the restructuring as financial murder on behalf of the Argentine government[8]. This perception as well as the fact that it took over three years for the problem to be effectively addressed underlines that unless the current legal framework is improved, the process of restructuring unsustainable sovereign debts in many instances will remain lengthy and costly for all participants involved.

11.2.2 Problems due to Renegade Creditors

A central problem for an efficient restructuring process is posed by renegade or hold-out creditors. Even if a majority of creditors agrees on a restructuring proposal with a debtor country, hold-out creditors have the ability to prevent the necessary debt exchange. The attempts by German investor H.W. Urban to block the Argentinean debt exchange are an example for the disruption minority creditors can cause by opting for litigation. His case built on the argument that the unilateral and coerced exchange offer by Argentina's authorities violates Rule 23 of the U.S. Federal Rules for Civil Procedure that requires good faith relations between

---

7 See Adam Thomson and Andrew Balls. 2005. "76% Back Argentina Debt Terms." *The Financial Times.* March 3, 2005
8 "Tough Deal." *The Economist.* March 3, 2005

creditors and debtors[9]. Collective action clauses, aggregation provisions and exit consents all aim at addressing the problems posed for successful debt restructurings by such hold-out creditors. Three exemplary cases describing minority creditors' profit maximising strategies are summarized below:

In the case of CIBC Bank & Trust Co. versus Banco Central do Brazil the former was able to secure full repayment of both principal and accrued interest by refusing to participate in the exchange of Brazil's Multi-Year Debt Facility Agreement (MYDFA) into different types of Brady Bonds[10]. The exchange became necessary in 1992 when Brazil was unable to meet its debt service obligations agreed under the MYDFA in 1988. Although the restructuring involved a reduction in principal, all other debt holders participated in the exchange. Only Cayman-based CIBC, representing the Dart family which had accumulated over USD 1.4 billion of debt at discounts of up to 60 percent, attempted to accelerate the debt and receive full repayment[11]. Although acceleration was blocked by the court following an intervention by the U.S. government, in 1994 the Dart family was awarded a payment of USD 77.6 million in cash and bonds for accrued interest with the claims on full principal repayment being left intact. By placing a Eurobond worth USD 1.28 billion and collateralised by the remaining USD 1.4 billion claims on principal in October 1996, CIBC eventually found a successful exit opportunity. The holdout strategy provided stellar profits for the Darts while all other creditors suffered a haircut on their investments.

The case of Pravin Banker Associates Ltd. versus Banco Popular de Peru (BPP) and the Republic of Peru involved only a fraction of the amounts challenged above. Although by stopping principal repayments on its outstanding debt obligations Peru had defaulted already in 1984, in 1990 the investment company Pravin Banker Associates acquired USD 9 million of Peruvian sovereign debt from the Mellon Bank of Pittsburgh at a discount of 73 percent, interest on which was still serviced via the state-owned commercial bank Banco Popular del Peru[12]. BPP continued to

9 See Daniel Tillotson. 2004. "Argentina – An Injunction to Halt Exit-Consent Abuses." *Wachnovia Securities Sovereign Research Bulletin*. November 1, 2004. New York, NY: Wachovia Securities LLC

10 See CIBC Bank & Trust Co. (Cayman) Ltd. vs. Banco Central do Brasil. 886 F. Supp. 1105, 1115–16 (S.D.N.Y., 1995)

11 Accelerating debt is the legal term for the initiation of legal proceedings against the borrower to achieve early repayment. When a borrower defaults on its debt service obligations, creditors can demand full repayment before maturity of the original contract. The terms of the Brazilian MYDFA required the consent of at least 50 percent of debt holders for initiating litigation and acting against the borrower's assets. After all other creditors tendered their claims, CIBC would theoretically have been left with 100 percent of MYDFA outstanding. By converting only a share of the tendered securities, the Banco Central do Brazil ensured that CIBC holdings remained below the 50 percent threshold.

12 See Pravin Banker Associates, Ltd. vs. Banco Popular del Peru and the Republic of Peru. 912F. Supp. 77 (US District Court, 1996)

pay interest on the USD 1.425 million portion of debt Pravin Banker Associates had kept after reselling the majority of its investment in the secondary market, but payments ceased when BPP became illiquid and was subsequently liquidated. Instead of participating in the liquidation, the investment company went to court to secure full repayment of both principal and interest thereby endangering Peru's efforts to restructure USD 8 billion of sovereign debts under the Brady Plan. Balancing between official U.S. interest in promoting a successful debt restructuring and maintaining debt enforceability under contract law, the court choose the latter and awarded the plaintiff over USD 2.1 million in 1996. After failing to get court permission for claiming the assets of Peruvian state-owned company Conade, the parties finally settled their claims outside court for a reduced amount. The case underlines the disruptive role even smallest creditors can play during debt restructuring proceedings. By holding a mere USD 1.4 million in debt acquired on the secondary market, Pravin Banker Associates was able to endanger a restructuring worth over 8000 times that amount.

The case most widely cited to describe renegade debtors' strategies is Elliott Associates L.P. versus Banco de la Nacion of Peru[13]. Specialised on distressed debt Elliot Associates already had successfully litigated against the government of Panama in 1995. Following Peru's announcement on debt restructuring in the same year and the ruling on Pravin Banker Associates Ltd. versus BPP, in early 1996 Elliot acquired USD 20.7 million of Peruvian debt at a 45 percent discount in the secondary market. On 8 October 1996, 10 days before final signature was to be put on Peru's Brady restructuring, Elliot initiated litigation proceedings in the United States demanding full repayment of principal and accrued interest. The claims were rejected at the first instance with the court arguing that the suitor had violated section 489 of New York Judiciary Law by acquiring the debt with the clear intention to sue. The decision was reversed by the Court of Appeals in October 1999 which argued that section 489 was not applicable since the plaintiff primarily sued for debt repayment. Elliott Associates initially attached its claims to Peruvian funds held at Chase Manhattan Bank and reserved to service Peru's new obligations under the Brady Plan. Despite initial failure at the Brussels Commercial Court, in September 2000 Elliott Associates was awarded a restraining order on Peru's fiscal agents Chase Manhattan and Euronext by the Court of Appeals. In order to prevent the restraining order from causing her to default on its Brady obligations, Peru settled with Elliott Associates three days before the final payment date. The investment

---

13 See Elliott Associates, L. P. vs. Banco de la Nacion. 194 F.3d 363 (Second Circuit, 1999)

company secured a payment of USD 58.4 million, easily outweighing the initial investment of USD 11.4 million and litigation costs[14].

11.2.3 Need for Reform

Even in the absence of hold-out creditors, collective action problems and information asymmetries arising in large and incoherent creditor groups make the process of restructuring sovereign debts lengthy, burdensome and disorderly. A disorderly process hurts developing countries by reducing economic growth and may restrict a country's access to international capital markets for a period of several years. Hutchinson and Neuberger attempt to identify the costs of sovereign default and subsequent financial crises. They find that the cumulative effect of *sudden stops*—a balance of payments crisis paired with an outflow of short-term capital—over a three-year period is a reduction in output of as much as 13 to 15 percent[15]. Further evidence on the negative correlation between sovereign defaults and economic growth has been found by Sturzenegger for debt defaults during the 1980s[16] and Barro who analysed the effects on growth of financial crises in East Asia[17]. Given changes in the composition of international creditor groups and the costs involved in disorderly restructuring efforts, the case for introducing measures to facilitate an orderly restructuring process is overwhelming.

For private enterprises an orderly process of debt restructuring is aided by the existence of specific bankruptcy procedures within national jurisdictions. Specific procedures are necessary since in case of default the interests of the parties involved are often diametrically opposed. When the ability of a borrower to service its debt obligations becomes questionable, the rational response by creditors is to refrain from advancing new loans or rolling over loans coming due. However, often it is precisely this response which actually causes the debtor's inability to honour its debt. Suspending debt service payments before default and restructuring obligations to achieve a sustainable debt burden is the obvious solution to this problem. Legal

---

14 See John Nolan. 2001. *Emerging Market Debt & Vulture Hedge Funds: Free-Ridership, Legal and Market Remedies.* Special Policy Report 3. September 29, 2001. Washington, DC: Financial Policy Forum

15 See Michael Hutchinson and Ilan Neuberger. 2002. *Sudden Stops and the Mexican Wave: Currency Crises, Capital Reversals and Output Loss in Emerging Markets* (2002). Working Paper PB-02-03. Centre for Pacific Basin Monetary and Economic Studies. San Francisco, CA: Federal Reserve

16 See Federico Sturzenegger. 2002. *Toolkit for the Analysis of Debt Problems* (2002). Working Paper. Centro de Investigación de Finanzas. Buenos Aires, Argentina: Universidad Torcuato di Tella

17 See Robert Barro. 2001. *Economic Growth in East Asia before and after the Financial Crisis.* NBER Working Paper 8330. Cambridge, MA: National Bureau of Economic Research

provisions like those included in Chapter 11 in the United States successfully adapt this approach in case of illiquid private debtors.

In case of sovereign debtors this process is far more complicated. As sovereign entities, countries' assets are generally protected from creditors. Consequently, when a sovereign borrower suspends its debt service payments, the most promising way for creditors to secure at least partial repayment is to engage in negotiations with the defaulting government. As restructuring often involves some form creditor loss, for each individual creditor the option to free-ride and choose litigation over accepting a haircut is naturally attractive.

11.3 Proposals to Facilitate Sovereign Debt Restructuring

The existence of formal debt restructuring procedures can overcome this collective action problem by forcing minority hold-outs to accept agreements backed by a majority of creditors and refrain from litigation and disruption of resolution efforts. A number of different proposals exist to achieve this objective and overcome free-rider problems: Apart from the proposal to create a formal Sovereign Debt Restructuring Mechanism, the debate centres on the effectiveness of an internationally agreed code of conduct and the inclusion of collective action clauses in sovereign debt issues.

11.3.1 A Code of Good Conduct

A code of good conduct (CGO) can serve as a non-statutory framework to outline procedures for dealing with borrowing countries' problems to service their debts while safeguarding that original contractual obligations are met to the furthest extent possible. A code of good conduct includes a list of best practices defining common principles that actors involved in debt restructurings would be expected to follow. Often interpreted as compromise between relying solely on the inclusion of collective action clauses in future debt issues and the establishment of a formal bankruptcy court, support for a code of good conduct has come from the private and the public sectors alike. A widely discussed blueprint was presented by Jean-Claude Trichet and the Banque de France in March 2003. An alternative CGC approach representing private creditors' interests has been proposed by the so-called Gang of Six[18] as part of *mutual efforts to strengthen crisis prevention and resolution in*

---

18 The Group of Six comprises the Institute of International Finance (IIF), the Trade Association for Emerging Markets (EMTA), the International Primary Market Association (IPMA), the Securities Industry Association (SIA), the Bond Market Association (TBMA), the International Securities Market Association (ISMA) and the Emerging Markets Creditor Association (EMCA).

emerging markets[19]. At their Berlin Meeting on November 20–21, 2004 the G-22 officially supported the *principles for stable capital flows and fair debt restructuring in emergent markets* drafted by *major sovereign issuers and international bonds and global leaders of private finance*[20].

The original Trichet proposal consisted of several core principles: The first called for an earlier and more *regular dialogue between debtors and creditors* in order to identify eventual liquidity problems early on and achieve larger creditor participation during restructuring negotiations. The second principle stressed the importance of fair information-sharing mechanisms to be put in place as *transparency of information* would allow all parties to reach an assessment on the debtor's financial and economic position. Particular emphasis was thirdly given to efforts safeguarding *the fair representation of creditors* during restructuring negotiations since without a large degree of representational fairness acceptance of the eventual agreements will be limited. Fourth, *creditor equality* has to be secured by implementing measures to ensure that creditors are treated comparably. Excluding preferential treatment for individual creditors is essential to overcome free-rider problems when hold-out creditors initiate litigation. The fifth principle insisted that any restructuring *agreement has to result in a sustainable debt structure in the medium term*. Creditors need to agree that short-term solutions leaving the debtor with unsustainable debt burdens fail to secure their claims in the future. Negotiations must be held in *good faith*, in essence requiring the willingness of creditors to accept a debt reduction if inevitable given debtors' sincere efforts to fulfil obligations to the maximum extent possible. As such, *fair burden sharing between creditors and debtors* is an essential principle. Moreover, during negotiations the *financial position of the debtor should be prevented from deteriorating*: In practice, this means a standstill on debt service payments. All parties involved were to finally aim to *make the process of restructuring timely and expeditious*[21].

The *principles for stable capital flows and fair debt restructuring in emergent markets* endorsed by the G-22 in November 2004 have realised the often-stated intention by main participants in international capital markets to establish a voluntary code of good conduct regarding sovereign debt restructuring. Drafted by private sector associations IIF and IPMA in collaboration with major sovereign issuers of

---

19 See IIF, EMTA, IPMA, SIA, ISMA, EMCA and TBMA. 2003. *Code of Conduct for Emerging Markets*. Part of a Discussion Draft from January 31, 2003. Washington, DC: Institute for International Finance: 1

20 Institute of International Finance and International Primary Markets Association. 2004. *Key Principles Agreed to Strengthen Emerging Markets Finance*. Press release issued on behalf of IIF, IPMA and Sovereign Issuers of International Bonds. New York, NY: November 22, 2004

21 For the Trichet proposal see Bertrand Couillanlault and Pierre-Francoise Weber. 2003. *Towards a Voluntary Code of Good Conduct for Sovereign Debt Restructuring*. International Monetary Relations Division. Paris: Banque de France

international debt they are more concise than the Trichet Proposal and consist of only four legally non-binding principles[22]. The first calls for *transparency* and *a timely flow of information* by sovereign debtors to provide a detailed and complete picture of their economic and financial position. This entails the disclosure of maturity and term structures of all sovereign external debt obligations in case a restructuring becomes necessary. The principles further demand a *close debtor-creditor dialogue and co-operation to avoid restructuring*. This requires regular dialogue and consultations between creditors and debtors, the provision of best practice investor relations services, the adherence to responsible fiscal and economic policy reforms by debtors as well as creditors' full support of those efforts. Achieving *good faith* in the dialogue between both parties requires restructuring negotiations to be conducted in a voluntary, good faith process led by the principle of sanctity of contracts. In this context the code includes detailed specifications regarding restructuring vehicles to be used, creditor committee policies and practices to be adhered to as well as several guidelines regarding both creditor and debtor actions during the restructuring process. The final principle demands the *avoidance of unfair discrimination among affected creditors* to ensure inter-creditor equality and the implementation of a fair voting process.

The principles aim to apply to several distinct types of situations. A subset can be applied even when dealing with temporarily illiquid but fundamentally solvent countries. The principles further intend to provide guidance for countries that face no immediate default but whose debt structure appears unsustainable in the long-term. But most importantly, the code of good conduct should serve as a roadmap for the restructuring process of countries that defaulted and are entering negotiations on debt restructuring during the payments standstill period. Although a crucial characteristic of any CGO is the fact that it is voluntary and not legally binding, the existence of a widely accepted code is likely to exert considerable pressure in terms of reputation on both creditors and debtors. The establishment of monitoring groups representing both public and private sector interests could further increase adherence to the central principles of a voluntary code[23].

Given its non-binding nature, a code of good conduct alone cannot eliminate the possibility that hold-out creditors might nevertheless press for litigation and disrupt restructuring processes. In contrast to collective action clauses or a formal SDRM, a voluntary code of good conduct lacks the instruments to force renegade creditors to accept a restructuring outcome that is supported by a large majority of creditors. A

---

22 Institute of International Finance and International Primary Markets Association. 2004b. *Principles for Stable Capital Flows and Fair Debt Restructuring in Emerging Markets.* New York, NY: Institute of International Finance

23 See Jacque De Larosiére. 2003. "Reality Hits Debt Restructuring Debate." *The Banker.* September 3, 2003

simultaneous implementation of collective action clauses would overcome this problem.

11.3.2 Collective Action Clauses

Collective action clauses allow binding a creditor minority to restructuring terms acceptable to a large majority of debt holders. By implementing such clauses in bond contracts between lenders and borrowers, renegade creditors can be prevented from disrupting an orderly process of debt restructuring. In their recommendations to facilitate orderly workouts for sovereign debtors in the aftermath of the Mexican crisis, Eichengreen and Portes advocated the use of this instrument already in 1995[24]. Since then, support for their use has grown to include a large number of both private and public sectors bodies. Three types of clauses are essential for facilitating an orderly workout process: collective representation clauses, majority enforcement clauses and majority restructuring clauses.

Collective representation or *engagement clauses* address co-ordination problems between creditors: They provide for the creation of a forum where creditors come together and identify diverging interests and common positions. Creditors will elect representatives entrusted to negotiate in the majority of creditors' name. *Majority enforcement clauses* define a minimum percentage of creditors required for initiating litigation against the debtor. In case of litigation the necessary fraction of creditors will nominate a trustee to file the law suit on their behalf. In addition, *sharing clauses* ensure that in case of a successful verdict, proceeds will be shared among all creditors, not just among those litigating; consequently, no creditor can benefit disproportionally from litigation. *Majority voting* or *restructuring clauses* directly aim at preventing hold-out creditors from exiting consensus. In case a specific majority, usually no less than 2/3 of creditors, agrees on restructuring terms with debtor representatives, the minority of dissenting shareholders is forced to participate in the transaction and prevented from disrupting negotiations and blocking restructuring agreements supported by the majority of creditors.

Emerging market debt is issued in several markets, but the largest volumes by far are offered in London and New York. In the U.K. collective action clauses have been a part of sovereign bond contracts since about 1870; their inclusion was a response to the sharp increase in the volume of tradable debt offered in the London market from the mid century onwards. In contrast, debt securities issued in New York under U.S. law have lacked collective action clauses. Authorities in the United States instead relied on the courts to prevent minority creditors from forcing enter-

---

24 See Barry Eichengreen and Richard Portes. 1995. *Crisis? What Crisis? Orderly Workouts for Sovereign Debtors*. London: Centre for Economic Policy Research

prises into unwarranted bankruptcy leading eventually to the installation of bankruptcy judges under the amended Bankruptcy Act[25]. The preference for unanimity requirements was based on fears that majority debt holders in possession of insider information could enforce restructuring solutions to the detriment of less informed minority debt holders[26]. The 1939 Trust Indenture Act finally made unanimous support a legal requirement for any restructuring effort for every type of bond. Eichengreen argues that the fact that sovereign bonds issued under New York law still lack collective action clauses in the majority of cases is a consequence of missing legal experience: When capital market lawyers in New York were drafting emerging market sovereign bond contracts in the early 1990s, they adopted the corporate bond frameworks they were experienced with instead of taking into account the particularities of sovereign debtors[27]. This lack of experience can be attributed to the fact that virtually no foreign sovereign bonds where issued in New York between the Great Depression and the1990s[28]; indeed, Brady bonds were the first such instruments issued in New York since World War II.

Although sovereign bonds issued in Japan and Luxembourg already include collective action clauses, in late 2001 around 70 percent of developing country debt outstanding still lacked provisions to address collective action problems among creditors[29]. The vast majority of developing country debt containing collective action clauses is issued in London. In order to change the terms of repayment, English law requires support by a majority of no less than 2/3 of those debt holders present at the first creditor meeting. Bond contracts devised under English law specify detailed procedures regarding the selection of creditor representatives to handle negotiations. Under U.S. law, decisions regarding changes in repayment schedules and structure of sovereign debt must have the support of all bond holders unanimously. In contrast to the *trustee* appointed under English law, a *fiscal agent* acts in an administrative role only under U.S. law. He is neither empowered to negotiate on behalf of the bond holders nor chosen to represent their interests.

---

25 It is sometimes pointed out that prior to the Great Depression sovereign debt issued in New York also included collective action clauses. However, this was the exception rather than the rule. The percentage of bonds with provisions facilitating collective action was little above 10 percent of total volume outstanding. See Torbjörn Becker, Anthony Richards and Yungyong Thaicharoen. 2001. *Bond Restructuring and Moral Hazard: Are Collective Action Clauses Costly?* IMF Working Paper WP/01/92. Washington, DC: International Monetary Fund

26 See Lee Buchheit and Mitu Gulati. 2002. *Sovereign Bonds and the Collective Will.* Working Paper. Georgetown-Sloan Project on Business Institutions. Washington, DC: Georgetown University

27 See Barry Eichengreen. 2003. *Restructuring Sovereign Debt.* Working Paper. Berkeley, CA: University of California at Berkeley

28 See Gray, Robert. 2003. *Collective Action Clauses.* Remarks prepared for delivery at UNCTAD Fourth Inter-Regional Debt Management Conference at Geneva. November 11, 2003

29 See Eichengreen (2003): 13

Accordingly, holders of bonds issued under U.S. jurisdiction retain almost complete freedom of action in case a sovereign borrower experiences difficulties in servicing its debt obligations. While investors can co-operate voluntarily, they retain the option to initiate litigation and disrupt negotiations between debtor country and a majority of creditors.

Incorporating collective action clauses in sovereign bond contracts clearly enhances the process of restructuring sovereign debt. The only significant potential drawback of a widespread introduction of collective action clauses comes in terms of moral hazard. Opponents of the instrument argue that any measure facilitating debt restructuring might increase moral hazard problems as debtor countries would feel incentives to push for restructuring despite being able to meet their debt service obligations. Reduced repayment security may thus result in an increase in the cost of borrowing and difficulties in placing debt issues with international investors. Both effects are clearly detrimental to developing country interests. Comparing yield spreads of bonds issued under New York law with bonds issued under English juris-diction, Eichengreen and Mody find that the inclusion of collective action clauses in bond contracts can have different effects on borrowing costs, depending on the creditworthiness of the borrowing country: For countries with strong credit ratings, their inclusion seems to lower borrowing costs; however, for weaker rated debtors the incorporation of collective action clauses led to an increase in borrowing costs[30].

These findings are shared only partly by an analysis of yield spread data from both primary and secondary markets for a sample of over 1500 sovereign bonds by Becker, Richards and Thaicharoen who find no evidence that the inclusion of collective action clauses in sovereign bond issues raises the cost of sovereign bor-rowing[31]. According to their results, the increase in borrowing costs for low grade debtors initially reported and subsequently updated by Eichengreen and Mody is exaggerated. Primary market data covering the period between 1990 and 2000 and secondary market yields between 1998 and 2000 indicate that sovereign bonds issued under English law are subject to an interest premium of no more than 10 and 25 basis points for higher and lower rated bonds respectively.

---

30 See Barry Eichengreen and Ashoka Mody. 2003. *Would Collective Action Clauses Raise Bor-rowing Costs?* NBER Working Paper 7458. Cambridge, MA: National Bureau of Economic Research and Barry Eichengreen and Ashoka Mody. 2000. *Would Collective Action Clauses Raise Borrowing Costs? An Update and Additional Results.* Update to NBER Working Paper W7458. http://emlab.berkeley.edu/users/eichengr/research/governinglaw6.pdf

31 See Becker, Richards and Thaicharoen (2001)

11.3.3 A Sovereign Debt Restructuring Mechanism

The most comprehensive approach to facilitate an orderly process to deal with un-sustainable sovereign debt burdens is the creation of a formal sovereign debt restructuring mechanism. At the National Economists' Club Annual Members' Dinner on November 26, 2001 Anne Krueger described the SDRM's primary purpose as being

> To create a catalyst that will encourage debtors and creditors to come together and restructure unsustainable debts in a timely and efficient manner. This catalyst would take the form of a framework offering a debtor country legal protection from creditors that stand in the way of necessary restructuring, in exchange for an obligation for the debtor to negotiate with its creditors in good faith and put in place policies that would prevent a similar problem arising in the future[32].

In Krueger's initial proposal a country struggling to meet its debt obligations would approach the IMF acting as a kind of sovereign bankruptcy court and seek a temporary standstill on its interest obligations and principal repayments. During this period debtors and creditors have the opportunity to negotiate a restructuring agreement that would reduce the burden of debt to sustainable levels. A temporary stand-still would be approved if the bankruptcy court, and essentially the IMF, would judge the applicant's debt burden unsustainable and acknowledge that neither official sector institutions nor capital markets were willing to provide further credit. The debtor would then be obliged to offer guarantees to ensure that during the stand-still period capital outflows would be prevented. As in the case of companies filing for chapter 11 under U.S. law, the existence of a formal SDRM would encourage creditors and debtors to arrive at restructuring agreements before default and resorting to the formal procedures becomes inevitable. The IMF would provide the framework for negotiations but refrain from influencing the negotiating process; a restructuring agreement would thus be reached by creditors and debtors alone.

IMF staff also explored the opportunity to establish an independent and impartial body to handle the administration of claims and facilitate the resolution of potential disputes among creditors and debtors. However, to safeguard *independence, competence, diversity and impartiality*, the composition of such a Sovereign Debt Dispute Resolution Forum is of vital importance[33]: To be perceived legitimate and

---

32 Anne Krueger. 2001. *International Financial Architecture for 2002: A New Approach to Sovereign Debt Restructuring*. Address given at the National Economists' Club Annual Members' Dinner. November, 26 2001. Washington, DC: International Monetary Fund

33 The Fund's executive board has acknowledged this point specifically. See International Monetary Fund. 2002. *IMF Board Discusses Possible Features of a New Sovereign Debt*

effective it would have to include not only representatives from both the debtor and the creditor side, but also recognized restructuring experts.

An effective SDRM would operate in adherence to four principles: Most importantly, the mechanism would need to prevent minority creditors from launching court action within national jurisdictions once the debtor entered the standstill period and ceased debt service payments. Otherwise, creditors would have an incentive to start a wave of rapid litigation in order to access limited assets and so considerably disrupt the negotiating process. The ban on litigation would be limited to a fixed period during which negotiations are taking place. The debtor country needs to assure creditors of adequate behaviour during the standstill period including the prevention of capital flight, good faith negotiations and an avoidance of discrimination between distinct creditor groups. A third necessary feature entails a provision to ensure that additional funds lent after the standstill period commenced would be granted preferred creditor status as priority over previous debt is essential to encourage private creditors to provide additional loans during a restructuring process. Finally, any formal mechanism would have to include some form of collective action provision to prevent dissenting minority creditors from frustrating a restructuring agreement supported by a large majority of creditors.

Several issues render the creation of a formal SDRM far more difficult than the implementation of a code of good conduct and collective action clauses. The ability to prevent renegade creditors from litigating in national courts requires the existence of a universally binding contract that supersedes national law. If only some countries eliminate the possibility of dragging sovereigns before national courts, renegade creditors would move to jurisdictions that allow for litigation during a standstill period. However, imposing a universally binding contract to prevent litigation by private creditors during a stand-off period is politically unfeasible. An alternative approach suggested by Anne Krueger is to include a provision of similar content into the IMF Articles of Agreement[34] which would nevertheless require supermajority support of no less than 85 percent of total votes.

While the IMF appears generally qualified to operate a sovereign debt restructuring mechanism, there are widespread reservations to grant it more and especially more legal powers. One argument often advanced in this respect is that given its status as fellow creditor, the Fund would not be perceived as impartial. Moreover, operating a SDRM would require the IMF to shoulder responsibilities it may struggle to discharge. Due to impartiality problems it would not be accepted as con-

---

Restructuring Mechanism. Public Information Notice 02/106. September 24, 2002. Washington, DC: International Monetary Fund

34 See Anne Krueger. 2001. *A New Approach to Sovereign Debt Restructuring.* Speech given at the Indian Council for Research on International Economic Relations held in Delhi. December 20, 2001. Washington, DC: International Monetary Fund

flict resolving authority regarding disputes between creditors among each other as well as between creditors and debtors. Furthermore, the Fund lacks the resources to provide verification services regarding creditor claims or voting procedures.

A related problem concerns the procedures of initiating a restructuring process. Although the initiative to enter a restructuring process should come from the debtor, it appears necessary to make initiation dependent on an impartial third-party assessment. If debtor countries could unilaterally decide to impose a standstill on debt service payments, moral hazard problems would increase and negatively affect developing countries' access to international capital markets. To safeguard impartiality, third-party assessments would need to be based on clear guidelines defining the circumstances under which a standstill period would be acceptable. Again, an agreement between debtors, creditors and the official sector on such guidelines will be difficult to find.

For creditors to accept a standstill period, debtor countries have to ensure that creditor interests will be defended during the negotiating process. This requires measures safeguarding that assets available to creditors in case of default will be protected. To prevent currency reserves from leaving the country, exchange controls can be an effective instrument. However, even if temporary, exchange controls impose considerable costs on the real economy as discussed in chapter 7. Although the Fund regards approved economic adjustment programs as the core instrument to ensure responsible economic behaviour on the debtor-side, stability programs alone are unlikely to effectively protect creditors' interests during negotiations.

Introducing a formal SDRM also requires determining the type of liabilities included in the standstill and an eventual restructuring agreement. Although the primary focus of any restructuring will clearly be on sovereign debt owed to international creditors, additional obligations may have to be included thus further complicating the restructuring process[35]. First, domestic creditors holding sovereign debt denominated in foreign currency are as likely to cause balance of payments problems by sending their capital abroad as foreign creditors. Foreign creditors are unlikely to agree on a restructuring proposal that includes a haircut when domestic creditors are being repaid in full. Second, in case exchange controls are implemented, the private sector may be prevented from repaying its obligations to foreign creditors. Accordingly, any agreement would have to include international debt owed by the private sector unless alternative solutions to this problem can be devised.

The problems indicated above complicate the introduction of a formal SDRM considerably. They could be addressed given widespread international consensus and the determination to create an effective framework to deal with unsustainable

---

35 See Krueger (2001)

burdens of sovereign debt. But given the fact that support for the implementation of a formal framework is not universal, chances of implementation are slim. Roubini and Setser point out that policymakers could also opt for a less stringent and ambitious mechanism, a so-called *SDRM-lite*[36]. In contrast to a framework along the lines of Anne Krueger's four principles, a reduced version should be far easier to implement in practice. In essence, a *SDRM-lite* would be a compromise between creating a SDRM and relying solely on collective action clauses. Central to its functioning would be the establishment of an aggregated voting process allowing for a single vote by the holders of all outstanding issues to decide on whether to approve or reject a restructuring proposal. Aggregated voting would significantly reduce the ability of holdout creditors to undermine agreements as they would need to accumulate a blocking share of all outstanding debt issues rather than of merely a single one. In a similar procedure, debt holders could vote on a potential ban on litigation during the standstill period. By altering the Fund's Articles of Agreement, aggregated votes could also be taken on debt securities lacking collective action clauses thereby addressing the problem that such provisions are currently part of only around 30 percent of sovereign bond contracts.

11.4 SDRM versus CAC and Code of Conduct

There is a broad consensus that improved procedures for restructuring unsustainable debt burdens would benefit both creditors and debtors. Only a minority accepts the view that the current situation cannot be improved upon. Anna Schwartz, for example, not only strictly opposes IMF proposals to create a formal SDRM, but argues that the problem of sovereign debt restructuring has been exaggerated altogether. Citing both private creditor and sovereign debtor representatives Schwartz points out that *neither sovereign countries nor private-sector investors have been clamoring for a sovereign country bankruptcy law* and in fact both actually oppose reform efforts[37].

The debate on how to achieve a more efficient and orderly process of dealing with unsustainable sovereign debt burdens has by now converged on the approaches described above: A statutory approach to establish a formal SDRM and a contractual, market-based approach entailing widespread use of collective action clauses and the introduction of a code of good conduct, although proponents of the former claim that a formal SDRM is as market-based a solution as the proposals supported

---

36 See Nouriel Roubini and Brad Setser. 2004. The Reform of the Sovereign Debt Restructuring Process: Problems, Proposed Solutions and the Argentine Episode. Working Paper. New York, NY: Stern School of Business

37 Anna Schwartz. 2003. "Do Sovereign Debtors Need A Bankruptcy Law?" *Cato Journal.* Vol. 23, No. 1: 91

by private sector interest groups. However, both approaches come in various forms as the distinction between *SDRM-heavy* and *SDRM-light* indicates. A market-based approach can be designed to account for private sector concerns to a smaller or larger extent. The former would entail the introduction of collective action clauses and a code of good conduct as drafted by the syndicate of private lender interest groups. A more balanced approach would see collective action clauses modelled after bonds issued under U.K. law and a code of good conduct along the lines of the draft presented by the Banque de France. Since a voluntary CGC is compatible with both proposals, the debate centres on the Fund's SDRM proposal versus collective action clauses as supported by both the private-sector and U.S. Treasury[38]. Depending on the mode of implementation, both approaches would considerably improve upon the current situation; however, each approach focuses on a different problem: Proponents of a formal SDRM or bankruptcy court primarily address the problem of holdout creditors disrupting negotiations between the debtor and a majority of creditors. The Treasury's proposal instead predominantly aims at defining ex-ante the procedures to be followed in case a restructuring becomes necessary[39].

Even proponents of developing a fully-fledged SDRM agree on the usefulness of collective action clauses in facilitating the process of sovereign debt restructuring. Their widespread support is not a novel development: The international community has officially encouraged a wider use of CACs at least since the G-10 submitted the Rey Report in 1995. Although initially opposed, the private sector in a letter to then IMFC Chairman Gordon Brown in April 2003 suggested the use of CACs *as the best way forward*[40], underscoring Anne Krueger's claim that even *creditors now accept that official financing is limited and that the choice is not between workout and bailout, but between an orderly restructuring and a disorderly one*[41].

11.4.1 Concerns on the Effectiveness of Collective Action Clauses

Opposition to relying on the introduction of collective action clauses and a code of good conduct instead of creating a formal restructuring mechanism rests primarily on two considerations. Firstly, even if from now on all new sovereign debt issues

38 For the Treasury's current position regarding the question SDRM versus CAC see John Taylor. 2002a. *Sovereign Debt Restructuring: A U.S. Perspective.* Speech given at the IIE. April 2, 2002. Washington, DC: Institute for International Economics

39 See Glenn Hubbard. 2002. *Enhancing Sovereign Debt Restructuring.* Remarks at the Conference on the IMF's Sovereign Debt Proposal. October 7, 2002. Washington, DC: American Enterprise Institute

40 IIF. 2003. *Letter by IIF Chairman Charles M. Daralla to Chairman of the IMFC Gordon Brown.* April 1, 2003. Washington, DC: Institute of International Finance: 3

41 Krueger (2001): 6

would include collective action clauses, it would take a long time until the reform would have worked itself through the system. As stated above, today only about 30 percent of all sovereign bonds outstanding contain such provisions, predominantly those issued in the United Kingdom and Canada. This leaves around USD 250 billion in bonds issued under New York or similar law with maturities of up to 10 years[42]. Many of those bonds are of medium-term maturity, implying that it would take years until the majority of sovereign bonds outstanding would contain collective action clauses. To overcome this problem would require a kind of *mega swap of current debt instruments for new debt containing such clauses*[43], a possibility unlikely to be implemented in practice.

However, a proposal originating from the private sector addresses exactly this problem: J. P. Morgan Chase analysts Ed Bartholomew, Ernest Stern and Angela Liuzzi propose a two-step mechanism that would allow restructuring unsustainable sovereign debt burdens without the need to pass new legislation[44]. In their proposal a debtor burdened with unsustainable debt obligations would in a first step offer bond holders to exchange their bonds for new Interim Debt Claims (IDC), bonds of short maturities that contain collective action clauses and allow for an orderly process of debt restructuring in a second step.

For the offer to be successful investors not participating in the initial exchange for IDCs would have to fare worse in the restructuring process than those who participated. Incentives like up-front cash payments to support the exchange as well as disincentives to retain the original bonds, such as the exit consents used in Ecuador's debt exchange, should therefore accompany the offer to encourage widest possible participation[45]. The fact that the new instruments would be far more liquid than the original paper as several distinct debt issues would be exchanged for a few standardised instruments should provide further incentives for creditors to participate. While the maturity of newly issued IDCs would be short but sufficient to allow for adequate negotiations on a subsequent restructuring, the initial exchange of old paper into IDCs would have to be executed as soon as possible after the debtor first approached its creditors. Although participation by the private sector cannot be guaranteed, the proposal requires no legislative changes and thus underlines the

---

42 See Roubini and Setser (2004): 5
43 Jack Boorman. 2002. *Sovereign Debt Restructuring: Where Stands the Debate?* Speech given at a conference co-sponsored by the Cato Institute and the Economist. October 17, 2002. New York, NY: The Cato Institute: 5
44 See Ed Bartholomew, Ernest Stern and Angela Liuzzi. 2002. *Two-Step Sovereign Debt Restructuring*. J. P. Morgan Chase Research Paper. January 28, 2002. New York, NY: J. P. Morgan Chase
45 See Stephen Choi and Mitu Gulati. 2004. *Innovation in Boilerplate Contracts: An Empirical Examination of Sovereign Bonds*. Working Paper. Berkeley, CA: University of California at Berkeley

ability of market-based approaches to address the problem of unsustainable sovereign indebtedness. At the very least it presents a possible path to follow until a majority of sovereign debt outstanding will include collective action clauses.

An important limitation of CACs is the problem that they only address collective action problems for individual issues. But in order to restructure sovereign debt burdens to sustainable levels a comprehensive approach, involving at least a large majority of outstanding debt, is necessary. When Argentina defaulted in December 2001, individual issues outstanding numbered no less than 90. Although the episode can be argued to represent an extreme case, most sovereign debtors have placed a substantial number of sovereign debt instruments with international investors. As individual issues are offered under different jurisdictions and distinct terms to diverse creditors, a durable solution would require the restructuring of essentially every issue outstanding. Negotiating individual agreements for each outstanding instrument, while theoretically and legally possible, is protracted, expensive, and complicated. If an agreement cannot be reached with investors in merely one or two individual issues, successful agreements with all other creditors might be frustrated. If full repayment would be granted to individual creditors, inter-creditor equality would be violated and could result in a rejection of the agreement by all other creditors as well. The expectation that by holding out investors in specific instruments may be fully repaid can thus create *first-mover problems*[46].

To overcome this problem a kind of *super collective action clause* that would allow reaching restructuring agreements on individual bond issues by supermajority consent would be required. However, super collective action clauses have only a slim chance of implementation given strong opposition by private creditors. Moreover, in some countries super collective action clauses would violate existing legislation; this is the case particularly in countries lacking statutory insolvency procedures[47]. The difficulties in aggregating different debt classes constitute the most important limitation of all approaches suggesting that a universal introduction of collective action clauses into sovereign bond issues could address the problem of sovereign insolvency effectively.

Proponents of market-based approaches agree on the importance of this issue. Although Jack Boorman suggests that the contingency clauses proposed by John Taylor include aggregation clauses which would effectively aggregate creditor claims across different bond issues for voting purposes[48], the position of the U.S.

46 See Barry Eichengreen and Ashoka Mody. 2003. *Is Aggregation a Problem for Sovereign Debt Restructuring?* Working Paper. Berkeley, CA: University of California at Berkeley: 3
47 See Anne Krueger. 2002. *New Approaches to Sovereign Debt Restructuring: An Update to Our Thinking.* Speech given at the Institute of International Economics. April 1, 2002. Washington, DC: International Monetary Fund: 5
48 Boorman (2002): 5

treasury laid out by then U.S. Undersecretary of Treasury for International Affairs, John Taylor, fails to include such a provision. In contrary, Taylor addressed the issue in a speech given to the EMTA on December 5, 2002 arguing that

> It is true that most proposals do not allow for collective action across different classes of debt. But this does not mean that the process would not work or that it would not provide sufficient clarity to attract additional investors and greatly improve predictability. Even without aggregation, the clauses can be helpful in describing a process for workouts without the added delay of developing a complex aggregation procedure[49].

The significance of the problem of aggregation is underlined by findings of Eichengreen and Mody who identified increased borrowing costs for weak borrowers as a consequence of a large number of debt instruments outstanding[50]. However, they find no significant correlation in a sample consisting of sovereign bonds issued in the period from 1991 to 2000 between yield spreads and the number of instruments outstanding for debtors with relatively high creditworthiness. This suggests that investors indeed see the number of borrowers' outstanding debt instruments as an indicator of future costs of restructuring; but only for borrowers likely to face problems these concerns are priced in.

Nonetheless, the problems posed by aggregation issues for market-based approaches to sovereign debt restructuring appear exaggerated. Uruguay's 2003 bond exchange highlights that even the issue of aggregation can be effectively addressed by market solutions. In the transaction, the government of Uruguay was able to exchange both domestic and international sovereign bonds, worth USD 1.6 and USD 3.75 billion respectively, into new debt instruments including collective action clauses in an orderly process. In this respect the episode provides a real-world example for the two-step approach suggested by Barholomew, Stern and Liuzzi: The exchange was voluntary and new debt instruments included both collective action clauses and exit consents. Moreover, and for the first time ever in an emerging market issue, the new bonds also included provisions allowing for aggregate voting over a range of different debt instruments. According to these provisions the government may decide to change the terms of several different bond issues if supported by an aggregate supermajority of no less than 85 percent of relevant debt holders. Minimum support required by creditors to alter the terms of individual issues is at

---

49 John Taylor. 2002. *Using Clause to Reform the Process Sovereign Debt Workouts: Progress and Next Steps.* Prepared Remarks at the EMTA Annual Meeting. December 5, 2002. Washington, DC: Department of Treasury: 3

50 See Barry Eichengreen and Ashoka Mody. 2003b. *Would Collective Action Clauses Raise Borrowing Costs?* NBER Working Paper 7458. Cambridge, MA: National Bureau of Economic Research

66.6 percent. Renegade creditors would need to acquire either 15 percent of all debt instruments included in the aggregate provisions or no less than 33.3 percent of each individual issue. In case more than 33.3 percent of an individual issue's debt holders reject an amendment, restructuring of the remaining issues can still proceed, while for the single issue amendments are still possible under the more regular 75 percent majority clause. The acceptance of this exchange offer by creditors and the fact that Uruguay was able to access international capital markets at pre-exchange interest costs in its aftermath[51], may be the strongest indicator yet that market-based solutions can be sufficient in addressing the problem of unsustainable sovereign debt burdens. It further underlines the importance of co-operation between both creditors and debtors and between creditors holding distinct instruments during the negotiating process.

Co-operation among the holders of distinct debt instruments would be facilitated by the creation of a *Sovereign Debt Dispute Resolution Forum* (SDDRF) as proposed by Anne Krueger. An SDDRF would function in a similar way as the World Bank's International Centre for Settlement of Investment Disputes by providing an impartial forum to resolve disputes arising between creditors and debtors as well as between different creditor classes. It could ensure inter-creditor fairness and provide legitimacy and credibility to the restructuring process. Anne Krueger suggested that composition of such a forum should be decided by the Fund's Board of Governors choosing from a short-list compiled by an independent nomination committee elected by the Executive Board[52]. However, for reasons of legitimacy and credibility, private-sector institutions like the IIF or EMTA should be able to nominate a number of representatives directly. The SDDRF would ideally be composed of an equal number of creditor and debtor-side representatives nominated directly by their respective constituencies. Although a SDDRF would lack a mandate to interfere in negotiations between creditors and debtors or to assess whether a restructuring leaves the remaining debt burden at sustainable levels, it would allow for improving co-operation among creditors and debtors without resorting to a formal bankruptcy court. A sensible approach in this respect would

---

51 The domestically-denominated USD 200 million issue, offered only 5 month after the debt exchange, was oversubscribed 2.5 times. See Carlos Steneri. 2003. *Voluntary Debt Reprofiling: The Case of Uruguay*. Paper prepared for the Fourth UNCTAD Conference on Debt Management. November 11–14, 2003. Geneva: United Nations Conference on Trade and Development: 25

52 See Anne Krueger. 2002. *Sovereign Debt Restructuring and Dispute Resolution*. Address to the Bretton Woods Committee Annual Meeting. June 6, 2002. Washington, DC: International Monetary Fund

be to initially create a voluntary body to foster the resolution of sovereign debt disputes to test the demand for and effectiveness of such a forum[53].

11.4.2 Market-based Approach as the Way Forward

Anne Krueger argued that only a formal sovereign debt restructuring mechanism allows for aggregating several classes of debt[54]. By including aggregation provisions Uruguay's 2003 restructuring undermines this line of argument. As Lerrick and Meltzer point out, *all of the protections provided by an elaborated sovereign bankruptcy court can be easily replicated in bond contracts*[55]. Moreover, requiring neither a universal treaty nor an amendment to the Fund's Articles of Agreement, a market-based approach is far easier to implement than any statutory proposal. Although both approaches would improve on the current practice of restructuring unsustainable sovereign debt burdens, political feasibility suggests concentrating efforts on fostering the inclusion of collective action clauses in all new sovereign debt issues, not only in bond but also in syndicated loan contracts. This course of action has the support of the U.S. Treasury, the major emerging markets trade associations[56] and emerging market issuers themselves who in the past feared adverse effects on their ability to tap international capital markets.

The case for a universal adoption of collective action clauses has been strengthened by Mexico becoming the first emerging market borrower to include collective action clauses in three sovereign bond offerings under New York law in early 2003. Oversubscribed and yielding similar returns to debt instruments lacking collective action clauses, the issue was well received by the markets[57]. Since then, Brazil has followed suit while Argentina indicated its intention to include collective action clauses in any future offerings.

As market initiatives by sovereign debtors since 2003 have strengthened the case for market-based approaches to sovereign debt restructurings, international support

---

53 See Randall Kroszner. 2003. "Enhancing Sovereign Debt Restructuring." *Cato Journal.* Vol. 23, No. 1
54 See Krueger (2002): 4–5
55 Adam Lerrick and Alan Meltzer. 2002. "Sovereign Default. The Private Sector Can Resolve Bankruptcy without a Formal Court." *Quarterly International Economics Report.* April 2002. Pittsburgh, PA: Carnegie Mellon Galliot Centre for Public Policy: 3
56 See Robert Gray. 2003. *Collective Action Clauses.* Remarks prepared for delivery at UNCTAD Fourth Inter-Regional Debt Management Conference. November 11, 2003. Geneva: United Nations Conference of Trade and Development
57 Mexico's Q1 2003 offerings contained a *majority action* provision at 75 percent. Given Mexico's current high level of creditworthiness this experience may not necessarily be applicable to weaker sovereign borrowers. For a detailed analysis of Mexico's offer see Anna Gelpern. 2003. "How Collective Action Is Changing Sovereign Debt." *International Finance Law Review.* May 2003

for a formal SDRM all but evaporated. Despite preliminary encouragement by then Treasury Secretary O'Neill after the idea's initial flotation in November 2001, support began vanishing during the following year. Although the proposal for a formal mechanism was altered three times to re-built international support by reducing the Fund's role, successive statements by the Treasury in favour of a market solution have eroded remaining support further. In light of opposition by the Treasury, the private sector and many emerging market governments, the Executive Board dropped the SDRM proposal in spring 2003[58].

---

58 Notwithstanding, Germany's Federal Ministries of Finance and Economic Cooperation and Development perceive market-based approaches insufficient to tackle the problems of sovereign debt restructuring and argues for continuous efforts to search for solutions based on the central features of a sovereign debt restructuring mechanism. See Bundesministerium der Finanzen. 2004. *60 Jahre Bretton Woods-Institutionen: Standortbestimmung und Ausrichtung.* Berlin: Bundesministerium der Finanzen: 23

12. A Proposal

The IMF can be no International Lender of Last Resort as defined by Walter Bagehot's criteria. Since it cannot create international currency and its resources are inevitably limited, the Fund cannot lend freely as money-issuing central banks can in national settings. Neither can it make use of a collateral requirement as rough indicator of whether a borrower is facing a liquidity crunch or a solvency problem. However, IMF procedures and lending policies can be reformed in a way enabling the Fund to empower emerging market central banks to act as effective lenders of last resort to their economies. Drawing on short-term liquidity assistance by the official sector central banks of fundamentally healthy economies could be put in a position to prevent financial sector collapse and to avoid a default on sovereign debt despite medium to long-term solvency. While not eliminating the possibility that financial crises will occur in the future, if implemented these reforms would go a long way in enhancing the stability of the global financial system. In adherence to Bagehot's principles a restructured IMF would not bail-out insolvent economies but ensure that the contagious effects on fundamentally healthy economies would be kept in check. Like an effective domestic lender of last resort, the Fund would not lend into, but around a crisis.

Under the reform proposal advanced below the Fund's capacity to reduce both frequency and severity of financial crises would be considerably enhanced. At the same time, the IMF would continue its valuable supervisory and monitoring work and the provision of technical assistance to developing economies. While combining the latter function with functions similar to those of an international lender of last resort requires considerable restructuring efforts, reforms may appear less radical than those suggested in a number of rival proposals. The reason is that for effectively discharging its supervisory and monitoring role, the Fund must remain involved in activities that are not necessarily required to enable developing country central banks to act as lender of last resort to their economies. The blueprint for a restructured IMF presented below draws on the arguments developed in chapters 2 to 11. While the reasoning behind each recommendation is summarized, a detailed discussion of individual conditions and recommendations is not duplicated and can be found in the afore mentioned chapters.

12.1 Underlying Principles

Two explicit targets guide this proposal to restructure the IMF. The first is to increase the Fund's effectiveness in addressing financial crises. The second is to ensure that it remains sufficiently equipped to continue its supervisory and monitoring role. By building on the lessons learned over the past decade and addressing those parts of critique on the Fund's response to recent financial crises that are justified, this proposal attempts to improve the Fund's effectiveness and legitimacy for the years to come.

12.1.1 Principles for Effective Liquidity Assistance

Improving the Fund's effectiveness requires to ensure that the provision of liquidity assistance by the IMF is based on several fundamental principles. Most importantly, effectiveness requires that international taxpayers' money is only employed when the probability of sustainable success in preventing or mitigating financial crises is high. If a crisis appears inevitable, further liquidity assistance is hard to justify. If default is inevitable, additional loans will benefit only a limited subset of creditors and saddle the receiving country with even more debt. Consequently, a reformed IMF should grant large-scale liquidity assistance exclusively to illiquid but fundamentally solvent economies as only for those economies short-term emergency loans are an effective instrument for preventing or mitigating financial crisis.

Increased effectiveness also requires the Fund to act faster in cases where timely liquidity assistance is necessary to prevent a fundamentally solvent country from default. Calming panics in financial markets and restoring investors' confidence further requires that assurances of forthcoming liquidity assistance are credible. To be credible, emergency loans have to be disbursed timely and to be of sufficient size to prevent fundamentally solvent institutions from defaulting. The lessons learned in Thailand, Indonesia and Korea suggest that the Fund's conditionality policy often counteracts these principles. Disbursing loans in tranches can mean that at the height of panic domestic central banks find themselves unable to access sufficient funds for acting as lender of last resort to their economies. Market participants may also doubt that national authorities will succeed in implementing the reforms required for further loan disbursements. Ex-post conditionality, therefore, can substantially reduce the effectiveness of emergency assistance in restoring investor confidence and ending capital flight from distressed economies.

Lastly, effective liquidity assistance requires that emergency funds are employed in ways most likely to achieve their objectives. This is important not only for reasons of legitimacy, but also given the fact that international funding is inevitably limited. The central aim of international liquidity assistance should be to enable domestic central banks to act as effective lenders of last resort for their economies; it is not to manipulate or intervene in international currency markets. Consequently, domestic central banks should be restricted to spend international funds along

Bagehotian lines, namely to prevent a default by solvent banks and governments on debt burdens sustainable in the medium to long-term. Domestic central banks should not be permitted to draw on international funds to intervene in the currency markets for the sake of keeping exchange rates at specific levels. In the majority of cases such efforts will prove futile as inevitable limits on IMF funding would render countries' commitment to specific currency pegs incredible. Only if the IMF restricts the permissible uses of its liquidity assistance to the provision of lender of last resort services can its resources suffice and its support be credible for international investors.

Box 12.1 Principles for Effective Liquidity Assistance	
Principle 1	Liquidity assistance should be disbursed only when the probability of averting or mitigating financial crisis is high.
Principle 2	To be effective and credible, liquidity assistance has to be disbursed timely and in sufficient amounts.
Principle 3	To take account of the inevitable scarcity of resources, employment of international funds has to be restricted to its most effective uses.

12.1.2 Principles for Effective Monitoring and Supervisory Work

At the same time, restructuring the IMF to allow for more effective liquidity assistance must not impede its ability to fulfil its essential role as provider of monitoring and advisory services. The data gathered in IMF surveillance activities is an important source of information for both the official sector and international investors when devising assistance and investment strategies respectively. While improvements in transparency and data dissemination standards have enabled the private sector to generate proprietary research regarding the major emerging economies, the costs of gathering economic and financial information on smaller low-income countries in-house are generally prohibitively high. Moreover, given its institutional weight and annual Article IV consultations, the Fund enjoys privileged access to information regarding member countries' economic and financial positions. Accordingly, the Fund is far better equipped to provide financial data and economic assessments on its 184 members than any other institution, both public and private[1]. But to ensure effective and comprehensive supervision and monitoring, Fund membership must remain universally attractive. In order to maintain the attrac-

---

1 See Domenico Lombardi. 2005. *The IMF's Role in Low-income Countries: Issues and Challenges.* IMF Working Paper WP/05/177. Washington, DC: International Monetary Fund: 5

tiveness of membership and encourage members to provide accurate and timely information, the Fund must support programs and provide loans even if of limited effectiveness in preventing and mitigating financial crises[2]. To retain universal membership, the IMF must provide some benefits to all of its members, not only to those most likely endangering global financial stability[3]. Finally, to be successful in gathering the necessary information to fulfil its supervisory and monitoring role, the Fund must also be perceived by all its members as legitimate institution that is not excessively geared towards a subgroup of members' interests.

Simultaneously, a restructured IMF must avoid impeding its role as credible provider of information on macroeconomic data and financial sector stability to international capital markets. To do so, the institution's interests have to remain aligned with its assessments of member countries' financial and economic positions. If the IMF ceases putting its own money at risk, the credibility of its assessments will be significantly reduced. Without credibility in international capital markets, the catalytic role of IMF involvement for private sector capital flows would be limited. Given the importance of private sector capital for developing economies, reform efforts must therefore also aim at retaining the Fund's catalytic capacity.

Box 12.2
Principles for Effective Monitoring and Supervision

Principle 4	The IMF should concentrate on its core mandate in fostering global financial stability. For reasons of effectiveness and to avoid duplication of tasks, it should shed most functions not required to achieve its core mandate.
Principle 5	To enable the Fund to continue its provision of monitoring and supervisory services, membership has to remain universally attractive and the institution itself perceived as legitimate.
Principle 6	To remain a credible provider of assessments on member countries' economic and financial stability, the Fund's interests have to remain aligned with the accuracy of its assessments.

The central mandate of the IMF is to foster global financial stability. The Fund is neither development bank nor international donor agency. For the sake of efficiency and transparency, the IMF should focus on its core mandate and not become

---

2 See Dani Rodrik. 1995. *Why Is There Multilateral Lending?* NBER Working Paper 5160. Cambridge, MA: National Bureau of Economic Research

3 Retaining the Fund's universal character has also been central in the then German government's position on reforming the Bretton Woods institutions. See Michael Kreile. 2000. "Deutschland und die Reform der Internationalen Finanzarchitektur." *Aus Politik und Zeitgeschichte.* B 37–38/2000. Bonn: Bundeszentrale für politische Bildung

involved in general development work. It should therefore cease offering most of its long-term and interest-subsidized facilities while letting development banks fill the void. Therefore it should continue to provide non-emergency facilities only to the extent necessary for retaining its credibility and effectiveness in discharging its monitoring and supervisory functions.

12.2 Membership Rules for a Restructured IMF

In alignment with the principles indicated above a restructured IMF would remain an inclusive organisation with almost universal membership. As such, it would continue to discharge the majority of its current functions. The central aspect of reform entails constitutional changes to improve the Fund's ability in preventing and mitigating financial crises. To achieve this goal, two degrees of membership should be introduced: A general membership for which all current members can easily qualify and an advanced stage for which only a subgroup of members is likely to qualify in the short-term.

12.2.1 General Membership

General membership at the IMF would require countries to meet two conditions in addition to current rules and regulations as laid down in the Articles of Agreement: First, membership would require countries to both subscribe and adhere to standards of transparency and data dissemination as defined by the IMF under the Special Data Dissemination Standard[4]. Second, all members must commit themselves to include standardised collective action clauses in all sovereign debt issues to facilitate a restructuring in case default becomes inevitable. Both conditions can be easily met by all members of the IMF.

The SDDS was introduced in 1996 to serve as guidance on the provision of economic and financial data to the public for countries seeking access to international capital markets. It identifies four dimensions of data dissemination, data, access, integrity and quality, and for each dimension defines several observable elements. Universal subscription to the standard will ensure improvements in the availability of timely and accurate economic and financial information thereby facilitating the functioning of financial markets both domestically and internationally. As of April 2005 over 60 IMF members have already voluntarily subscribed to the SDDS.

---

4 See IMF. 1996. *Guide to the Data Dissemination Standards.* Washington, DC: International Monetary Fund and IMF. 1998. *The Special Data Dissemination Standard: Updated Guidance.* February 1998. Washington, DC: International Monetary Fund

Collective action clauses facilitate the restructuring process in case member countries have saddled themselves with unsustainable debt levels and are forced to restructure either after or preferably before defaulting on their obligations. Collective action clauses allow to reach restructuring agreements by majority consent and to circumvent the problem of rogue creditors. The use of collective action clauses has substantially increased over the past few years; indeed, they appear to already independently become best practice in credit agreements between international creditors and developing country borrowers. Although not all IMF members issue debt in international capital markets, each country should nevertheless commit to include collective action clauses in the case it decides to offer sovereign debt at a later stage.

Box 12.3
Conditions for General Membership

Condition 1	Members must subscribe to the Special Data Dissemination Standards as defined by the IMF.
Condition 2	Members must commit to include collective action clauses in all sovereign debt they issue in international capital markets.

General membership would entail access to all current activities in the fields of surveillance and technical assistance. The Fund would continue to monitor economic and financial developments in its members' economies and issue policy advice under annual Article IV consultations. Similarly, it would continue to provide technical expertise to its members regarding the organisation of their financial systems; implementation of the Fund's advice would remain voluntary. The IMF would also continue to lend foreign currency to its members in balance-of-payments difficulties under Stand-By Agreements (SBA) and Poverty Reduction and Growth Facilities (PRGF) up to a maximum amount of 300 percent of a member's quota. All other facilities would be abolished. The maximum threshold would be absolute and exceeding it strictly excluded under IMF regulations. Terms and conditions on the facilities would remain largely unchanged.

Maintaining both PRGF and SBA facilities bind IMF resources and do not contribute to the Fund's effectiveness in responding to financial crises. In most instances Stand-By Agreements are likely to prove ineffective in the prevention and mitigation of financial crises since 300 percent of a members' quota are insufficient to restore calm in a solvent, but illiquid economy. Furthermore, conditionality requirements mean that only a fraction of the maximum amount can be disbursed upfront, reducing the effectiveness of stand-by agreements in mitigating financial crises even further. The PRGF is an instrument of development policy rather than an instrument to provide liquidity assistance in times of financial distress. Its subsidized interest rates counteract the principles an effective lender of last resort should follow and is suited to achieve World Bank rather than IMF objectives. As both facilities' effectiveness in weathering financial crises is limited, there is a powerful case for their abolition. Indeed, the Meltzer Commission advised Congress that all long-term facilities offered by the IMF should be abolished to avoid mission-creep and duplication of other agencies' programs[5].

Nevertheless both SBA and PRGF should be retained to ensure that the Fund can continue to discharge its supervisory and monitoring function: To maintain the IMF as an effective forum for international monetary cooperation, as wide as possible a membership is necessary. Its monitoring and supervisory role ideally requires universal membership. While for more developed emerging economies IMF membership is essential to retain access to international capital markets, particularly developing countries which rarely interact with international capital markets need alternative incentives to aspire membership. Currently membership is attractive not only in order to receive subsidized loans but also given the fact that most funding by international development banks is dependent on whether the borrowing country has in place a stability program with the IMF. Similarly, Paris Club debt rescheduling and debt forgiveness under the Highly Indebted Poor Country Initiative requires low-income countries' involvement in concessionary stability programs with the IMF. By abolishing the PRGF, incentives for developing countries to uphold membership would be substantially reduced.

The existence of IMF programs is also required for reasons of credibility: IMF assessments on members' economic and financial position are a vital decision-making criterion for international investors and the concept of catalytic finance depends on the Fund's credibility when expressing its confidence in the future course of a country's economy. IMF assessments can only be credible if its incentives are aligned with those of private creditors and credibility requires the IMF to put its own money at risk. That conditionality policy also provides incentives for policy reform is an additional benefit. Similarly, if funds disbursed under SBA or PRGF improve the capability of local central banks to act as lender of last resort for the domestic financial sector, this is a welcome side effect, but not the facilities' primary intention.

12.2.2 Access to Large-scale Liquidity Assistance

In order to increase the stability of the international financial system and reduce the frequency and severity of financial crises the IMF also needs to offer liquidity

---

5 See International Financial Institutions Advisory Commission (2000): 41

assistance in excess of the 300 percent ceiling in terms of a country's quota. *Extended Liquidity Assistance Facilities* (ELA) should enable domestic central banks to function as effective lender of last resort to their economies if liquidity shortages arise. As developing countries' external debt is often denominated in foreign currency and sufficient levels of foreign currency reserves are not always available, central banks in developing countries can be restricted in their ability to act as lender of last resort to their economies. To address this problem, external liquidity assistance must be available on short notice and in sufficient amounts. Assistance in excess of the 300 percent ceiling is warranted as experience from past financial crises shows that to calm financial panics available liquidity must be substantial. If markets judge emergency loans pledged by the international community insufficient, panic is unlikely to subside and confidence among international investors cannot be restored. While the exact amounts required to restore confidence are impossible to determine, a suitable approximation is an amount sufficient to cover both a country's short-term external sovereign and financial sector liabilities.

Extended Liquidity Assistance should only be granted if a domestic lender of last resort is likely to be an effective instrument for preventing or mitigating financial crisis. As demonstrated by Walter Bagehot, short-term liquidity assistance should be advanced to illiquid, but fundamentally solvent borrowers only. Since assessing the solvency of economies is almost impossible, a thorough solvency test must be substituted by an approximation based on suitable indicators. Today the majority of financial crises result as a consequence of either sovereign default or a collapse of a country's financial system. Consequently, an economy should be assumed fundamentally solvent and short-term liquidity assistance perceived as effective instrument if, and only if, sovereign indebtedness is at sustainable levels and the financial sector is fundamentally healthy.

If sovereign debt is at unsustainable levels, short-term loans cannot solve the problem but merely postpone a default. In this case restructuring or debt forgiveness is preferable. If the financial sector of an economy is vulnerable, financial crises can occur even if sovereign indebtedness is at sustainable levels. The bankruptcy of a single bank can trigger the collapse of the whole financial system. Short-term loans by a lender of last resort can prevent unwarranted panic from turning into crisis and triggering a collapse of the financial system if the banking sector is fundamentally stable; but emergency loans will be ineffective if the financial system is vulnerable in the first place due to the widespread existence of insolvent banks. In a healthy banking sector the vast majority of banks and financial institutions are solvent and unlikely to become distressed during non-crisis times. If a majority of banks is close to insolvency, stability can only be restored by restructuring the financial sector.

A domestic lender of last resort can introduce collateral requirements as a rough test of solvency. As shown in chapter 7, at the international level and for economies instead of banks this approach is not feasible. The alternative is to determine financial and economic criteria which, if met, indicate that an economy is fundamentally solvent and that short-term liquidity assistance would be effective in preventing a collapse of the financial sector. Like a collateral requirement, but in contrast to the Fund's current policy of ex-post conditionality, *pre-qualification* allows for timely, indeed almost instant, disbursal of emergency loans. The discussion on the concept of a lender of last resort in chapter 4 suggests that the earlier emergency loans are disbursed, the more effective liquidity assistance will be in calming financial panics. Consequently, pre-qualification is the approach endorsed in this reform proposal to ensure that disbursing emergency loans is an appropriate response. Under reformed IMF regulations, only members meeting previously specified pre-qualification criteria would be eligible for Extended Liquidity Assistance. In alignment with this reasoning, pre-qualification criteria are devised to indicate whether an economy's burden of sovereign debt is sustainable and whether its financial sector is fundamentally healthy. To access ELA facilities member countries must therefore meet two sets of requirements: sovereign stability criteria and criteria indicating financial sector stability.

12.2.2.1 Sovereign Stability Criteria

To indicate the sustainability of their sovereign indebtedness countries should meet the three criteria discussed in detail in chapter 8. Firstly, the level of external indebtedness must lie below applicable maximum thresholds, secondly, short-term debt must not make up more than a quarter of total debt and finally, foreign currency reserves have to be maintained at a unity ratio to the country's short-term external debt obligations.

Research by World Bank economists suggests that, depending on the quality of its institutions and economic policies, for different countries different levels of external debt are sustainable. Consequently, different thresholds and debt ratios are employed for different countries when assessing whether a member's external debt burden can be perceived as sustainable. For countries whose quality of institutions and economic policies is comparatively strong, the level of external indebtedness perceived sustainable is higher than for countries whose quality of institutions and policies is relatively poor. The thresholds adapted correspond to those devised by IMF and IDA in their proposal for a debt sustainability framework for low-income countries. The quality assessment of a country's institutions and economic policies corresponds to the World Bank's Country Policy and Institutional Assessments.

External debt burdens are assumed sustainable if the three-year average value of three out of four debt ratios is below the appropriate thresholds defined in Table 12.1. Requiring to meet three out of four criteria ensures that both debt stock and debt service ability is taken into account while drawing on three-year averages ensures that one-off shocks in a single year do not distort the fundamental picture.

Table 12.1
Thresholds for Sustainable Levels of External Indebtedness (%)

	Country Institutional and Policy Assessment		
	Poor	Medium	Strong
NPV of debt-to-GDP	30	45	60
NPV of debt-to-exports	100	200	300
Debt service-to-exports	15	25	35
Debt-servive-to-revenue	20	30	40

Source: IMF and IDA

By meeting a maximum threshold of short-term debt to total debt of 25 percent members additionally indicate a healthy debt structure in terms of maturity. As experienced over and over again, countries can be forced into default as a consequence of maturity mismatches in their debt structures even when total debt burdens are sustainable. Similar reasoning applies to the unity reserve requirement: Financial panics often occur because speculators expect a country to lack sufficient foreign currency reserves to service short-term debt obligations. Drawing their lessons from financial crises during the 1990s, many emerging economies today hold foreign currency reserves substantially in excess of their short-term external debt service requirements. Pre-qualification should require members to maintain at least a level of foreign currency reserves sufficient to service external debt service obligations coming due over a period of three months. Over an appropriate transition period, most countries should be able to rebalance their debt structures in order to avoid excessive currency or maturity mismatches and qualify for advanced membership at a restructured IMF.

12.2.2.2 Criteria Indicating Financial Sector Stability

To qualify for short-term liquidity assistance above the 300 percent ceiling, members should be required to meet three additional criteria that indicate a minimum level of financial sector stability: On the one hand, national authorities have to ensure that financial institutions operating in their economy meet appropriate capital adequacy standards and adequate cash reserve ratios. On the other, national authorities need to safeguard that their financial sectors are open to international competition.

In order to reduce financial sector vulnerability, supervisory authorities in developing countries should implement compulsory capital adequacy ratios of 15 percent. To account for the fact that return volatility is far higher in developing than in industrialised economies, capital adequacy requirements are set substantially above the 8 percent level defined in the Basel II capital adequacy framework as the latter's focus is primarily on financial institutions in OECD countries. To determine the amount of capital necessary to meet the 15 percent requirement financial institutions in developing countries should employ an approach based on the Basel Standardized Approach but modified to account for characteristics of less developed financial sectors. As shown in chapter 8, unless modified, the Basel II Standardized Approach is of limited suitability for developing countries and emerging economies.

While capital adequacy requirements aim to safeguard a minimum level of prudence in banks' portfolio composition, adequate reserve requirements strengthen bank's resilience when liquidity in the financial system becomes scarce. Although reducing profitability, adequate cash reserves significantly reduce banks' vulnerability to runs and potential default in case foreign creditors call their loans unexpectedly and all at once. As all banks operating in the financial sector would have to meet identical reserve requirements, domestic competition would not be distorted. A cash reserve requirement of 15 percent of assets balances benefits of increased stability with the cost of capital gains foregone. In combination with capital adequacy requirements, sufficient reserve requirements will increase financial sector stability regardless of the degree of banking sector development. While for less developed financial systems reserve requirements often are the most effective regulatory instrument, in more advanced financial systems capital adequacy ratios are central to safeguard a minimum level of financial sector stability.

To qualify for extended liquidity assistance a country's financial sector also needs to be open to international competition. Empirical evidence suggests that barriers of entry for foreign financial institutions are negatively related to financial sector stability. Entry of foreign banks fosters financial sector development by introducing competition that in turn raises efficiency at local institutions and can break-up excessively close relations between banks and corporations. Efficiency is further enhanced by the introduction of best practices and international managerial experience. In addition, by investing foreign capital into the domestic banking sector, foreign banks can strengthen the capital structures of local banks and increase depth and liquidity of domestic capital markets. Although internationalisation of the financial sector is often perceived as unilaterally benefiting vested interests of industrial countries' financial sectors, empirical evidence suggests that for developing countries the benefits from lowering barriers to entry into their financial sectors generally outweigh costs.

Box 12.4
Conditions for Advanced IMF Membership

Condition 1	Members must not surpass more than one of the four applicable three-year average maximum sustainability thresholds of sovereign indebtedness as defined in IMF and IDA's debt sustainability framework.
Condition 2	Short-term sovereign debt, defined as debt maturing within a period of three months, must not surpass 25 percent of a member's total sovereign indebtedness.
Condition 3	Members must maintain an adequate level of foreign currency reserves; the minimum level is an amount sufficient to meet three months of external debt service obligations of both the sovereign and the financial sector.
Condition 4	Members have to implement effective financial sector regulation ensuring that banks maintain a 15 percent capital adequacy ratio. Capital requirements are to be determined by a standardized approach based on Basel II, but altered to account for the specifics of developing country financial sectors.
Condition 5	Members must implement a cash reserve requirements demanding financial institutions to keep 15 percent of total assets in cash or cash equivalents
Condition 6	Member countries have to ensure their financial sectors are open to the entry of foreign competitors and allow for foreign investment into local financial institutions.

12.3 Lending Rules Governing IMF Facilities

In addition to pre-qualification requirements for both general and advanced IMF membership, a careful design of the lending rules governing the use of IMF facilities is necessary to increase the Fund's effectiveness in crisis prevention and management while keeping moral hazard problems in check.

12.3.1 Lending Rules Governing PRGF and SBA Facilities

All IMF members qualify for liquidity support under Stand-By Agreements or the Poverty Reduction and Growth Facility. The maximum amount a country can draw under these facilities is strictly fixed at the current level of 300 percent of its quota. Terms and conditions applicable to both facilities remain largely unchanged; only interest charges for funds lent under Stand-By Agreements are to be raised above the market rate of interest. Funds can be drawn either to facilitate debt restructuring or to bolster the central bank's capability as lender of last resort. IMF funds may not be used by central banks to intervene in the currency markets for the sake of manipulating currency values. Disbursal of both facilities continues to be guided by the policy of conditionality; funds are released in tranches subject to borrowers meeting previously agreed policy conditions to foster economic reform. The maturity of Stand-By Agreements remains at a range of between 12 and 18 months; interest payable would be at a premium of 100 basis points above market rates. For funds disbursed to low-income countries under the Poverty Reduction and Growth Facility interest charges would be maintained at a concessional level of 50 basis points while maturity could be extended to periods of up to 10 years.

12.3.2 Lending Rules Governing ELA Facilities

Large-scale liquidity assistance should enable central banks in developing countries to act as effective lender of last resort to their domestic financial sectors and governments. Its effectiveness in doing so depends on several factors and requires several conditions to be met. Two are already met when a country qualifies for Extended Liquidity Assistance: Sovereign indebtedness is at sustainable levels and the financial sector is fundamentally healthy during non-crisis times. Additional requirements can be addressed by incorporating suitable incentives into the framework of lending rules applicable to funds disbursed under the ELA facility. Three are of particular importance: First, international liquidity assistance has to be sufficient to prevent the financial sector from collapse and restore confidence. Second, lending rules must ensure that central banks employ international funds effectively. And third, moral hazard effects arising from the availability of liquidity assistance for both borrowing countries and international investors have to be kept in check. Lending rules governing the use, maturity and interest charges applicable to ELA facilities must be designed to ensure that these additional requirements are met.

12.3.2.1 Ensuring Liquidity Assistance in Sufficient Amounts

The existence of Extended Liquidity Assistance is necessary as in most financial crises PRGF and SBA facilities are not sufficient to restore confidence in the financial markets. If during a banking panic depositors expect the central bank to be unable to provide all solvent institutions with short-term liquidity, bank runs will continue. This is why Bagehot advised the Bank of England to lend freely and to say so. The same applies to a restructured IMF: Bank runs and violent capital outflows will only subside if investors are persuaded that short-term liquidity is available to solvent institutions in sufficient amounts. Ideally, the amount of funds available under the ELA facility would be unlimited; in practice it must be at least sufficient to restore confidence in the financial system. While determining the exact amount required is impossible, the combined amount of short-term external debt owed by the financial sector as well as the government less foreign currency reserves is a good approximation. To increase confidence and credibility, the maximum amount of liquidity assistance available to qualified countries under the ELA facility should be set at 150 percent of short-term external debt obligations falling due over a period of three months less foreign currency reserves.

For the sake of efficiency, funds should be disbursed in full and upfront. The earlier liquidity assistance is disbursed during a crisis, the more effective funds will be in mitigating it. In a crisis' early stages only few banks will be in need of short-term liquidity to avoid default. The longer a crisis lingers, the more institutions fall into distress and more emergency loans are needed to prevent the financial sector from collapsing. Qualified members should therefore receive funds instantly without having to meet any further policy conditions as they indicated fundamental solvency by meeting pre-qualification requirements. Since ex-post conditionality severely limits the Fund's effectiveness in preventing and mitigating financial crises, substituting it by pre-qualification substantially strengthens its capabilities.

As IMF resources—even if substantially bolstered—are inevitably limited, terms and conditions applicable to ELA facilities have to ensure that IMF resources are employed as efficiently as possible. Emergency loans should flow back to the Fund as soon as they have become dispensable and the crisis has been arrested. Consequently, ELA facilities should be lent exclusively at short-term maturities, with a maximum maturity of up to 6 months. If a financial crisis results from asymmetric information or herd behaviour, within six months and given the existence of emergency assistance the panic will be likely to subside. Otherwise, the crisis may be fundamentally justified rather than the consequence of a liquidity crunch. In general, ELA facilities should be non-renewable. Only under extraordinary circumstances a supermajority of executive directors should be able to extend maturity once for an additional 6 month period. Maturity for ELA facilities is therefore considerably shorter that the 12 to 30 months of the Fund's abolished Contingent Credit Line but close to the 18 months maximum maturity suggested by the Independent Task Force Report.

12.3.2.2 Ensuring Liquidity Assistance Is Employed Effectively

Since the Fund's central task is to increase global financial stability, lending rules must also ensure that borrowing countries put international liquidity assistance to its most effective uses in preventing or mitigating financial crises. More specifically, countries receiving international assistance need to employ it for the sake of preventing a collapse of the financial sector and a default on sovereign debt obligations. To achieve this end, domestic central banks have to make loans available in a way ensuring that solvent financial institutions do not have to declare bankruptcy due to a short-term lack of liquidity and that governments are not forced to default on a sustainable debt burden due to currency or maturity mismatches in their debt structures. As emergency funds available are limited, the use of ELA facilities must be restricted to the most effective ways of achieving these objectives.

This restriction implies that all other uses of international liquidity assistance are strictly excluded. Accordingly, central banks should not be allowed to lend on IMF funds to non-financial institutions or official development projects. While both uses can have their individual merits, the central objective of liquidity assistance by a restructured IMF is to increase global financial stability; it is not to foster development by any other means like financing infrastructure projects or providing finance to ease the upstart of private sector initiatives. Such tasks are the domain of the World Bank, its regional equivalents and of commercial banks operating in developing countries. The IMF has neither the funds nor the professional expertise to engage in conventional development assistance. If it had, its involvement would lead to an inefficient duplication of structures and functions of other international organisations.

Enabling central banks of developing countries to act as lender of last resort is the only way limited funding can be sufficient to prevent financial sector collapse or sovereign default. Although the successful maintenance of currency pegs can help to prevent a number of entities from financial distress, the probability that intervening in currency markets will be successful in the medium to long-term is limited. Furthermore, there is little reason to believe that central bank officials can determine the fair value of a currency more accurately than currency markets themselves. The funds required to sustainably defend an overpriced currency peg are essentially unlimited and the international community is unwilling to provide an international institution with unlimited funding. Experience from emerging market currency crises has shown that if funds available to maintain an overpriced peg are known to be limited, efforts of maintaining it will ultimately prove futile.

Therefore lending rules should stipulate that ELA facilities are employed exclusively for two purposes: First, to prevent governments from defaulting on the short-term portion of fundamentally sustainable sovereign debt. And second, to enable domestic central banks to act as effective lender of last resort. The latter requires central banks to adhere to the Bagehot Rules demanding that a lender of last resort should make available short-term loans to illiquid, but solvent institutions only against good collateral and at penalty rates. Employing ELA facilities to intervene in the currency markets should be strictly excluded. Although excluding individual violations of these rules may be impossible, requiring central banks to detail their uses of official sector liquidity assistance together with regular monitoring would go a long way in making violations the exception rather than the rule.

12.3.2.3 Reigning In on Debtor-side Moral Hazard

Lending rules should also ensure that members draw on international liquidity assistance only as a last resort when no other means of short-term credit is available. In order to provide incentives for members facing liquidity problems to examine all alternative sources of liquidity, interest charges applicable to ELA facilities should be set above the market rate of interest. If interest charges would be at subsidized rates, as is the case with many current IMF facilities, members have incentives to draw on international liquidity assistance as a low-cost source of financing. Moreover, penalty rates on official sector liquidity assistance encourage borrowers to repay their debts as early as possible, either out of replenished reserves or by refinancing through alternative sources of capital. By making ELA facilities subject to a penalty rate, incentives would be created for members to negotiate stand-by facilities with commercial lenders to draw on in times of crisis. Argentina can serve as an example for this prudent strategy[6]. While some countries will find entering such agreements easier than others, particularly countries able to pledge natural resources or future foreign currency income streams as collateral should have little difficulties in negotiating stand-by facilities with commercial lenders. Penalty interest rates should be set to ensure that all countries able to negotiate stand-by facilities with the private sector have an incentive to do so before drawing on international taxpayers' money.

---

6 In 1996 the central bank of Argentina entered into stand-by agreements with several foreign banks, opening the possibility to draw on external resources when foreign currency reserves would become substantially depleted. By late 1997 Argentina had negotiated unconditional credit lines with 13 commercial banks worth around $7 billion. Under the agreement, Argentina had the right to swap government debt for U.S. dollars at an effective interest rate of 205 basis points above Libor and an additional commitment fee of 33 basis points. Importantly, stand-by agreements where not subject to a normally common contract clause allowing banks to withdraw from their commitment in case of serious adverse material changes, like financial crises.

While there is wide agreement on the importance of penalty rates, absolute numbers are rarely suggested. The Meltzer Commission merely stated that the penalty rate should be a premium above the yield on borrowers' sovereign debt one week before it applied for IMF assistance. To uphold the attractiveness for countries to negotiate stand-by agreements with the private sector, interest payable on ELA facilities should be clearly above interest charged by the private sector. However, a premium of 200 basis points in addition to the higher of either a country's latest lending agreement with private sector entities or the yield on the sovereign's debt a week before applying for international assistance appears appropriate. As a result, while the premium would be equal for all borrowers, absolute interest charged would differ depending on a borrowing country's market rate of interest. If under extraordinary circumstances the Executive Board agrees to extend the lending period from 6 to 12 months, the interest premium charged should be increased by a further 100 basis points.

Box 12.5
Lending Rules Governing Extended Liquidity Assistance

Rule 1	The use of ELA facilities by local central banks is restricted to the provision of effective lender of last resort services along Bagehotian lines. Central banks must not employ ELA facilities to intervene in the currency markets.
Rule 2	ELA facilities are subject to a penalty interest charge of 200 basis points above the applicable market rate of interest.
Rule 2	Maturity of loans disbursed under ELA facilities is restricted to 6 months. Under extraordinary circumstances loans can be renewed once for 6 additional months subject to consent by a supermajority of executive directors. In this case an additional interest premium of 100 basis points becomes applicable.

12.4 Funding Issues and Transition Period

A proposal to restructure the IMF into an institution operating similarly to an international lender of last resort would be incomplete without addressing two important issues: The first is the question of how much funding a restructured IMF would require to fulfil its mandate. The second is the problem that some members would require a considerable period of time until being in a position to meet the pre-qualification criteria established above.

12.4.1 Funding Issues

It is impossible to derive the actual amount of funding necessary for the IMF to enable the central banks of qualified members to act as effective lenders of last resort to their economies. Enabling an single illiquid, but fundamentally solvent economy to avoid defaulting on its external debt obligations requires at least an amount matching short-term external debt obligations of both the sovereign and the banking sector less foreign currency reserves held at the central bank. To increase the credibility of official sector liquidity assistance and to restore confidence in the financial markets, funds available for liquidity support should be above the minimum amount required to avoid default. Consequently, necessary funding can be approximated by identifying maximum liquidity gaps over the past decade and adding an amount of between 25 and 50 percent for the sake of credibility.

As argued in chapter 6 an estimate of required funding for the IMF to enable developing country central banks to act as lenders of last resort to their economies in a range between USD 250 and 350 billion seems suggestive. A commitment capacity of USD 350 billion should ensure that the Fund can credibly commit to effectively support every member facing short-term liquidity problems and meeting pre-qualification criteria; in comparison, the Fund's current commitment capacity is at around USD 165 billion. As it is unlikely that the Fund would ever have to support more than a few members at the same time, a share of the required commitment capacity could take the form of stand-by agreements with the central banks of major industrial economies. Via consecutive quota increases IMF commitment capacity should be raised to USD 250 billion with stand-by agreements ensuring access to a further USD 100 billion worth of loans from international central banks put in place.

12.4.2 Transition Period

Currently only a minority of developing countries would meet all pre-qualification requirements to advanced membership at a restructured IMF. While some conditions can be fulfilled with relative ease by most current members, others would require substantial reforms and time for their implementation. A five-year transition period seems a reasonable time frame to allow countries adapting to the new requirements. During this period, countries could initiate the policy reforms necessary in order to meet the conditions required to gain advanced IMF membership. By pursuing prudent financial and economic policies major emerging economies should be able to meet most criteria indicating the sustainability of both the level and the structure of sovereign debt and build up an adequate level of foreign currency reserves. Countries burdened by unsustainable levels of sovereign debt would be able to do so following restructurings under the HIPC or similar initiatives; as these countries are of lesser importance for global financial stability, a longer transition period would not increase the vulnerability of the global financial system.

Greater difficulties for developing countries arise in meeting the conditions for a fundamentally healthy financial sector, namely in ensuring that banks meet adequate capital ratios and reserve requirements. In their efforts to increase banking sector stability and competitiveness, developing countries will need support by the international community. Particularly the World Bank and bilateral development assistance would have to further concentrate their focus on developing country banking sectors; they would be required to finance more projects that contribute to the stability and competitiveness of financial institutions in the developing world. The international community would need to increase technical assistance in advising developing countries on the creation of the legislation and institutions necessary for the functioning of successful market-based economies such as supervisory, monitoring and regulatory authorities, but also effective bankruptcy laws and accounting standards; at least for the transitory period, this might require development banks and similar agencies to shift additional resources into this field.

One of the greatest problems in this regard will be a lack of funding available to developing country banks for shoring up their balance sheets to meet capital adequacy ratios and reserve requirements. Even if national authorities formally implement required regulations, a lack of financial resources can render these efforts futile. Opening financial sectors to international competition and foreign investments opens one source of funding: Through foreign direct investments in developing country banks, foreign capital becomes available for financial institutions to increase both reserves and capital ratios.

However, in many instances subsidies by the public sector to recapitalize banks may prove inevitable. Although such transactions are generally detrimental to market discipline and involve moral hazard problems, one-off subsidies may prove a sensible strategy if they help countries to satisfy pre-qualification requirements and break opposition to financial sector reform by vested interests. A transactional design which would minimize unwanted moral hazard effects has been suggested by Calomiris[7]: Under his proposal originally developed for the Japanese banking sector, the government would invest for a limited period into preferred equity of under-capitalized banks; the amount invested would match the funds banks are able to raise by issuing common stock to the public. As long as the government retains its stake, banks would refrain from paying dividends to holders of common stock while the government would forego its dividend payments to subsidize recapitalization. By

---

7 See Charles Calomiris. 1998. "Reducing Moral Hazard: Introducing Market Signals to Banking Supervision." *Economic Perspectives. USIA Electronic Journal.* Vol. 3, No. 4

restricting its capital injection to the amount individual banks can raise in the market, authorities can draw on market signals to determine which banks are worth recapitalizing and which should be closed down in order to reduce banking sector vulnerability.

13. Epilogue: Chances of Implementation

Over the last twelve chapters this analysis has attempted to explore the concept of an international lender of last resort from a variety of angles. The various aspects analysed suggest that in an international context a lender of last resort operating strictly in accordance with Bagehot's principles is practically unfeasible. At the same time the preceding chapters aimed at establishing that the creation of an institution performing a function similar to that of an international lender of last resort is not only theoretically possible but also practically feasible given support by the international community.

However, a realistic assessment of the current political environment must concede that a comprehensive reform of the IMF along the lines of this proposal is rather unlikely. While some features of the proposal are likely to command support with the Fund's major shareholders, its central recommendation to make large-scale liquidity assistance dependent on borrowing countries meeting pre-specified qualification criteria faces strong opposition. This is not surprising since pre-qualification would restrict the ability of G-7 members to use IMF facilities as instrument to foster individual foreign policy objectives. While qualified countries would have automatic access to liquidity assistance above the 300 percent ceiling available to all IMF members, countries failing to meet qualification criteria would be denied large-scale liquidity assistance—regardless of their strategic importance to the Fund's dominant members.

The case for reforming the IMF by replacing the principle of ex-post conditionality with the principle of pre-qualification or ex-ante conditionality rests on effectiveness. By introducing pre-qualification the Fund's credibility and effectiveness as crisis manager would be considerably enhanced. Only ex-ante conditionality allows for a timely disbursal of emergency loans since strict collateral requirements are unfeasible in an international context. And only ex-ante conditionality is likely to enhance market confidence and to rebuild the institution's credibility and legitimacy. The trade-off is a reduction in policy flexibility and control over IMF resources for the Fund's major shareholders since their ability to use the IMF as a political slush fund would be curtailed. Currently, concerns of loosing control and policy flexibility outweight the desire to improve the Fund's effectiveness in reducing the frequency and severity of financial crises. But recent developments both inside and outside the Fund suggest that the likelihood of IMF lending policies moving towards a new paradigm is increasing. Regional monetary cooperation in Southeast Asia is likely to provide a growing impetus for the Fund's major shareholders to increase international cooperation and to agree on significant reforms to the international financial architecture. At the same time, comments and policy proposals by IMF staff suggest that the advantages of putting more emphasis on ex-ante conditionality are getting more recognition even inside the IMF.

13.1 Opposition to Reform

The reasons why reform has been so limited are at least twofold: Firstly, G-7 countries, the Fund's most powerful members, have not put their weight behind a substantial reform of the global financial architecture. They are reluctant to do so as the changes advocated in this proposal go along with a loss in their ability to use the Bretton Woods institutions to further individual economic and strategic interests. Secondly, developing countries which would benefit from significant reforms of the IMF lack the power to push for their implementation. Likewise, supporters of reform in the developed world are not represented in the central levels of financial decision making, particularly in industrial countries' ministries of finance[1].

13.1.1 Opposition by Developed Countries and the G-7

Without support by the United States significant reforms at the IMF are impossible. As described previously the U.S. and G-7 representatives at the IMF can veto any decision of importance. Currently, U.S. policy makers appear opposed to a fundamental reform that would enhance the Fund's ability to act like an international lender of last resort to the global financial system. Their position is shared by most G-7 countries including Germany. Opposition is based on at least three considerations. Most importantly, the U.S. administration is unwilling to accept any reductions in their control over IMF policy and their ability to use the Bretton Woods institutions as an instrument to foster individual interests. In addition, neither the U.S. nor its fellow G-7 members are willing to increase the Fund's financial resources. Adding to this reluctance on part of the executive is the fact that influential financial sector interests are fundamentally opposed to any reform which might inhibit the profitability of its foreign exchange and derivative operations[2].

Opposition concentrates on the proposal's central building block: the introduction of ex-ante conditionality for large scale emergency assistance. Objectives and other aspects of the proposal are less controversial and have been partially implement already with the backing of the Fund's largest shareholders. Efforts have been made to strengthen members' incentives to reduce their vulnerability to financial crises, a

---

1 See Stephany Griffith-Jones and Jose Ocampo. 2003. *What Progress on International Financial Reform. Why So Limited?* Stockholm: Almqvist & Wiksell International
2 See Heribert Dieter. 2005. *Die Zukunft der Globalisierung.* Baden-Baden: Nomos: 339–340

stronger focus has been put on financial systems, debt structures and adequate exchange rate regimes and transparency and data dissemination have improved considerably. The position of U.S. policy makers regarding pre-qualification is represented by the Treasury's reaction to the Meltzer Commission's majority report which included the recommendation to make IMF assistance dependent on countries meeting a set of pre-qualification criteria[3]. The Bush administration has signalled more openness for reform, but at the same time opposes pre-qualification and has in practice followed similar policies as its predecessor.

Treasury justified its opposition to the central recommendations of the Meltzer commission on several grounds. Regarding prequalification it criticised that the IMF would be unable to implement stability programs in countries that fail to meet qualification criteria and its support restricted to a very limited set of strong emerging market economies. It also rejected the conditions proposed by the Meltzer Commission as overly narrow and argued that the criteria would not have prevented crises stemming from other causes. In addition, moral hazard problems were claimed to increase as eligible member countries would face incentives to concentrate on pursuing imprudent policies not covered by pre-qualification criteria. Maintaining the Fund's conditionality policy has instead been perceived essential for encouraging countries to tackle their economic problems and ensuring that IMF resources are not misappropriated and repaid on time[4].

The technical arguments set forth by the Treasury do not discredit the principle of ex-ante conditionality. They are only partially convincing regarding recommendations by the Meltzer Commission and even less so regarding the proposal developed in this thesis. Firstly, the proposal explicitly aims at preventing the IMF from granting large scale liquidity assistance to countries which fail to meet pre-qualification criteria as the failure to do so would suggest that liquidity support is unlikely to be effective. In contrast to the qualification criteria suggested in the Meltzer Report, this proposal includes as central criterion a maximum threshold of sovereign indebtedness, ensuring that liquidity assistance will not merely increase an already unsustainable burden of sovereign debt. While it is undeniable that conditionality policy has its merits, the Treasury does not address the problem that the Fund's conditionality policy makes effective crisis management almost impossible. Moreover, the majority of incentives ex-post conditionality provides for countries to improve their economic policies are maintained since countries would be encouraged to meet qualification criteria. The strong support by both IMF staff and the

---

3 See Department Treasury. 2000. *Response to the Report by the International Financial Institution Advisory Commission.* June 8, 2000. Washington, DC: Department of Treasury
4 See Department of Treasury (2000): 17–19

Fund's major shareholders for the Contingent Credit Line facility suggests that the effectiveness of a pre-qualification approach is at least implicitly acknowledged.

The advantages of ex-ante conditionality have been discussed in depth in the previous chapters; but even the counter-arguments mentioned above indicate that opposition to this approach rests on political rather than on technical considerations. Significantly altering the Fund's approach to crisis management involves a similarly significant reduction in the control its largest shareholders currently exert over IMF policies. Increasing the Fund's effectiveness in reducing frequency and severity of financial crises may be welcome in general but not at the price of reducing the opportunities to use the institution to enhance individual policy interests. As the Treasury stated in the opening paragraph of its response to the recommendations made in the Meltzer Report, the *IFIs are among the most effective and cost-efficient means available to advance U.S. policy priorities worldwide*[5].

The record of IMF reform since the Asian Crisis underlines that U.S. policy makers support reforms to increase IMF efficiency as long as they do not impede U.S. capacity to control the Fund's major lending decisions. In contrast to the Clinton administration which made active use of the IMF during its time in office and was particularly reluctant to reform the institution, the Bush administration initially put IMF reform high up on its agenda. Traditionally more sceptical regarding the role of international organizations in general and international financial organisations in particular, under Secretary O'Neill Treasury's reform efforts focussed on reducing the role of the IMF rather than on increasing its effectiveness in preventing and mitigating financial crises. The most important reforms enacted by the IMF with strong support by the Treasury comprised a clarification of the limits and criteria for large-scale liquidity assistance and the streamlining of conditionality restricting conditions to a limited number of macroeconomic policies. In addition, efforts were made to expand the use of short-term loans and to make use of interest premia to encourage timely repayment[6].

While these reforms are in line with the recommendations advanced in this proposal and increase the institution's effectiveness and transparency, no progress has been made regarding the introduction of pre-qualification as the Fund's guiding principle. Moreover, the new rules were broken as soon as foreign policy considerations entered the picture. Despite the stated intention to refrain from large-scale liquidity assistance regardless of such policies' chance of success, IMF lending since 2001 continued to be based on political rather than on economic consider-

---

5 Department of Treasury (2000): 1
6 See Randal Quarles. 2005. *IMF Reform – Toward an Institution for the Future.* Statement before the Subcommittee on International Trade and Finance. June 7, 2005. Washington, DC: Senate Banking Committee

ations. Large loans were advanced to countries of strategic importance such as Pakistan or Turkey which received two rescue packages within two years despite the country's ambiguous economic fundamentals. In a similar vain large rescue packages were advanced to Brazil and Argentina in 2001 before Argentina was left to default in December the same year. Nevertheless, the default of Argentina shows that by lending around the crisis instead of continuing to lend into it, contagious effects on fundamentally sound economies can be mitigated. In this respect, only the assistance package for Uruguay to cope with the fallout of Argentina's default followed the underlying rationale of this proposal.

The limited likelihood that this proposal would find support by G-7 policy makers also stems from their reluctance to increase IMF funding. As argued in chapter 6, to act as credible lender of last resort the Fund's resources would have to be increased. While necessary funding would be by no means unlimited, an increase in IMF commitment capacity would be required. As liquidity assistance will be sought by developing countries and emerging economies only, policy makers in developed countries perceive no immediate pay-off from replenishing the Fund's resources. While an increase in the stability of the global financial system benefits developed and developing countries alike, the benefits for industrial countries are less tangible as spending more money on international cooperation and international organisations is unlikely to yield more votes in the electorate.

Indeed, given its scepticism towards international financial institutions, the current administration explicitly aims at reducing the Fund's ability to advance large loan packages to developing country members. According to Undersecretary of Treasury for International Affairs John Taylor *the Bush administration set out to establish the presumption that the IMF—rather than official creditor governments— is responsible for providing large scale loan financing. This provides an overall budget constraint and thereby an overall limit on loan assistance, recognizing that IMF resources are limited*[7].

While this stance should be welcomed in the case of countries whose economic problems render liquidity assistance ineffective, it also reduces the Fund's ability to arrest liquidity crises in fundamentally solvent economies. Although an increase in global financial stability is clearly in the interest of the Fund's major shareholders, reforms lack influential constituents such as the financial sector or exporting industries. This is surprising as particularly the former would benefit from more clarity regarding IMF lending decisions and signals regarding the economic position of developing and emerging market economies.

---

7 John Taylor. 2004. *New Directions for the International Financial Institutions.* Address at the Conference Global Economic Challenges for the IMF's New Chief. American Enterprise Institute. June 10, 2004. Washington, DC: Department of Treasury

13.1.2 The Lacking Clout of Developing Economies

The majority of developing countries and particularly emerging market economies would benefit from reforming the IMF into a quasi international lender of last resort. Only for countries of high strategic importance to the United States and its G-7 partners that follow unsound economic policies the current IMF lending policies seem preferable. Countries instead inclined to follow prudent fiscal and monetary policies and strengthen their financial sectors would receive additional incentives and direction for reform. By meeting pre-qualification criteria they could signal to international creditors the quality of their policies and thus gain access to private capital at more attractive terms. The statement by Guillermo Ortiz, Governor of the Bank of Mexico, indicates that the reform proposal would be likely to find support by many emerging market policy makers:

> There is a missing piece in the institution's toolkit: a substitute for the CCL. None of the existing Fund facilities is designed to encourage members to implement sound economic policies, while at the same time helping those with strong fundamentals cope with exogenous shocks[8].

While some emerging market economies may prefer current IMF lending policies, the fact that the scope for large scale liquidity assistance by the Fund has been significantly reduced makes the proposal described above far more attractive than the status quo. The proposed framework should be particularly welcome by countries critical of the excessive conditionality requirements insisted on by the IMF during the Asian Crisis. By qualifying for extended liquidity assistance these countries could access short-term liquidity assistance instantly without any intrusion into their sovereignty.

Moreover, the capacity of developing countries and emerging economies to build effective coalitions for advancing common interests has so far been limited. The problem of African nations in agreeing on a common stance regarding a reform of the U.N. Security Council is a point in case. The existence of collective action problems among developing countries is not surprising since their diversity in size and level of economic development means that their interests are not necessarily aligned. Emerging market economies like China and India naturally have different interests than states in Sub-Saharan Africa or Central Asia. Given the fragility of the balance of power in many geographical regions, developing countries can oppose reforms of mutual interests by considering relative rather than absolute gains. In addition, many developing countries are dependant on the support of industrial countries and thus

---

8 Guillermo Ortiz. 2005. *The IMF – Panacea for Every Illness?* Speech given at the Joint IMF-Bundesbank Symposium "The IMF in a Changing World.2 Frankfurt: Bundesbank

reluctant to join coalitions that pursue agendas opposed by countries with the ability to grant preferential trade agreements or development assistance. Certainly problems of coalition building and international cooperation apply to developed and developing countries alike and there is no shortage of examples of failed cooperation efforts among industrial countries; however, regarding the problem of global financial stability, interests of industrial countries are far more aligned than those of developing countries and emerging market economies.

Broad consent among all types of developing countries only exists regarding the question of adequate representation at international organisations' decision-making levels. The skewed distribution of quotas and votes at the IMF prevents developing countries and emerging market economies from effectively pushing for altering the Fund's operational procedures and lending policies. Given limited voting power even unanimous support by a coalition of developing countries would be insufficient to foster changes against the will of the Fund's major shareholders. Without a re-allocation of quotas and voting weights at both the Executive Board and the Board of Governors, developing countries' influence on IMF policy will remain limited. As a re-allocation of quotas requires the consent of the Fund's largest shareholders, the likelihood of significant change in the balance of power within the IMF is miniscule. For the same reasons a radical reform that would restructure the IMF into an institution operating like an international lender of last resort is politically unfeasible in the short to medium term.

13.2 The Potential for Gradual Reform

However, even without a radical reform of the IMF and its Articles of Agreement, gradual reforms to the Fund's procedures would go a long way in increasing the Fund's legitimacy and effectiveness in increasing global financial stability. The proposal described in chapter 12 suggests operational procedures that would allow the IMF to fulfil a similar function for the global financial system as central banks do as lenders of last resort to their domestic economies. While the Fund would retain its capacity to support developing countries in weathering current account crises, its ability to both prevent and arrest capital account crises in emerging markets would be significantly enhanced.

Although support for changes in the Fund's procedures is currently lacking in G-7 governments and finance ministries, the emergence of regional cooperation in South East Asia may contribute to a gradual change in the position of G-7 governments regarding much needed reforms at the International Monetary Fund.

13.2.1 Regional Monetary Cooperation

Following the Asian Financial Crisis support for regional monetary cooperation in Southeast Asia has been on a rise. This trend can be attributed not only to deep-seated resentments regarding their inability to tackle the crisis in 1997–98 without external help and the Fund's subsequent incursions into national sovereignty, but also to the perception that progress in reforming the international financial architecture has been slow and cumbersome. The large increase in central banks' currency reserves indicates that East Asian economies are determined to increase their ability to deal with external shocks and capital flow reversals in the future without having to resort to liquidity assistance by the IMF and accepting the accompanying conditions. It also means that confidence in the ability of the IMF to increase global financial stability is limited. If this trend strengthens and important emerging economies turn away from the Fund, its ability to influence the economic policy of its members will be severely curtailed. As a result, the world's industrial countries would loose their most effective instrument to influence developing countries' policies and enhance global financial stability. Increasing monetary integration at a regional level is likely to increase the willingness of the Fund's major shareholders to gradually reduce their opposition to reforms that would increase both legitimacy and effectiveness of the IMF.

The trend of regional monetary cooperation is likely to continue as for the economies involved there are clear advantages of strengthening their cooperation. Regarding the objective to reduce vulnerability to financial crises, the most important step may be the creation of a regional liquidity fund. Dieter suggests the creation of a regional liquidity fund as the first step in a framework for monetary regionalism; it could be realised by central banks depositing between 10 and 20 percent of their currency reserves at a regional lender of last resort[9]. Such an arrangement would allow participating central banks to arrest liquidity crises in their economies by providing emergency loans to the financial sector drawing not only on own but also on cooperating partners' currency reserves. The mere existence of a regional liquidity fund would reduce the vulnerability of participating economies to speculative attacks on their currency. More importantly, participating economies could access ample liquidity without having to cede to structural reform conditions as regularly imposed by the IMF. Furthermore, a pooling of currency reserves allows for insuring against liquidity crunches at a far lower cost than would be incurred by holding sufficient amounts of currency reserves unilaterally. The World Bank suggests that the annual carrying cost for central banks of holding USD 1 billion in currency reserves amounts to USD 25 million. For a country like China

---

9 See Dieter (2005): 285

currency reserves approach USD 1000 billions suggesting an annual opportunity cost of nearly USD 25 billion[10].

Table 13.1
Foreign Currency Reserves in East Asia

	2002	2003	2004
China	291	408	615
Hong Kong	112	118	124
Indonesia	31	35	35
Malaysia	34	45	66
Philippines	13	14	13
Singapur	82	96	112
South Korea	121	155	199
Thailand	38	41	49
Japan	670	674	699
Tawain	162	207	233
Total	1555	1792	2145

Source: Joint BIS-IMF-OECD-World Bank Statistics: August 2005

The effectiveness of a regional liquidity fund depends on the ability of participating central banks to raise sufficient foreign currency reserves. As countries are likely to be reluctant to contribute a large share of national currency reserves to a common fund, the likelihood of realisation is highest for regions whose countries hold significant amounts of foreign currency reserves. Since the Asian Crisis central banks in East Asia have accumulated substantial amounts foreign currency reserves. By contributing no more than 10 percent of currency reserves, East Asian central banks could create a liquidity fund of over USD 200 billion, an amount outweighting the IMF's current commitment capacity.

For countries participating in a regional liquidity fund the attraction of IMF membership would be severely reduced. Although they would be unlikely to renounce membership, the Fund's clout over its economic policies would decline considerably. Japan's flotation of a proposal to create an Asian Monetary Fund in September 1997 underlines that the advantages of monetary cooperation are widely acknowledged in the region. The proposal received a warm welcome by many Southeast Asian countries and was supported by all members of Asean and South

---

10 See World Bank. 2005. *Global Development Finance 2005*. Washington, DC: The World Bank: 60. World Bank estimates assume an average interest spread between 2-year treasuries and emerging market bonds of comparable maturity of 250 basis points. Assuming a yield differential of 6 percent Dieter arrives at significantly higher carrying costs: USD 60 million per billion foreign currency reserves held.

Korea[11] at the regional finance ministers' meeting in Hong Kong on November 21, 1997. In it original form it suggested creating a USD 100 billion liquidity fund whose membership would consist of China, Hong Kong, Japan, South Korea, Australia, Indonesia, Malaysia, Singapore, the Philippines and Thailand and could act independently of the IMF. Japan's proposal of an Asian Monetary Fund was strictly opposed by the United States and the IMF who managed to frustrate it by active lobbying in the region. Instead of an Asian Monetary Fund the so-called Manila Framework was agreed upon—a watered down effort comprising commitments by Asian countries to improve economic surveillance and technical assistance, implementing measures to strengthen the Fund's capacity in crisis management and to create an additional arrangement to supplement IMF resources. However, the fact that the United States offered Asian economies enticements in the form of increased quotas at the IMF and concessions regarding access to the NAB for opposing the Japanese proposal[12] suggests that increased monetary cooperation could make a reform of the IMF more likely.

A variety of reasons explain why the trend towards regional monetary cooperation in Southeast Asia is not only continuing but strengthening. Dieter points out that increasing efforts towards more effective cooperation to a great extent stem from the experiences made during the Asian Crisis and its aftermath[13]. The crisis underlined that a lack of cooperation can lead to a sudden loss of sovereignty if the only source of external assistance is to be found in the IMF. The Fund's policies, particularly its conditionality policy, were perceived as unsuitable and dominated by U.S. interests. While the Fund strictly opposed the capital controls implemented successfully by Malaysia, it identified as core culprits of the Asian Crisis the practices of regimes long closely associated with the United States. In addition, the IMF has increasingly been perceived as not being up to the task of effectively reducing the frequency and severity of financial crises. Reforms have been limited and in the case of Contingent Credit Lines badly designed. Access to sufficient liquidity assistance in times of crisis remains doubtful at best and still depends on the goodwill of the Fund's major shareholders. And despite persistent claims to address the obvious imbalances of quotas and voting rights, progress has been lacking.

It therefore is not surprising and only consequent that Asian policy makers are determined to enhance their capacities in addressing the problem of financial crises by enhancing regional cooperation[14]. Regarding the creation of alternative sources

---

11 See Philipp Lipscy. 2003. "Japan's Asian Monetary Fund Proposal." *Stanford Journal of East Asian Affairs.* Vol. 3, No. 1: 94
12 See Lipscy (2003): 94
13 See Dieter (2005): 306–307
14 See Yung Chul Park and Yunjong Wang. 2001. *Reform of the International Financial System and Institutions in Light of the Asian Financial Crisis.* G-24 Discussion Paper Series.

for liquidity assistance several steps have already been taken. In March 2000 finance ministers of ASEAN extended the ASEAN Swap Arrangement originally created in 1977 to a volume of USD 1 billion and admitted all members that joined ASEAN in the meanwhile. Two months later ASEAN+3 finance ministers agreed to negotiate lines of bilateral liquidity support under the Chiang Mai Initiative. In Mai 2001 the first concrete agreements were implemented with Japan announcing bilateral swap agreements with Thailand, South Korea and Malaysia worth USD 3, 2, and 1 billion respectively. Although access to the largest part of these facilities still requires consent by the IMF, these developments highlight the willingness of Asian policy makers to take pro-active steps to increase their ability to effectively address financial crises in the future. Similar arrangements were negotiated for USD 2 billion between China Thailand, South Korea and Japan.

While these developments underline Asian countries' general willingness to increase regional monetary cooperation, significant progress is by no means imminent. Cooperation between nation states is always a difficult and slow-moving process and Eastern Asia is no exception. National pride, regional competition and a general reluctance to renounce sovereign prerogatives all suggest that progress will continue to be slow. Moreover, the United States are unlikely to abandon their scepticism regarding regional cooperation in Asia and efforts to undermine proposals similar to that of an Asian Monetary Fund. However, the fact that regional monetary cooperation is not only in the interests of Southeast Asian economies, but also wanted and practically feasible may well contribute to a gradual decline in G-7 opposition regarding reforms that would improve the Fund's reputation and credibility as the central and most effective instrument to reduce global financial instability.

13.2.2 Changes Inside the IMF

Support for a gradual reform of the Fund's operational procedures also appears to build inside the IMF and even U.S. policy making circles. On the one hand, the Fund's procedures have been improved in several ways over the last four years. Crisis prevention capabilities have increased, excesses in policy conditionality have been reigned in on and the willingness to arrange massive rescue packages appears to have been considerably declined. On the other, comments by IMF staff suggest that even the principle of ex-ante conditionality may be considered more favourably than official IMF statements in the past implied.

With its new *Guidelines on Conditionality* the IMF has underlined its intention to streamline and reduce both number and scope of policy conditions attached to its

UNCTAD and Center for International Development Harvard University. Geneva: United Nations Conference for Trade and Development: 15

loans. It declared that *in setting program-related conditions, the Fund will be guided by the principle that the member has primary responsibility for the selection, design, and implementation of its economic and financial policies*[15]. It also committed to tailor programs and conditions more to the individual circumstances of the member involved and to take into account its domestic social and political objectives without ceding to aim at consistency in the application of policies and uniform treatment of its members. Fund-supported programs will be directed primarily at two macroeconomic objectives: First, to solve balance of payments problems without impeding national and international prosperity. And second, to achieve medium-term viability while enhancing economic growth. Policy conditions attached to IMF support must be within the member's control and critical to achieve the program's objectives or its monitoring. Conditions must consist of macroeconomic and structural measures in the Fund's core area of responsibility: monetary, fiscal, and exchange rate policies and macroeconomic stabilisation, but also closely related structural issues particularly regarding financial sector stability. Moreover, conditions must be either outcome or action-based. While these guiding principles still allow for considerable flexibility on behalf of the IMF, their application will enhance effectiveness and reduce unnecessary intrusions into members' sovereignty. Although they highlight the Fund's continuing emphasis on ex-post conditionality, they also suggest that both IMF staff and its major shareholders have accepted that conditionality policy can be both ineffective and counterproductive.

At the same time, the introduction of Contingent Credit Lines and the *Framework for Exceptional Access* indicate that Fund staff and shareholders perceive the advantages of rules-based lending and pre-qualification. The attempt to introduce the CCL, although unsuccessful due to flawed design, shows an implicit agreement that pre-qualification would be effective in providing incentives for members to pursue prudent macroeconomic policies. The Framework for Exceptional Access represents an acknowledgement that enhancing the predictability and clarity of IMF lending decisions is vital to increase the stability of the global financial system. The four criteria defined to justify exceptional access to IMF funds by members in capital account crises have been designed to ensure as far as possible that exceptional access will be successful in arresting financial crises: Exceptional access must be necessary, there must be a high probability that the member's debt burden will remain sustainable, that the member will regain access to international capital markets during the program's duration and that members' reform efforts have good prospects of success[16]. Similarly, the pre-qualification criteria defined in this reform proposal aim to ensure that only fundamentally solvent countries will receive large-

---

15 See IMF (2002): 1
16 See IMF (2004): 4

scale liquidity assistance by the IMF. They are based on the rationale that only liquidity crises can be arrested by liquidity assistance while solvency crises require a restructuring for sustainable resolution.

The central difference between both approaches is that the Fund's framework for exceptional access is too flexible and not binding: The IMF and its shareholders retain the flexibility to advance large-scale rescue packages to countries of strategic importance, even if the chances of success are limited or the necessity in doubt. Indeed, immediately after the framework became operational in September 2003, the Fund swerved from its stated intentions. Neither Argentina's USD 9 billion three-year Stand-By Agreement approved in September 2003, nor Brazil's 15 month extension on December 12 the same year met all four criteria laid down in the Framework for Exceptional Access[17]. This undermines the credibility of the IMF and its new framework considerably by reducing incentives to follow policies that ensure their eligibility to exceptional liquidity assistance during capital account crises. Members important to G-7 countries' strategic interests can justifiably assume that in case of crisis they will receive support regardless of the shape of their economies. For less influential countries the legitimacy of the Fund is reduced as they feel overreached. At the same time, predictability for international investors decreases while moral hazard problems are heightened since moral hazard plays may again become a rewarding strategy.

Recent comments made by IMF staff indicate that there is full awareness of this problem within the organisation itself. Furthermore, the underlying rationale of the proposal laid out in the previous chapters seems to be shared by key personnel at the Fund. As declared by Raghuram Rajan, Economic Counsellor and Director of the IMF Research Department

> In capital account crises, the Fund should intervene primarily in situations where the problem is temporary illiquidity or where there is a significant possibility of rapid structural change. But if it is hard to tell, even in the midst of a crisis, whether the underlying factors are temporary or more structural, the facts that emerge are unlikely to help decisionmaking. In such a case, discretion can only be harmful as it exposes the Fund to internal and external pressures to intervene. Not only will the decision be biased as a result of discretion, it also will be noisy because it will not be based on underlying fundamentals. Bias and unpredictability are not the best attributes of sound decisionmaking[18].

---

17 See IMF (2004): 3
18 Raghuram Rajan. 2005. "Institutional Reform and Sovereign Debt Crises." *Cato Journal.* Vol. 25, No. 1: 21–22

He goes on to continue that

> If a country follows sound policies and undertakes needed reforms there should be a presumption that if it faces a crisis, it is likely to be a liquidity crisis, or a solvency problem (such as a permanent terms of trade shock) that is not of its own making. The Fund should intervene in the former, and will be providing insurance in the latter case (with the country then making needed adjustments on its own accord), not an entirely bad use of Fund resources. Offering a contingent stream of lending, based on past policy choices, would also provide incentives for continuous improvement in policies.

Given awareness both within the IMF and among its largest shareholders that the Fund's effectiveness in enhancing global financial stability would benefit from less discretionary and more rules-based lending, a gradual move towards a new approach to crisis prevention and management thus may be more realistic than it seems at the outset. While the Fund's major shareholders remain unlikely to support reforms that would eliminate their ultimate discretion over IMF lending decisions, a practice of rules-based lending might well emerge over time. If violations to the lending rules recommended in this proposal would become truly exceptional, greater clarity of IMF policy responses would be given for both investors and developing country governments alike. The Fund would rebuild its legitimacy and increase its credibility and influence in advising its members on economic policy. Its capacity as crisis manager would be improved while incentives for developing country governments and emerging market economies to follow prudent economic policies would contribute to more effective efforts in crisis prevention. All this would go a long way in increasing global financial stability and reducing both frequency and severity of financial crises.

Appendix

Abbreviations

ADB	Asian Development Bank
ASEAN	Association of Southeast Asian Nations
ASEAN+3	ASEAN, China, Japan, Korea
BCBS	Basel Committee on Banking Supervision
BCP	Basel Core Principles on Effective Banking Supervision
BCRA	Banco Central de la Republica Argentina
BFSR	Bank Financial Strength Ratings
BIS	Bank for International Settlements
BWI	Bretton Woods Institution
CAC	Collective Action Clause
CCL	Contingent Credit Line
CGO	Code of Good Conduct
CIPA	Country Policy and Institutional Assessment
CPI	Corruption Perceptions Index
CRB	Central Ratings Based Approach
EFF	Extended Fund Facility
ELA	Extended Liquidity Assistance Facility
EMBI	Emerging Markets Bond Index
EMS	European Monetary System
EMTA	Trade Association for the Emerging Markets
EMU	European Monetary Union
ESAF	Enhanced Structural Adjustment Facility
ESCAP	UN Social and Economic Commission for Asia and the Pacific
ESF	Exchange Stabilisation Fund
EU	European Union
FATF	Financial Action Task Force
FCC	Forward Commitment Capacity
FLIRB	Front-loaded Interest Reduction Bond
FRBNY	Federal Reserve Bank of New York

FSAP	Financial Sector Assessment Program
G-5	Group of Five
G-7	Group of Seven
G-10	Group of Ten
G-22	Group of 22
GAB	General Agreements to Borrow
GDP	Gross Domestic Product
GFN	Gross Financing Need
GKO	Gosudarstvennye Kratkosrochnye Obligatsii
HIPC	Heavily Indebted Poor Country
IASC	International Accounting Standards Committee
ICIC	International Credit Insurance Corporation
IDA	International Development Association
IDC	Interim Debt Claim
IFC	International Finance Corporation
IFIAC	International Financial Institutions Advisory Commission
IIF	Institute of International Finance
IIE	Institute for International Economics
IIP	International Investment Position
IMF	International Monetary Fund
IMFC	International Monetary and Financial Committee
IRB	Internal Ratings Based Approach
ISF	International Stabilization Fund
LIBOR	London Interbank Offered Rate
MERCOSUR	Mercado Común del Sur
MYDFA	Multi-Year Debt Facility Agreement
NAB	New Arrangements to Borrow
NAFTA	North American Free Trade Agreement
NBER	National Bureau of Economic Research
NGO	Non-Governmental Organisation
OECD	Organisation for Economic Cooperation and Development
OFZ	Obligatsii Federal'nykh Zaemov
PIA	Power to Initiate Action
PPA	Power to Prevent Action
PRGF	Poverty Reduction and Growth Facility

PRI   Partido Revolucionario Institucional

ROSC   Reports on the Observance of Standards and Codes

SAF   Structural Adjustment Facility

SASAC   State-Owned Assets Supervision and Administration Commission

SBA   Stand-by Agreement

SDDRF   Sovereign Debt Dispute Resolution Forum

SDDS   Special Data Dissemination Standard

SDR   Special Drawing Right

SDRM   Sovereign Debt Restructuring Mechanism

SOE   State-Owned Enterprise

SPV   Special Purpose Vehicle

SRF   Supplemental Reserve Facility

UCITS   Undertakings for Collective Investments in Transferable Securities

UN   United Nations

UNDP   United Nations Development Programme

WTO   World Trade Organisation

Bibliography

Adams, Timothy. 2005. *The US View on IMF Reform*. Speech presented at the IIE Conference on IMF Reform. September 23, 2005. Washington, DC: Institute for International Economics

ADB. 2001. *Key Indicators 2001: Growth and Change in Asia and the Pacific*. Manila, Philippines: Asian Development Bank

Admati, Anat and Paul Pfleiderer. 1988. "A Theory of Intraday Patters: Volume and Price Variability." *The Review of Financial Studies*. Vol. 1, No. 1: 3–40

Aghevli, Bijhan B. 1999. "The Asian Crisis: Causes and Remedies." *Finance and Development*. Vol. 36, No. 2. Washington, DC: International Monetary Fund

Aizenman, Joshua and Jaewoo Lee. 2005. *International Reserves: Precautionary vs. Mercantilist Views, Theory and Evidence*. IMF Working Paper WP/05/198. Washington, DC: International Monetary Fund

Akerlof, George. 1970. "The Market for Lemons: Quality Uncertainty and the Market Mechanism." *Quarterly Journal of Economics*. Vol. 84, No. 3: 488–500

Andrews, A. Michael. 2005. *State-Owned Banks, Stability, Privatisation and Growth: Practical Policy Decisions in a World without Empirical Proof* (2005). IMF Working Paper 05/10. Washington, DC: International Monetary Fund

Arner, Douglas W. 1996. *The Mexican Peso Crisis: Implications for the Regulation of Financial Markets*. Essays in International Financial & Economic Law, No. 4. London: The London Institute of International Banking, Finance & Development Law

Arrow, Kenneth. 1963. "Uncertainty and the Welfare Economics of Medical Care." *The American Economic Review*. Vol. 53, No. 5: 941–969

Bagehot, Walter. 1999. *Lombard Street: A Description of the Money Market*. New York, NY: John Wiley & Sons

Balls, Andrew. 2005. "The US Diplomacy behind China's Revaluation." *Financial Times*. July 24, 2005

Banco Nacional de Desenvolvimento Economico e Social (BNDES). 2002. *Privatization in Brazil 1990–2002*. Rio de Janeiro: Banco Nacional de Desenvolvimento Economico e Social http://www.bndes.gov.br/english/studies/priv_brazil.pdf

Banerjee, Abhijit. 1992. "A Simple Model of Herd Behaviour." *Quarterly Journal of Economics* 107: 797–817

Banzhaf, John. 1965. "Weighted Voting Doesn't Work." *Rutgers Law Review* 19: 317–343

Barth, James, Gerard Caprio and Ross Levine. 2001. *Bank Regulation and Supervision: What Works Best?*. World Bank Working Paper. Washington, DC: The World Bank

Barro, Robert. 2001. *Economic Growth in East Asia before and after the Financial Crisis*. NBER Working Paper 8330. Cambridge, MA: National Bureau of Economic Research

Barro, Robert and Jong-Wha Lee. 2002. *IMF Programs: Who Is Chosen and What Are the Effects?* NBER Working Paper W8951. Cambridge, MA: National Bureau of Economic Research

Barth, James, Gerard Caprio and Ross Levine. 2001. *A New Database*. World Bank Working Paper. Washington, DC: The World Bank

Bartholomew, Ed, Ernest Stern and Angela Liuzzi. 2002. *Two-Step Sovereign Debt Restructuring*. J. P. Morgan Chase Research Paper. January 28, 2002. New York, NY: J. P. Morgan Chase

Basel Committee for Banking Supervision. 2004. *International Convergence of Capital Measurement and Capital Standards. A Revised Framework*. Basel: Bank for International Settlements

Basu, Sanjoy. 1977. "The Investment Performance of Common Stocks Relative to Their Price-Earnings Ratios: A Test of the Efficient Markets." *Journal of Finance*. Vol. 32, No. 3: 663–682

Becker, Torbjörn, Anthony Richards and Yungyong Thaicharoen. 2001. *Bond Restructuring and Moral Hazard: Are Collective Action Clauses Costly?* IMF Working Paper WP/01/92. Washington, DC: International Monetary Fund

Benston, George. 1999. "Banking Fragility, Effectiveness, and Regulation in Less-Developed Countries." In Hunter et al. 1999. *The Asian Financial Crisis: Origins, Implications, and Solutions*. Boston, MA: Kluwer Academic Publishers

Berg, Andrew and Catherine Pattillo. 1999. *Are Currency Crises Predictable? A Test*. IMF Staff Paper 46/2. Washington, DC: International Monetary Fund

Bikchandani,Sushil, David Hirshleifer and Ivo Welch. 1992. "A Theory of Fads, Fashion, Custom, and Cultural Change as Informational Cascades." *Journal of Political Economy* 100: 992–1026

Bird, Graham, Antonella Mori and Dane Rowlands. 2000. "Do the Multilaterals Catalyize Other Capital Flows?" *Third World Quarterly*. Vol. 21, No. 3: 483–503

Bird, Graham and Dane Rowlands. 2003. *Financing Balance of Payments Adjustments: Options in the Light of the Illusory Catalytic Effect of IMF Lending*. Working Paper. Guilford: University of Surrey

Blustein, Paul and Sandra Sugawara. 1997. "Seoul Accepts $55 Billion Bailout Terms." *The Washington Post*. December 4, 1997

Bonchek, Mark and Kenneth Shepsle. 1997. *Analysing Politics: Rationality, Behavior and Institutions*. New York, NY: W.W. Norton

Boorman, Jack. 2002. *Sovereign Debt Restructuring: Where Stands the Debate?* Speech given at a conference co-sponsored by the Cato Institute and the Economist. October 17, 2002. New York, NY: The Cato Institute

Bordo, Michael. 1983. *The Lender of Last Resort: Some Historical Insights*. NBER Working Paper 3011. Cambridge, MA: National Bureau of Economic Research

Bordo, Michael. 1986. *Financial Crises, Banking Crises, Stock Market Crashes and the Money Supply: Some International Evidence, 1870–1933*. In Forrest Capie and Geoffrey Wood. 1986. *Financial Crises and the World Banking System*. New York, NY: St. Martin's Press

Bordo, Michael D. 1999. "International Bailouts versus Rescues: A Historical Perspective." *Cato Journal*. Vol. 18, No. 3: 363–375

Bordo, Michael and Lars Jonung. 2000. *Lessons for EMU from the History of Monetary Unions*. London: Institute of Economic Affairs

Bordo, Michael and Barry Eichengreen. 2002. *Crises Now and Then: What Lessons from the Last Era of Financial Globalization?* NBER Working Paper No. 8761. Washington, DC: National Bureau of Economic Research

Borensztein, Eduardo, Marcos Chamo, Olivier Jeanne, Paolo Mauro and Jeromin Zettelmeyer. 2004. *Sovereign Debt Structure for Crisis Prevention.* IMF Research Paper. Washington, DC: International Monetary Fund

Brealey, Richard and Evi Kaplanis. 2002. *The Impact of IMF Programs on Asset Values.* Working Paper. London: London Business School

Browning, Edgar and Jacquelene Browning. 1992. *Microeconomic Theory and Applications.* New York, NY: Harper Collins

Broz, Lawrence and Michael Hawes. 2003. *Domestic Interests of International Monetary Fund Policy.* Paper delivered at the Public Lectures Committee for the UCLA Department of Political Science. June 2, 2003. Los Angeles, CA: University of California

Brunnengräber, Achim (Ed.). 2003. *Globale öffentliche Güter unter Privatisierungsdruck: Festschrift für Elmar Altvater.* Münster: Westfälisches Dampfboot

Bryant, John. 1980. "A Model of Reserves, Bank Runs, and Deposit Insurance." *Journal of Banking and Finance* 4: 335–344

Buchanan, James. 2001. *The Origins and Development of a Research Program.* Webpage. Fairfax, VA: Public Choice Society. http://www.pubchoicesoc.org/about_pc.html

Buchheit, Lee and Mitu Gulati. 2002. *Sovereign Bonds and the Collective Will.* Working Paper. Georgetown-Sloan Project on Business Institutions. Washington, DC: Georgetown University

Buira, Ariel. 2002. *The Governance of the International Monetary Fund.* In Inge Kaul, Pedro Conceicao, Katell Le Goulven and Ronald Mendoza. 2002. *Providing Global Public Goods.* Oxford: Oxford University Press

Buira, Ariel. 2002. *The Governance of the IMF in a Global Economy.* Working Paper. Washington, DC: G-24. http://www.g24.org/buiragva.pdf

Buira, Ariel. 2002. *A New Voting Structure for the IMF.* Working Paper. Washington, DC: Intergovernmental Group of Twenty Four

Buira, Ariel. 2004. *Should the Governance of the IMF Be Reformed?* Presentation at the IMF Book Forum on February 5, 2004. Washington, DC: International Monetary Fund

Bulow, Jeremy and Kenneth Rogoff. 2005. *Grants versus Loans for Development Banks.* Paper presented at the American Economic Association Meetings in Philadelphia. January 7, 2005.

Bundesministerium der Finanzen. 2004. *60 Jahre Bretton Woods-Institutionen: Standortbestimmung und Ausrichtung.* Berlin: Bundesministerium der Finanzen

Bureau of Public Affairs. 1995. *Article 6: Mexico Agreement Signing Ceremony.* Washington, DC: Department of State Dispatch. Vol. 6, No. 11, March 13, 1995.
http://dosfan.lib.uic.edu/ERC/briefing/dispatch/1995/html/ Dispatchv6no11.html

Burnside, Craig, Martin Eichenbaum and Sergio Rebelo. 1998. *Prospective Deficits and the Asian Currency Crisis.* NBER Working Paper No. 6758. Cambridge, MA: National Bureau of Economic Research

Burnside, Craig, Martin Eichenbaum, and Sergio Rebelo. 1999. "What Caused the Recent Asian Currency Crises?" In Hunter et al. 1999. *The Asian Financial Crisis: Origins, Implications, and Solutions.* Boston, MA: Kluwer Academic Publishers

Bussiére, Matthieu and Christian Mulder. 1999. *External Vulnerability in Emerging Market Economies: How High Liquidity Can Offset Weak Fundamentals and Effects of Contagion.* IMF Working Paper 99/88. Washington, DC: International Monetary Fund

Caballero, Ricardo J. 1996. "Coping with Chile's External Vulnerability: A Financial Problem." In Norman Loayza and Raimundo Soto. 1996. *Economic Growth: Sources, Trends, and Cycles.* Santiago de Chile: Central Bank of Chile

Calomiris, Charles. 1998. *Blueprints for a New Global Financial Architecture.* Washington, DC: American Enterprise Institute

Calomiris, Charles. 1998. "The IMF's Imprudent Role As Lender of Last Resort." *Cato Journal.* Vol. 17, No. 3: 275–294

Calomiris, Charles. 1998. "Reducing Moral Hazard: Introducing Market Signals to Banking Supervision." *Economic Perspectives. USIA Electronic Journal.* Vol. 3, No. 4

Calomiris, Charles. 1999. "Building an Incentive-compatible Safety Net." *Journal of Banking and Finance.* Vol. 23, No. 10: 1499–1519

Calomiris, Charles and Alan Meltzer. 1999. "Fixing the IMF – Reforming the International Monetary Fund." *The National Interest* 56: 88–96

Calomiris, Charles. 2000. *Prepared Testimony of Dr. Charles W. Calomiris.* Hearing on the Final Report of the International Financial Institution Advisory Commission. March 9, 2000. Washington, DC: Senate Banking Committee

Canadian Team for the Russian Public Expenditure Project. 2002. *A Taxonomy for Budgetary Control of Stated-owned Enterprises.* February 2002. http://www.globalcentres.org/html/docs/PER%20Taxonomy%20FINAL%20Feb%2028.pdf

Cantor, Richard and Frank Packer. 1996. "Determinants and Impacts of Sovereign Credit Ratings." *The Journal of Fixed Income.* Vol. 6, No. 3

Capie, Forrest and Geoffrey Wood. 1986. *Financial Crises and the World Banking System.* New York, NY: St. Martin's Press

Capie, Forrest. 1998. "Can There Be an International Lender-of-Last-Resort?" *International Finance.* Vol. 1, No. 2: 311–325

Capie, Forrest. 2000. "Can There Be an International Lender-of-Last-Resort?" In Charles Goodhart and Gerhard Illing (Eds.). 2000. *Financial Crises, Contagion, and the Lender of Last Resort. A Reader.* Oxford: Oxford University Press: 437–484

Caprio Gerad, Jonathan Fiechter, Robert Litan and Michael Pomerleano. 2004. *The Future of State-Owned Financial Institutions.* Brookings Conference Report No. 18. Washington, DC: The Brookings Institution. http://www.brook.edu/comm/conferencereport/cr18.htm

Caprio, Gerard, Jonathan Fiechter, Robert E. Litan, and Michael Pomerleano. 2004. *The Future of State-Owned Financial Institutions.* Policy Brief No. 18–2004. Washington, DC: The Brookings Institution

Cavallo, Michelle and Giovanni Majnoni. 2001. *Do Banks Provision for Bad Loans in Good Times? Empirical Evidence and Policy Implications.* World Bank Working Paper 2619. Washington, DC: The World Bank

Chalk, Nigel. 2002. *The Potential Role for Securitizing Public Sector Revenue Flows: An Application to the Philippines.* IMF Working Paper. Washington, DC: International Monetary Fund

Chang, Roberto and Andrés Velasco. 1998a. *Financial Crises in Emerging Markets: A Canonical Model.* NBER Working Paper No. 6606. Cambridge, MA: National Bureau of Economic Research

Chang, Roberto and Andrés Velasco. 1998b. *Financial Fragility and the Exchange Rate Regime.* NBER Working Paper No. 6469. Cambridge, MA: National Bureau of Economic Research

Chari, V. V. and Patrick J. Kehoe. 2001. *Hot Money.* Research Department Staff Report 228. Minneapolis, MN: Federal Reserve Bank of Minneapolis

Choi, Stephen and Mitu Gulati. 2004. *Innovation in Boilerplate Contracts: An Empirical Examination of Sovereign Bonds.* Working Paper. Berkeley, CA: University of California at Berkeley

Chosun. 2004. "South Korea's State Assets Exceed W200 Trillion in 2003." *The Chosun Journal.* May 6, 2004. http://english.chosun.com/w21data/html/news/200405/200405060023.html

Chuhan, Punan and Federico Sturzenegger. 2004. *Default Episodes in the 1980s and 1990s: What Have We Learned?* Draft chapter for *Managing Volatility and Crisis: A Practitioner's Guide.* Washington, DC: The World Bank

Claessens, Stijn, Asli Demirgüç-Kunt and Harry Huizinga. 1998. *How Does Foreign Entry Affect the Domestic Banking Market.* World Bank Working Paper. Washington, DC: The World Bank

Claessens, Stijn and Tom Glaessner. 1998. *Internationalization of Financial Services in Asia*. Paper presented at the conference "Investment Liberalisation and Financial Reform in the Asia-Pacific Region" in Sidney, Australia. August 29–31, 1998

Cohen, Daniel. 1997. *Growth and External Debt: A New Perspective on the African and Latin American Tragedies*. Discussion Paper No. 1753. London: Centre for Economic Policy Research

Cole, Harold L. and Timothy J. Kehoe. 1996. A *Self-Fulfilling Model of Mexico's 1994–95 Debt Crisis*. Research Department Staff Report 210. Minneapolis, MN: Federal Reserve Bank of Minneapolis

Cole, Harold L. and Timothy J. Kehoe. 1998. *Self-Fulfilling Debt Crises*. Research Department Staff Report 211. Minneapolis, MN: Federal Reserve Bank of Minneapolis

Coleman, James. 1973. "Loss of Power." *American Sociological Review* 38: 1–17

Cooper, Richard. 1984. "A Monetary System for the Future." *Foreign Affairs*. Vol. 63, No. 1: 166–184

Copelovitch, Mark. 2003. *Domestic Interests and the International Lender of Last Resort: The Political Economy of IMF Crisis Lending*. Paper prepared for the Annual Meeting of the American Political Science Association. August 28–31, 2004

Corsetti, Giancarlo, Paolo Pesenti and Nouriel Roubini. 1998. *Paper Tigers? A Model of the Asian Crisis*. NYU Working Paper. New York, NYU: New York University

Corsetti, Giancarlo, Paolo Pesenti and Nouriel Roubini. 1998. *What Caused the Asian Currency and Financial Crisis*. Part I and Part II. NBER Working Papers No. 6833 and 6844. Cambridge, MA: National Bureau of Economic Research

Corsetti, Giancarlo, Bernardo Guimaraes and Nouriel Roubini. 2003. *International Lending of Last Resort and Moral Hazard: A Model of IMF's Catalytiv Finance*. NBER Working Paper 10125. Cambridge, MA: National Bureau of Economic Research

Cottarelli, Carlo and Curzio Giannini. 2002. *Bedfellows, Hostages, or Perfect Strangers? Global Capital Markets and the Catalytic Effect of IMF Crisis Lending*. IMF Working Paper WP/02/193. Washington, DC: International Monetary Fund

Cottareli, Carlo. 2005. *Efficiency and Legitimacy: Trade-Offs in IMF Governance*. IMF Working Paper WP/05/107. Washington, DC: International Monetary Fund

Couillanlault, Betrand and Pierre-Francoise Weber. 2003. *Towards a Voluntary Code of Good Conduct for Sovereign Debt Restructuring*. International Monetary Relations Division. Paris: Banque de France

Council on Foreign Relations. 1999. *Safeguarding Prosperity in a Global Financial System: The Future International Financial Architecture*. Independent Task Force Report. New York, NY: Council on Foreign Relations

Crockett, Andrew. 1997. "Why Is Financial Stability a Goal of Public Policy?" In Federal Reserve Bank of Kansas City. 1997. *Maintaining Financial Stability in a Global Economy*. Kansas City, MO: Federal Reserve Bank of Kansas City

Da Costa e Silva, Jose Ricardo. 2002. *Currency Crises in Emergent Markets and Minsky Financial Fragility Theory: Is There a Link?* Working Paper. St. Louis, MO: Washington University

Dani Rodrick, Dani. 1996. *Why Is There Multilateral Lending?* Annual World Bank Conference on Development Economics. Washington, DC: The World Bank

De Larosiére, Jaques. 2003. "Reality Hits Debt Restructuring Debate." *The Banker*. September 3, 2003

Dell'Arricia, Giovanni, Enrica Detragiache and Raghuram Rajan. 2005. *The Real Effect of Banking Crises*. IMF Working Paper WP/05/63. Washington, DC: International Monetary Fund

Dell'Ariccia, Giovanni, Isabel Schnabel & Jeromine Zettelmeyer. 2002. *Moral Hazard and International Crisis Lending: A Test*. IMF Working Paper 02/181. Washington, DC: International Monetary Fund

Demirguc-Kunt, Asli and Enrica Detragiache. 1999. *Does Deposit Insurance Increase Banking System Stability? An Empirical Investigation*. Policy Research Working Paper 2247. Washington, DC: The World Bank

Desai, Padma. 2003. *Financial Crisis, Contagion and Containment: From Asia to Argentina*. Princeton, NJ: Princeton University Press

Diamond, Douglas and Philipp Dybvig. 1983. "Bank Runs, Deposit Insurance, and Liquidity." *Journal of Political Economy* 91: 401–419

Dieter, Heribert. 2002. *Nach den Finanzkrisen*. SWP-Studie S 16. Berlin: Stiftung Wissenschaft und Politik

Dieter, Heribert. 2003. "Das globale öffentliche Gut Finanzielle Stabilität: Wege zur Reduzierung der Turbulenzen auf den internationalen Finanzmärkten." In: Achim Brunnengräber (Ed.). 2003. *Globale öffentliche Güter unter Privatisierungsdruck: Festschrift für Elmar Altvater*. Münster: Westfälisches Dampfboot: 85–108

Dieter, Heribert. 2005. *Die Zunkunft der Globalisierung*. Baden-Baden: Nomos

Disyatat, Piti. 2001. *Currency Crises and the Real Economy: The Role of Banks*. IMF Working Paper No. 01/49. Washington, DC: International Monetary Fund

Djiwandono, J. Soedradjad. 1999. "Causes and Implications of the Asian Crisis: An Indonesian View." In Hunter et al. 1999. *The Asian Financial Crisis: Origins, Implications, and Solutions*. Boston, MA: Kluwer Academic Publishers

Dooley, Michael P. 1998. *A Model of Crises in Emerging Markets*. International Finance Discussion Papers 630. Washington, DC: Federal Reserve

Dooley, Michael. 1999. "Origins of the Crisis in Asia." (1999). In Hunter et al. *The Asian Financial Crisis: Origins, Implications, and Solutions*. Boston, MA: Kluwer Academic Publishers

Dooley, Michael, David Folkerts-Landau and Peter Garber. 2003. *An Essay on the Revised Bretton Woods System*. NBER Working Paper No. 9971. Cambridge, MA: National Bureau of Economic Research

Dreher, Axel and Roland Vaubel. 2001. *Does the IMF Cause Moral Hazard and Political Business Cycles? Evidence from Panel Data*. Beiträge zur angewandten Wirtschaftsforschung No. 598–01. Mannheim: Universität Mannheim

Dreher, Axel. 2004. *Does the IMF Cause Moral Hazard? A Critical Review of the Evidence*. Unpublished Paper

Duska, Ronald. 1992. "Why Be a Loyal Agent? A Systemic Ethical Analysis." In Norman Bowie and Edward Freeman. 1992. *Ethics and Agency Theory*. Oxford: Oxford University Press

Eatwell, John, Murray Milgate and Peter Newman (Eds.). 1991. *The New Palgrave: A Dictionary of Economics*. London: Macmillan

Eichengreen, Barry and Richard Portes. 1995. *Crisis? What Crisis? Orderly Workouts for Sovereign Debtors*. London: Centre for Economic Policy Research

Eichengreen, Barry, Andrew Rose and Charles Wyplosz. 1995. "Exchange Rate Mayhem: The Antecedents and Aftermath of Speculative Attacks." *Economic Policy* 21: 249–312

Eichengreen, Barry, Andrew Rose and Charles Wyplosz. 1996. *Contagious Currency Crises*. NBER Working Paper No. 5681. Cambridge, MA: National Bureau of Economic Research

Eichengreen, Barry. 1996. *Globalizing Capital*. Princeton, NJ: Princeton University Press

Eichengreen, Barry. 1999. *Towards a New International Financial Architecture: A Practical Post-Asia Proposal*. Washington, DC: Institute for International Economics

Eichengreen, Barry and Ashoka Mody. 2000. *Bail-Ins, Bailouts and Borrowing Costs*. Paper prepared for the First Annual IMF Research Conference, November 9–10, 2000. Washington, DC: International Monetary Fund

Eichengreen, Barry and Ashoka Mody. 2000. *Would Collective Action Clauses Raise Borrowing Costs? An Update and Additional Results*. Update to NBER Working Paper W7458. Unpublished Paper. http://emlab.berkeley.edu/users/eichengr/research/governinglaw6.pdf

Eichengreen, Barry. 2003. *Restructuring Sovereign Debt.* Working Paper. Berkeley, CA: University of California

Eichengreen. Barry and Ashoka Mody. 2003a. *Is Aggregation a Problem for Sovereign Debt Restructuring?* Working Paper. Berkeley, CA: University of California

Eichengreen, Barry and Ashoka Mody. 2003b. *Would Collective Action Clauses Raise Borrowing Costs?* NBER Working Paper 7458. Cambridge, MA: National Bureau of Economic Research

ESCAP. 2002. *Bulletin on Asia-Pacific Perspectives 2002/03.* Bangkok, Thailand: United Nations Social and Economic Commission for Asia and the Pacific

Evrensel, Ayse. 2002. "Effectiveness of IMF-supported Stabilization Programs in Developing Countries." *Journal of International Money and Finance* 21: 565–578

Evrensel, Ayse and Ali Kutan. 2004. *Creditor Moral Hazard in Equity Markets: A Theoretical Framework and Evidence from Indonesia and Korea.* Working Paper. Portland, OR: Portland State University

Evrensel, Ayse and Ali Kutan. 2004. *Financial Sector Returns and Creditor Moral Hazard: Evidence from Indonesia, Korea and Thailand.* Working Paper. Portland, OR: Portland State University

Evrensel, Ayse and Ali Kutan. 2004. *Testing Creditor Moral Hazard in Sovereign Bond Markets: A Unified Theoretical Approach and Empirical Evidence.* Working Paper. Portland, OR: Portland State University

Falkus, Malcolm. 1999. *Historical Perspectives of the Thai Financial Crisis.* UNEAC Asia Papers No. 1. Armidale, Australia: University of New England

Fama, Eugene, Lawrence Fisher, Michael Jensen and Richard Roll. 1969. "The Adjustment of Stock Prices to New Information." *International Economic Review.* Vol. 10, No. 1: 1–21

Fama, Eugene. 1970. "Efficient Capital Markets: A Review of Empirical Work." *Journal of Finance*: Vol. 25, No. 2: 383–417

Fama, Eugene and Kenneth French. 1988. "Dividend Yields and Expected Stock Returns." *Journal of Financial Economics.* Vol. 22, No. 1: 3–25

Fama, Eugene. 1991. "Efficient Capital Markets: II." *Journal of Finance.* Vol. 49, No. 3: 283–306

Fama, Eugene and Kenneth French. 1992. "The Cross Section of Expected Stock Returns." *Journal of Finance.* Vol. 47, No. 2: 427–466

Feldstein, Martin. 1998. "Refocusing the IMF." *Foreign Affairs.* Vol. 77 No. 2: 20–33

Feldstein, Martin. 1999. *Self-Protection for Emerging Market Economies*. NBER Working Paper No. 6907. Cambridge, MA: National Bureau of Economic Research

Fernández-Arias, Eduardo and Ricardo Hausmann. 2000. *The Redesign of the International Financial Architecture from a Latin American Perspective: Who Pays the Bill?* Working Paper No. 440. Washington, DC: Inter-American Development Bank

Fetter, Frank Whitson. 1965. *The Development of British Monetary Orthodoxy 1797–1875*. Cambridge, MA: Harvard University Press

Fischer, Stanley. 1999. *On the Need of an International Lender of Last Resort*. Paper prepared for delivery at the joint luncheon of the American Economic Association and the American Finance Association. New York, NY: January 3, 1999

Fischer, Stanley. 2000. *Presentation to the International Financial Institution Advisory Commission*. February 2, 2000. Washington, DC: International Monetary Fund. http://www.imf.org/external/np/speeches/2000/020200.htm

Fischer, Stanley. 2002. *Financial Crises and Reform of the International Financial System*. NBER Working Paper 9297. Cambridge, MA: National Bureau of Economic Research

Flandreau, Marc (Ed.). 2003. *Money Doctors. The Experience of International Financial Advising 1850–2000*. New York, NY: Routledge

Flood, Robert and Peter Garber. 1984. "Collapsing Exchange-Rate Regimes: Some Linear Examples." *Journal of International Economics* Vol. 17: 1–13

Fons, Jerome. 1999. "Improving Transparency in Asian Banking Systems." In Hunter et al. 1999. *The Asian Financial Crisis: Origins, Implications, and Solutions*. Boston, MA: Kluwer Academic Publishers

Frank, Robert. 1991. *Microeconomics and Behavior*. New York, NY: McGraw-Hill

Frankel, Jeffrey A. and Andrew K. Rose. 1996. *Currency Crashes in Markets: Empirical Indicators*. NBER Working Paper No. 5437. Cambridge, MA: National Bureau of Economic Research

Frankel, Jeffrey. 1999. "Soros' Split Personality: Scanty Proposals from the Financial Wizard." *Foreign Affairs*. Vol. 78, No. 2

Friedman, Milton and Anna Schwartz. 1963. *A Monetary History of the United States 1867–1969*. Princeton, NJ: Princeton University Press

Gai, Prasanna and Ashley Tailor. 2004. *International Financial Rescues and Debtor Moral Hazard*. Working Paper No. 217. London: Bank of England

Galiani, Sebastián, Paul Gertler, Ernesto Schargrodsky and Frederico Sturzenegger. 2003. *The Benefits and Costs of Privatization in Argentina: A Microeconomic Analysis*. Research Network Working Paper 454. Washington, DC: Inter-American Development Bank

Garrison, Roger W. 1996. "Central Banking, Free Banking, and Financial Crises." *Review of Austrian Economics.* Vol. 9, No. 2: 109–127

Garten, Jeffrey. 1998. "Needed: A Fed for the World." *The New York Times.* September 23, 1998

Garten, Jeffrey E. 1999. "Lessons for the Next Financial Crisis." *Foreign Affairs.* Vol. 78, No. 2: 76–92

Gelpern, Anna. 2003. "How Collective Action Is Changing Sovereign Debt." *International Finance Law Review.* May 2003

Ghosh, Atish, Timothy Lane, Marianne Schulze-Ghattas, Ales Bulír, Javier Hamman and Alex Mourmouras. 2002. *IMF-Supported Programs in Capital Account Crises.* Washington, DC: International Monetary Fund

Giannini, Curzio. 1999. *Enemy of None But a Common Friend of All? An International Perspective on the Lender-of-Last-Resort Function.* IMF Working Paper WP 99/10. Washington, DC: International Monetary Fund

Gil-Diaz, Francisco. 1998. "The Origin of Mexico's 1994 Financial Crisis." *Cato Journal.* Vol. 17, No. 3: 303–313

Goldstein, Morris. 1998. *The Asian Financial Crisis: Causes, Cures, and Systematic Implications.* Policy Analysis in International Economics 55. Washington, DC: Institute for International Economics

Goldstein, Morris. 2000. *IMF Structural Programs.* Paper prepared for NBER conference on "Economic and Financial Crises in Emerging Economies." Woodstock, VT. October 19–21, 2000

Goodfriend, Marvin and Robert King. 1988. "Financial Deregulation, Monetary Policy and Central Banking." In Haraf, W. and R. M. Kushmeider (Eds.). 1988. *Restructuring Banking and Financial Services in America.* Lanham, MD: American Enterprise Institute and UPA

Goodhart, Charles. 1969. *The New York Money Market and the Finance of Trade 1900–1913.* Cambridge, MA: Harvard University Press

Goodhart, Charles. 1972. *The Business of Banking 1891–1914.* London School of Economics and Political Science. London: Weidenfeld and Nicolson

Goodhart, Charles. 1988. *The Evolution of Central Banks.* Cambridge, MA: The MIT Press

Goodhart, Charles and Gerhard Illing (Eds.). 2000. *Financial Crises, Contagion, and the Lender of Last Resort. A Reader.* Oxford: Oxford University Press

Gould, Erica. 2003. "Money Talks: Supplementary Financiers and International Monetary Fund Conditionality." *International Organisation.* Vol. 57, No. 3: 551–586

Gray, Robert. 2003. *Collective Action Clauses*. Remarks prepared for delivery at UNCTAD Fourth Inter-Regional Debt Management Conference. November 11, 2003. Geneva, Switzerland: United Nations Conference of Trade and Development

Greenspan, Alan. 1999. *Efforts to Improve the "Architecture" of the International Financial System*. Testimony given before the Committee on Banking and Financial Services. May 20, 1999. Washington, DC: House of Representatives

Grieco, Joseph. 1988. "Anarchy and the Limits of Cooperation: A Realist Critique of the Newest Liberal Institutionalism." *International Organization*. Vol. 42, No. 3: 485–507

Griffith-Jones, Stephany and Jose Ocampo. 2003. *What Progress on International Financial Reform. Why So Limited?* Stockholm: Almqvist & Wiksell International

Group of 22. 1998. *Report of the Working Group on Strengthening Financial Systems*. Washington, DC: G-22

Group of 22. 1998. *Report of the Working Group on Transparency and Accountability*. Washington, DC: G-22

Haldane, Andrew and Jörg Scheibe. 2003. *IMF Lending and Creditor Moral Hazard*. Working Paper 216. London: Bank of England

Haldane, Andy. 1999. "Private Sector Involvement in Financial Crises: Analytics and Public Policy Approaches." *Financial Stability Review*. London: Bank of England

Hanke, Steve. 2003. "Iraq, Regime Changes and Currency Boards." *The National Post*. May 28, 2003

Hanke, Steven H. and Kurt Schuler. 1999. *A Dollarization Blueprint for Argentina*. Foreign Policy Briefing No. 52. Washington: The Cato Institute

Hanke, Steven. 2000. "Please, No More 'New' IMFs." *The Wall Street Journal*. March 21, 2000

Hasenclever, Andreas, Peter Mayer and Volker Rittberger. 1997. *Theories of International Regimes*. Cambridge: Cambridge University Press

Hayo, Bernd and Ali Kutan. 2001. *Investor Panic, IMF Actions, and Emerging Stock Market Returns and Volatility: A Panel Investigation*. Working Paper B27. Bonn: Centre for European Integration Studies

Herbert Simon. 1982. *Models of Bounded Rationality*. Cambridge, MA: MIT Press

Hotelling, Harold. 1931. "The Economics of Exhaustable Resources." *Journal of Political Economy* 39: 137–175

Hubbard, Glenn. 2002. *Enhancing Sovereign Debt Restructuring*. Remarks at the Conference on the IMF's Sovereign Debt Proposal. October 7, 2002. Washington, DC: American Enterprise Institute

Humphrey, Thomas M. and Robert E. Keleher. 1984. "The Lender of Last Resort: A Historical Perspective." *Cato Journal*. Vol. 4, No. 1: 275–318

Hunter, William, George Kaufman, and Thomas Krueger. 1999. *The Asian Financial Crisis: Origins, Implications, and Solutions*. Boston, MA: Kluwer Academic Publishers

Hunter, William. 1999. "The Korean Banking Crisis: Picking Up the Pieces." In Hunter, William, George Kaufman and Thomas Krueger. *The Asian Financial Crisis: Origins, Implications, and Solutions*. Boston, MA: Kluwer Academic Publishers

Hutchinson, Michael and Ilan Neuberger. 2002. *Sudden Stops and the Mexican Wave: Currency Crises, Capital Reversals and Output Loss in Emerging Markets*. Working Paper PB-02-03. Centre for Pacific Basin Monetary and Economic Studies. San Francisco, CA: Federal Reserve

Hyman, David. 1993. *Microeconomics: Analysis and Applications*. Boston, MA: Irvin

IDA and IMF. 2004. *Debt Sustainability in Low-Income Countries – Proposal for an Operational Framework and Policy Implications*. February 3, 2004. Washington, DC: International Monetary Fund

IMF. 1996. *Guide to the Data Dissemination Standards*. Washington, DC: International Monetary Fund

IMF. 1998. *The Special Data Dissemination Standard: Updated Guidance*. February 1998. Washington, DC: International Monetary Fund

IMF. 2000. *Debt- and Reserve-Related Indicators of External Vulnerability*. Paper Prepared by the Policy Development and Review Department. March 23, 2000. Washington, DC: International Monetary Fund

IMF. 2000. *Report to the IMF Executive Board of the Quota Formula Review Group*. April 28, 2000. Washington, DC: International Monetary Fund

IMF. 2001. *A New Approach to Sovereign Debt Restructuring: Preliminary Considerations*. November 30, 2001. Washington, DC: International Monetary Fund

IMF. 2002. *Access Policy in Capital Account Crises*. Report prepared by the Policy Development and Review and Treasurer's Departments. July 29, 2002. Washington, DC: International Monetary Fund

IMF. 2002. *A Sovereign Debt Restructuring Mechanism – Further Reflections and Future Work*. Washington, DC: International Monetary Fund

IMF. 2002. *Global Financial Stability Report: A Quarterly Report on Market Developments and Issues*. March 2002. Washington, DC: International Monetary Fund: 49–50

IMF. 2002. *Guidelines on Conditionality*. September 25, 2002. Washington, DC: International Monetary Fund

IMF. 2002. *IMF Board Discusses Possible Features of a New Sovereign Debt Restructuring Mechanism.* Public Information Notice 02/106. September 24, 2002. Washington, DC: International Monetary Fund

IMF. 2003. *Access Policy in Capital Account Crises – Modifications to the Supplemental Reserve Facility (SRF) and Follow-up Issues Related to Exceptional Access Policy.* January 14, 2003. Washington, DC: International Monetary Fund

IMF. 2003. *Assessing Public Sector Borrowing Collateralized on Future Flow Receivables.* Paper prepared by FAD, ICM, LEG, and PDR. June 11, 2003. Washington, DC: International Monetary Fund

IMF. 2003. *Quota Distribution – Selected Issues.* Report prepared by the Finance Department. Washington, DC: International Monetary Fund

IMF. 2003. *Report of the IMF Executive Board to the International Monetary and Financial Committee on Quotas, Voice and Representation.* Report prepared by the Finance and Secretary's Department. September 12, 2003. Washington, DC: International Monetary Fund

IMF. 2003. *Review of Access Policy under the Credit Tranches and the Extended Fund Facility.* Report prepared by the Policy Development and Review and Treasurer's Departments. January 14, 2003. Washington, DC: International Monetary Fund

IMF. 2004. *Review of Exceptional Access Policy.* Report prepared by the Policy Development and Review and Finance Departments. March 23, 2004. Washington, DC: International Monetary Fund

IMF. 2004. *Sovereign Debt Structure for Crisis Prevention.* Paper prepared by the Research Department. Washington, DC: International Monetary Fund

Institute of International Finance. 2003. *Letter by IIF Chairman Charles M. Daralla to Chairman of the IMFC Gordon Brown.* April 1, 2003. New York, NY: Institute of International Finance

Institute of International Finance, EMTA, IPMA, SIA, ISMA, EMCA and TBMA. 2003. *Code of Conduct for Emerging Markets.* Part of a Discussion Draft from January 31, 2003. New York, NY: Institute of International Finance

Institute of International Finance and International Primary Markets Association. 2004a. *Key Principles Agreed to Strengthen Emerging Markets Finance.* Press release issued on behalf of IIF, IPMA and Sovereign Issuers of International Bonds. New York, NY: November 22, 2004

Institute of International Finance and International Primary Markets Association. 2004b. *Principles for Stable Capital Flows and Fair Debt Restructuring in Emerging Markets.* New York, NY: Institute of International Finance

International Financial Institution Advisory Commission. 2000. *Report of the International Financial Institution Advisory Commission*. Washington, DC: Senate Committee on Banking, Housing, and Urban Affairs

Iwasaki, Yoshihiro. 1999. "Whither Thailand?" In Hunter, William, George Kaufman and Thomas Krueger. 1999. *The Asian Financial Crisis: Origins, Implications, and Solutions*. Boston, MA: Kluwer Academic Publishers

James, Harold. 1996. *International Monetary Cooperation since Bretton Woods*. Oxford: Oxford University Press

Jeanne, Olivier and Charles Wyplosz. 2001. *The International Lender of Last Resort: How Large is Large Enough?* 2001. Paper presented at the NBER conference on Management of Currency Crises in Monterey, CA. March 28–31, 2001

Jeanne, Olivier and Jeromin Zettelmeyer. 2001. "International Bailouts, Moral Hazard and Conditionality." *Economic Policy* 30: 407–432

Jeanne, Olivier and Jeromin Zettelmeyer. 2004. *The Mussa Theorem (and other results on IMF induced moral hazard)*. Paper written for the IMF Conference in Honour of Michael Mussa. June 4–5, 2004. Washington, DC: International Monetary Fund

Jeegadesh, Narasimhan and Sheridan Titman. 1993. "Returns to Buying Winners and Selling Loosers: Implications for Stock Market Efficiency." *Journal of Finance* 48: 65–92

Jensen, Michael and William Meckling. 1976. "Theory of the Firm: Managerial Behaviour, Agency Costs and Ownership Structure." *Journal of Financial Economics* 3: 303–360

Kahneman, Daniel and Amos Tversky. 1979. "Prospect Theory: An Analysis of Decision under Risk." *Econometrica*. Vol. 47, No. 2: 263–291

Kamin, Steven. 2002. *Identifying the Role of Moral Hazard in International Financial Markets*. International Finance Discussion Paper 736. Washington, DC: Board of Governors of the Federal Reserve System

Kaminsky, Graciela, Saul Lizondo and Carmen M. Reinhard. 1997. *Leading Indicators of Currency Crises*. IMF Working Paper No. 97/79. Washington, DC: International Monetary Fund

Kaminsky, Graciela L. and Sergio L. Schmunkler. 2002. *Short-Run Pain, Long-Run Gain: The Effects of Financial Liberalization*. World Bank Working Paper No. 2912. Washington, DC: The World Bank

Kaufman, Henry. 1998. "Preventing the Next Global Financial Crisis." *The Washington Post*. January 28, 1998

Kaul, Inge, Isabelle Grunberg and Marc Stern. 1999. "Defining Global Public Goods." In Inge Kaul, Isabelle Grunberg and Marc Stern (Eds.). *Global Public Goods*. Oxford: Oxford University Press: 2–19

Kaul, Inge, Isabelle Grunberg and Marc Stern (Eds.). 1999. *Global Public Goods*. Oxford: Oxford University Press

Kaul, Inge, Pedro Conceicao, Katell Le Goulven and Ronald Mendoza. 2002. *Providing Global Public Goods*. Oxford: Oxford University Press

Kendall, Maurice. 1953. "The Analysis of Economic Time Series, Part I. Prices." *Journal of the Royal Statistical Society* 96: 11–25

Keohane, Robert. 1984. *After Hegemony*. Princeton, NJ: Princeton University Press

Keohane, Robert. 1989. *International Institutions and State Power*. Boulder, CO: Westview Press

Ketkar, Suhas and Dilip Ratha. 2001. *Development Financing During a Crisis: Securitization of Future Receivables*. Economic Policy and Prospects Group. Washington, DC: The World Bank

Killick, Tony, Moazzam Malik and Marcus Manuel. 1991. *What Can We Know about the Effects of IMF Programmes?* Working Paper 47. London: Overseas Development Institute

Killick, Tony. 1995. *IMF Programmes in Developing Countries – Design and Impact*. London: Routledge

Kindleberger, Charles P. and Jean-Pierre Laffargue (Eds.). 1982. *Financial Crises: Theory, History and Policy*. Cambridge: Cambridge University Press

Kindleberger, Charles P. 2000. *Manias, Panics and Crashes: A History of Financial Crises*. 4th Edition. New York, NY: John Wiley & Sons

Kodres Laura E. and Matthew G. Pritsker. 1998. *A Rational Expectations Model of Financial Contagion*. Board of Governors of the Federal Reserve Finance and Economics Discussion Series 98–48. Washington, DC: Federal Reserve

Köhler, Horst. 2000. *Address to the Board of Governors of the Fund*. September 26, 2000 in Prague. Washington, DC: International Monetary Fund

Kose, M. Ayhan, Eswar Prasad and Marco Terrones. 2003. *Financial Integration and Macroeconomic Volatility*. IMF Working Paper No. 03/50. Washington, DC: International Monetary Fund

Kraay, Aart and Vikram Nehru. 2004. *When Is External Debt Sustainable?* Policy Research Working Paper 3200. Washington, DC: The World Bank

Krasner, Stephen (Ed.). 1983. *International Regimes*. Ithaca, NY: Cornell University Press

Kreile, Michael. 2000. "Deutschland und die Reform der Internationalen Finanzarchitektur." *Aus Politik und Zeitgeschichte*. B 37–38/2000. Bonn: Bundeszentrale für politische Bildung: 12–20

Kroszner, Randall S. 1995. *Free Banking: The Scottish Experience as a Model for Emerging Economies.* World Bank Working Paper 1536. Washington: The World Bank

Kroszner, Randall. 2003. "Enhancing Sovereign Debt Restructuring." *Cato Journal.* Vol. 23, No. 1: 79–86

Krueger, Anne. 2001. *International Financial Architecture for 2002: A New Approach to Sovereign Debt Restructuring.* Address given at the National Economists' Club Annual Members' Dinner. November 26, 2001. Washington, DC: International Monetary Fund

Krueger, Anne. 2001. *A New Approach to Sovereign Debt Restructuring.* Speech given in Delhi at the Indian Council for Research on International Economic Relations. December 20, 2001. Washington, DC: International Monetary Fund

Krueger, Anne. 2002. *New Approaches to Sovereign Debt Restructuring: An Update to Our Thinking.* Speech given at the Institute of International Economics. 1 April 2002. Washington, DC: International Monetary Fund

Krueger, Anne. 2002. *Sovereign Debt Restructuring and Dispute Resolution.* Address to the Bretton Woods Committee Annual Meeting. June 6, 2002. Washington, DC: International Monetary Fund

Krugman, Paul. 1979. "A Model of Balance-of-Payment Crises." *Journal of Money, Credit and Banking* 11: 311–325

Krugman, Paul. 1996. *Are Currency Crises Self-fulfilling?* NBER Macroeconomics Manual. Washington, DC: National Bureau of Economic Research

Krugman, Paul. 1999. *The Return of Depression Economics.* New York, NY: W. W. Norton & Company

Krugman, Paul. 2001. *Crises: The Next Generation.* Draft prepared for Razin Conference. Tel Aviv University. March 25–26, 2001

La Porta, Rafael and Florencio Lopez-de-Silanes. 1997. *The Benefits of Privatization: Evidence from Mexico.* NBER Working Paper 6215. Cambridge, MA: National Bureau of Economic Research

Laidler, David. 2002. *Two Views of the Lender of Last Resort: Thornton and Bagehot.* Paper presented at a conference on the *Lender of Last Resort* at the University of Paris. September 23–24, 2002

Lane, Timothy and Steven Phillips. 2000. *Does IMF Financing Result in Moral Hazard?* IMF Working Paper 00/168. Washington, DC: International Monetary Fund

Lane, Timothy, Atish Gosh, Javier Hamann, Steven Phillips, Marianne Schulze-Ghattas, and Tsidi Tsikata. 1999. *IMF-supported Programs in Indonesia, Korea, and Thailand: A Preliminary Assessment.* IMF Occasional Paper. Washington, DC: International Monetary Fund

Lang, William and Douglas Robertson. 2000. *Analysis of Proposals for a Minimum Subordinated Debt Requirement.* Economic and Policy Analysis Working Paper No. 2000–4. Washington, DC: Department of Treasury

Lau, Lawrence and Joseph Stiglitz. 2005. "China's Alternative to Revaluation." *The Financial Times.* April 25, 2005

Leech, Dennis. 2002. *Voting Power in the Governance of the International Monetary Fund.* Annals of Operations Research 109, 375–397. Amsterdam: Kluwer Academic Publishers

Leech, Dennis and Robert Leech. 2004. *Voting Power in the Bretton Woods Institutions.* Warwick Economic Research Paper. Warwick: University of Warwick

Lerrick, Adam and Alan Meltzer. 2002. "Sovereign Default. The Private Sector Can Resolve Bankruptcy without a Formal Court." *Quarterly International Economics Report.* April 2002. Pittsburgh, PA: Carnegie Mellon Galliot Centre for Public Policy

Levine, Ross. 1996. "Foreign Banks, Financial Development, and Economic Growth." In Claude E. Barfield (Ed.). 1996. *International Financial Markets: Harmonization versus Competition.* Washington, DC: American Enterprise Institute

Lipscy, Philipp. 2003. "Japan's Asian Monetary Fund Proposal." *Stanford Journal of East Asian Affairs.* Vol. 3, No. 1: 93–104

Litan, Robert. 1999. "Does the IMF Have a Future. What Should It Be?" In Hunter, William, George Kaufman and Thomas Krueger. 1999. *The Asian Financial Crisis: Origins, Implications, and Solutions.* Boston, MA: Kluwer Academic Publishers

Lombardi, Domenico. 2005. *The IMF's Role in Low-income Countries: Issues and Challenges.* IMF Working Paper WP/05/177. Washington, DC: International Monetary Fund

Majnoni, Giovanni, Margaret Miller and Andrew Powell. 2004. *Bank Capital and Loan Loss Reserves under Basel II: Implications for Latin America and Carribbean Countries.* World Bank Working Paper 3437. Washington, DC: The World Bank

Malido, Webster. 2003. *African Countries Demand for Democracy in IMF, World Bank.*

Marchesi, Silvia. 2002. *Adoption of an IMF Programme and Debt Rescheduling. An Empirical Analysis.* Working Paper. Siena: Universitá di Siena

Masson, Paul R. 1999. *Multiple Equilibria, Contagion and the Emerging Market Crises.* IMF Working Paper No. 99/164. Washington, DC: International Monetary Fund

McBrady, Matthew and Mar Seasholes. 2001. "Bailing In." *Journal of Restructuring Finance*. Vol. 1, No. 1

McTaggart, Douglas, Christopher Findlay and Michael Parker. 1992. *Economics*. Sydney, Australia: Addison-Wesley

Meltzer, Allan H. and Adam Lerrick. 2001. *Beyond IMF Bailouts: Default without Disruption*. Quarterly International Economics Report, May 2001. Pittsburgh, PA: Carnegie Mellon University

Meltzer, Allan. 1991. *U.S. Policy in the Bretton Woods Era*. Homer Jones Lecture. St. Louis, MO: Federal Reserve Bank of St Louis

Meltzer, Allan. 1998. *What's Wrong with the IMF? What Would Be Better?* Paper prepared for the "Asia: An Analysis of Financial Crisis" conference. October 8–10, 1998. Chicago, IL. Federal Reserve Bank of Chicago

Mikesell, Raymond. 1994. "The Bretton Woods Debates: A Memoir." *Essays in International Finance*. No. 192, March 1994. Princeton, NJ: Princeton University

Miller, Gary and Terry Moe. 1986. "The Positive Theory of Hierarchies." In Herbert Weisberg (Ed.). 1986. *Political Science: The Science of Politics*. New York, NY: Agathon Press

Milton Friedman. 1953. *A Case for Flexible Exchange Rates. Essays in Positive Economics*. Chicago, IL: University of Chicago Press

Mina, Wasseem and Jorge Martinez-Vasquez. 2002. *IMF Lending, Maturity of International Debt and Moral Hazard*. Working Paper. Atlanta, GA: Georgia State University

Minsky, Hyman P. 1982. "The Financial Instability Hypothesis: Capitalistic Processes and the Behaviour of the Economy." In Charles P. Kindleberger and J. P. Laffargue (Eds.). 1982. *Financial Crises: Theory, History and Policy*. Cambridge: Cambridge University Press

Mishkin, Frederic S. 2000. *The International Lender of Last Resort: What are the Issues?* Paper prepared for the Kiel Week Conference "The World's New Financial Landscape: Challenges for Economic Policy." June 19–20, 2000. Kiel: Kiel Institute of World Economics

Mitnick, Barry. 1992. "The Theory of Agency and Organizational Analysis." In Norman Bowie and Edward Freeman. 1992. *Ethics and Agency Theory*. Oxford: Oxford University Press

Mody, Ashoka and Diego Saravia. 2003. *IMF Doctor: Better at Prevention than Cure?* Working Paper. Washington, DC: International Monetary Fund

Moen, Jon. 2001. *Panic of 1907*. EH.Net Encyclopedia, edited by Robert Whaples. August 15, 2001. http://www.eh.net/graphics/encyclopedia/rawdata.backup.12162003/moen.panic.1907

Morris, Stephen and Hyun Song Shin. 2003. *Catalytic Finance: When Does It Work?* Cowles Foundation Discussion Paper No. 1400. New Haven, CT: Cowles Foundation for Research in Economics at Yale University

Mussa, Michael. 2002. *Reflections on Moral Hazard and Private Sector Involvement in the Resolution of Emerging Market Financial Crises.* Paper presented at the Bank of England Conference on the Role of the Official and Private Sectors in Resolving International Financial Crises, July 23–24, 2002. London: Bank of England

Nam, D. W. 1999. *The Distinct Nature of the Korean Crisis.* Paper prepared for presentation at the 11th Conference of the Korea U.S. Business Council at the Maui Prince Hotel. January 19, 1998. Maui, Hawaii. http://www.dwnam.pe.kr/6imf02.html

Nolan, John. 2001. *Emerging Market Debt & Vulture Hedge Funds: Free-Ridership, Legal and Market Remedies.* Special Policy Report 3. September 29, 2001. Washington, DC: Financial Policy Forum

Oatley, Thomas and Jason Yackee. 2000. *Political Determinants of IMF Balance of Payments Lending: The Curse of Carabosse?.* Working Paper. Chapel Hill, NC: University of North Carolina

Oatley, Thomas. 2002. *Commercial Banks and the International Monetary Fund: An Empirical Analysis.* Working Paper. Chapel Hill, NC: University of North Carolina

Odell, Kerry and Marc D. Weidenmeier. 2001. *Real Shock, Monetary Aftershocks: The San Francisco Earthquake and the Panic of 1907.* Claremont Colleges Working Papers in Economics. Claremont, CA: Claremont College

Ortiz, Guillermo. 2002. *Recent Emerging Market Crises: What Have We Learned?* 2002 Per Jacobsson Lecture. Basel: Per Jacobsson Foundation

Ortiz, Guillermo. 2005. *The IMF – Panacea for Every Illness?* Speech given at the Joint IMF-Bundesbank Symposium "The IMF in a Changing World." Frankfurt: Deutsche Bundesbank

Park, Yung Chul and Yunjong Wang. 2001. *Reform of the International Financial System and Institutions in Light of the Asian Financial Crisis.* G-24 Discussion Paper Series. UNCTAD and Center for International Development Harvard University. Geneva: United Nations Conference for Trade and Development

Patillo, Catherine, Hélène Poirson and Luca Ricci. 2002. *External Debt and Growth.* IMF Working Paper WP/02/69. Washington, DC: International Monetary Fund

Paul Stiglitz. 2003. *The Roaring Nineties.* New York, NY: W. W. Norton & Company

Piermartini, Roberta. 2004. *The Role of Export Taxes in the Field of Primary Commodities.* Geneva: World Trade Organization

Pollack, Andrew. 1997. "Package of Loans Worth $55 Billion Is Set for Korea." *The New York Times*. December 4, 1997

Powell, Andrew. 2004. *Basel II and Developing Countries: Sailing through a Sea of Standards*. World Bank Policy Research Working Paper 3387. Washington, DC: The World Bank

Prasad, Eswar, Kenneth Rogoff, Shang-Jin Wei and M. Ayhan Kose. 2004. *Financial Globalization, Growth and Volatility in Developing Countries*. NBER Working Paper No. 10942. Cambridge, MA: National Bureau of Economic Research

Quarles, Randal. 2005. *IMF Reform – Toward an Institution for the Future*. Statement before the Subcommittee on International Trade and Finance. June 7, 2005. Washington, DC: Senate Banking Committee

Radelet, Steven and Jeffrey Sachs. 1998. *The East Asian Financial Crisis: Diagnosis, Remedies, Prospects*. Brookings Papers on Economic Activity No. 1: Washington, DC: The Brookings Institution

Radelet, Steven and Jeffrey Sachs. 1998. *The Onset of the East Asian Financial Crisis*. NBER Working Paper No. 6680. Cambridge, MA: National Bureau of Economic Research

Raffer, Kunibert. 1990. "Applying Chapter 9 Insolvency to International Debts: An Economically Efficient Solution with a Human Face." *World Development* 18: 301–311

Rajan, Raghuran. 2005. "Institutional Reform and Sovereign Debt Crises." *Cato Journal*. Vol. 25, No. 1

Ratha, Dilip. 2003. *Financing Development through Future-Flow Securitization*. Prem Notes No. 69. Washington, DC: The World Bank

Ratha, Dilip. 2003. *Workers' Remittances: An Important and Stable Source of Development Finance*. Global Development Finance 2003. Washington, DC: The World Bank

Ribakova, Elina. 2005. *Liberalization, Prudential Supervision, and Capital Requirements: The Policy Trade-Offs*. IMF Working Paper WP/05/136. Washington, DC: International Monetary Fund

Rodrik, Dani. 1995. *Why Is There Multilateral Lending?* NBER Working Paper 5160. Cambridge, MA: National Bureau of Economic Research

Rodrik, Dani and Andrés Velasco. 1999. *Short-term Capital Flows*. NBER Working Paper 7364. Cambridge, MA: National Bureau of Economic Research

Rogoff, Kenneth. 1999. *International Institutions for Reducing Global Financial Instability*. NBER Working Paper 7265. Cambridge, MA: National Bureau of Economic Research

Rogoff, Kenneth. 2002. "Moral Hazard in IMF Loans: How Big a Concern?" *Finance and Development*. Vol. 39, No. 3. Washington, DC: International Monetary Fund

Rojas-Suarez, Liliana. 2001. *Can International Capital Standards Strengthen Banks in Emerging Markets?* Washington, DC: Institute for International Economics

Rojas-Suarez, Liliana. 2004. *Domestic Financial Regulations in Developing Countries: Can they Effectively Limit the Impact of Capital Account Volatility?* Washington, DC: Centre for Global Development

Rosengreen, Eric. 1999. "Will Greater Disclosure and Transparency Prevent the Next Banking Crisis?" In William Hunter, George Kaufman, and Thomas Krueger. 1999. *The Asian Financial Crisis: Origins, Implications, and Solutions*. Boston, MA: Kluwer Academic Publishers

Ross, Steven. 1973. "The Economic Theory of Agency: The Principal's Problem." *American Economic Review*. Vol. 63, No. 2: 134–139

Roubini, Nouriel and Brad Setser. 2004. *Bail-outs or Bail-ins? Responding to Financial Crises in Emerging Markets*. Washington, DC: Institute of International Economic

Roubini, Nouriel and Brad Setser. 2004. *The Reform of the Sovereign Debt Restructuring Process: Problems, Proposed Solutions and the Argentine Episode*. Working Paper. New York, NY: Stern School of Business

Rowland, Peter. 2004. *Determinants of Spread, Credit Ratings and Creditworthiness for Emerging Market Sovereign Debt: A Follow-Up Study Using Pooled Data Analysis*. Working Paper. La Paz, Bolivia: Banco de la Republica

Rowland, Peter and José Torres. 2004. *Determinants of Spreads and Creditworthiness for Emerging Market Sovereign Debt: A Panel Data Study*. Working Paper. La Paz, Bolivia: Banco de la Repubblica

Rozeff, Michael and William Kinney. 1976. "Capital Market Seasonality: The Case of Stock Returns." *Journal of Financial Economics* 3: 379–402

Rubin, Robert E. 2004. *In an Uncertain World: Tough Choices from Wall Street to Washington*. New York, NY: Random House

Ruogu, LI. 2004. *Reform the Governance of the IMF*. Speech given on the Seminar on Governance of the Bretton Woods Institutions. October 1, 2004. Beijing, China: The People's Bank of China

Rustomjee, Cyrus. 2004. "Why Developing Countries Need a Stronger Vote." *Finance & Development*. September 2004. Washington, DC: International Monetary Fund

Salant, Stephen and Dale Henderson. 1978. "Market Anticipations of Government Policies and the Price of Gold." *Journal of Political Economy* 86: 627–648

Sayers, Richard S. 1976. *The Bank of England 1891–1944*. Cambridge: Cambridge University Press

Schaefer, Brett D. and John P. Sweeney. 1999. *The IMF Strikes out on Brazil*. Executive Memorandum No. 569. Washington, DC: The Heritage Foundation http://www.heritage.org/Research/InternationalOrganizations/EM569.cfm

Scharfstein, David and Jeremy Stein. 1990. "Herd Behaviour and Investment." *The American Economic Review*. Vol. 80, No. 3: 465–479

Schmukler, Sergio L., Pablo Zoido and Marina Halac. 2003. *Financial Globalization, Crises, and Contagion*. Working Paper. Washington, DC: The World Bank

Schneider, Benu. 2003. *The Road to International Financial Stability: Are Key Financial Standards the Answer?* New York, NY: Palgrave Macmillan

Schneider, Benu. 2004. *The Road to International Financial Stability: Are Key Financial Standards the Answer?* Presentation held at the IMF Book Forum "Standards and Codes: Can they Prevent Financial Crises?" May 27, 2004. Washington, DC: International Monetary Fund

Schuknecht, Ludger. 1999. "A Trade Policy Perspective on Capital Controls." *Finance and Development*. Vol. 36, No. 1. Washington, DC: International Monetary Fund

Schwartz, Anna J. 2000. "Earmarks of a Lender of Last Resort." In Charles Goodhart and Gerhard Illing (Eds.). 2000. *Financial Crises, Contagion, and the Lender of Last Resort. A Reader*. Oxford: Oxford University Press

Schwartz, Anna. 1999. "Is There a Need for an International Lender of Last Resort?" *Cato Journal*. Vol. 19, No. 1: 1–6

Schwartz, Anna. 2003. "Do Sovereign Debtors Need a Bankruptcy Law?" *Cato Journal*. Vol. 23, No. 1: 87–100

Shapley, Lloyd and Martin Shubik. 1954. "A Method for Evaluating the Distribution of Power in a Committee System." *American Political Science Review* 48: 787–792

Shiller, Robert. 2001. *Irrational Exuberance*. New York, NY: Broadway Books

Shiller, Robert. 2002. *From Efficient Market Theory to Behavioural Finance*. Cowles Foundation Discussion Paper No. 1385. New Haven, CT: Yale University

Solomon, Robert. 1977. *The International Monetary System, 1945–1976: An Insider's View*. New York, NY: Harper & Row

Soros, George. 1997. Avoiding a Breakdown: Asia's Crisis Demands a Rethink of International Regulation." *The Financial Times*. December 31, 1997

Soros, George. 1998. *The Crisis of Global Capitalism*. New York, NY: Public Affairs

Spence, Michael and Robert Zeckhauser. 1971. "Insurance, Information and Individual Action." *American Economic Review.* Vol. 61, No. 2: 380–387

Sprague, Oliver M. W. 1910. *History of Crises under the National Banking System.* Washington, DC: National Monetary Commission

Standard and Poor's. 2002. *Sovereign Defaults: Moving Higher Again in 2003?* Research Note published by S&P Sovereigns. New York, NY: Standard and Poor's

Steneri, Carlos. 2003. *Voluntary Debt Reprofiling: The Case of Uruguay.* Paper prepared for the Fourth UNCTAD Conference on Debt Management. November 11–14, 2003. Geneva: United Nations Conference on Trade and Development

Stiglitz, Joseph. 2001. *Globalization and Its Discontents.* London: Allen Lane

Stone, Charles and Anne Zissu. 1999. "Engeneering a Way around the Sovereign Ceiling." *The Securitization Conduit.* Vol. 2, No. 2 & 3

Strange, Susan. 1986. *Casino Capitalism.* Oxford: Blackwell

Strathern, Paul. 2001. *Dr Strangelove's Game: A Brief History of Economic Genius.* London: Penguin Books

Sturzenegger, Federico. 2002. *Toolkit for the Analysis of Debt Problems.* Working Paper. Centro de Investigación de Finanzas. Buenos Aires, Argentina: Universidad Torcuato di Tella

Sturzenegger, Frederico and Jeromin Zettelmeyer. 2005. *Haircuts: Estimating Investor Losses in Sovereign Debt Restructurings, 1998–2005.* IMF Working Paper WP/05/137. Washington, DC: International Monetary Fund

Sushil Bikhchandani, David Hirshleifer and Ivo Welch. 1992. "A Theory of Fads, Fashion, Custom, and Cultural Change in Informational Cascades." *Journal of Political Economy* 100: 992–1026

Taylor, John. 2002a. *Sovereign Debt Restructuring: A U.S. Perspective.* Speech given at the IIE. April 2, 2002. Washington, DC: Institute for International Economics

Taylor, John. 2002b. *Using Clause to Reform the Process Sovereign Debt Workouts: Progress and Next Steps.* Prepared Remarks at the EMTA Annual Meeting. December 5, 2002. Washington, DC: Department of Treasury

Taylor, John. 2004. *New Directions for the International Financial Institutions.* Address at the Conference Global Economic Challenges for the IMF's New Chief. American Enterprise Institute. June 10, 2004. Washington, DC: Department of Treasury

Thacker, Strom. 1999. "The High Politics of IMF Lending." *World Politics.* Vol. 52, No. 1: 38–75

Thaler, Richard. 1992. *The Winner's Curse: Paradoxes and Anomalies of Economic Life.* Princeton, NJ: Princeton University Press

The Banker. 2000. "The New IMF: Too Many Architects?" October 2, 2000. http://www.thebanker.com/news/fullstory.php/aid/138/The_new_IMF:_too_many_architects_.html

Thomson, Adam and Andrew Balls. 2005. "76% Back Argentina Debt Terms." *The Financial Times.* March 3, 2005

Thornton, Henry. 1939. *An Enquiry into the Nature and Effects of the Paper Credit of Great Britain.* New York, NY: Rinehart and Company

Tillotson, Daniel. 2004. "Argentina – An Injunction to Halt Exit-Consent Abuses." *Wachovia Securities Sovereign Research Bulletin.* November 1, 2004. New York, NY: Wachovia Securities LLC

Tirole, Jean. 2002. *Financial Crises, Liquidity, and the International Monetary System.* Princeton, NJ: Princeton University Press

Tobin, James. 1999. "Prologue." In Mahbub ul Haq, Inge Kaul and Isabelle Grunberg (Eds.). 1996. *The Tobin Tax: Coping with Financial Stability.* Oxford: Oxford University Press

Todaro, Michael and Stephen Smith. 2003. *Economic Development.* Boston, MA: Addison-Wesley

Tompson, William. 1999. "The Bank of Russia and the 1998 Rouble Crisis." In Vladimir Tikhomirov (Ed.). 1999. *Anatomy of the 1998 Russian Crisis.* Contemporary Europe Research Center. Carlton, Australia: University of Melbourne

Trebat, Thomas. 1983. *Brazil's State-Owned Enterprises.* Cambridge: Cambridge University Press

Turner, Jonathan. 1991. *The Structure of Sociological Theory.* Belmont, CA: Wadsworth

Ueda, Kazuo. 1998. "The East Asian Economic Crisis: A Japanese Perspective." *International Finance.* Vol. 1 No.2: 327–338

Uegaki, Akira. 2000. "Russia as a Newcomer to the International Financial Market: 1992–2000." *Acta Slavica Iaponica.* Tomus 21: 23–46

Ul Haq, Mahbub, Inge Kaul and Isabelle Grunberg (Eds.). 1996. *The Tobin Tax: Coping with Financial Stability.* Oxford: Oxford University Press

United Nations Department of Treasury. 2000. *Response to the Report by the International Financial Institution Advisory Commission.* June 8, 2000. Washington, DC: Department of Treasury

United Nations Development Program. 2003. *Worker Remittance as an Instrument for Development.* Comparative Research, December 2003. New York, NY: United Nations Development Program http://www.undp.org/surf-panama/referrals.htm

United States General Accounting Office. 1996. *Mexico's Financial Crisis: Origins, Awareness, Assistance, and Initial Efforts to Recover.* Report to the Chairman, Committee on Banking and Financial Services. House of Representatives. Washington, DC: United States General Accounting Office

Valdes-Prieto, Salvador and Marcelo Soto. 1997. *The Effectiveness of Capital Controls: Theory and Evidence from Chile.* Working Paper. Santiago de Chile: Pontificia Universidad Católica de Chile

Van Houtven, Leo. 2002. *Governance of the IMF. Decision Making, Institutional Oversight, Transparency, and Accountability.* IMF Pamphlet Series No. 53. Washington, DC: International Monetary Fund

Vaubel, Roland. 2003. *Principal-Agent-Probleme in internationalen Institutionen.* HWWA Discussion Paper 219. Hamburg: Hamburgisches Welt-Wirtschafts-Archiv

Vreeland, James. 2002. *Institutional Determinants of IMF Agreements.* Working Paper. Department of Political Science. New Haven, CT: Yale University

Weisbrot, Mark. 2005. "The IMF Has Lost Its Influence." *International Herald Tribune.* September 23, 2005

Wendt, Alexander. 1992. "Anarchy Is What States Make of It: The Social Construction of Power Politics." *International Organization.* Vol. 46, No. 2: 391–425

White, Lawrence H.. 1984. *Free Banking in Britain: Theory, Experience, and Debate, 1800–1845.* Cambridge: Cambridge University Press

Williamson, John. 2005. *Curbing the Boom-Bust Cycle: Stabilizing Capital Flows to Emerging Markets.* Policy Analyses in International Economics 75. Washington, DC: Institute for International Economics

Wolf, Martin. 2004. "We Need a Global Currency." *Financial Times*: August 4, 2004

Wolf, Martin. 2004. *Why Globalization Works.* New Haven, CT: Yale University Press

Wood, John H. 2003. "Bagehot's Lender of Last Resort: A Hollow Hollowed Tradition." *The Independent Review.* Vol. 7, No. 3: 343–351

World Bank. 2005. *Global Development Finance 2005.* Washington, DC: The World Bank

Wyplosz, Charles. 1998. *Globalized Financial Markets and Financial Crises.* Paper presented at the conference "Coping with Financial Crises in Developing and Transition Countries: Regulatory and Supervisory Challenges in a New Era of Global Finance" organised by the Forum on Debt and Development. Amsterdam. March 16–17, 1998

Wyplosz, Charles. 1999. "International Financial Instability." In Inge Kaul, Isabelle Grunberg and Marc Stern (Eds.). *Global Public Goods*. Oxford: Oxford University Press

Wyplosz, Charles. 2005. "How to Rebuild the Stability Pact." *Financial Times*. January 31, 2005.

Yergin, Daniel and Joseph Stanislaw. 1998. *The Commanding Heights: The Battle for the World Economy*. New York, NY: Touchstone

Zettelmeyer, Jeromin and Joshi Priyadarshani. 2005. *Implicit Transfers in IMF Lending, 1973–2000*. IMF Working Paper 05/08. Washington, DC: International Monetary Fund

Zhang, Xiaoming. 1999. *Testing for "Moral Hazard" in Emerging Markets Lending*. IIF Research Papers No. 99–1. Washington, DC: Institute for International Economics